# Infantry Combat in Livy's Battle Narratives

Sam Koon

BAR International Series 2071
2010

Published in 2016 by
BAR Publishing, Oxford

BAR International Series 2071

*Infantry Combat in Livy's Battle Narratives*

ISBN 978 1 4073 0632 2



BAR Publishing is the trading name of British Archaeological Reports (Oxford) Ltd. British Archaeological Reports was first incorporated in 1974 to publish the BAR Series, International and British. In 1992 Hadrian Books Ltd became part of the BAR group. This volume was originally published by Archaeopress in conjunction with British Archaeological Reports (Oxford) Ltd / Hadrian Books Ltd, the Series principal publisher, in 2010. This present volume is published by BAR Publishing, 2016.

Printed in England

BAR
PUBLISHING

BAR titles are available from:

BAR Publishing
122 Banbury Rd, Oxford, OX2 7BP, UK
EMAIL info@barpublishing.com
PHONE +44 (0)1865 310431
FAX +44 (0)1865 316916
www.barpublishing.com

**CONTENTS**

## ACKNOWLEDGEMENTS

This book is developed from my PhD thesis at the University of Manchester. As such I would like to thank firstly my supervisor, Dr Andrew Fear, for all his help, and my examiners Professor Tim Cornell and Professor Philip Sabin for all their advice and encouragement. I would also like to thank Professor Stephen Oakley, Dr John Briscoe and Dr James Thorne for reading various drafts of my thesis and offering valuable advice.

On a more personal note, I wish to thank my parents, William and Angela Koon, my sister, Dr Hannah Koon, and my girlfriend, Kathryn Green, for all their help and support. Finally, I would like to thank all my friends in Manchester and elsewhere who gave me encouragement, but especially Dr Ian Harrison and Dr Jamie Wood.

## Chapter 1: Introduction

The period known as the mid-Republic, ranging roughly from the beginning of the second Punic War to tribunate and murder of Tiberius Gracchus in 133BC, was a time of great expansion in the Roman world. In order to comprehend better the nature of Roman imperialism in this period, it is important to understand how the Romans fought in battle. The Roman army included cavalry and light troops, but the main strength of the legion lay with its heavy infantry. For decades scholars have argued over the mechanics of mid-Republican infantry combat. In the early twentieth century there was fierce debate among the great German military historians Delbrück and Kromayer and Veith. Building on this debate, throughout the last century a general consensus arose over the mechanics of infantry combat. These models were grand-tactical and produced rather static images of massed groups of highly disciplined soldiers relentlessly advancing against any enemy which crossed their path. So pervasive were these models that this remains the most popular image of the Roman heavy infantry.

In 1976, with the publication of *The Face of Battle*, John Keegan proposed a methodology for analysing combat, which aimed to challenge the traditional command-centred and grand-tactical approach to battle narration and bring accounts out of the stereotypical and into, as far as possible, the realm of reality. His aim was to catch a glimpse of the combat experience of the individual soldier within the wider context of a pitched battle. As such his focus was not on generals, logistics, strategy or tactics, but rather on the sub-tactical mechanics and physical environment of the battle and how these may have affected the psychology of the individual soldier. This pioneering work sparked a new school of thought in ancient military history and inspired a number of soldier's-eye-view histories, particularly in the field of Greek battle, where there are contemporary accounts, but also some on Roman warfare. Two of the most innovative of the scholars inspired by Keegan's approach, Philip Sabin and Adrian Goldsworthy, have done a great deal in the past decade to chip away at the monolithic traditional conception of Roman infantry combat and have shown that the mechanics of the formation as a whole can only be understood by focusing on the experience of the individual soldier.[1] These works are based on theoretical and psychological principles, archaeology and also the literary evidence of individual battles in isolation or from pieces of information taken from a range of ancient sources covering a considerable period of time. Although these new models are persuasive they have not convinced all scholars working on ancient military history and have not yet filtered down into popular consciousness.

In my opinion, for any model of ancient battle to be convincing it must be derived predominantly from the surviving ancient sources. These sources are chiefly literary in nature, and as such can never fully describe the reality of ancient combat. They can, however, offer a reflection of that reality by reproducing a consistently realistic vision of combat. It may never be possible to understand exactly what happened in any particular ancient battle, but by analysing the battle narratives within the sources, it is possible to reconstruct a realistic image of ancient battle in general. This book, therefore, is an attempt to bring these debates back further into the literary field by analysing the combat narratives of the most prolific writer on mid-Republican battle: Livy. In addition it will try both to restore Livy's reputation as a military source and to bridge the current conceptual gap between the literary, archaeological and theoretical approaches to mid-republican infantry combat.

The initial two chapters form a sort of extended introduction and justification of the methodology employed. The first discusses the source-based, archaeological, theoretical and psychological parameters of Roman infantry battle, against which any model of combat must be judged. It examines the traditional model and introduces some of the newer ones proposed over the last decade. The second chapter primarily offers a defence of Livy against the charge of crippling military ignorance and a justification for using his accounts as the focus of my analysis. Livy's methodology, use of sources and method of constructing his battle accounts will be examined and briefly contrasted with the techniques of some of his predecessors.

The third, fourth and fifth chapters form the bulk of the literary analysis. The method employed here is a close examination of Livy's combat vocabulary and the contexts in which it is found in an attempt to understand better how he envisaged the combat he describes. Livy's vision of combat is put into context in the following two chapters by directly comparing it to those of Polybius and Caesar, representing respectively the Greek and Latin literary traditions of battle narration. The study concludes that Livy's vision of battle is a synthesis of these literary traditions, which reflects the generic realities of Roman mid-republican infantry combat. A model derived from this analysis, when used in conjunction with the archaeological evidence is not only convincing, but also conforms better to the parameters of mid-Republican infantry battle than traditional models of combat and corresponds well with the new range of more theoretical hypotheses.

[1] Keegan (1976); Sabin (1996), (2000) and Goldsworthy (1996).

## Chapter 2: Close range clashes of the Roman mid-Republican heavy infantry: the state of the question

For generations the mechanics of mid-Republican Roman infantry combat have been the source of fierce debate. From the German scholars of the late 19th and early 20th centuries to their English speaking successors of the 20th and early 21st, there have been as many models of infantry combat as their have been scholars of the Roman army. These various models of infantry combat have caused many differing interpretations of the ancient source material and led to the intense squabbles which surround reconstructions of mid-Republican infantry battle.

This chapter will introduce the main points of contention and show that there is little about Roman infantry battle that can be taken for granted. The chapter is divided into three main sections. The first acts as an explanation of, and an introduction to, the problems and debates surrounding the Roman infantry formation as presented in the surviving source material, which predominantly stem from assumptions based on the various opposing models of Roman combat. The second sets limits on possible models of infantry combat by introducing several parameters of mid-Republican infantry combat against which models must be judged. These parameters can be divided into two general areas. The first is the archaeological evidence for how the Roman heavy infantryman was armed and how this may have affected his mode of combat. The second includes the many theoretical limitations such as duration of battle, casualty figures, mobility of battle-lines and the role of reserve ranks.

In the third section the major modern interpretive models of combat are examined. First the 'traditional' model of Roman infantry battle and then some of the important developments advanced in the last decade. An analysis of the strengths and weaknesses of these models will highlight a methodological path that should be followed in order to improve our understanding of mid-Republican infantry combat.

### 1. The problems of infantry formation within the sources

The Romans employed a peculiar infantry formation during the mid-Republic known as the manipular legion. This formation was neither the densely-packed, continuous mass of a Greek phalanx nor the loose swarm of a 'barbarian horde'. Unfortunately, despite a number of descriptions in our ancient sources, no consensus has been reached on many issues fundamental to reconstructing this formation. Here three of the more important will be introduced to show the extent of the confusion and the range of conflicting interpretations. Surprisingly few of our assumptions about mid-Republican battle mechanics are on safe ground.

### *The* quincunx *formation*

Polybius offers us the clearest description of the mid-Republican Roman army in book 6 of his history. The structure of the army he describes is now known as a double-consular manipular army, consisting of four Roman legions with four accompanying allied units of similar size, known as *alae* because they usually fought on the wings of the legions.[2] Polybius' legion had a theoretical strength of 4,200 men distributed into light infantry, *velites*, and a three line system of heavy infantry, the *hastati*, *principes*, and *triarii*. These rows lined up one in front of the other, with the *hastati* at the front and the *triarii* at the rear.[3] The *hastati*, the youngest men of the heavy infantry, numbered 1,200 and were armed with a sword, an oval shield, and two *pila* (one light and one heavy throwing javelin, with a range of roughly 20 to 30m).[4] The second line, the *principes*, was made up of men in the prime of their life, who were equipped in a similar way to the *hastati* and were equal in number. The third line, the *triarii*, consisted of the oldest soldiers, who numbered 600 and were armed in a similar way to the first two lines except they carried a thrusting spear (*hasta*) instead of *pila*. Polybius states that each line was divided into ten maniples, the basic tactical unit of the legion, made up of 120 men for the *hastati* and *principes*, with 60 men in the maniples of the *triarii*.[5] The remaining men, 1,200 in all, comprised the *velites*, light infantry armed with a sword, javelins and a small shield. These were the youngest and poorest of the legionaries, and divided proportionally amongst each of the maniples, being used in battle as skirmishing troops in front of the heavy infantry.[6]

For each of the three lines ten centurions were elected, the *prior* centurions, and then a further ten, the *posterior* centurions. The centurions then appointed an equal number of rearguard officers (*optiones*). Each maniple had two centurions and two *optiones*, and finally two of the bravest men from each maniple were appointed standard bearers;[7] thus it is usually agreed that each maniple had a bipartite structure, made up of two centuries of sixty men each (thirty for the *triarii*).

---

[2] On the allies see most recently Dobson (2008) 51-3.

[3] Polybius' terms for the different infantry lines (6.21.6-10): he calls the *velites* γροσφμάχοι; for the heavy infantry he uses transliterated terms: the *hastati* are ἁστάτοι, the *principes*, πρίγκιπες, and the *triarii*, τριαρίοι. The order in which Polybius ranks his three lines appears correct; the same order occurs in his own narrative (14.8.5 and 15.9.7), in Livy's narrative (30.8.5, 30.32.11 and 30.34.10) and also in Ovid (*Fasti* 3.128.32) and Varro (*De Lingua Latina* 5.89).

[4] Equipment of the heavy infantry: 6.23. Range of *pila*: Connolly (2000) 43-46.

[5] At 6.24.5 Polybius uses the terms τάγμα, σπεῖραν or σημαίαν for this unit, rather than transliterating *manipulus*, but these terms correspond to the maniple.

[6] On the three line distribution and quantification of the legion: 6.21.6-10. Division of each line into maniples: 6.24.3-5 and maniple as the smallest tactical unit: 6.35.12; Livy 26.5.15, 6.1; 42.34. Equipment of the *velites*: 6.22; skirmishing of the *velites*: 3.73.1-3 and 6; 11.22.9-10, etc; cf. most recently Sekunda (2007) 351. On division amongst the maniples: 6.24.4; Walbank (1957) 707; Dobson (2008) 49.

[7] For a discussion of the debate over where the standards were placed in battle see Oakley (1998) 509-510.

Polybius states that the centurion first elected (πρῶτος αἱρεθεις) commanded the right side of the maniple and the second (δεύτερος) commanded the left, unless one centurion was incapacitated in which case the other commanded the maniple as a whole. Polybius' terms correspond to the Latin terms for the first and second picked centurions, *prior* and *posterior centurio.* [8] Walbank suggests that arrangement would be impractical as the legion's tactical structure would then have relied on fate, and so proposes that each centurion led their own men into battle, but the *prior* centurion commanded the maniple as a whole, with the *posterior* taking over if the *prior* became incapacitated.[9]

Polybius' description of the Roman formation at the battle of Zama (202) offers some idea of how the legion normally lined up for battle:

> "Scipio drew up his army in the following fashion. In front he placed the *hastati* with certain intervals between the maniples and behind them the *principes*, not placing their maniples, as is the usual Roman custom, opposite to the intervals separating those of the first line, but directly behind these latter at a certain distance owing to the large number of the enemy's elephants. Last of all he placed the *triarii*".[10]

This unusual formation shows that the normal battle order was a three line system, each line divided into ten maniples, with gaps between each maniple. It also implies that the maniples of the *principes* normally lined up behind the gaps of the first line, and assuming that the maniples of the third lined up behind the gaps of the second, it is generally believed that the 'parade-ground' formation of the legion had a *quincunx* or chessboard appearance. The primary function of this formation was to aid the advance of the legion over rough ground and to avoid bunching. While there is no evidence in the sources concerning the size of these gaps, Delbrück believed that the intervals need only have been small to gain the required advantage over rough ground. It is now generally thought that the gaps were a similar width to the maniples themselves since they appear to be used to bring up maniples of the second line for relief.[11] The width of the maniple depends on the amount of space taken up by each man, an issue addressed below, but it is generally assumed that each maniple lined up with a frontage of twenty and a depth of six men (a depth of three for the *triarii*). The distance between each of the three lines is also debated, with Connolly suggesting as much as 200 metres while Warry believes the distances could vary from nothing up to 76 metres.[12]

A further point of contention is whether or not the two centuries lined up side-by-side in this formation or one in front of the other. Delbrück, with his small intervals between maniples, suggested that the centuries were stationed side by side. Recently though, with the generally accepted view that the intervals were larger than those hypothesised by Delbrück, many scholars have suggested that the centuries could not have lined up side-by-side as the total frontage of the legion would then be too large. Instead it has been suggested that before battle commenced the *prior* centuries lined up in front of the *posterior* centuries to create the quincunx formation and allow an orderly advance. These intervals would then be filled immediately before the first attack by the rear centuries moving left and forward.[13] This interpretation is based on the translation of *prior* and *posterior* as 'forward' and 'rear' centurions, and the assumption that the infantry fought in an unbroken line. Neither of these assertions necessarily holds up. The word *prior* in Latin is often used in opposition to *posterior* to mean 'superior to', 'preferable to' or simply, as in this case, 'first picked', with *posterior* meaning 'next in order'.[14] This usage corresponds to Polybius' πρῶτος and δεύτερος centurions. The names of the centurions simply relate to the two stages of election and the superiority of the *prior* centurion. These titles do not necessarily imply that the centuries lined up in file, one in front of the other.[15] The only real indication of battlefield disposition would be that the *prior*, 'superior', centurion was positioned on the far right of the maniple, the place of honour in ancient warfare.

Secondly, this interpretation is based on the assumption that the legion must have fought with an unbroken line. Fundamentally this again stems from Delbrück, who believed that the *quincunx* formation may have been possible on the 'parade ground' but not in battle:

> "[this formation would have been] completely impossible under war conditions, since in the approach march the intervals would all be lost, here becoming too large, there too small. Even if the *hastati* should succeed in reaching the enemy with the correct intervals, that would still result in the most foolish battle formation one can imagine. Each

[8] Cf. Livy 42.34.7f.

[9] Election of centurions and *optiones*: 6.24.1-6, command of the maniple: 6.24.8. On the impracticality of this: Walbank (1957) 707-708, Daly (2002) 60.

[10] 15.9.6-8: πλὴν ὁ μὲν Πόπλιος ἔθηκε τὰς τάξεις τῶν ἰδίων δυνάμεων τὸν τρόπον τοῦτον. πρῶτον μὲν τοὺς ἁστάτους καὶ τὰς τούτων σημαίας ἐν διαστήμασιν, ἐπὶ δὲ τούτοις τοὺς πρίγκιπας, τιθεὶς τὰς σπείρας οὐ κατὰ τὸ τῶν πρώτων σημαιῶν διάστημα, καθάπερ ἔθος ἐστὶ τοῖς Ῥωμαίοις, ἀλλὰ καταλλήλους ἐν ἀποστάσει διὰ τὸ πλῆθος τῶν παρὰ τοῖς ἐναντίοις ἐλεφάντων· τελευταίους δ᾽ ἐπέστησε τοὺς τριαρίους.

[11] Delbrück (trans. 1975) 273. Against this: Walbank (1967) 454; Adcock (1970, [1940]) 9; Keppie (1998, [1984]) 39; Connolly (1998) 128; Daly (2002) 61; etc.

[12] Connolly (1989) 162; Warry (1980) 111; Keppie (1998) 39; Daly (2002) 61.

[13] Delbrück (trans. 1975) 272-3. For the newer interpretation: Connolly (1998) 142; Warry (1980) 112; Daly (2002) 61. The various difficulties with this reconstruction will be discussed further in the second half of this chapter.

[14] *Prior*: *Oxford Latin Dictionary* (*OLD*) s.v. 5 and 7; *posterior*: *OLD* s.v. 3 and 4.

[15] Compare Cicero's explanation of why three of the six cavalry centuries were called *prior* and three *posterior* (*De Re Publica* 2.36).

> maniple would immediately be enveloped on both flanks and pressed together".[16]

Although most would disagree with the size of intervals employed while the legion advanced, Delbrück's view that the Romans must have fought with an unbroken line still remains popular in modern scholarship.[17] Nonetheless there are some who have tried to argue against this. The first were Kromayer and Veith, who suggested that a battle-line in which the intervals remained would actually be an advantage in the initial collision as, by pressing into the gaps, the opposing troops stationed in a continuous line would expose themselves to attack from Roman troops on three fronts. As we shall see below, the Roman forces were far better equipped to fight in all directions than members of a traditional phalanx, whose strength lay merely in driving forward in one direction. They suggested then that the intervals in the Roman line would neutralise the charge of a phalanx, its main offensive advantage.[18] Adcock later suggested that even if the enemy were Gauls, whose primary attack was a massed charge, the enemy would enter the line through the intervals but be held up by the covering maniples of the second line and be unable to envelop the maniples, instead finding themselves facing Romans on three sides.[19] For these reasons some recent scholars agree that the intervals in the battle-lines remained during battle, though without exact spacing.[20]

In opposition to this Daly has suggested that enemy troops armed with longer range missiles than the Roman *pila* could take advantage of intervals in the Roman first line by attacking the covering maniples in the second line without endangering themselves.[21] This would seem to add much to the debate, but the enemy's ability to do this depends not only on the range of their missile weapons, but also on the distance between the first and second Roman lines, and unfortunately there is no ancient evidence for either of these variables. The lack of ancient evidence to answer these fundamental questions is the main problem facing historians and as such the debate over whether the gaps in the Roman lines were retained in a battle situation remains fierce, and depends entirely on one's assumptions about the mechanics of infantry combat. For this reason Wheeler has suggested that "in the current state of our evidence a real solution to the problem is impossible".[22]

### *Line-spacing*

A second contentious issue with the Roman mid-Republican infantry formation concerns the amount of space taken up by each individual legionary. Polybius offers the following description:

> "Now in the case of the Romans also each soldier with his arms occupies a space of three feet in breadth, but as in their mode of fighting each man must move separately, as he has to cover his person with his long shield, turning to meet each expected blow, and as he uses his sword both for cutting and thrusting it is obvious that a looser order is required, and each man must be at a distance of at least three feet from the man next to him in the same rank and those in front of and behind him, if they are to be of proper use." (Paton, 1926).[23]

Polybius' account is clear. He states that because of the particular fighting style of the Romans they needed an open formation. Unlike some other ancient combat systems, this style allowed the Romans to fight in all directions and also both singly or in formation, by using their swords for cutting as well as stabbing and moving their shields in all directions to repel enemy blows. In this open formation, each infantryman took up a space of six feet (1.8m) along the front of the battle-line, and needed to be three feet (0.9m) from the man in front and behind him (plus an unspecified depth taken up by the man himself).[24] For many though Polybius' clear account is untenable, again due to assumptions based on models of combat mechanics. The traditional view of Roman infantry combat, as we shall see later in this chapter, dictates that battle began with an initial massed charge of the entire Roman front line. Such a charge, if it were to take place, would be less effective in Polybius' open order than in a close-order formation, as the density of the formation would be greater. For this reason some scholars prefer to reject Polybius' account in favour of the close-order line-spacing suggested by Vegetius. This is justified by the claim that much of the battle order of Vegetius' "ancient legion" came from Cato the Censor's *De Re Militari*.[25] Vegetius states that:

---

[16] Delbrück (trans. 1975) 293.

[17] Connolly (1998); Warry (1980); Daly (2002).

[18] Kromayer and Veith (1912) 358-9.

[19] Adcock (1970) 10.

[20] Sabin (2000) 1-17 and Goldsworthy (2000) 55-60, who notes that Rome's opponents must also have had similar gaps in their lines to enable them to move.

[21] Daly (2002) 61.

[22] Wheeler (1979) 306.

[23] 18.30.6-9: ἵστανται μὲν οὖν ἐν τρισὶ ποσὶ μετὰ τῶν ὅπλων καὶ Ῥωμαῖοι· τῆς μάχης δ᾽ αὐτοῖς κατ᾽ ἄνδρα τὴν κίνησιν λαμβανούσης διὰ τὸ τῷ μὲν θυρεῷ σκέπειν τὸ σῶμα, συμμετατιθεμένους αἰεὶ πρὸς τὸν τῆς πληγῆς καιρόν τῇ μαχαίρᾳ δ᾽ ἐκ καταφορᾶς καὶ διαιρέσεως ποιεῖσθαι τὴν μάχην προφανὲς ὅτι χάλασμα καὶ διάστασιν ἀλλήλων ἔχειν δεήσει τοὺς ἄνδρας ἐλάχιστον τρεῖς πόδας κατ᾽ ἐπιστάτην καὶ κατὰ παραστάτην, εἰ μέλλουσιν εὐχρηστεῖν πρὸς τὸ δέον.

[24] For his measurements Polybius uses the term πους, which means foot. In Gulbekian (1987) 359-360, the author states that there were three standard measurements for the Greek foot: "The "Attic" of 294.1 ± 1.0 mm (used in Asia Minor and Southern Italy), the "Doric" of 326.9 ± 1.4 mm (Used in Greece and Sicily), and the "Ionic" of 348.7 ± 1.5mm." These correspond to 11.8", 13.1" and 13.9". It is unclear whether Polybius was using the Attic, Doric, Ionic or even the Roman foot (roughly 11.7"). Therefore, here, we shall assume that when Polybius writes τρεῖς πόδας, surely not an exact measurement in itself, he means a measurement of approximately three modern feet, 36" or 0.9m.

[25] On the claim see for example Milner (1996) xviiff, and Gilliver (1999) 104. Even the most recent scholars attempting to move away from this traditional thinking are forced into accepting Vegetius' figures because they accept initial massed charges, though not of the whole line: Goldsworthy (1996) 179; Sabin (1996) 71.

> "Since it has been explained how the battle-lines ought to be drawn up, now I will explain the distances and the measurements of this arrangement. In a field a thousand paces wide [approximately five thousand feet] one battle-line will contain 1,666 foot soldiers because the individual soldiers each occupy three feet. But if you should wish to arrange six battle lines in a field of a thousand paces, 9,996 soldiers are needed. If, however, you should wish to direct this number of men into three battle-lines you will cover 2,000 paces; but it is better to make more battle-lines than to spread out the army. We have said that six feet in depth ought to intervene behind the individual battle-lines, and that the soldiers themselves standing in position occupy each man one foot. Therefore, if you should arrange six battle-lines, an army of 10 thousand men will occupy 42 feet in depth and 1,000 paces in length". (Stelten, 1990).[26]

Here it is claimed that individual soldiers occupied a three foot frontage (0.9m) and one-foot depth (0.3m), with six feet (1.8m) between the ranks; offering the close-order formation necessary for an effective initial massed charge. But there are a number of problems with this passage. Firstly there is no acknowledgement of the various divisions of the Roman army; rather Vegetius describes troops standing in a long unbroken line. As shown above, while Polybius' description of the Roman battle-line included intervals between the maniples, Vegetius' formation does not. Even if one takes the prevalent view that these intervals were filled immediately prior to battle, a front line of 1,666 men has no relation to how a legion would be distributed on a battlefield. Vegetius is merely describing how to fit ever increasing numbers of troops within a one and a half kilometre wide space, with a varying depth depending on the number of men: the Roman legion becomes a phalanx. Secondly, although it is claimed that Vegetius was using a Republican source, the passage preceding his discussion of line spacing seems to describe a battle-line very different from that of the mid-Republic:

> "The law of military formation is this: that the trained and veteran soldiers, whom they previously called *principes*, are located in the first line; in the second line are arranged the bowmen, wearing breastplates, and the best soldiers, with spears and lances, whom formerly they used to call the *hastati*. However, the individual soldiers in a straight line were accustomed to have three feet between them... so that the battle-line is not capable of being seen through and so there is space for handling the weapons... [these two lines] like a solid wall, must be compelled neither to give ground nor at times to pursue, lest they upset the ranks, but rather to meet the approaching enemy and repel or rout him by standing and fighting... [There follows a discussion of three more lines of light infantry missile troops, until] the sixth line, behind all others was held by very strong soldiers who have shields and are protected by every type of armour; whom the ancients called the *triarii*" (Stelten, 1990).[27]

In this passage the *principes* form the front line with the *hastati* and archers (*sagittarii*) making up the second. There follow three lines of light infantry, the first two lines are armed with bows or light javelins, which Vegetius calls the *ferentarii* and the *levis armatura* respectively, the fifth line, which he calls the *fundibulatores*, hurl stones with a sling, and the final line is composed of the *triarii*.[28] Vegetius' description of the Roman battle-line is very different from the three line system of *hastati*, *principes* and *triarii* described in both Polybius and Livy. Rawson claims that it is "unlikely in the extreme" that Vegetius is right in changing the order of Polybius' first two lines. She further suggests that Vegetius' descriptions of the arms of the legionary appear to be based on the imperial period. Finally, she claims that, even if Vegetius used Cato, "Cato has found a very inaccurate transmitter; Vegetius was not an experienced soldier and was tendentious in his desire to reform the army of his time on the basis of that of the very vaguely defined great days of old".[29] His description may refer, in a rather confused way, to the army of his own day or perhaps in some way reflects the very early Republican phalanx of the Servian army, but it does not describe the mid-Republican legion. [30] It should not be used as evidence that the line spacing in the mid-Republic was a close-order three feet per man and certainly not used in preference to Polybius' clear statement.

Polybius was a man both experienced and interested in military matters, who had seen Roman troops in action and was on intimate terms with Roman elite military families.[31] He describes an open infantry formation with a line-spacing of six feet per man and so any model of Roman infantry battle should involve a form of combat

[26] 3.15: *Explanato qualiter debeant acies instrui, nunc podismum mensuramque ipsius ordinationis exponam. In mille passibus campi una acies mille sescentos sexaginta sex suscipiet pedites, propterea quia singuli pugnatores ternos occupant pedes. Quod si sex acies in mille passibus campi volueris ordinare, novem milia nongenti nonaginta sex pedites sunt necessarii. Si autem in terno hunc numerum volueris tendere, duo milia passum conprehendes; sed melius est plures acies facere quam militem spargere. Senos pedes a tergo inter singulas acies in latum diximus interpatere debere, et ipsi bellatores stantes singulos obtinent pedes. Ideoque si sex acies ordinaveris, quadraginta duo pedes in latum et mille passus in longum decem milium hominum tenebit exercitus.*

[27] 3.14: *Instructionis lex est; ut in primo exercitati et veteres milites collocentur, quos antea principes vocabant; in secundo ordine circumdati catafractis sagittarii et optimi milites cum spiculis vel lanceis ordinentur, quos prius hastatos vocabant. Singuli autem armati in directum ternos pedes inter se occupare consueverunt... ut nec acies interluceat et spatium sit arma tractandi... hi enim ad vicem muri nec cedere nec sequi aliquando cogendi sunt, ne ordines turbent, sed venientes adversaries excipere et stando pugnandoque repellere vel fugare... sextus ordo post omnes a firmissimis et scutatis et omni generearmorum munitis bellatoribus tenebatur; quos antique triarios appellabant.*

[28] This six line formation may reflect the six battle line arrangement discussed in 3.15, for which 9,996 men were needed.

[29] Rawson (1971) 18.

[30] For a recent argument against the existence of an early-Republican Roman phalanx see Rich (2007).

[31] Walbank (1979) 12-15.

conforming to this open-order formation, even if this means rethinking traditional models of combat.

***The line-relief system***

The final controversy which we will address is how the Romans replaced or relieved their front-line troops. Our sources make it clear that Romans preferred a multiple-line system over the physical and psychological advantages of a deep formation such as the phalanx, but they remain silent about the thinking behind this tactical decision. One conceivable reason may have been battlefield psychology. It is an axiom that the longer an infantry unit remains close to the enemy the more likely it is to lose its cohesion and break. In general men tend to follow their natural instincts in battle, with the braver men moving to the front, the most timid drifting to the rear, while the majority remain in the middle ready at any moment either to follow the front ranks into victory or the more timid into flight. In ancient battle, what historians and theorists call the 'killing zone' (the distance beyond the user's body that a weapon can strike the enemy) was limited, so only the front few ranks would be engaged in the fighting at any one time. The rear ranks would be forced to watch the approaching danger passively, awaiting their turn to fight, which would come only when the men in front were killed, injured or exhausted. The nineteenth century French military theorist and officer Ardant Du Picq describes the pressure of such a position:

> "These men were subjected to the poignant emotions of combat without being supported by the animation of the struggle. They were thus placed under the moral pressure of the greatest of anxieties. Often they could not stand it until their turn came; they gave way".[32]

The great depth of a phalanx would have initially been psychologically encouraging to the phalangites and certainly intimidating to the enemy. But the vast majority of its members would have remained for much of the battle in this terrible state of anxiety, becoming increasingly likely to flee as the stress was amplified over time. Battles involving a phalanx tended to be short precisely for this reason; if the initial charge of the phalanx was unsuccessful it was just a matter of time before it broke. The Roman three-line system was different. It addressed the problem of battlefield anxiety that plagued the phalanx by ensuring that the stress-levels of the majority of troops remained relatively low by keeping them as a reserve or support line, at a relatively safe distance from the enemy. Another advantage of this system over the phalanx was that it allowed multiple attacks because of the ability to replace tired units with fresh ones.

Livy offers us the most complete account of the line-relief process for the mid-Republican legion, although he places the account anachronistically in the context of the Servian army:

> "[T]he *hastati* were the first of all to engage. If the *hastati* were unable to defeat the enemy, they retreated slowly and were received into the intervals between the companies of the *principes*. The *principes* then took up the fighting and the *hastati* followed them. The *triarii* knelt beneath their banners, with the left leg advanced, having their shields leaning against their shoulders and their spears thrust into the ground and pointing obliquely upwards, as if their battle-line were fortified with a bristling palisade. If the *principes*, too, were unsuccessful in their fight, they fell back slowly from the battle-line on the *triarii*. (From this arose the adage, "to have come to the *triarii*," when things were going badly.) The *triarii* rising up after they had received the *principes* and *hastati* into the intervals between their companies, would draw their companies together and close the lanes, as it were; then, with no more reserves behind to count on, they would charge the enemy in one compact array" (Foster, 1926). [33]

This account occurs within a more general digression about changes within the Roman military system. There are a number of difficulties surrounding this digression, such as the implication that there were fifteen maniples in each of the three lines, or that Livy has the *rorarii* and *accensi*, both terms which necessarily denote light-armed troops, fighting as heavy infantry similar to the *triarii*.[34] However, these problems all involve Livy's description of the constitution of the legion, its size and the change from a phalanx to a manipular based army, rather than the description of the line relief process itself. In fact, the general picture of the manipular system derived from this passage complements Polybius' descriptions of the Roman infantry. Livy describes a three-line system of *hastati*, *principes* and *triarii*, with the divisions based upon age and experience, and with the *triarii* alone fighting with spears and in an unbroken line, in a similar way to Polybius. So despite some difficulties, this

[32] du Picq (trans. 1987) 79. Cf. Goldsworthy (2000) 59-60.

[33] Livy 8.8.9-12: *ubi his ordinibus exercitus instructus esset, hastati omnium primi pugnam inibant. si hastati profligare hostem non possent, pede presso eos retro cedentes in interualla ordinum principes recipiebant. tum principum pugna erat; hastati sequebantur; triarii sub uexillis considebant, sinistro crure porrecto, scuta innixa umeris, hastas suberecta cuspide in terra fixas, haud secus quam uallo saepta inhorreret acies, tenentes. si apud principes quoque haud satis prospere esset pugnatum a prima acie ad triarios se sensim referebant; inde rem ad triarios redisse, cum laboratur, prouerbio increbruit. triarii consurgentes, ubi in interualla ordinum suorum principes et hastatos recepissent, extemplo compressis ordinibus uelut claudebant uias unoque continenti agmine, iam nulla spe post relicta, in hostem incidebant.*

[34] For a full discussion of the problems of this account, see Rawson (1971) 26-31; Oakley (1998) 451-466, especially 459-60 on the confusion over Livy's definitions of *ordo* and *vexillum*. In 8.8.4 Livy states that an *ordo* was made up of 60 men with two centurions and a *vexillarius*, which would only hold true for Polybius' third line. However it is possible that Livy considered an *ordo* to be a century of 60 men, and that his second centurion is in fact an *optiones*. Against this idea stands 8.8.5-6 where it appears that *ordo* and *manipulus* are equivalent. On *rorarii* see Oakley (1998) 469-470, and 471 on *accensi*.

passage remains one of great importance to the question of the Roman line relief system.

For those who believe that the *quincunx* formation remained in battle this passage appears to present few problems. Adcock's reading of this passage claims that the front ranks of the *hastati* began the fighting, with the rear ranks supplying relief to the injured or exhausted. The *hastati*, when beaten, could retreat through the intervals in the second line, as the *principes* advanced for a second assault. The *hastati* then formed the second line, still with their intervals intact. The *principes*, if defeated, could then retire slowly, into the gaps of the *hastati*, forming one united battle-line. This line, as a whole, could then retreat with their ranks intact. On a signal, the combined line of the *hastati* and *principes* would quickly break-up and retire through the intervals in the *triarii*, as this final line of veterans advanced, closed their gaps and formed a single compact array. This would allow the whole army to retreat in safety.[35] Indeed, as Adcock claims, Livy's account seems to imply that the legion did usually fight with the line intervals intact. The *hastati* are received into the line of the *principes* without mention of them changing from a continuous line back into the quincunx formation; Livy claims they merely retreat back through the gaps of the second line. He only mentions the *triarii* fighting as a continuous line, making no mention of the first two lines 'closing their lanes'.

Nevertheless there are some problems with this interpretation of Livy's passage. The main offensive advantage of a line replacement system should be to bring in fresh troops to fight against those already weary from battle. But with this interpretation, as the intervals in the lines remain intact, the fresh troops of the *principes* would face equally fresh enemy troops (those stationed before the intervals in the *hastati*), and so would gain little offensive advantage. A way round this would be to suggest the advantage came not through fresh troops fighting weary men, but by bringing in the more experienced troops of the *principes* to face the same type of enemy.

An alternative interpretation is that the *hastati* retreat back into the gaps of the second line, and battle is immediately joined by both groups. This is a line-reinforcement system, which added force to the fighting of the first line rather than relieving tired troops. With the exhausted *hastati* continuing to fight all the advantages of a line replacement system would be lost. Again there are problems with this interpretation as well. For had Livy intended his description to be a line-reinforcement system, one would expect the *principes* to advance into the gaps in the front line to add more force to the attack, rather than having the *hastati* retreat (*retro cedentes*) into the *principes*. In addition, the retreating *hastati*, if they had not lost their formation entirely, would at least be in some form of disorder, which could easily be passed on to the *principes*.[36]

It is possible then that both of these interpretations may have some grain of truth, that the Roman system offered either line reinforcement or replacement, depending on the circumstances of battle. In any case, these interpretations, and indeed Livy's account itself, seem dry and more suited to men on the training ground than under the stress of combat.

Those who take the view that the Romans fought with an unbroken line have an even harder time explaining the line-relief system. The most damaging objections are that there is no explanation in the sources of how the Romans could fill the gaps created by the *quincunx* system, nor is there any evidence that the Romans fought with an unbroken battle-line, except when the *triarii* joined the battle. Some historians have created highly complex line-relief systems in an attempt to merge Livy's description with their own assumption that the battle-line was continuous. These will be examined later in this chapter. Alternatively it has been argued that the *hastati* did not reopen their intervals to allow line replacement, but rather the *principes* filtered through the *hastati*.[37] This would be possible with Polybius' open formation, but as we have seen, the traditional assumption that battle involved an initial masse charge dictates a close-order formation. Scholars have thus been forced to invent ways in which the line could be converted from close-order to open, despite there being no evidence for such a manoeuvre in our sources.[38]

As we have seen, debate over the Roman mid-Republican infantry formation tends to be fierce. For each of these three fundamental questions there are opposing interpretations of the evidence. Each reading depends on the individual reader's assumptions about the mechanics of infantry fighting. Although due to the nature of our sources no real solution to these problems will ever be acceptable to everyone, nonetheless it is important for our knowledge of Roman warfare and the mid-Republican period as a whole to try to develop the most convincing model possible from the available evidence. It is the contention of this book that such a model must be based directly on the ancient source material, while simultaneously taking into account the archaeological and theoretical parameters of infantry combat, which will now be examined.

## 2. The parameters of Roman infantry battle

This section will examine a series of archaeological, theoretical and psychological parameters which should limit the range into which a plausible model of infantry combat can fall. The first parameter to be analysed will

[35] Adcock (1970) 10-11.

[36] Livy's description of the fighting at the battle of Veseris (8.9.14) perhaps supports the view that the *hastati* and *principes* could fight together as one line.

[37] Connolly (1989) 163.

[38] For examples of how this manoeuvre could be achieved see Walbank (1967) 589, Connolly (1998) 142, Daly (2002) 63.

be the surviving archaeological evidence for Roman infantry equipment in the mid-Republican period. Although this evidence is sparse, it can be used to reveal possible ways in which the Roman legionary may have fought and how it might have affected him on the battlefield.

### *Archaeological parameters*

*Sources of evidence*

The archaeological evidence for the mid-Republican period is rather limited but has been growing in recent years with improved identification of material. Nevertheless, Bishop and Coulston offer the following warning:

> "given the paucity of evidence for this period, it is all too easy to generalise from the particular, but the temptation to over-simplify the equipment of the Republic is best kept at bay by reference to the immensely complicated picture archaeology has given us of a comparatively short period in the early Principate".[39]

There are a small number of archaeological sites producing material from the Republican period, with a predominance of finds from the bases around Numantia. The five camps at Renieblas range from 195-75 BC, with camps I and II dated as early- to mid-second century, camp III identified as that of the consul Fulvius Nobilior, dating from 153-152 BC, and camps IV and V dated to about 80BC. The site of Castillejo was used in 137 BC by Gaius Hostilius Mancinus and in 134-133 by Scipio Aemilianus. The camp at Peña Redonda also dates to the siege of Numantia. A hoard of weapons, including three swords and many *pila*, found at Grad near Šmihel, Slovenia, date from the late third or early second century BC. There is also a deposition of Roman equipment at Entremont in France. These are the main sites producing material for the mid-Republican period.[40] Some later Republican sites have also been used to help produce a picture of the mid-Republican legionary. These include the supposed *Castra Caecilia* at Cáceres el Viejo, thought to date from the Sertorian wars, and the weapons found in the vicinity of Alesia, dating for the middle of the first century BC.[41] The main iconographical evidence for the period is provided by the Aemilius Paullus monument, raised in Delphi after his defeat of Perseus at Pydna in 168BC, and the Altar of Domitius Ahenobarbus, dating from around 115BC.[42] It is from this small body of evidence that we can try to reconstruct the Republican soldier.

*Swords*[43]

The most famous sword used in this period is what has come to be known as the *gladius Hispaniensis*.[44] It is generally accepted that the Romans produced this sword after they encountered a similar weapon in Spain.[45] It is a short sword with a long point and both edges sharpened. There are a few examples of this type of sword which still survive intact from the Republican period.[46] One such example was found in Delos and dates from 69 BC. It measures 760mm in length including the tang, the blade measures 631mm, with a short triangular point, and is approximately 57mm wide. The sword still has its scabbard, which has suspension rings and two buckles. Still evident are the remains of a charred wooden pommel, held in place by seven rivets. Swords found in France share characteristics of the Delos sword: straight blades with lengths of between 600 and 670mm, similar scabbards and suspension systems, but with longer triangular points. The swords found at Šmihel, dating from earlier in the period, are also similar in shape and dimensions (blades range in length from 622 to 661mm; in width 40 to 45mm at the broadest point; with a long triangular point).[47] Later early imperial examples tend to have a wider variation, with lengths between 400 and 550mm, excluding the tang. The blade widths taper from 54-75mm to 48-60mm, with the length of the point varying between 96 and 200 mm.[48] It seems likely that a similar variation would have existed during the mid-Republican period. Finds of Celtic long swords on Spanish sites in apparently Roman contexts may suggest the use of this weapon by some Roman forces. In the same way, an example of the Spanish single-edged *Falcata* found at Cáceres el Viejo may also suggest Roman use.[49]

---

[39] Bishop and Coulston (1993) 48. On the potential weaknesses of an archaeological approach to ancient warfare in general see most recently Whitby (2007) 72-81.

[40] Bishop and Coulston (2006). On Numantia and Renieblas see Schulten (1927 and 1929); Dobson (2008); Curchin (1991) 34-9; Keay (1988) 36. Castillejo: Keay (1988) 38; Peña Redonda: Keay (1988) 40. Šmihel: Horvat (1997); Kmetic *et al* (2004). Entremont: Coutagne (1987), 64-5; Rivet (1988) 40.

[41] Cáceres el Viejo: Keay (1988) 43 and Ulbert (1985). Alesia: Feugère (trans. 2002) 68; Reddé *et al* (1995); Sievers (1995); Brouquier-Reddé (1997).

[42] The Aemilius Paullus monument shows two legionaries with shields. On the frieze of this monument see Kähler (1965). The Altar of Ahenobarbus shows four infantrymen, one cavalryman and one officer. On this monument in general see Coarelli (1968); for the dating, Coarelli (1968) 338-343; Torelli (1982) 15. For photographs of both see:http://www.romanarmy.com/cms/component/option,com_easygallery/act,categories/cid,73/Itemid,135/ .

[43] On swords see Quesada Sanz (1997); Horvat (1997) Fig. 10; Feugère (trans. 2002) 79-80; Feugère (1994); Bishop and Coulston (2006) 54-56; Lang (1988); Le Bohec (1997); Connolly (1997), etc.

[44] Main literary sources discussing the *gladius hispaniensis*: Suda, s.v. *machaira*; Polybius, 2.30.8, 2.33.6, 3.114.2-4, 6.23.6; Claudius Quadrigarius, Fr. 10b; Livy 7.10.5, 22.26.5, 31.34.1-5, 38.21.13; Aulus Gellius, *N. Att.* 9.13.4. Quesada Sanz (1997) 254, 268, follows the Suda and believes that this was adopted around the time of the Hannibalic War.

[45] Sandars (1913) 205-94 argues that this axiom is a myth.

[46] Feugère (1994) ; Connolly (1997) 49-56; Quesada Sanz (1997).

[47] France: Feugère (1994) Figs. 10 and 11; Slovenia : Horvat (1997) 113, Fig. 10. For similar swords found in Spain : Quesada Sanz (1997).

[48] Bishop and Coulston (2006) 78. On early imperial changes in sword type see Lang (1988).

[49] Bishop and Coulston (1993) 54. On Celtic swords see Schulten (1929) pls. 25.9; 26.6 (scabbard); on the *falcata* found at Cáceres el Viejo see Ulbert (1985) pl. 25, 201. The fortress at Cáceres el Viejo was meant for one legion, but as Keppie suggests in his review of Ulbert's work, "from the presence of substantial numbers of Iberian broaches, the legion

The way in which these swords were used in battle has important implications for reconstructions of the infantry formation and the mechanics of Roman combat. Bishop and Coulston believe that the Roman short sword implies a close-order style of combat, with the sword used predominantly for stabbing rather than slashing in the manner of the Celtic long sword.[50] This can be supported by the evidence of Vegetius, who claims that the Roman sword's main function was stabbing:

> "They [the ancient Romans] learned to strike not with the edge, but with the point. For the Romans not only easily beat those fighting with the edge, but even made mock of them, for a cut, whatever its force, seldom kills, because the vitals are protected by both armour and bones. But a stab driven 2 inches in is fatal; for necessarily whatever goes in penetrates the vitals. Secondly while a cut is being delivered the right arm and flank are exposed; whereas a stab is inflicted with the body remaining covered, and the enemy is wounded before he realises it. That is why, it is agreed, the Romans used chiefly this method for fighting".[51]

Using the sword in this way would imply a very close-order infantry formation. The line-spacing per man would only need to be slightly wider than his shield, corresponding perhaps to the three feet spacing advocated by Vegetius.[52] In opposition to this, Polybius claims that:

> "The shields of the Celts and Spaniards were very similar, but their swords were entirely different, those of the Spaniards thrusting with as deadly effect as they cut, but the Gaulish sword being only able to slash and requiring a long sweep to do so" (Paton, 1922).[53]

> "Besides the shield they [the Romans] also carry a sword, hanging on the right thigh and called a Spanish sword. This is excellent for thrusting, and both of its edges cut effectually, as the blade is very strong and firm" (Paton, 1923).[54]

Polybius believes that the Roman sword was used both for stabbing *and* cutting. He uses the term κέντημα, from κεντέω 'stab', to signify an action with the point of the sword, and καταφορᾶ, the downward stroke of a sword, to denote cutting as opposed to thrusting.[55] The general shape of republican swords appears to support Polybius' statement. Straight blades with sharpened edges measuring over 600mm and triangular points, make the sword suitable for both cutting and thrusting. Some of the surviving swords show slight waisting of the blade, which may suggest they had been worn down by repeated sharpening, consistent with a cutting weapon.[56]

The finds of the *falcata* and long Celtic swords are also interesting. The Spanish *falcata*, a type of saber, although originally a slashing sword, had been developed by the mid-Republican period into a sword for both cutting and thrusting. This was done by extending the cutting edge round the point and along the back for about one third the length of the blade. This allowed the *falcata* to be used in a similar way to Polybius' description of the Spanish sword.[57] The long Celtic sword was solely a slashing weapon and could not be used effectively for stabbing. If these finds were more that souvenirs and instead indicate periodic Roman adoption of these types of weapons, it would imply that at least some of the legionaries were using the slashing action implied by Polybius.

Gabriel and Metz have attempted to quantify the lethal capabilities of ancient weapons. Their tests showed that a well built man using the *gladius* in a slashing motion could generate an impact energy of 101 footpounds (fpds), while a thrust from a *gladius* could only generate 21.3 fpds.[58] As it requires less than 2fpds to penetrate naked human flesh, if the force is concentrated in 1 square inch, both forms of attack would be lethal.[59] But against any form of body protection, slashing with a *gladius* would be more effective than thrusting. Nonetheless, the impact energy required to penetrate iron armour is 251fpds, so neither attack could wound areas of the body protected in this way.[60] In order to kill an enemy the *gladius* would have to be thrust into the unprotected groin area or face, while a slashing action would allow the legionary to

shared the site with some Spanish auxiliaries" (Keppie (1987) 401). Although these finds occurred in Roman contexts, they were not necessarily weapons used by Romans on active service, but could have been taken as souvenirs.

[50] Bishop and Coulston (1993) 53; (2006) 56. They do however include the warning: "we ought not to allow the fervour of later writers for the stabbing action to mislead us into seeing the sword as unifunctional" ((2006) 56).

[51] Vegetius 1.12: *Praeterea non caesim sed punctim ferire discebant. Nam caesim pugnantes non solum facile vicere sed etiam derisere Romani. Caesa enim, quovis impetu veniat, non frequenter interficit, cum et armis vitalia defendantur et ossibus; at contra puncta duas uncias adacta mortalis est, necesse est enim ut vitalia penetret quicquid inmergitur. Deinde,dum caesa infertur, brachium dextrum latusque nudatur; puncta autem tecto corpore infertur et adversarium sauciat, antequam videat.Ideoque ad dimicandum hoc praecipue genere usos constat esse Romanos.*

[52] 3.14.6. Oakley (1998) 134-136 follows Vegetius in believing that the Roman sword was only used for stabbing. Cf. Livy 7.10.5-9, where Manlius kills his Gaul with two stabs to the groin while the Gaul's wild slashing bounces off Manlius' armour.

[53] Pol. 3.114.2-3: τῶν δ᾽ Ἰβήρων καὶ Κελτῶν ὁ μὲν θυρεὸς ἦν παραπλήσιος, τὰ δὲ ξίφη τὴν ἐναντίαν εἶχε διάθεσιν· τῆς μὲν γὰρ οὐκ ἔλαττον τὸ κέντημα τῆς καταφορᾶς ἴσχυε πρὸς τὸ βλάπτειν, ἡ δὲ Γαλατικὴ μάχαιρα μίαν εἶχε χρείαν τὴν ἐκ καταφορᾶς, καὶ ταύτην ἐξ ἀποστάσεως.

[54] 6.23.6-7: ἅμα δὲ τῷ θυρεῷ μάχαιρα· ταύτην δὲ περὶ τὸν δεξιὸν φέρει μηρόν, καλοῦσι δ᾽ αὐτὴν Ἰβηρικήν. ἔχει δ᾽ αὕτη κέντημα διάφορον καὶ καταφορὰν ἐξ ἀμφοῖν τοῖν μεροῖν βίαιον διὰ τὸ τὸν ἀβελίσκον αὐτῆς ἰσχυρὸν καὶ μόνιμον εἶναι.

[55] LSJ s.v. Vegetius also differentiates the two actions of a sword, using *caesa* (from *caedere*) for a slash and *puncta* (from *pungere*) for a stab.

[56] Waisted blades: one of the swords from Šmihel (Horvat (1997) 113, Fig. 10) as well as examples from Giubiasco (Connolly (1997) 50, Fig. 8), Vrhnika, Caminreal and Alesia (Rapin (2001)).

[57] Sandars (1913) 240.

[58] Gabriel and Metz (1991) 59.

[59] Gabriel and Metz (1991) 63.

[60] Gabriel and Metz (1991) 63.

attack the neck and head. With a cutting action, the *gladius* could also be used to disable the enemy by slicing the arms or legs. Against a protected chest a powerful slash could knock an enemy off balance, while a slashing blow to the head would disorient the enemy or knock him unconscious. In order to use the *gladius* to its greatest effect in battle, it should be used in both a thrusting and a cutting motion.[61] Our limited archaeological evidence seems to support Polybius' statement. With this more expansive style of sword-play each man would require more space to fight, necessitating an open formation such as Polybius' six feet line-spacing.[62]

Unfortunately, due to the lack of evidence for the swords in the republican period it is impossible to do more than speculate about how it was used and how this may have affected the style of combat. The evidence we do have supports Polybius' description of the Roman fighting style. It also suggests that the sizes and types of the swords were not standardised in this period. This variation may have its root in the nature of the mid-Republican legion: this army was a citizen militia, rather than a professional army, and each man was required to arm themselves. Expensive equipment would have been passed down from father to son, or looted from the enemy, leading to a wider variety of sword types in use at any one time.[63] It is important to view this army as made up of individuals, rather than a monolithic block. Personal preferences and variation in equipment would lead to different types of sword fighting, some may have slashed and cut, and others may have preferred to stay behind their shield and stabbed at the enemies' faces and groins. The model of infantry combat should not be proscriptive as the type of fighting and the formation employed may have varied depending on the circumstances of the battle.

*Pila*

The second most important offensive weapon of the mid-Republican infantry man was the *pilum*, which is again described by Polybius:

> "In addition [to the shield and sword], each heavy infantryman has two *pila*, a bronze helmet and greaves. The *pila* are of two sorts – stout and fine. Of the stout ones some are round and a palm's length in diameter and others are a palm square. The fine *pila*, which they carry in addition to the stout ones, are like moderate sized hunting spears, the length of the haft in all cases being about 3 cubits [ca. 1.3m]. Each is fitted with a barbed iron head of the same length as the haft. This they attach so securely to the haft, carrying the attachment halfway up the latter and fixing it with numerous rivets, that in action the iron will break sooner than become detached, although its thickness at the bottom where it comes in contact with the wood is a finger's breadth and a half [ca. 2.9cm]; such great care do they take about attaching it firmly" (Paton, 1923).[64]

The *pilum* was a close-range javelin that used weight, rather than velocity, to provide its penetrating power. The pyramidal head found on most *pila* (sometimes barbed as Polybius mentions) reveals that it was designed as an armour-piercing weapon.[65] Its primary function was to penetrate an enemy shield, then, aided by the long narrow shank following behind the larger head, the point would carry on through to the body of the enemy. A useful by-product of this design was that the shank tended to bend upon impact, disabling the weapon, so it could not be re-used by the enemy. In some cases the enemy's shield would also be put out of action, leaving him defenceless.[66] Modern experiments carried out by Connolly, reveal that a *pilum* weighed around 1kg and had an effective range of less than 30m. He found that at point blank range (5m) a *pilum* could easily pierce a 7mm thick birch plywood target. In some of the tests bending of the shank occurred similar to that found in surviving examples.[67]

The origin of the weapon has been much debated, but no satisfactory consensus has been reached.[68] The earliest surviving Republican examples date from the late third century and were found at Castellruf in Spain and Talamoniaccio in Italy. The most famous examples are from the Roman camps around Numantia and there are also finds from Gaul at Entremont and Alesia.[69] A complete example of the heavy *pilum* comes from Renieblas. "With a head 60mm (2in) long, a shank of 554mm (22in), and a tang 90mm (3.5in) long and 55mm (2in) broad, it was fastened to its shaft by means of two rivets through the tang, 35mm (1.5in) apart".[70] Renieblas also has a complete example of the lighter *pilum*, which

[61] Livy 31.34.1-5 describes the horrific wounds caused by *gladii* used in this way: "now they [the Macedonians] saw bodies dismembered by the Spanish sword (*gladio hispaniensi*) arms torn away with the shoulders, heads separated from bodies with the neck sliced all the way through, intestines laid bare, and other repulsive wounds"

[62] i.e. shield width plus right arm length plus blade length; 6ft spacing: 18.30.6-9.

[63] On variation in equipment in general see Gilliver (2007).

[64] 6.23.9-11: πρὸς δὲ τούτοις ὑσσοὶ δύο καὶ περικεφαλαία χαλκῆ καὶ προκνημίς. τῶν δ᾿ ὑσσῶν εἰσιν οἱ μὲν παχεῖς, οἱ δὲ λεπτοί. τῶν δὲ στερεωτέρων οἱ μὲν στρογγύλοι παλαιστιαίαν ἔχουσι τὴν διάμετρον, οἱ δὲ τετράγωνοι τὴν πλευράν. οἵ γε μὴν λεπτοὶ σιβυνίοις ἐοίκασι συμμέτροις, οὓς φοροῦσι μετὰ τῶν προειρημένων. ἁπάντων δὲ τούτων τοῦ ξύλου τὸ μῆκός ἐστιν ὡς τρεῖς πήχεις. προσήρμοσται δ᾿ ἑκάστοις βέλος σιδηροῦν ἀγκιστρωτόν, ἴσον ἔχον τὸ μῆκος τοῖς ξύλοις· οὗ τὴν ἔνδεσιν καὶ τὴν χρείαν οὕτως ἀσφαλίζονται βεβαίως, ἕως μέσων τῶν ξύλων ἐνδιδέντες καὶ πυκναῖς ταῖς λαβίσι καταπερονῶντες, ὥστε πρότερον ἢ τὸν δεσμὸν ἐν ταῖς χρείαις ἀναχαλασθῆναι τὸν σίδηρον θραύεσθαι, καίπερ ὄντα τὸ πάχος ἐν τῷ πυθμένι καὶ τῇ πρὸς τὸ ξύλον συναφῇ τριῶν ἡμιδακτυλίων· ἐπὶ τοσοῦτον καὶ τοιαύτην πρόνοιαν ποιοῦνται τῆς ἐνδέσεως.

[65] On republican *pila* in general see: Bishop and Coulston (1993) 48-51, (2006) 50-53; Brouqier-Reddé (1997); Sievers (1997); Fuegere (1994) and (trans. 2002) 80-83; Connolly (1997).

[66] Caesar, *B Gall.* 1.25.3.

[67] Connolly (2000) 43-46.

[68] There are arguments for a Samnite (Reinach (1907)), Spanish (Schulten (1911)) and Etruscan (Connolly (1981) 100) origin.

[69] Spain: Ìlvarez Arza and Cubero Argente (1999); Italy: Luik (2000); Gaul: Reddé *et al* (1995) 148-9; Fuegere (1994).

[70] Bishop and Coulston (1993) 50.

was usually socketed. "The length of the head of the weapon from Renieblas measured 20mm (0.75 in) to its broadest point, from where it measured 232mm (9in) to the socket base; which was 20mm (0.75in) in diameter".[71]

The *pilum* poses two main problems for the reconstruction of mid-Republican Roman infantry combat. The first will be discussed here, the second within the section on Roman shields. The problem is whether the Roman infantryman carried two *pila* into battle, and how this was possible. Goldsworthy states the issue clearly: "it is difficult to see how a man could have had time to throw more than one *pilum*, when both he and the enemy ranks were approaching over a distance of, at most 30 metres, at a run".[72] Connolly attempts to quantify this problem, "in the final charge both armies must have been advancing in excess of 10 km per hour with a closing speed of about 25 km per hour or seven metres per second".[73] If Connolly's estimates are correct, the Roman infantryman would be left four seconds in which to throw both of his *pila* and ready himself for the clash. In response to this issue Goldsworthy suggests that the heavy infantryman carried only one *pilum* into battle.[74] As often, Delbrück was the first to propose this solution, claiming that:

> "it is an undoubted misunderstanding of Polybius when he gives each legionary two *pila*, a light one and a heavy one (6.23). Not every legionary is outfitted with two *pila*, but there are two different types of *pilum*; aside from the light one that the legionary takes into the field, there is a still heavier one, which is used for the defence of fortifications".[75]

Delbrück provides no evidence for his claim that the heavier *pilum* was only used for defending fortifications. His assertion, as well as Goldsworthy's, seems to contradict the evidence of Polybius. Modern studies rely on Polybius' accounts directly as the most reliable evidence for the mid-Republican legion and so it is misguided to discard Polybius' evidence simply because it does not correspond with the established views of infantry combat.

The problem stems from a traditional assumption that Roman infantry battle began with a massed charge. Were this assumption removed, the issue would disappear. Zhmodikov has attempted to do just that.[76] He argues that legionary combat was based far more on missile exchange than hand-to-hand combat, and that this exchange was *not* confined to the start, but was a continuous feature of a battle. This model of missile warfare removes the initial massed charge of the whole infantry line and with it the problem of the *pila*. It is necessary in this model that each man carried two *pila* (at least!).[77] Although not entirely convincing, Zhmodikov's model highlights the value of thinking outside traditional assumptions. A model of Roman infantry combat should be derived from, rather than imposed on, the evidence of our sources.

*Spears*

The *triarii*, unlike the *hastati* and *principes* were armed with a long thrusting spear rather than *pila*. This had an iron head, with a variety of shapes, a wooden shaft and a butt. The head was obviously used for thrusting, but the butt could be used to protect the shaft when it was stuck into the ground or as a secondary weapon if the head broke off. There are examples of spear heads from this period, but it is impossible to distinguish Roman from allied or enemy weapons.[78]

*Shields*

The most important form of defensive equipment in the Roman infantryman's panoply was his oval-shaped shield, known in Latin as a *scutum*. This type of shield is described in detail by Polybius:

> "The convex surface of [the shield] measures two and a half feet in width and four feet in length, the thickness at the rim being a palm's breadth [ca. 7.5cm].[79] It is made of two planks glued together, the outer surface being then covered first with canvas and then with calf-skin. Its upper and lower rims are strengthened by iron edging which protects it from descending blows and from injury when rested on the ground. It also has an iron boss fixed to it which turns aside the more formidable blows of stones, pikes, and heavy missiles in general" (Paton, 1923).[80]

A similar shield was found in 1900 at Kasr el-Harit in Fayûm, Egypt, which was originally thought to be Celtic.[81] Owing to its remarkable similarity to the sculptural representation of Roman shields on the altar of Domitius Ahenobarbus and the monument of Aemilius Paullus it is now thought to be Roman, from the mid-

[71] Bishop and Coulston (1993) 50. For different varieties of *pila* see Bishop and Coulston (1993) 50; Connolly (2000) 43-46.

[72] Goldsworthy (1996) 199.

[73] Connolly (2000) 46.

[74] Goldsworthy (1996) 199; followed by Daly (2002) 64.

[75] Delbrück (trans. 1975) 280.

[76] The traditional view of an initial massed charge and Zhmodikov's argument will be examined in detail in the final section of this chapter.

[77] Zhmodikov (2000) 67-78.

[78] Bishop and Coulston (1993) 52.

[79] Treloar (1971) argues that this measurement refers to the depth of the curvature of the shield rather than the thickness of the rim.

[80] 6.23.2-5: οὗ τὸ μὲν πλάτος ἐστὶ τῆς κυρτῆς ἐπιφανείας πένθ᾽ ἡμιποδίων, τὸ δὲ μῆκος ποδῶν τεττάρων, τὸ δ᾽ ἐπ᾽ ἴτυος [πάχος] ἔτι καὶ παλαιστιαῖον - ἐκ διπλοῦ σανιδώματος ταυροκόλλῃ πεπηγώς, ὀθονίῳ, μετὰ δὲ ταῦτα μοσχείῳ δέρματι περιείληται τὴν ἐκτὸς ἐπιφάνειαν. ἔχει δὲ περὶ τὴν ἴτυν ἐκ τῶν ἄνωθεν καὶ κάτωθεν μερῶν σιδηροῦν σιάλωμα, δι᾽ οὗ τάς τε καταφορὰς τῶν μαχαιρῶν ἀσφαλίζεται καὶ τὰς πρὸς τὴν γῆν ἐξερείσεις. προσήρμοσται δ᾽ αὐτῷ καὶ σιδηρᾶ κόγχος, ἣ τὰς ὁλοσχερεῖς ἀποστέγει πληγὰς λίθων καὶ σαρισῶν καὶ καθόλου βιαίων βελῶν.

[81] Kimmig (1940), including photographs of the shield. See also Sekunda (1991) 80-83, who claims that similar shields were in general use in the Ptolemaic army.

Republican period. This shield is described by Bishop and Coulston:

> "1.28m long (4ft; 4.3 Rft) and 0.635m wide (2ft; 2.1Rft), was fashioned from plywood of three layers of wooden strips, possibly birch wood, laid with the outer ones horizontal. The nine or ten vertical strips were between 60 and 100mm (2.33 and 4 in) in breadth, the 40 horizontal ones 25-50mm (1-2 in). An interesting aspect of the shield's form, and one which directly affected the dynamic of its behaviour, was the fact that it was thicker in the centre than at the edges (giving it strength near the boss and flexibility near the rim). Both inner and outer surfaces were covered with lamb's wool felt (the inner covering overlapping that on the outer face by 50-60mm (2-2.33 in); the edges were not bound with metal. The shield had a wooden 'barleycorn' boss with a vertical rib (*spina*) attached with iron nails above and below it on the shield face, and a horizontal handgrip behind the boss. The remains of the rings used for attaching carrying straps were also found inside the shield".[82]

The reason for designating the Kasr el-Harit shield as Roman, rather than Celtic, involves its horizontal handgrip. This is very similar to a representation on the Altar of Ahenobarbus showing a soldier holding a shield with a horizontal handgrip.[83] The Kasr el-Harit shield also has a wooden boss which extends into a spine along the vertical axis of the shield. Frames 13 and 20 of the Aemilius Paullus frieze appear to represent a similar type shield, as do the shields of the first, second and fifth Roman legionary figures on the Ahenobarbus altar.

The Kasr el-Harit shield differs slightly from those described by Polybius. It is narrower by half a foot, was made of three layers rather than Polybius' two, was covered in lamb's wool felt rather than calf skin, and the edges were not bound with metal for protection.[84] Polybius' shield includes an iron boss in the centre to turn away missiles, whereas the Kasr el-Harit shield has a wooden boss and spine for this purpose. These differences may indicate that there were at least two types of Republican legionary shield, making it likely that, as with swords, there may have been some variation among shield-types. With no uniform type of shield, various similar types may have been used to perform the same tasks.[85]

Shield widths of roughly 2.5ft (0.75m) would affect line spacing, though they can be used equally to support both Vegetius' 3ft and Polybius' 6ft spacing. With Vegetius' spacing, the shield would leave a gap of 0.5ft between one shield and another, in which space only a stabbing action would be possible. With Polybius' spacing a Roman shield would leave about 3.5ft, enough room for a 1.5-2ft blade to be wielded in a cutting motion without interfering with one's neighbour. The size of the Roman shield offers no hard evidence for the line spacing or the fighting style of the Roman infantry; rather it underlines the plausibility of both.

The horizontal handgrips of Kasr el-Harit shield and the shield on the Altar of Ahenobarbus also reveal some clues about the shield's use. The handgrip is protected on the outside by a boss, iron in Polybius' description and wooden on the Kasr el-Harit shield. Polybius claims that the purpose of this boss was to "[turn] aside the more formidable blows of stones, pikes, and heavy missiles in general".[86] So the function of the shield was to defend against missile fire from all directions. The horizontal handgrip is suitable to this task as it allows the bearer to raise it above the head and across both sides of the body to deflect missiles. This can be seen in frame 24 of the Aemilius Paullus frieze, where a soldier wields a shield with a horizontal handgrip above his head.[87] It is unclear whether the soldier is defending himself against a missile attack, but this frame does show that the Roman shield could be handled in this way. This type of handgrip offers a freer range of movement than the vertical arm strap of the hoplite shield used in a Greek phalanx. Such freedom of movement with the shield would necessitate an open formation, such as that described by Polybius. Reconstructions of this type of shield weigh about 10kg, which, although heavy, is not too heavy for a trained soldier.[88] A similar shield, though flat with a *vertical* handgrip was found at Doncaster weighing 9kg.[89] This shield dates to 300 years later than the mid-Republican period but it does show that such a weight was not unfeasible.

The Greek hoplite shield was held by a vertical strap and had a bowl shape, allowing the bearer to press his left shoulder against the shield and transfer a large proportion of his body weight through it. This meant that the shield could be used offensively to drive forward into the enemy and knock him off balance. The flat outer surface enabled the rear ranks to push on the backs of those in front of them, adding their own weight to the massed drive forward of the whole formation. This was the archetypal form of combat for a phalanx and is known by the Greek term for 'pushing', an *othismos*.[90]

The Roman shield could certainly be used offensively to 'punch' the enemy and for individual pushing, but not for

[82] Bishop and Coulston (1993) 58-9.

[83] Kähler (1965) frames 6, 7 and 24 show representations of similar shields with horizontal handgrips on the Aemilius Paullus monument.

[84] The lack of a metal binding on the Kasr el-Harit shield appears impractical in a battle situation. Against a slashing blow, the wood could easily splinter making the shield practically useless. It is possible then that it was not a real shield but rather a votive offering.

[85] This variation is perhaps reflected by Livy 44.35.21, where the Romans appear to be fighting with the *scutum ligusticum*, a long, light rectangular shield (cf. Diodorus 5.39.7).

[86] 6.23.5.

[87] Kähler (1965) 24.

[88] Connolly (1998) 131.

[89] Buckland (1978) 247-69.

[90] Recently, even this traditional view of massed pushing in a hoplite battle has been questioned, cf. Krentz (1985b) 51-55, 61 and (1994) 47, Goldsworthy (1997) and Van Wees (2004) 189. Against this see Luginbill (1994).

an initial massed charge and *othismos*.[91] The horizontal handgrip, held either against the body with the arm flat against the left side or with the arm outstretched in front of the body, would have made it very difficult for the Roman legionary to charge into the enemy. With the shield held against the body, running towards and crashing into the enemy with the left shoulder would be very awkward owing to the length of the *scutum*, as the bottom lip would constantly bang into the left shin and get tangled up in the legs. Even with greaves (lower leg protectors) this would be uncomfortable.[92] Crashing into an enemy with the left arm outstretched would lead to broken forearms and wrists. The very shape of the *scutum*, a long oval, the use of greaves and the weight of the rest of the Roman panoply, would make running awkward and a massed and coordinated infantry charge very difficult, if not impossible. Unlike the Greek equivalent, the Roman shield, with its wooden or iron boss, would not spread weight evenly across its surface, making it a hindrance within an *othismos*. If the Roman rear ranks tried to add their weight to the drive forward, they would have to force their shield bosses into backs of the men in front of them, both an uncomfortable and dangerous tactic.[93] The archaeological evidence of the Roman shield suggests that the Roman form of combat would not usually involve a coordinated massed charge at the enemy followed by a shield drive. Instead the evidence implies a more open and individualistic style of fighting in which the shield was used predominantly to deflect enemy blows from all directions, as Polybius states, and to punch the enemy in hand-to-hand combat.

The horizontal handgrip also brings in to question Polybius' statement that a heavy infantryman carried two *pila* into battle. This handgrip would make it difficult to also carry a *pilum* in the left hand. This has lead some to discard Polybius' statement and suggest that the heavy infantryman only carried one *pilum* in battle, leaving the other in camp. But rejecting Polybius' claim need not be necessary. A relief from the Flavian period shows an auxiliary holding a javelin in one hand and carrying two further javelins, which seem to be attached to the inside of his shield.[94] These javelins are not *pila* and the relief is a depiction of a soldier from a period over two hundred years later than the mid-Republic, but the republican *pila* could have been held in a similar way. The Kasr el-Harit shield has the remains of rings for attaching carrying straps. In battle these carrying straps may have been adjusted to hold the second *pilum*. Connolly believes that the second *pilum* could have been held by the left thumb against the inner surface of the shield rather than by straps, although he admits from his own experience that this was difficult.[95] If the second pilum was held in the shield hand, the size and weight of this javelin would have affected the manoeuvrability of the shield and made running even more difficult for the legionary. A simple solution may be that second *pilum* was placed on the ground before an attack, and picked up again afterwards when the ranks had reformed.[96]

*Other protective equipment*

The Roman infantryman wore a helmet, body armour and greaves (possibly only one). The most common type of helmet in the mid-Republic was the *Montefortino* helmet (named after the place where it was first found). This helmet was adopted in the fourth century from a Celtic design. It is basically a hemispherical copper alloy bowl beaten into shape, with a small neck-guard and triangular cheek pieces.[97] These cheek pieces covered the ears and must have made it difficult to hear orders in the midst of a battle. This limitation may have had an effect on the type of combat employed. Men who could not hear would be less likely to respond to an attack initiated by an aural order, than to optical stimuli from the few soldiers stationed within their limited range of sight. For this reason grand tactical manoeuvres initiated by this type of order, such as a massed charge, which depends on the whole line moving as one coordinated unit, would have been difficult to carry out effectively. Instead simpler, smaller scale, self-motivated attacks would have been more likely, as when one of the braver men moved out of the battle-line to attack, soldiers stationed around him would respond to this visual stimulus and follow in his wake.

On top of the helmet was a crest knob which Polybius claims held long feathers in order to strike fear into the enemy by making a man appear taller.[98] The evolution of this type of helmet broadly involved the neck-guard increasing in size down to the Principate. Connolly argues that the fighting position of the infantryman became more upright as the neck-guard became larger. So he suggests that the mid-Republican soldier, with a small neck-guard, would have fought in a crouched position with his head up to protect the neck as much as possible. In this fighting position the legionary would be more likely to use a thrusting action with the sword and line up in a close-order formation.[99] This position would be extremely uncomfortable and difficult to fight in for any length of time, as well as exposing the infantryman to

[91] Note Livy 9.41.18-19: "They did their work more with shields than with swords, swinging them from the shoulder and knocking down their enemies with the bosses" (Foster, 1926) (*scutis magis quam gladiis geritur res; umbonibus incussaque ala sternuntur hostes*) Cf. 4.37.10, 30.34.3, 34.46.10, etc. Also see, Gellius 9.13.4 = Claud. Quad. 10b (Peter) describing single combat between a Roman and a Gaul, in which the Roman 'punches' his shield twice against his enemy's shield. Oakley (1998) 766, discusses this offensive use of the shield, including a list of passages from other Latin writers. Goldsworthy (1997) 19-20, and Van Wees (2004) 190, argue that this form of individual 'punching' or 'pushing' was more likely than massed pushing in hoplite battle.

[92] Polybius 6.23.8.

[93] Goldsworthy (1996) 206-8.

[94] Bishop and Coulston (1993) 29 fig 5a.

[95] Connolly (1998) 142.

[96] Cf. Livy 6.12.8: 'let us place our *pila* at our feet and arm our right hands with swords' (*Pilis ante pedes positis gladiis tantum dextras armemus*). At 10.29.6 Livy suggests that *pila* could be picked up between attacks, though the *pila* in this account had previously been thrown rather than placed on the ground.

[97] Quesada Sanz (1997); Feugere (trans. 2002) 70-3; Bishop and Coulston (2006) 65-6.

[98] 6.23.12-13. On display see Gilliver (2007).

[99] Connolly (1991) 362.

attacks from above.[100] The development of the larger neck-guard itself suggests that the infantry actually fought in a position where the back of the neck was vulnerable, making Connolly's intentional crouched position less convincing.

Two types of mid-Republican body armour are described by Polybius:

> "The common soldiers wear in addition a breastplate of brass a span square [c.230mm],[101] which they place in front of the heart and call the heart-protector, this completing their accoutrements; but those who are rated above ten thousand drachmas wear instead of this a coat of chain-mail" (Paton, 1923).[102]

Similar breastplates, both rectangular and round have been attested by finds in Campania, Puglia and Abruzzon-Molise. A round bronze plate was also found near Numantia.[103] Both the Aemilius Paullus monument and the Altar of Ahenobarbus show soldiers wearing ring-mail. The cuirasses are thigh length, again making running difficult, with shoulder doubling for extra protection against slashing weapons, and were worn with a belt, to transfer some of the weight from the shoulders.

The final pieces of protective equipment mentioned by Polybius are greaves.[104] Although there are no examples of greaves in the Republican archaeological record, Bishop and Coulston suggest that the Roman legionary may have only worn one greave, on the left leg.[105] The combination of greave, shield, and helmet offered complete armour coverage of the infantryman's left side. This full coverage of the left side may tempted the legionary to expose as little of his vulnerable right side as possible. This could be achieved by making one's frontal spacing as small as possible and using the sword only for stabbing, perhaps reflected in Vegetius' close-order line-spacing.

The archaeological evidence of the mid-Republican army is open to debate. We have seen that the Roman sword can be taken to support both a close-order and an open-order infantry formation, and perhaps suggests that the formation could vary depending on the circumstances of battle. This argument can not be resolved through archaeology alone. At times the archaeological evidence can offer some less contentious insights into the mechanics of Roman infantry battle. The shape of the Roman shield made running difficult. The horizontal handgrip, though useful when carrying the shield on the march, limited the offensive use of the shield. It could be used to 'punch' the enemy or to deflect missiles and blows from the sword, but could not be used to crash into the enemy and drive him backwards in an *othismos*. The use of greaves and thigh-length chain mail further limited ability of the legionary to run, as did carrying *pila* and the weight of the panoply as a whole. The archaeological evidence suggests that a massed charge and shield drive would not have been the usual form of infantry fighting. It is important to take these archaeological parameters in to account when developing a model of Roman infantry combat, using them to shape the model in conjunction with the literary evidence and the theoretical parameters.

***Theoretical parameters***

In his article of 2000, Philip Sabin examined certain theoretical parameters for Roman heavy infantry combat, arriving at four main features against which all models of Roman infantry battle should be tested.[106] These were: the duration of the battles; casualty figures on either side; the mobility of the two battle-lines; and the role of reserve or support ranks behind those initially engaged. Before analysing some of the more popular combat models, it will be useful to discuss these theoretical limitations.

*Duration*

Our sources suggest that Roman infantry clashes were sometimes decided very quickly with one battle-line becoming disrupted during, or even before, the first attack. Livy's descriptions of the Allia and Herdonea show the Roman line giving way soon after the battle began, and Ibera and Agrigentum show initial disruptions in the enemy line.[107] Far more frequently though battles between heavy infantrymen were drawn out affairs lasting many hours before one line became so disrupted that they turned and fled. Sabin offers Caesar's claim that a clash between cohorts of legionaries at Ilerda lasted for five hours to support the hypothesis that combat between heavy infantry troops could often be measured in hours rather than minutes. In addition to this, Plutarch claims that Pydna was an unusually swift battle, lasting only one hour, and Vegetius states that Roman battles usually lasted between two and three hours. Zhmodikov has gathered a large number of Livian references to battle durations to further corroborate this hypothesis.[108]

---

[100] Goldsworthy (1996) 217-18, Daly (2002) 187.

[101] Walbank (1957) 706: the καρδιοφύλαξ was roughly 9 inches square.

[102] 6.23.14-15: οἱ μὲν οὖν πολλοὶ προσλαβόντες χάλκωμα σπιθαμιαῖον πάντῃ πάντως, ὃ προστίθενται μὲν πρὸ τῶν στέρνων, καλοῦσι δὲ καρδιοφύλακα, τελείαν ἔχουσι τὴν καθόπλισιν· οἱ δ᾽ ὑπὲρ τὰς μυρίας τιμώμενοι δραχμὰς ἀντὶ τοῦ καρδιοφύλακος σὺν τοῖς ἄλλοις ἁλυσιδωτοὺς περιτίθενται θώρακας.

[103] Bishop and Coulston (2002) 63-4. Italian finds: Connolly (1981) 101 Figs. 9-14; Burns (2003) 71-2. Numantia: Schulten (1927) Pls. 44,19;50; Schulten (1929) 257-9, Pl. 26,19;22.

[104] 6.23.8

[105] Bishop and Coulston (2002) 64-65.

[106] Sabin (2000) 1-17.

[107] Sabin (2000) 4; Livy 5.38, 23.29, 25.21, and 25.40. Goldsworthy (1996) 201-6 offers similar instances for late Republican and early imperial battle.

[108] Sabin (2000) 4; Caesar, *B Civ.* 1.45, Plutarch, *Aem.* 22, and Vegetius 3.9. Zhmodikov (2000), 67-78: Two hours: 25.19.15, 36.38.3; three hours: 22.6.1, 42.7.5; four hours: 23.40.9, 24.15.3, 24.42.2; four + hours: 8.38.10, 9.44.11, 10.12.5, 10.29.8, 27.2.7, 35.1.5, 40.50.2; and long battles, of unknown length: 7.33.13, 25.15.14, 27.12.10, 27.14.6, 28.15.2, 34.28.11, 40.32.6.

Additional evidence for the duration of heavy infantry battle can be gained from the 'internal clock' provided by the grand tactical manoeuvres which occur in a number of our Roman battle narratives. For example, Sabin suggests that it must have taken at least an hour, and probably far longer, at Cannae, for Hannibal's cavalry to defeat the Roman cavalry, ride round to the opposite wing and drive off the Italian cavalry, before, finally, attacking the Roman infantry in the rear. Any model of the mechanics of Roman infantry battle must take into account that combat of this type could drag on for a number of hours.[109]

*Relative casualty rates*

In 1985 Krentz produced a study of casualty rates in hoplite engagements, which concluded that the victors lost an average of five per cent while the defeated side generally lost fourteen per cent of their total.[110] Sabin suggests that in Roman battle casualty rates on the losing side were frequently of a far greater magnitude, often with losses of over half the total strength; citing as evidence for this the 20,000 killed and similar number captured by the Romans at Zama; and Cynoscephalae, where Philip's force of 25,000 men lost 8,000 to the sword with 5,000 taken prisoner.[111] Even taking into account exaggeration and number rounding within our sources, the casualty rates among the defeated in Roman battles do appear far heavier than their hoplite counterparts. This divergence may be explained by what happened in each case when one side broke. In hoplite battles the fleeing troops often threw away their shields allowing them to outrun more easily their heavily-burdened pursuers. Whereas in Roman battles the losers often found themselves encircled by their enemy's echelon tactics making escape impossible. Where fleeing troops could escape, they would often be ridden down in a long pursuit by faster enemy cavalry as at Zama or Pydna.[112]

Sabin also examines casualty rates for the victors during Roman infantry combat. Apart from the severe casualties which occurred in the 'Pyrrhic victories' of the early third century BC, he claims that in many cases the rate was similar to that found in hoplite battle, around five per cent.[113] The casualty figures of 700 dead at Cynoscephalae, 350 at Magnesia, 100 at Pydna, 230 at Pharsalus, and 1,000 at Munda, suggest that during this period of Roman military dominance, as victors, they lost an even smaller percentage of their troops.[114] Although these figures may be coloured by patriotic exaggeration, and a failure to include the number of wounded or perhaps even the casualties suffered by the non-Roman auxiliaries, they do suggest a "much greater asymmetry of losses than in hoplite warfare".[115] From this Sabin surmised that:

> "One of two conclusions seems inescapable – either the losses during the fighting itself were heavily one-sided, with one antagonist's troops being killed without being able to make effective reply, or else *both* sides suffered relatively limited overall casualties before the rout, with the real danger for the losing troops (especially those incapacitated by wounds) coming only after they turned and fled. These two models in fact represent two ends of a spectrum, and the likeliest interpretation is that different clashes could fit virtually anywhere along that spectrum".[116]

There were some long lasting battles which yielded relatively low mutual casualty figures compared to the enormously asymmetrical rates shown above: such as Ilerda, lasting some five hours, where Caesar's legionaries suffered 70 dead and 600 wounded, while Pompey lost 200 and an unknown number of wounded. At Jotapata fighting went on all day, with the Romans losing 13 dead and many wounded, while the Jews lost 200 and had 600 wounded.[117] Any credible model of Roman heavy infantry combat must explain both the asymmetrical slaughter of battles such as Cannae, Zama or Pydna, and also that Roman battle could last for many hours without usually producing greater *mutual* slaughter than hoplite battles.[118]

*Mobility of the fighting lines*

In Roman battles the infantry lines could pull away from the fighting and give ground intentionally or under pressure from the enemy line without breaking entirely. At Cannae the centre of the Carthaginian infantry line

[109] Sabin (2000) 4-5; Polybius, 3.113-16, cf. Polybius 11.1 for Nero's infantry manoeuvre at the Metaurus and Caesar *B Gall.* 2.18-27 for Labienus beating the Atrebates and Viromandui, seizing the Gallic camp and sending the Tenth Legion to relieve Caesar's forces.

[110] Krentz (1985a). Cf. Gabriel and Metz (1991) 83-91. The Athenian losses at Delion were around fourteen per cent, and in few other battles "do even the beaten side appear to have suffered more than the Athenians at Delion, and casualties amongst the winners seem sometimes to have been perhaps as low as 2 per cent" (Lazenby (1991) 10). Cf. Lazenby (1985) 128-9, 133-4, 136-8, 143, 143-4, 148, 152-3 and 160, for casualty figures in other hoplite battles.

[111] Sabin (2000) 5. Polybius 15.14, 18.27; Livy 33.4. At Trasimene and Cannae the Romans themselves suffered terrible loses of about sixty per cent of their force (Polybius 3.84-5: nearly fifteen thousand casualties and the same number of prisoners at Trasimene, Polybius 3.117: some seventy thousand died in one day at Cannae).

[112] Sabin (2000) 5; Polybius 15.9-14 and Livy 30.32-5; Plutarch, *Aem.* 21-2. Lazenby (1991) 101, agrees that the lower casualty rates among the losers in hoplite warfare resulted from the limited use of cavalry and that hoplites were unsuitable for pursuit.

[113] Sabin (2000) 5; Plutarch, *Pyrrh.* 17, 21; Polybius 1.34, 3.74, 3.84-5, 3.3.117, 9.3, 15.14. The 5,700 dead suffered by the Carthaginians at Cannae (3.177) equated to eleven per cent of their total force, but can be explained by the effort needed to destroy such a large Roman army.

[114] Polybius 18.27; Livy 37.44; Plutarch, *Aem.* 21; Caesar, *B Civ.* 3.99; *B Hisp.* 31.

[115] Sabin (2000) 6.

[116] Sabin (2000) 6.

[117] Sabin (2000) 6; Caesar, *B Civ.* 1.46; Josephus 3.150-4.

[118] The huge asymmetrical casualty figures tend to occur in the battles of the middle Republic rather than the late Republic. This could be explained by a change in our sources and the type of battle recorded. Casualty rates recorded for a battle of conquest may be exaggerated by patriotism, while the figures of a civil war may be intentionally reduced. On the other hand they may reflect a real change in casualty rates, perhaps caused by modifications in the fighting style of the legion itself, which should be addressed by any combat model.

was driven back from a convex to a concave formation by Roman pressure, with the result that the Roman infantry became surrounded and were forced to fight on three flanks. The battles of Cynoscephalae and Pydna also show the Roman heavy infantry's ability to withdraw in step. In both of these cases the Romans gave ground to the advancing Macedonian phalanx until it was drawn on to uneven ground and its formation was disrupted.[119]

For these withdrawals to have had grand tactical significance Sabin suggests that they must have involved hundreds rather than tens of yards. Caesar shows that Celtic and Gallic troops could withdraw over vast distances at a run before reforming their line in a more favourable position, for example the Helvetii withdrew a mile from their initial clash with the Romans before resuming the battle.[120] It is difficult to imagine more heavily armed troops, such as the Romans, being able to withdraw in such a way in the face of offensive opposition. Sabin claims there would have been a more measured retreat of heavily armed troops, withdrawing in step while facing the enemy line. To support this he cites passages from Polybius and Appian.[121] Sabin notes that the means by which troops were 'pushed back' in practice is especially difficult to discern, given the possible confusion between metaphor and reality within our ancient battle narratives.[122] Nevertheless, any convincing model of Roman infantry combat must offer an explanation of how battle-lines of heavy infantry could move backwards and forwards over hundreds of yards while maintaining some semblance of order and formation.

*Role of the reserve ranks*

The Greek phalanx was a single battle-line, which could be formed into a variety of depths either to drive the enemy back with their 'weight' advantage, or merely to add defensive strength to the formation.[123] As was shown above, the Romans used a multiple line system, either the manipular formation or the later *triplex acies* of Caesar's legion. There are two important consequences of this multiple line system.

The first is simply that the Romans, unlike most other ancient armies, seem to have preferred this formation and so any model must explain this preference. These reserve lines could be employed within grand tactical manoeuvres, but the most important use of the multiple line system was "to allow fresh troops to replace or reinforce tired ones in the front line itself".[124] This process is described by Livy for the manipular legion.[125] Caesar's descriptions of Ilerda and Pharsalus also suggest that fresh cohorts could be used to replace tired ones in the late Republican legion.[126] Sabin suggests that the advantage of having fresh troops fighting tired ones gave a Roman army the edge over a numerically superior enemy massed in a single line. This assertion is supported by Ardant du Picq's discussion of Roman tactics:

> "The best tactics, the best dispositions were those that made easiest a succession of efforts by assuring the relief of units in action, actually engaging only the necessary units and keeping the rest as a support or reserve outside of the immediate sphere of moral tension".[127]

A convincing model of Roman infantry combat must be one in which the advantages of fresh troops in a relatively shallow line outweighs the physical and psychological advantages of a deep formation. The second consequence is that a model of fighting must be one in which it is feasible for the front line to withdraw and reserve lines to make a passage through to the front in the face of enemy aggression. As Sabin states, "any model of infantry combat at the level of individual soldiers which makes it easier to understand how the line relief process may have worked will be much more convincing as a consequence".[128]

## 3. The models of Roman infantry combat

This chapter began by introducing the difficulties of reconstructing the Roman infantry formation from our literary sources. It demonstrated that each opposing interpretation of these sources stemmed directly from assumptions founded on very different models of combat mechanics, thus highlighting the fundamental importance of developing a more convincing combat model for the study of the republican Roman army. There followed an examination of the archaeological and theoretical parameters of Roman infantry battle, against which any model of combat, whether derived directly from the ancient evidence, psychological considerations or comparative material from more modern warfare, must be judged. We are now in a position to examine some of the more influential current combat models.

### *The 'traditional' model of Roman infantry combat*

[119] Sabin (2000) 6; Polybius 3.113-15; Livy 33.8-9; Plutarch, *Aem.* 20.
[120] Caesar, *B Gall.* 1.25-6, cf. 2.23 and Livy 22.47.
[121] Sabin (2000) 6; Polybius 2.68 and Appian, *BC* 4.128.
[122] Sabin (2000) 6. On the topic of metaphor in battle narratives see Lendon (1999).
[123] Xenophon implies the Spartan line at Nemea was sixteen deep (*Hell.* 4.2.18), the Boiotians at Delion were twenty-five deep (Thuc. 4.93.4), whereas Epameinondas made his line fifty men deep at Leuktra (Polyaenus 2.3.15). Cawkwell (1978) suggests that especially deep phalanxes could provide a reserve used for flanking tactics (154-5), while Lazenby states that "there is no evidence that the rear ranks of a hoplite phalanx were ever used in this way, and there must be some other explanation for the importance attached to depth" (1991) 98. See Hanson (1989) 172, cf. 171-184, and Luginbill (1994), who suggest that the importance of depth was for pushing from the rear ranks.
[124] Sabin (2000) 7; grand tactical manoeuvres: the Metaurus, the Great Plains, Zama, Cynoscephalae (Polybius 11.1, 14.8, 15.14, 18.26); Second Chaeronea (Plutarch, *Sulla* 19) and Pharsalus (Caesar, *B Civ.* 3.89-94).
[125] Livy 8.8; the problems of this account have been discussed above.
[126] Caesar, *B C* iv. 1.45-6, 3.94.
[127] du Picq (trans. 1987), 79.
[128] Sabin (2000) 7.

The mechanics of the Roman manipular battle sequence have been debated for many years and as such there are numerous models of infantry combat. Each of these models varies slightly, but the majority have one fundamental similarity, an initial massed charge. It is unnecessary to analyse each of the models as the problems with one resonate with the other models of a similar type. Instead just one model will be examined representing all the models based around an initial massed charge: Peter Connolly's reconstruction of a "standard battle sequence" for the mid-Republican Roman infantry. As any model must do, Connolly has attempted to bring together and explain many of the characteristics of Roman battle by the adoption of a simple, generic system of battle. Although there is debate over the particulars, Connolly's model represents, as far as there can be one, a general consensus of traditional opinion over how the Roman infantry fought in battle, and this 'traditional model' remains very influential.[129] Due to the wide scope of his study as a whole, Connolly's model is necessarily rather short and generic in scope and should not be criticised for its lack of evidence or appreciation of the subtleties of individual battles. But owing to the influence of this particular model and its reflection of traditional thought on Roman infantry combat some of its inherent weaknesses need to be unmasked. Connolly's battle sequence is really in two parts, the initial clash of the infantry and the line relief system. These two stages will be discussed separately.

*The initial clash of the infantry*

Connolly describes the initial stages of combat in the following way:

> "On emerging from camp each legion formed up in three unbroken lines with the centuries side by side. Before battle the consul would address his troops...On a signal the *posterior* centuries turned about face and fell in behind their *prior* centuries, opening up the gaps in the line. When the signal to prepare for battle was given, the *velites* left their maniples, passed through the gaps and ran forward to harass the advancing enemy, hurling a constant shower of javelins. The purpose of this was to try to break up the enemy formation in anticipation of the charge of the heavy infantry...When the enemy came within range of the heavy infantry, the trumpeters sounded the recall and the *velites* retreated through the gaps...
>
> The rear centuries of the *hastati* now moved up to close the gaps and began clashing their *pila* against their shields as if impatient to get to grips with the enemy. The trumpets blared, the *hastati* raised their war cry and, cheered on by the rest of the army, rushed in hurling first their thin and then their thick *pila*. In the confusion that followed this hail of heavy javelins, the *hastati* drew their swords and charged into the enemy, throwing the whole weight of their bodies against their shields in an attempt to knock their opponents off balance. Then, allowing their long shields to rest on the ground whilst still leaning their left shoulders against them and trying to force the enemy back, they fought behind the shield".[130]

Basically Connolly's model takes the traditional form of the Roman heavy infantry hurling their *pila* to disrupt the enemy, then charging as a massed formation of the whole first line and crashing in to the enemy with their shields. All the weight of their bodies was put behind the shield to knock their opponent off balance. Finally, resting the shield on the ground, while still leaning their left shoulder against it and pushing the enemy back, they began stabbing, viciously, with their short swords.

This model is clear and engaging, but when judged against the parameters of battle some issues arise. The first is the difficulty of hurling both *pila* in, or retaining one *pilum* during, a charge, which has already been discussed. Add to this, as we have seen, Zhmodikov's research into Livy's battle narratives suggests that *pila* fire was actually a continuous feature of infantry battle, rather than merely a precursor to the charge.[131]

Secondly, in Connolly's model the *hastati* charge as one continuous line. During such an attack, formation is likely to be lost immediately due to the psychological strains of the battlefield. It would take immense courage and discipline to mount a coordinated charge of the entire front line. Hans Van Wees realises the inadequacies of such a model for classical Greek warfare. He claims:

[129] Examples of the differences of opinion over particulars: Delbruck (trans. 1975) 272-80, envisions the manipular legion as a fifteen man deep phalanx "with links", and would disagree with Connolly's line relief system, but generally the two agree that the Romans fought with a continuous line in closed-formation (3ft spacing), with a volley of *pila* followed by a massed charge of the whole line and shield drive. John Warry (1980) 111, has a slightly different line relief system and, unlike in Connolly's model, the *hastati* are able to withdraw from the fighting, rest and then attack again, though he does not fully explain how this is done. Warry agrees that the Roman infantry engaged with a massed charge, following a volley of *pila*, in a close-order formation and a continuous line, but his charge begins at about 150yds (137 m). Keppie (1998) 38-9, agrees in general with Connolly, though makes no attempt to explain how this battle system would work in reality. Adcock (1970) 9-10, argues that the maniples retained their intervals in battle, but he would agree with Connolly's massed charge, as he claims "the attack of the Romans began with a short charge of the *hastati* of the front line prepared by one or two volleys of *pila*" (10). Furthest from Connolly's model is Parker (1961, [1928]) 15-20, who argues that the Roman infantry fought in open (6ft) order, with the *quincunx* spacing intact, and using the Roman sword equally for cutting and thrusting, yet he still believes that the initial attack was a charge of the whole *hastati* following a volley of *pila*.

The influence of this traditional thought, and Connolly's model specifically, can be seen recently in Lendon (2005) 424. In the bibliographical notes Lendon offers pp. 129-42 of Connolly's work and Daly (2002) 56-73, which at times follows Connolly, as two "good, accessible descriptions in English of the manipular legion and considerations of the problems it presents". The influence of this 'traditional' model to a wider audience can be seen in the computer game *Rome: Total War* (The Creative Assembly, Sept. 2005), in which the fighting of the middle and late Republican legion follows this system of combat closely.

[130] Connolly (1998) 142.

[131] Zhmodikov (2000)

> "human psychology suggests that very few hoplites would have charged blindly onwards until their shields or spears hit an immovable object, and human physiology suggests that those who did would have ended up sprawling on the ground, if not skewered on an opponent's weapon".[132]

A similar tendency would be true for Roman battle. Only the bravest men would push forward in the charge, while the more timid would naturally hold back. The majority of the infantry would come somewhere between these two extremes, meaning the line would hit the enemy at different times. A massed charge in theory is designed to intimidate the enemy into flight, or, failing that, to hit their opponents as one dense mass, delivering a hammer blow to scatter the enemy. In reality such a charge would turn into a spattering of the braver men hitting an immovable wall of enemy, followed at various intervals by the rest of the legion, resulting in chaos. The two opposing lines, having lost their cohesion, would mix together and men would find themselves deep inside the enemy's formation alone or in small groups. This large-scale mixing of troops along the battle-line would make it extremely difficult for the two formations to disengage successfully and make a second attack.

John Keegan, discussing Du Picq and nineteenth century warfare, supports this idea that large masses of soldiers do not smash into each other.

> "Either because one [side] gives way at the critical moment, or because the attackers during the advance to combat lose their fainthearts and arrive at the point of contact very much inferior in numbers to the mass they are attacking. In either case, the side which turns and runs does so not because it has been physically shaken but because its nerve has given".[133]

The difference between ancient and modern warfare is great, but similar psychological factors must have affected the combatants. It is unlikely that legionary battle could have involved an initial massed charge while still, as we have seen, lasting for hours without one side losing its nerve and giving way.

Thirdly, Connolly accepts Polybius' six feet per man spacing, but claims that the infantry could form up in close-order "when the Romans went for the massed breakthrough…so that they could use their weight to its maximum effect".[134] He cites the battles at the River Trebia and Cannae as examples of this massed breakthrough, and though it is not stated specifically, it follows that the initial massed charge would also have been in close-order. The crouched fighting position proposed by Connolly elsewhere and discussed above also requires a close-order formation.[135] This close-order formation is based on the rather spurious evidence of Vegetius, but is necessary for the assumption of an initial massed charge. This has forced Connolly and others to invent a manoeuvre for converting the line-spacing from 6 to 3 feet. There is no evidence for such a manoeuvre in the sources and it also contradicts Polybius. While Connolly is probably right that line-spacing could vary depending on battlefield conditions, this would have been in a much more informal way. Certainly the examples of the Trebia and Cannae, both terrible defeats for Rome, suggest that close-order line-spacing was not an advantage, as it did not leave enough room for the legionaries to use their weapons effectively.

The fourth issue concerns the role of the shield within this model. The function of the shield is described by Connolly as follows:

> "it was not meant to be wielded. When the legionary charged, he generally held his shield with a straight arm and with his left shoulder resting against it. When he reached the enemy, he hit him full-on with his shield, throwing the whole weight of his body against it, and tried to knock his adversary over. He would then rest his shield on the ground and, crouching down, fight from behind it".[136]

This description directly contradicts Polybius, who clearly states that the purpose of the shield was for deflecting blows from all directions, and therefore *must* have been wielded. The archaeological evidence for the shield demonstrates that the horizontal handgrip would have made Connolly's fighting style very awkward, if not impossible. Connolly's initial clash was the pre-cursor to 'massed breakthroughs', in which the Romans used their combined weight to maximum effect by pushing the enemy backwards. This form of attack is an *othismos*, for which the Roman shield boss was entirely unsuitable.

In such an *othismos*, entailing an initial massed clash of men followed by pushing with shields and stabbing with the swords, one would expect far higher *mutual* casualty rates than can be found in our sources, owing to the close proximity of large numbers of soldiers to attacks from deadly weapons over such long periods of time. In addition, this form of combat would be very difficult to maintain for the lengths of time described in the sources. Fuller estimates that a man could only be constantly engaged in fighting for fifteen minutes before becoming exhausted, while Goldsworthy estimates an even shorter time.[137] In Connolly's model all of the *hastati* are constantly engaged, with the rear ranks pushing on those in front of them, until they are replaced by the *principes*, who may not become involved in the fighting for an hour or more, as happened at Zama.[138] Continuous fighting for such extended periods of time would be very difficult to maintain for the rears ranks doing the pushing and

[132] Van Wees (2004) 188.
[133] Keegan (1976) 69.
[134] Connolly (1998) 142.
[135] Connolly (1991) 362.
[136] Connolly (1998) 131.
[137] Fuller (1965) 91; Goldsworthy (1996) 224.
[138] Polybius 15.9-14, Livy 30.32-5.

absolutely impossible for the front ranks actually engaged in hand-to-hand combat.

It may be possible to imagine a situation in which the two opposing formations, both shoving in this direct shield-to-shield *othismos*, would become forced so close together as to make the use of weapons impossible. While this situation would explain both the low mutual casualty rates and the great length of Roman battles, it would make it very difficult for the lines to pull apart to allow for line replacement, which was fundamental to the Roman combat system. Lazenby claims that there could be a certain ebb and flow at the pushing stage of hoplite battles. He cites Herodotus' description of the Greeks flinging the Persians back four times in the pushing over Leonidas' body. [139] Unfortunately not only is the fighting not against hoplites, the movement is on a small scale over a localised section of the battle-line, not the formation as a whole. Similar small-scale oscillation could have occurred within a Roman *othismos*, but this is not the large-scale movement forward and backwards over hundreds of metres without breaking seen in our sources. Such a feat would be very difficult with this *othismos* model of combat.

Finally, not only would this massed pushing make it difficult for the two lines to remain cohesive and to separate from each other to allow line replacement, but it would also make the Roman three-line system redundant. The multiple line system implies that reserves were more important than pushing strength. In traditional models the Roman first line, though only six men deep, would be forced to push against formations of far greater depth. An extreme example of this is Warry's description of the legion fighting a pike phalanx, in which a six-man deep close-order legion rushes towards a sixteen-man deep Macedonian phalanx. [140] At the point of engagement, "the legionaries would take the impact of the pikes on their *scuta*. A pushing match develops which normally favours the deeper formation".[141] A situation in which a six-man, or even three-man, deep Roman formation attempts to push back a sixteen-man deep Macedonian pike phalanx seems absurd, showing little appreciation for the importance of reserves in the multiple-line system and begs the question of why the Romans engaged in the first place, if, as Warry says, a pushing match usually favoured the deeper formation. If the Romans regularly attempted to drive back an enemy battle-line they would have employed far deeper formations to add weight to the shove. On the few occasions that the Romans did employ deep formations, which would promote such a pushing style, the battles ended in disaster, such as the battle of Tunis in 255 and at Cannae in 216.[142] This view that the whole Roman line would rush on to the spears of the enemy phalanx and try to push them back is equally absurd and contradicts our sources. Livy describes the fighting between the Romans and Macedonians at Pydna, stating that:

> "If they [the Romans] had attacked frontally in solid line against an orderly phalanx, as happened to the Paelignians who at the beginning of the battle recklessly met the guard troops [armed with pikes], the Romans would have spitted themselves on the spears and would not have withstood the solid line" (Schlesinger, 1951).[143]

For these various psychological, archaeological and theoretical reasons the traditional model of an initial massed charge followed by a shield drive, whether against a similarly armed enemy like the Carthaginians or a Macedonian pike phalanx, appears to be implausible within a practical battle situation.

*The line relief system*

Connolly's description of the legion's reinforcement system is also very influential. It is based on his belief that the legion fought in an unbroken line, Polybius' statement that the senior centurion was stationed on the right of his maniple,[144] and the titles of the two centurions in each maniple (*prior* and *posterior*). [145] These factors lead him, and others, to believe that centuries lined up one in front of the other while approaching the enemy, but engaged side-by-side in a continuous line. To explain how this worked in practice, he has offered a theoretical manoeuvre in four phases:

1. The legion is drawn up in three continuous lines, *hastati* at the front, *principes* in the middle and *triarii* at the rear. On the order the *posterior* centuries move backwards and then to the right to form up behind their *prior* centuries, creating gaps in the line. The *velites* leave their maniples, form up in front of the legion and begin battle.

2. After skirmishing, they then withdraw through the gaps. The *posterior* centuries of the *hastati* move to the left and then forward to fill the gaps of the line; the senior (*prior*) centurion is stationed on the right, with the junior (*posterior*) in the middle of the maniple. The *hastati* charge the enemy and drive forward with their shields.

3. At times the first charge was sufficient to break the enemy line. If it failed, the trumpets sounded the recall as soon as the momentum was dissipated. The

[139] Lazenby (1991) 100. Herodotus 7.225.1.

[140] Warry states that "the Roman maniples, in open order, may be 12 deep or more (this would vary according to the opponent)", the maniples would then move into close-order, making them 6 deep. He also believes that before the battle the two centuries lined up one in front of the other but engaged side-by-side. In this case an open-order maniple could be 12 deep *before* battle, but on engagement the *posterior* century moved forward, making the maniple six deep in open-order. Therefore in close-order Warry's maniple may only have been three deep.

[141] Warry (1980) 126-7.

[142] Polybius 1.33-4; 3.110-117.

[143] 44.41.9: *Qui si universa acie in frontem adversus instructam phalangem concurrissent, quod Paelignis principio pugnae incaute congressis adversus caetratos evenit, induissent se hastis nec confertam aciem sustinuissent.*

[144] Polybius 6.24.8.

[145] As already discussed this translation may be mistaken.

*posterior* centuries disengage, retreat until they are level with the rear of the *prior* centuries; they then turn to the right, presenting their left (protected) sides to the enemy and move across behind their *prior* centuries. The whole line retreats through the intervals in the second line. The *principes* move forward, their *posterior* centuries move to the right and then forward to fill the gaps left by the *hastati*. When a continuous line is formed the *principes* charge.

4. If the *principes* were also defeated, the legion could perform its final replacement manoeuvre. The *hastati*, stationed now behind the *principes*, would break ranks, pass through the gaps in the *triarii* and reform behind them. The *posterior* centuries of the *principes* would disengage, retreat until level with the end of the *prior* centuries, then turn to their left and move across behind them. The *principes* then withdraw through the intervals in the third line. The *triarii* fill the gaps in their own line, and the whole legion could now retreat in good order behind the spears of the *triarii*.[146]

This is an impressive theoretical reconstruction of the line replacement system, but it seems rather too complicated to be performed in the face of the enemy. The mid-Republican legion was a conscript rather than a professional army and, though trained, a manoeuvre of this complexity could easily lead to chaos. The fundamental argument against the use of the quincunx formation in battle is that it would allow the enemy to penetrate deep into the Roman formation, yet Connolly and his followers seem to believe that this would not occur when the *posterior* centuries, somehow, detached themselves from the fighting and withdraw into succeeding line.

This theory becomes even less likely when the system is deconstructed by stages. As the *principes* replace the *hastati* (step 3), Connolly is forced to make the *posterior* centuries of the second line move to the *right* of their *prior* centuries in order to fill the gaps vacated by the *hastati* and to stop the whole formation drifting to the left. In this way the junior (*posterior*) centurions of the second line are now stationed on the right of the maniple, contradicting Polybius' statement that the senior centurion held this position, one of the bases of the Connolly model. In addition, as the *principes* retreat the *posterior* centuries withdraw until they are level with the end of the *prior* centuries, then turn to their *left* and move across behind the front ranks. In this case half of the *principes* must turn their shields *away* from the enemy and leaving their vulnerable right sides open to attack. It is highly unlikely that the best troops of the legion would either be allowed or allow themselves to face such a reckless endangerment.

A further problem with this system is the limited number of attacks that could be made by the infantry. Connolly states that "some times the first charge was sufficient to break the enemy line. If it failed, the trumpets sounded the recall as soon as the momentum was dissipated". This implies that the *hastati* engaged with one decisive charge, which, if this failed, was followed by an attack of the *principes* and finally the *triarii*. As has already been shown, Roman battles could last for many hours. If our modern estimates for the amount of time a man could be constantly engaged are true (fifteen minutes), it is unlikely that this model of three consecutive charges could produce a battle lasting much longer than an hour. Connolly's system is impressive and may have been possible on the parade ground, but it appears unfeasible in the face of the enemy.

### *The 'new' models of Roman infantry combat*

Over the last decade some scholars have derived new models of combat. These tend to envisage battle as more tentative than the massed infantry charges proposed by the 'traditional' model. In the following section two of the more influential of these will be introduced.

#### *Zhmodikov and missile warfare*

According to the generally accepted view of Roman battle, infantry combat consists of two phases: missile fighting and hand-to-hand combat, the first stage leading directly to the second and lasting for far less time. In 2000 Alexander Zhmodikov attempted to refute this accepted model, claiming that missile fighting was a continuous feature of Roman battle and was far more prominent factor than previously assumed. Zhmodikov based his hypothesis on some of the parameters discussed above. As has been shown, literary evidence suggests that Roman battle typically lasted hours rather than minutes. This is supported by the Roman use of a multiple-line system for their infantry formation. This system provides the opportunity for line relief, which would be less important during a short engagement. Zhmodikov claims that a long duration for battle corresponds better with missile fighting than fighting with swords, as:

> "Hand-to-hand fighting between massed formations on level ground could not last long, because it required enormous physical and moral efforts from the participants. Several hours are too long for sword fighting, even taking into account the interchanging of the legion lines".[147]

The role ascribed by Polybius to *pila* is unclear. By far the most prominent weapon used by the Roman infantry in Polybius' accounts is the sword, while he mentions the use of *pila* in battle only once.[148] For this reason Zhmodikov dismisses the Greek historian, noting that there is no direct evidence that Polybius was an

[146] Paraphrased from Connolly (1998) 141-142; followed by Daly (2002) 61-62.

[147] Zhmodikov (2000) 71.

[148] *Pila*: 1.40.12; Swords: 2.30.8, 2.33.6, 15.13.1, 18.30.7, etc.

experienced military officer nor that he had ever seen the Roman army in pitched battle.[149] He relies instead on Livy for corroborating evidence. Although Livy provides descriptions of *pila* volleys followed by sword fighting, corresponding with traditional theories, there are numerous passages which imply that missile fire was not confined to the few seconds before an infantry charge. Such passages include the large number of military leaders whom Livy claims were injured or killed by missile weapons, often long after the battle had begun.[150] Although this could be a literary *topos*, adding interest to the narrative, it does show that Livy believed it possible for missile exchange to continue through out a battle. Zhmodikov also claims that the enemies of the early Roman legion all fought with missile weapons and would have influenced the development of the Roman army towards this form of warfare.[151] Based on this evidence and the claim that swords are not often mentioned in Livy's battle narratives, Zhmodikov asserts that Roman battles were, at least sometimes, long missile fights rather than hand-to-hand slaughter with swords.[152]

This argument is quite compelling for it relieves some of the issues surrounding the massed infantry charge and explains how Roman battle could last many hours with low mutual casualty rates. Nevertheless, the dismissal of Polybius' conviction that the Roman infantry were primarily swordsmen is unjustified and the fact that Livy does not specifically mention sword fighting in some battles does not allow us to "suppose that those were also fights with missiles".[153] Livy does not often mention sword fighting specifically, but the reason for this may be that his audience would have assumed the use of swords. As will be shown in the following chapter, Livy's audience would have had experience of Roman combat, either directly or indirectly, meaning that Livy had less need to explain the dominance of the sword among the Roman infantry than Polybius, who was trying to account for Roman dominance to a Greek audience. Instead Livy employs terms which *imply* hand-to-hand fighting with swords such as *caedere* ('to cut down') or terms like *impetus*, which Veith understood as '*Einbruch mit dem Schwert*' and is used hundreds of times by Livy to describe Roman infantry attacks.[154]

Daly, in his critique of this theory, convincingly claims that Zhmodikov's use of evidence is questionable.[155] Many of Zhmodikov's examples are drawn from the first decade of Livy. Though the battles in this decade follow the same combat formula Livy uses throughout his work, specific details, such as the methods by which a certain commander was injured or killed, are of dubious authenticity.[156] A number of his examples refer to the deaths of Roman commanders and so are difficult to use as evidence for a general theory of Roman missile warfare. These references show only that enemy troops were using missiles throughout the battle, and it does not necessarily follow that the Romans relied on the same tactics. These descriptions of how Roman commanders were killed may also have been altered by descendants of the deceased, Livy's annalistic sources or even Livy himself, for patriotic purposes. In sum, the theory of missile warfare is an interesting and important one, as it relieves the conceptual burden of an initial massed charge, but it does not hold up under close scrutiny.

### *Sabin, Goldsworthy and the dynamic stand-off*

In 1996, and with a fuller account in 2000, Philip Sabin proposed another theory of Roman infantry combat dismissing the traditional axiom of an initial massed charge of the whole line. Building on his research into the theoretical parameters of Roman battle and some aspects of Adrian Goldsworthy's model, which suggested that drawn-out infantry combat would be punctuated by lulls, during which the two sides could draw back from each other to rest and replace the wounded, Sabin developed a model of combat in the form of a dynamic stand-off.[157]

Based on "psychological considerations and deductions from more recent experience", Sabin suggests that close range hand-to-hand fighting with swords would have been a highly unstable state, requiring massive injections of physical and psychological energy, and was only made tolerable by the use of shields and protective armour. Therefore, he argues, there must have also been a "more physically and psychologically sustainable 'default state' within protracted Roman infantry contests, into which the combatants would naturally relapse".[158] This default state would take the form of a small separation of a few metres between the two lines forming a 'safety distance', which would allow insults and missiles to be exchanged but would not be close enough for hand-to-hand combat. Sabin argues that:

> "in most Roman battles the lines *did* sporadically come into contact, as one side or the other surged forward for a brief and localized flurry of hand-to-hand combat. The flurry of combat would end when one side got the worst of the exchange, and its troops would step back to re-impose the 'safety distance' while brandishing their weapons to deter immediate enemy pursuit.
>
> This kind of dynamic stand-off punctuated by episodes of hand-to-hand fighting could continue for some time until one side finally lost its ability to resist, thereby breaking the bonds of mutual

[149] Zhmodikov (2000) 68. The common view is that Polybius was brought to Carthage by Scipio as a friend but also as a military expert: Walbank (1979) 14.

[150] Zhmodikov (2000) 68-70.

[151] Zhmodikov (2000) 72-4.

[152] Zhmodikov (2000) 71. Livy's mention of swords in battle: 9.13.2, 9.35.6, 9.39.6, 22.4.7, 28.2.6.

[153] Zhmodikov (2000) 70.

[154] Kromayer and Veith (1928) 430. For Livy's use of *impetus* see chapter 4 below.

[155] Daly (2002) 216-7. See also Oakley (2005b) 518, for his criticisms of Zhmodikov's model.

[156] On the combat formula employed by Livy see chapter 2 below.

[157] Sabin (1996) and (2000); Goldsworthy (1996).

[158] Sabin (2000) 14.

> deterrence and encouraging the opposing troops to surge forward and begin killing in earnest, their gnawing tension and fear now released and converted into an orgy of blood lust. The most common mechanism for such a transformation would obviously be the panic of the losing troops due to the breaching of their line, a psychological shock such as the death of the general, or the sheer accumulation of casualties and fatigue".[159]

As evidence for this model, Sabin cites Livy's account of the battle of Zama with its repeated charges, steady advances and withdrawals before the final rout.[160] As a theoretical model the dynamic stand-off fits the parameters of Roman infantry battle very well, and certainly better than the traditional model. It explains how battles could last for many hours with only relatively low mutual casualties, since, before the rout, hand-to-hand fighting would only occur sporadically, while the majority of the missiles thrown in the default state could be deflected by shields. This model would also explain how battle-lines could move backwards and forwards over hundreds of metres without breaking, because as one side repeatedly came off worse in the small-scale localised exchanges and were forced to step back to re-instate the safety distance, over time, the line would be metaphorically 'pushed' back over great distances. The Roman sub-units of centuries and maniples would offer the ideal basis for these small-scale flurries of localised combat. A theory of a natural stand-off punctuated by periodic localised attacks would more plausibly enable the Romans to fight with gaps in their lines than a model involving a massed charge. It would also allow the second line to move up between the maniples of the first to either fight along side, or take over the combat from, the *hastati*, as the front line would not constantly be engaged.[161]

Sabin's convincing model of a dynamic stand-off is described vividly by Goldsworthy.[162] It corresponds to and explains many of the parameters of battle discussed in this chapter and as such it will be the foundation on which this study will build. The model represents an emerging consensus that Roman infantry combat was more tentative and sporadic than previously assumed.[163] This consensus is based on theoretical models founded on psychological considerations and comparative material, with a few selected ancient references that appear to fit the theory. Sabin himself states that "the 'pure' approach of relying on ancient sources alone as a guide to ancient battle mechanics is so sadly deficient", and in some ways he is correct.[164] Nevertheless, it is my belief that for a model of infantry combat not only to be convincing but universally acceptable, it must be firmly grounded in our sources. The aim of the rest of this work is to show that a close examination of the literary and archaeological source material can lead to a model of combat which is consistent with this growing consensus.

There are three approaches which allow us to get close to how the Roman mid-Republican heavy infantry fought. At the present time the archaeological evidence for the mid-Republican legion remains rather limited and without further discoveries any model derived from this approach alone will necessarily be inconclusive. A model which fulfils the theoretical parameters of Roman battle is on firmer ground. But although theory is important, it is not in itself evidence, and so a literary analysis will relieve our reliance upon theory. A systematic analysis of the vocabulary our sources use to describe infantry combat is a fresh approach towards extending the use of our ancient material, which will complement the archaeological and theoretical methods. This book is an attempt to derive a model of combat directly from our ancient sources using a comprehensive analysis of Livy's battle narratives, with parallel accounts from Polybius and comparative passages of Caesar where appropriate. This will take into account the theoretical parameters encompassed by Sabin's hypothesis and our archaeological parameters. The purpose of this analysis is to bring the growing consensus forward from its theoretical basis into a more convincing and tangible model of infantry combat. Only with a combination of all three of these approaches, archaeological, theoretical and literary, will it be possible to propose a truly convincing model of mid-Republican infantry combat.

---

159 Sabin (2000) 14-15, cf. Sabin (1996) 72-3.
160 In fact, there are a number of problems with this description which put the accuracy of the account into question. This will be discussed later in chapter 4.
161 Sabin (2000) 17.
162 Goldsworthy (2000) 55-60.
163 Sabin (2000) 17.
164 Sabin (2000) 15.

## Chapter 3: Livy and Republican battle narratives

The extant books of Livy's enormous compendium of Roman history are our most abundant source for early and mid-Republican battle accounts. Livy records and narrates more battles than any other ancient writer and for many of these his is the only surviving account. Throughout this corpus of battle narratives certain key terms appear repeatedly in his descriptions of Roman heavy infantry attacks, with a regularity that suggests more than mere chance translation of his sources. These terms constitute Livy's rhetorical formula for describing Roman infantry fighting and are controlled by his literary vision of combat: how he imagined the mechanics of infantry fighting. The aim of this study is to gain insight into Livy's vision of combat through an analysis of his vocabulary and to explore the way in which his descriptions relate to the archaeological, theoretical and psychological parameters of battle examined in the previous chapter.

Despite his prolificacy, Livy is generally undervalued as a military writer and often thought of as unreliable and even inept. The argument advanced throughout this study is that Livy is actually a valuable source for military history and that his vision of Roman combat is a reliable reflection of reality. An interpretation of his method of describing battle, when combined with other more respected military sources, such as Polybius and Caesar, can provide new insights into Roman infantry combat and allow us to derive a new, more convincing model of mid-Republican battle mechanics.

Before such an analysis can be performed, the charge of military ignorance often levied against Livy must be addressed and some reasons offered for the credibility of his battle accounts. In this chapter there will be an examination of his methodology and use of sources in order to demonstrate that he was not blindly following the text in front of him. Rather, he was an intelligent historian conscientiously using parallel accounts and his own understanding of combat to explain his main source and offer an authentic, or at least credible, description of Roman infantry battle. Owing to the fragmentary survival of many of his sources, it is not possible to trace the exact origin of Livy's vision of infantry combat. But by examining the method of describing battle in some of his predecessors' narratives, such as Polybius and Caesar, it can be determined that Livy was trying to produce a realistic expression of the fighting. Further, through a comparison of the texts it will be possible to estimate how far these writer's literary visions of combat influenced Livy's own.

### 1. Livy's military ignorance

The first thing to address is the supposed military ignorance of Livy. Walsh in his work on Livy's historical methods proposed that Livy should not be judged by modern standards of history, or even those of Polybius, but rather on the Isocratean ideas of clarity, brevity and plausibility. [165] Livy was an academic rhetorician-historian, whose work should both inform and entertain, and therefore his history should be judged on literary and rhetorical merit as well as reliability.[166] Despite this, it is commonly held that Livy took no part in military affairs, which even Walsh believes caused a "crippling... ignorance of military matters". [167] The main reason for believing that Livy was never a soldier is the sheer volume of his work. But other than his exceptional output very little is known about his life and so there is no real evidence for this supposition.

As Walsh states "[Livy] remains the most nebulous figure of all the greater historians of the ancient worlds".[168] He is believed to have been born either in 59 or 64BC at Patavium (modern Padua in Northern Italy) and died in AD17.[169] It is likely he spent most of his working life in Rome writing his history of the Roman people in 142 books from the fall of Troy to 9BC.[170] Livy is generally thought to have begun writing around the time of the battle of Actium and continued until the end of his life.[171] He seems to have published his work in groups of five books, with the first pentad, possibly a second edition, dating between 27 and 25BC and the second pentad to before 23.[172] Such a timeframe for composition implies an average output of about three large books every year for most of his life, which has led many to assume he could have taken no part in politics or warfare. This is not necessarily the case. [173] There is no evidence he did not have some kind of public role and as an educated member of the elite, coming to age during the civil war period, it is likely he would have had at least some military experience.

---

[165] See Quint. *Inst.* 257. Brunt (1993) 181-209, rejects the idea that Isocrates was responsible for historiography being a branch of rhetoric.

[166] Walsh (1970 [1961]) 23-26. See also Mcdonald (1957) 163; Oakley (1997) 83-85; Lipovsky (1981) 9-14; Woodman (1988). Cf. Wiseman (1979) 27-40, who claims that rhetoric and history were inseparable, and that many exaggerations and distortions would be accepted as historical fact. For a discussion on the development of Latin historiography see Walsh (1970 [1961]) 20-45. Cf. Prosen (1965). Prosen proposes that both Livy and Sallust should be seen as rhetorician-historians, and that Livy's literary skills particularly outshone his historical ability. On 'history' as entertainment see Cicero *De Or.* 2.59, *Fam.* 5.12.4-5; Vitruvius 5 *praef.* 1; Pliny *Ep.* 5.8.4; Tacitus *Ann.* 4.33.3, etc.

[167] Walsh (1961) 157. Cf. Mcdonald (1957) 161: "In military matters [in Livy] we see the blind leading the blind...".

[168] Walsh (1961) 1.

[169] Jerome/Eusebius, *Chron. Ad Ann. Abr.* 1958 provides the date 59; Syme (1959) 414-5 argues for 64 and puts back the date of his death to AD12.

[170] Walsh (1961) 18-9; Syme (1958) 137 and (1959) 428 claims he spent most of his life in Patavium and only infrequently came to Rome.

[171] For dating see Walsh (1961) 4-5. Woodman (1988) 128-34, Kraus (1994) 5; Kraus and Woodman (1997)74 n. 2, argue for a pre-31 date, while Luce (1965), Ogilvie (1971) and others argue for post Actium.

[172] On the structure of Livy's work see Stadter (1972) and Syme (1959) 401-10. On the possibility of a second edition of the first pentad see Luce (1965).

[173] Kraus (1994) 1 n.1 rightly claims that "it is perhaps naive to argue on the basis of his battle descriptions that he did not [have any experience of battle]".

As a historian he was famous in his own life time and his work seems to have superseded previous histories.[174] He appears to have had some relationship with the imperial family; he knew the future emperor Claudius and was chided as a Pompeian by Augustus.[175] While not an Augustan propagandist, his history reflects the central ideas of the contemporary elites: patriotism, concern for moral decay and the need for regeneration, the value of the past and a growing optimism for the future after the civil wars. Of the original 142 books only 35 survive extant (1-10, 21-45), but we also have a series of late antique summaries, or *periochae*, of most of the books.[176] The surviving books cover the years 753-293 and 219-167 BC, making Livy the most important Latin author for the history of the mid-Republican period.[177]

Walsh's evidence for Livy's ignorance is a series of accusations that tend to be overly critical and at times quite unjustified. His charges include various 'mistranslations' and apparently elementary mistakes, that on the surface are quite compelling. Before examining Livy's methodology and literary influences, some defence against these charges must be attempted. This will show that Livy was, if not a military expert, at least a conscientious student and recorder of combat, and that far from being dismissed, his vision of infantry conflict could offer important insight into Roman battle mechanics.

One of Walsh's main attacks is against Livy's ignorance of Roman weapons. He claims that "Livy thinks that the *pilum* was thrust as well as thrown".[178] This is based on a passage in Livy's famous comparison of Alexander's forces and the Roman army:

> '[Alexander's] men have been armed with targets and sarissas; the Romans with a *scutum*, which offers more protection to the body, and the *pilum*, *haud paulo quam hasta vehementius ictu missuque telum*.[179]

Walsh claims that this phrase implies the *pilum* was a more powerful weapon than the *hasta* when thrown or used for thrusting. But this is not the only way to read the statement. The word *ictus* can mean the impact of a thrown *pilum*, as can be seen from Caesar's use of the term: *B Gall.* 1.25: '[the Gauls were encumbered] because many of their shields had been pierced and pinned together by **one blow** (***uno ictu***) of the *pila*'.[180] Livy's use of the term does not necessarily mean he thought the *pilum* was either thrust like a spear or thrown, but simply that the impact of the *pilum* when thrown was more powerful than a thrust from the *hasta*, or even that when both weapons were thrown the impact of the *pilum* was the more powerful. A better translation of the phrase would be '...the *pilum*, which is much more powerful on impact when thrown than the *hasta*'. Walsh's assumption of Livy's military ignorance appears to have led him to misrepresent the Latin. In addition, even if Walsh is correct and Livy did believe the *pilum* was thrust as well as thrown, there is no reason to assume that the *pilum* could not be used as a thrusting weapon. In fact in Plutarch's description of Pharsalus the men of Caesar's tenth legion use their *pila* in just this way:

> "[Caesar told them that] whenever the enemy's cavalry charged they should run out through the front ranks, though without casting their *pila* as the best soldiers usually did in their eagerness to draw their swords, but to strike upwards with their *pila* and wound the faces and eyes of the enemy."[181]

Under the stress of combat it is possible that this weapon could be used as a thrusting spear to fend off an advancing enemy and the idea certainly does not deserve Walsh's scorn.

Livy's mention of the *pilum* appears in the wider context of a rhetorical digression on whether Alexander's army, had he lived and turned his attentions west, could have defeated his contemporary Roman forces (9.19). Walsh charges Livy with imagining that "Alexander's army was composed entirely of the Phalanx".[182] This is certainly not the case as Livy actually calculates the Macedonian army as thirty thousand men and four thousand horse.[183] This is similar to the overall totals given by Arrian (*Anab.* I.11) and show's Livy's awareness of the importance of cavalry; though Alexander generally deployed a higher ratio of cavalry to infantry than this in battle.[184] Even if Walsh were correct, it would still not mean Livy was completely ignorant of military matters. In the Hellenistic world the phalanx was far more dominant on the battlefield than under Alexander, who relied on his cavalry far more than later Hellenistic monarchs. Such a claim, if it were true, may suggest that Livy was ignorant of Alexander's army, but not of the Hellenistic armies which followed. An awareness of Hellenistic battle might have led to the logical assumption that Alexander's battle-line was similar. It would have been wrong, but certainly not deserving of the charge of military ignorance. In either case Walsh's accusation is unfounded.

---

[174] Pliny, *Ep.* 2.3.8 records the story of a man from Cadiz travelling the all way from Spain just to look at him.

[175] Suetonius *Claudius* 41.1; Tacitus *Annals* 4.34.3. On this joke and Livy's relationship with Augustus in general, see Badian (1993).

[176] All except 136 and 137.

[177] For a recent account of the little we can know about Livy see Kraus (1994) 1-4. For Livy as a historian see amongst others Walsh (1961); Luce (1977); Ogilivie (1965) and (1971); Oakley (1997-2005); Briscoe (1973-2008); Kraus and Woodman (1997); etc. On the *periochae* see Begbie (1967).

[178] Walsh (1970 [1961]) 157.

[179] 9.19.7: *Arma clipei essent illis sarsaeque: Romano scutum, maius corpori tegumentum, et pilum, haud paulo quam hasta vehementius ictu missuque telum.* On this Alexander digression in general see Morello (2002).

[180] *Quod pluribus eorum scutis **uno ictu** pilorum transfixis et colligates. OLD* s.v. 1 proposes that *ictus* can be a blow from a missile.

[181] Plutarch, *Pompey*, 69.2-3.

[182] Walsh (1970 [1961]) 157.

[183] 9.19.5: *triginta milibus hominum et **quattuor milibus equitum**.*

[184] At Granicus (334) for example he deployed 5,100 cavalry with just 13,000 infantry. See Sabin (2007) 129-133; Bosworth (1980) 98-99.

In his famous article about 'howlers' in Livy, Walsh provides more detail for his charges of incompetence based on supposed mistranslations of Polybius' Greek.[185] At 38.7.10 Livy describes fighting in a tunnel at the siege of Ambracia, where he has the Ambracians defending themselves with stretched-out goat-hair coverings and doors.[186] Polybius, Livy's source for the passage, has the soldiers fighting with two different types of shield.[187] Walsh suggests that Livy 'carelessly' confused the word θυρεοὺς with θύρας meaning 'doors'. This could have been a mistake in translation, perhaps owing to hasty composition or even a lack of comfort with the language. On the other hand, Briscoe believes that in fact the word may have been corrupted within Livy's text of Polybius.[188] A further example of this phenomenon occurs at 42.46.7: in Livy Rhodian envoys approach Thebes, Coronea and Haliartus, but Polybius has Thisbae, Coronea and Haliartus.[189] Walbank claims that "evidently the *lectio facilior* 'Thebes' had already ousted the correct form in Livy's text of Polybius".[190] It is certainly possible then that Livy's text of Polybius already had corruptions and that some of the so-called 'mistakes' may not have arisen from careless mistranslation but rather the state of his text.

Returning to the original passage, the term γέρρα can mean either an oblong shield covered with ox-hide, to which *ciliciis* ('rough cloaks') may approximate, or a wattled screen.[191] With the use of these 'make-shift' shields, defending oneself with doors may not have seemed too absurd to Livy. That Livy does not find the defensive use of doors extraordinary highlights his general policy of acceptance when it came to his main source, which shall be examined below. It may have seemed strange to Livy that his Polybian text included fighting with doors, but as it was not entirely implausible he made the conscious decision to include the detail.

Briscoe claims that "Polybius' Greek, in vocabulary at least, differs considerably from that of the classical Athenian writers, and one must be constantly on the look-out for unusual meanings".[192] This would be particularly true for technical terminology, the meanings of which may have changed by the time of Livy's writing. Some of the 'mistranslations' charged against Livy could be explained by unusual vocabulary. A well-known example of this occurs in Livy's account of Cynoscephalae. Polybius comments that, since the Romans were close upon them, the Macedonians were to lower their spears in order to attack.[193] In contrast, Livy has the Macedonians grounding their spears (*hastis positis*).[194] Walsh admits that Livy interpreted καταβαλλω understandably to mean 'throw down' rather than Polybius' technical meaning of 'to lower', which is very rare.[195] But Walsh despairs over his additional explanation that the length of the pikes was a hindrance and so the Macedonians were ordered to engage with swords.[196] Livy's explanation of this unusual order offers clues about both his use sources and his own understanding of infantry combat.

The attempted clarification shows that he was not blindly following the text in front of him, but rather that he thought about his sources and tried to explain for his readers any anomalies within the text. The passage also indicates Livy's assumption that close-combat normally took the form of hand-to-hand fighting with swords. After the initial terrifying advance of the pike phalanx and the first clash with the enemy, the long Macedonian pike would have been a hindrance in individual and small group combat. Livy's explanatory note at least shows that he was reflecting thoughtfully on his sources. He was of course wrong; the Hellenistic phalanx depended on keeping the enemy at bay with their pikes and was helpless when their formation was lost. Interestingly, the Roman army did fight in this form of individual and small-group close-combat. This passage then perhaps suggests Livy's general understanding of infantry fighting was fundamentally the combat of the Roman legion.[197] Livy's mistake suggests that although he may have been ignorant of Hellenistic fighting techniques, he was nonetheless a conscientious historian whose vision of combat reflects the Roman method of fighting.

Neither of these examples should necessarily be called a 'howler'; rather, they are mistakes which highlight Livy's use of his sources. In both cases he may have found the text in front of him rather odd, the first because of a possible corruption, and the second because of a failure to understand technical military language. Nevertheless, in both cases he chose to include the episodes in his narrative. This reveals a general policy of acceptance towards his sources. In the case of fighting within the tunnel, defending oneself with a door may have been within the realms of possibility and so Livy made the decision to include the story. The phalanx grounding their spears before an attack was more problematic. In Livy's mind it was Polybius who had made a mistake. He tried

[185] Walsh (1958) 83-88. For a recent re-evaluation of this see Briscoe (forthcoming).

[186] *nunc ciliciis praetentis nunc foribus raptim obiectis.*

[187] Pol., 21.28.11: θυρεοὺς καὶ γέρρα.

[188] Briscoe (2008) 44. On the possibility of such a corruption see Adams (2003) 5.

[189] Livy 42.46.7: *Thebes et Coroneam et Haliartum*; Pol. 27.5.2: Κορώνειαν καὶ Θίσβας, ἔτι δ᾽ Ἁλίαρτον.

[190] Walbank (1979) 298.

[191] Briscoe finds the translation of γέρρα as *ciliciis* surprising and would expect something like *uineae* instead (2008) 44.

[192] Briscoe (1993) 41. Walsh on the other hand states that "although no one could call the prose style of Polybius elegant, it provides no great difficulty to anyone familiar with Greek" (1958) 88.

[193] 18.24.9: καταβαλοῦσι τὰς σαρίσας

[194] 33.8.13.

[195] Luce (1977) 40. n. 13: "The technical military usage is rare; it does not find its way into the Liddell and Scott entry, for example". Cf. Adams (2003)5.

[196] Walsh (1958) 84-85; cf. Briscoe (1973) 263. 33.8.12-13: *Caetratos et Macedonum phalangem hastis positis, quarum longitudo impendimento erat, gladiis rem gerere iubet.*

[197] While discussing Livy 6.12.8-10, where the Romans put down their *pila* to get to the hand-to-hand more quickly, Oakley (1997) 510, claims that the *gladiis rem gerere* at 33.8.13 "suggests that he [Livy] assumed that the Macedonians used the same tactics as the manipular legion is made to adopt in our passage".

to rectify Polybius' error by offering the best explanation he could imagine. Neither of these are examples of a military ignorance in Livy. They instead demonstrate that he relied on his sources, thought conscientiously about the text and did not believe them infallible. His main task in writing his history was to bring together the earlier knowledge he had found within his sources. When he saw a problem or a mistake he did not simply omit it, but used other sources or his own understanding of Roman close-combat to try to elaborate on and explain the unusual feature of his main source.

Walsh further attacks Livy over his description of the battle dispositions at Zama.[198]Livy states that Hannibal's lines included auxiliaries, Carthaginians and "then, removed to the last line and separated by an open space as well, the Italic troops, of whom it was uncertain whether they were allies or enemies" (Moore, 1949).[199] Polybius writes that "last of all [were] the troops he had brought over from Italy at a distance of more than a stade from the front lines"; these 'men from Italy' Polybius later calls the "most efficient and steadiest of his troops" (Paton, 1925).[200] In Polybius' version the second line is made up of recently levied troops from Carthage and Africa, and the third are the veterans Hannibal *brought back from* Italy. Livy appears to have confused Polybius' second line with Hannibal's veterans and believes that the third line was made up of *actual* Italians. This is clearly a mistake and Walsh is right to chastise Livy for his explanation of why they were in the rear, which is the last place one would want to place uncertain troops. This explanation does reveal a certain amount of naivety on the part of Livy, but again this passage highlights his use of source material. Livy was confused about which troops comprised Polybius' final line, which he would have seen as the Greek historian's mistake. Following his general policy of acceptance and elaboration, Livy attempted to explain this strange position of Italian troops. His explanation is wrong and naïve but the fact that there is an explanation at all shows that he was actively thinking about his sources rather than blindly translating them.

There are a number of other indictments offered by Walsh to support his claim that Livy was a negligent historian. These involve his siege descriptions and some non-military 'mistranslations', which are less important for the present study.[201] These charges of negligence or even ignorance can be explained, if the method of constructing his histories proposed by Luce is correct, by Livy's habit of writing from memory or even by a simple lack of interest in the particular topic at hand.[202] Walsh and others, believing Livy had no experience in warfare and, perhaps subconsciously, following the Polybian precept that military history can only be written by military men, believe Livy was ignorant of warfare and therefore blame every mistake on this perceived ignorance. Livy did make mistakes, but these are very few in respect to the enormous volume of work he produced.

A closer look at these errors shows a historian carefully grappling with his sources and attempting to understand, and explain them to his audience. These few mistakes do not imply a 'crippling' military ignorance but rather an attempt to clarify battles found within his sources. If they do not prove crippling ignorance, neither do they prove that Livy was an expert in military matters, but nevertheless they should not preclude his use as a military source. The mistakes highlight Livy's method of acceptance, elaboration and explanation of Polybius' battle accounts. To attack Livy for including these errors in his own text is to force a modern view of literary criticism on to an ancient historian.

Walsh claims "it is clear that Livy scrutinises his sources without the insight of a military expert; he relies completely on their evidence, reproducing what he reads with stylistic elaboration".[203] As we have seen this is not the case. Livy is prepared to change the evidence of his sources, and appears to scrutinise them with the eye of, if not a military expert, at least an intelligent amateur keen to produce a credible, coherent and authentic reflection of battle. His purpose was to reproduce what he had read, but also to elaborate on his research using other sources and his own imagination to explain the battle narratives of his primary source to his readers, while recreating a clear and authentic literary representation of combat. These are the conditions on which he should be judged, and under which he succeeds admirably.

### 2. Livy's battle descriptions

Livy's battle descriptions fall into two groups: short, monotonous accounts and large-scale, more detailed narratives. Where Livy has only brief accounts from his sources he is unable to expand too much on these bare bones. All he is able to do is adapt his source information according to his literary vision and formula for describing battle. This is the reason for the many short, repetitive battle descriptions found throughout the work.[204] Where he has more detailed and complex sources, such as Polybius, Livy attempts to simplify these accounts for his audience. Although the accounts of both groups vary in size, accuracy and detail, they generally conform to the same descriptive formula, which will be examined in the following chapters.[205]

The aim of Livy's battle descriptions was to produce a clear, uncomplicated account of the sequence of events

[198] Walsh (1970 [1961]) 157.
[199] 30.35.9: *Italicos intervallo quoque diremptos, incertos socii an hostes essent, in postremam aciem summatos.*
[200] 15.11.2: ἐπὶ δὲ πᾶσι τοὺς ἐξ Ἰταλίας ἥκοντας μεθ᾽ αύτοῦ, πλεῖον ἤ στάδιον ἀποστήσας τῶν προτεταγμένων.
15.16.4: τοὺς δὲ μαχιμωτάτους καὶ στασιμωτάτους τῶν ἀνδρῶν.
[201] See Walsh (1958) 83-88 and (1970 [1961]) 158.
[202] Luce (1977).
[203] Walsh (1970 [1961]) 158.
[204] It is possible that, when Livy records a battle very briefly, he was imitating the style of a military communiqué. See Oakley (1997) 139 n. 146.
[205] For more general examinations of the style of Livy's battle descriptions see for example: Kraus and Woodman (1997) 67-8; Oakley (1997) 83-4; Walsh (1961) 191-204.

and the tactics employed. At the same time he tried to hold the interest of his audience by describing the battle dramatically, especially by depicting the psychological experiences of the participants. In order to achieve clarity Livy regularly divides the battle into sections, describing the events at the two wings and the centre of the battle-line as if they were engaged at different times. For the same reason the narratives are also divided into various stages by the use of adverbs such as *primo*, *mox*, *deinde*, etc.[206] Although this is a literary construct and is not an accurate reflection of any particular battle, it a sensible method for clearly and systematically analysing the events of a conflict.

Ancient battle accounts tend to focus on plotting the main sequence of events and so rarely describe in detail how individuals or small groups fought. They generally resort instead to metaphors or generic statements to explain the situation of large sections of the battle-line. A more detailed description of close combat was often unnecessary as the majority of the audience would have had direct experience of a similar form of hand-to-hand fighting. A modern reader, without the benefit of such experience, has to try to reconstruct this form of combat by piecing together the periodic, more detailed descriptions scattered amongst the surviving material. This can best be done by examining closely the formula an individual author employed for describing battle, which offers clues to the way in which they imagined the combat. As we shall see in the coming chapters Livy's formula represents a consistent vision of Roman combat which corresponds well to the archaeological and theoretical parameters of battle.

A further difficulty with ancient combat narratives is that battle is chaotic. It is never possible to record exactly what happened when many thousands of individuals fought for several hours over distances of a few kilometres. For this reason every ancient author had to decide how to construct his narratives, usually succumbing to the use of certain literary conventions specific to the culture in which he wrote. For this reason ancient accounts of battles tend to fall into a similar pattern. Livy is no exception. Many of his accounts fall into an identical pattern, based around the battle formula which will be examined in later chapters. Livy is often criticised for this replication and repetition within his battle accounts, with some claiming that the similar pattern of his battle narratives suggests they were simply literary creations, rather than representations of the reality of battle. But this in itself is no reason to dismiss Livy's accounts altogether.[207] For instance, there are only a limited set of tactical variables in a pitched battle between similarly armed heavy infantry, so the similarities of his battle accounts may actually reflect the limited and repetitive reality of heavy infantry engagement.[208] If Livy's battle accounts were purely literary constructs with no attempt to reflect the reality of the conflict one would expect wide variation between the narratives to keep his readers entertained. As this study will show, there is actually very little variation in the mechanics of heavy infantry combat in Livy's accounts. He instead adds drama to these repetitive descriptions by highlighting unusual details such as cavalry fighting on foot, sudden and dramatic changes of weather, duels between champions, or unexpected ambushes and timely interventions by relieving troops.[209]

Caesar also has a standard formula to describe battle which he repeats throughout his work. His battle narratives vary widely in terms of details but essentially they form a repetition of a common formula. This is usually taken by scholars to reflect the reality of infantry combat, while Livy's similar method is reproved for monotony.[210] The reason for this is presumably the general assumption that he was ignorant of military affairs. This is not a fair assessment of Livy's work, which should equally be used to shape our understanding of Roman combat.

As Livy's battle accounts conform to this formula some scholars have dismissed them as literary fiction.[211] Certainly the events of an individual battle may not have occurred in exactly the way Livy describes but when taken as a whole, the details found in Livy's battle descriptions reflect the wider realities of combat. In this Livy is no different from any writer of battle narratives, ancient or modern. It is never possible to describe exactly what happened in any particular battle, a writer can only hope to be consistent, base the account on the available evidence and to provide a credible image of the fighting.[212] Livy's battle accounts, as we shall see, fulfil these expectations.

---

[206] Walsh (1970 [1961]) 198. Walsh claims that the use of these adverbs is primarily a characteristic of Livy's battle accounts; and Oakley (1997) 127, maintains that this technique is used throughout the work in general.

[207] Roth's argument in support of Livy's siege narratives holds true for his battle narratives. Roth (2006) 49: "despite the importance of understanding narrative from a literary perspective, commentators should not assume a story is necessarily untrue if its narrative or language is stylized. Even the most accurate and objective account must follow conventions of writing. It may be that a focus on rhetorical elements have led some commentators to miss the fact that Livy's narratives reflect underlying realities of siege warfare".

[208] "It should be remembered that only a limited number of situations and outcomes are possible in a battle-scene and at least in the predictability of their battle-scenes the annalists may not have been false to the facts" Oakley (1997) 83-84. A similar point is made by Roth (2006) 57.

[209] For more on these dramatic techniques see Walsh (1970 [1961]) 200-204. Oakley (1997) 84, offers a list of standard motives which occur in the military narratives of books 6 to 10. Many of these recur throughout the extant books. The lists in Plathner (1934) record similar standard motifs in Livy's battle descriptions.

[210] Keegan (1976) 63-5.

[211] See Woodman's discussion of 'The Literature of War' (1998) 1-20, in which he puts forward the thesis that the procedure of Roman historians was closer to that of modern creative writers than of historians. I believe he should not be alarmed about such literary constructs. Ancient Roman historians offer authentic details, which, though not necessarily true of an individual battle, do offer a realistic image of combat in general.

[212] On the various problems of battle narratives in general see Keegan (1976) 13-77.

From pontifical records, inscriptions and monuments there is a large amount of authentic information which has survived in Livy and the annalists, including lists of magistrates, rituals and religious events.[213] Nevertheless, the quantity of this information is not enough to construct a detailed military and political narrative. Much of the information found in Livy and his sources must have been invented using a process of plausible reconstruction. Oakley claims that:

> "to bring an event alive the narrative historian has to use his imagination as sensitively as he can; and it is possible to argue that just as a modern historian makes plausible inferences from his evidence, so too the annalists were inferring what they believed must have happened – only their concept of plausibility was shaped by their literary and rhetorical training."[214]

These reconstructions are not just a series of blatant inventions. Cornell argues that the outline of Roman history was well known to educated Romans and therefore the annalists "had only limited scope for tampering with the received facts, and that they did not, in fact, greatly alter the basic outline of events that had been handed down to them. They were not free to invent anything they pleased."[215] This argument is equally valid for battle descriptions. Livy was writing for a Roman audience which had a collective military experience and were raised on a fundamental military ethos. His descriptions must have been perceived as credible by his readers, since in order for literature to be convincing it must operate within the limits of what its audience were prepared to accept. It follows that his descriptions of battle and thus his literary vision of combat would have been at least plausible reconstructions of Roman battle.

Livy's combat vocabulary and vision of Roman combat are consistent throughout the extant books. By analysing his battle descriptions it is possible to derive a model of combat which corresponds well with the parameters of battle examined in the previous chapter. In addition, there are many similarities between Livy's vision of battle and those of Polybius and Caesar. Caesar is, of course, describing a later form of combat, nevertheless his work is a reflection of a wider Latin literary tradition, which may have influenced Livy. To create a plausible narrative Livy would have worked within the literary and rhetorical framework his audience were accustomed to.[216] Any similarities between Livy's literary vision of battle and these two authors will reinforce the claim that Livy's combat descriptions reflect the general reality of Roman battle.

[213] For a full account of this authentic information see Oakley (1997) 22-72.

[214] Oakley (1997) 76. On this method of plausible reconstruction see Oakley (1997) 76-79; Luce (1977) 140-141; and Roth (2006) 55ff. for siege narratives.

[215] Cornell (1986) 57.

[216] Cf. Oakley (1997) 10, discussing Livy's description of a sack of a city.

### 3. Livy's methodology

There is a rather damning consensus about Livy's methodology, that he knew little about Roman history and blindly followed whichever source he had in front of him. Witte suggests that:

> "just as Livy began the composition of his work without having prepared himself much in advance and in particular failed to give at the start an outline of the contents, so he passed hurriedly from event to event, from scene to scene without taking the trouble to combine the separate accomplishments of the Roman people into larger, integrated units".[217]

Syme suggests that Livy was on the whole content to follow his sources for material.[218] Similarly Walsh states that, when Livy used Polybius in the later books, "a clear and somewhat damning picture emerges of a mind rapidly and mechanically transposing the Greek, and coming to full consciousness only when grappling with the more congenial problems of literary presentation".[219] We have already seen that, at least for his battle accounts, this is not the case. Livy was not blindly following his sources; rather he was conscientiously recording them while expanding and explaining various anomalies and points of interest.[220]

We would expect that, if Livy indeed had not read ahead and was reliant solely on the source in front of him, the battle narratives within the work would depend entirely on the source at hand for both the detail and the description of combat. If this were the case, wide variation would be likely not only between battle accounts in the first ten books and the later 'Polybian' decades, but also within the individual books themselves, whenever Livy changed his main source. But in fact, although the details of the battles may change depending on the source, the descriptive style and mechanics of Roman combat remain, for the most part, fairly standard throughout the extant books.[221] This can only mean that Livy was imposing his own vision of battle and assumptions about close-combat on to his sources, in turn suggesting that he not only had done some preparatory reading, but also that he read battle accounts in his sources with a mind to adapting them to this vision of combat. For this reason a different account of his methodology is necessary.

[217] Witte (1910) 418-19, translated into English by Luce (1977) xviii.

[218] Syme (1958) 148.

[219] Walsh (1970 [1961]) 144.

[220] On this debate see Lipovsky (1981) 6-25.

[221] The battles in the later books, for which Polybius is the main source, tend to be more detailed in matters of topography and tactics than the battles in the first decade. This is due mainly to the supremacy of Polybius over Livy's other sources, but could also be explained by the fact that earlier battles are less historical, and that the most important and decisive battles, to which Livy would naturally devote more space, tend to have occurred during the mid-Republic, with Polybius as the main source. Still, even the smaller semi-mythological battles of the early books conform to what could be called a 'Livian' style of battle narration.

Luce, in an attempt to restore Livy's reputation as a historian, produced a hypothetical account of Livy's working methods, based mainly on his use of Polybius' narrative.[222] Luce's main contention is that Livy did not write serially, moving forward sentence by sentence, nor did he only consult secondary sources after working through his main one. Luce admits that Livy worked quickly and often carelessly but claims that he was still able to adapt his sources in a wide variety of ways. After choosing his main source he on some occasions translated fully, at others condensed the material or even recast it completely. Livy made his own decisions over which parts to omit and at which points additions and substitutions were to be made from other sources, and in this process of adaptation "he felt free to colour and shape the material".[223]

According to Luce's model, Livy went through three stages of preparation before writing. In the first stage he blocked out material into periods: 1-15 on early Rome, 16-30 the Punic Wars and 31-45 the Eastern Conquests, and continued in a similar way until book 120. This presupposes preliminary reading of his sources on a large scale in order to gather enough material to fill units of at least fifteen books for the entire history of the city of Rome, some seven hundred and fifty years. This early reading allowed Livy to set out the material for the long sections such as 'early Rome' into pentads and then books, and also to choose which episodes deserved special treatment or development. The second stage of composition involved re-reading the main sources for each section in more detail; Luce suggests, at least for the later books, that he probably read in units of a consular year. From this he was able to determine the sequence in joining source material, set out his plans for adaptation and find odd notices in other sources which he could bring in to supplement his main source. The third stage involved the actual composition of the work. Luce suggests that, having read a small section, Livy would write this up from memory: "Livy thus worked through Polybius unit by unit, and keeping the information in his mind, wrote his adaptation without referring back to the source very often to refresh his memory".[224] The main evidence for this is the surprising frequency with which variations occur in short lists, such as those of cities or the names of individuals.[225] This suggests that Livy not only read widely before beginning his composition but also had a pre-existing idea of how he wanted his history to come together. Although he did rely on a main source, he wrote in small units from memory which allowed him to adapt, omit or add to his sources from his imagination. This may also be true of his battle narratives, certainly the consistency of his rhetorical formula suggests that he was adapting his sources rather than directly translating what was in front of him. That he read widely about battle and then wrote from memory with his own vision of battle in the forefront of his mind may explain some of the differences and 'mistakes' we have seen between Livy and his main source.

Briscoe, in his 1978 review of Luce's work, calls this methodology "an extraordinary flight of fancy", whereas both Walsh and Ogilvie, with a few reservations, approve.[226] Ogilvie states that the value of Luce's reconstruction "is to show that he [Livy] did not stick to a single annalistic thread at a time but has critical and frequent recourse to a wide variety of material. He did not just stumble on Polybius by accident after book 22". Walsh believes that Luce's model offers a "refreshing independence which leads to fresh insights into the reasons for and techniques of elaboration, compression, and omission".[227] Although Luce's model is hypothetical, it is nevertheless plausible and seems to fit well with what we have seen so far of Livy's battle narratives. Most importantly, it goes a long way towards restoring Livy's reputation as a historian, in the ancient rather than modern sense of the term, as both a collator of information and a literary entertainer.

### 4. Livy's sources

Ogilvie, discussing books 1 to 5, offers a standard analysis of Livy's sources:

> "As it is probable that at any moment Livy is following one authority and one only, so it is unlikely that the total number of authorities generally consulted by him will be very large. As well as making lordly allusions to *veterrimos auctores* (2.18.5, 8.30.7) he does indeed cite Fabius Pictor (1.44.2, 55.8, 2.40.10) and L. Calpurnius Piso (1.55.8, 2.32.3, 58.1) but the former wrote in Greek, a language with which Livy was not altogether familiar, while there was no call to consult the latter directly since he provided the main material for Valerius Antias' history".[228]

This represents the conventional view of the work as a whole: that Livy used late sources, such as Valerius Antias, C. Licinius Macer and Q. Aelius Tubero, which embodied previous research and saved him the trouble of using earlier authorities like Pictor and Piso. In addition it is claimed that Livy avoided using Pictor directly because he wrote in Greek, the chief evidence being mistranslations of Polybius, and the final charge is that he consulted relatively few authorities.

[222] Luce (1977) particularly 185-229.
[223] Luce (1977) 151.
[224] Luce (1977) 214. Cf. Oakley (1997) 16-19, believes that Livy would have had a copy of Polybius in front of him while he wrote. Oakley also claims that a comparison of Livy and the fragments of Piso and Quadrigarius reveals a number of verbal similarities, suggesting that a comparable method also applied to Livy's composition of books 6 to 10.
[225] Such as Polybius 18.3.12: P. has (1) Echinus, (2) Phthiotic Thebes, (3) Pharsalus, and (4) Larissa, whereas Livy (32.33.16) has (2), (1), (4), (3). For more examples see Luce (1977) 214 , especially note 44.

[226] Briscoe (1978) 228.
[227] Ogilvie(1979) 59; Walsh (1978) 173.
[228] Ogilvie (1965) 6-7. Cf. Walsh (1970 [1961]) 115 and 119; Walsh (1974) 14; and Burck (1971) 43 n. 13, who claims that Livy did not use Fabius Pictor or L. Cincius directly.

The accusation that Livy was uncomfortable with Greek is doubtful. He was educated as a member of the elite in a society which emphasised the study of Greek, and his extensive use of Polybius in the fourth and fifth decades suggests a willingness to employ Greek sources.[229] Livy does make errors in translating Polybius' Greek but, as has been shown above, these are relatively few and do not justify Ogilvie's charge. Luce suggests that the report of the battle of Lake Trasimene at 22.7.2-4 confirms Livy's direct use of Fabius Pictor. Livy claims that fifteen thousand Romans fell in the battle compared to two and a half thousand Carthaginians, and then writes that:

> "some writers report even greater casualties on both sides. But I, besides not wishing to make unfounded exaggerations, which all too many writers are prone to do, have selected as my particular authority a man who lived through the war: Fabius".[230]

Luce reasonably assumes that the later Sullan historians would not place the moderate casualty figures of the first Roman historian alongside their own hugely exaggerated figures as their falsification would be too obvious. For this reason he claims that Livy not only had read Fabius Pictor, but also consulted his work during the composition process.[231] Northwood recently reviewed all the passages where Livy claims to have used early sources, not just Fabius, and argued compellingly that Livy did consult these directly rather than receiving this information from later annalistic writers.[232]

For the first ten books it is generally agreed that Livy consulted the late annalists Valerius Antias, Claudius Quadrigarius, Macer and Tubero.[233] He also seems to have used Fabius Pictor and the Gracchan annalist L. Calpurnius Piso; in Luce's opinion directly, but for Walsh and others, only at second hand through one of his later sources. For the third decade there is more agreement over Livy's sources. He seems to have used Polybius for events in Greece, Sicily and Africa, with Coelius Antipater for campaigning in Italy and Spain in the first part of the Second Punic War and Valerius Antias and Claudius Quadrigarius increasingly in the second part of the war for a Roman perspective, especially as sources for Senatorial administration. There are also references to Pictor (22.7.4), Piso (25.39.12-13) and Cincius Alimentus (21.38.3), though these authorities would have supplied Livy with only a small amount of information.[234] For the fourth and fifth decades Livy used Polybius for eastern affairs, which account for two-thirds of books 31 to 45, with Antias and Quadrigarius for political and diplomatic events in the West. There is also convincing evidence for Livy's use of Cato, at least for his Spanish campaign in 195, but he also appears to have influenced Livy in other matters.[235]

It is generally assumed that, like other ancient writers, Livy would select a source to follow as his main authority for a particular section of his work and use other sources not to 'check' errors in the main source, but rather to supplement it. Livy is not often critical of statements in his secondary sources which do not occur in his main source; instead he uses this material as an additional supply of information. Livy would choose the authority he would use for his main source during his preliminary reading, based on several criteria: credibility, fame of the writer, closeness to the period, potential for literary adaptation, and fullness.[236] He would then use one or more sources for additional information not found in the main source or in some cases make substitutions where his main source was less detailed. Unlike modern scholars, Livy seems to have had an attitude of general acceptance towards his sources. Though he praises Polybius (30.45.5), he appears to have not regarded him as vastly superior to his Roman sources.[237] For example, as Livy was well aware, Antias was guilty of exaggerating his casualty figures, but for Livy he was right until proved wrong.[238] Therefore, although Livy was at the mercy of his sources he was, at least, able to make omissions from his main source, and additions or even substitutions from his secondary sources. We have already seen this policy at work within the context of his battle descriptions. Livy follows his main source closely, in these cases Polybius; but when he saw an error or an anomaly he generally chose to record this and attempt an explanation for it using his own experiences and imagination or perhaps other minor sources. In this way he is following his practice of acceptance and elaboration.

The fragmentary nature of these sources makes it impossible to explain fully from where Livy received his literary vision of, and rhetorical tools for describing, battle. The annalists supplied political details, especially the machinations of the senate, general movement of armies on campaign and usually inflated casualty figures. They did not appear to have offered Livy the rhetorical tools through which he was able to describe battle. Even Coelius Antipater, whom, it is generally agreed, Livy employed as a main source for campaigning in Italy and Spain during the initial years of the Second Punic War, does not appear from the surviving fragments to have offered much on the mechanics of battle. Although, of course the surviving fragments are a minute sample of

---

229 Luce (1977) 170.

230 *Multiplex caedes utrimque facta traditur ab aliis; ego praeterquam quod nihil auctum ex uano uelim, quo nimis inclinant ferme scribentium animi, Fabium, aequalem temporibus huiusce belli, potissimum auctorem habui.*

231 Luce (1977) 162. See also Ogilvie (1965) 3-16; Tränkle (1971); Astin (1978) 302-7; Oakley (1997) 62ff.

232 Northwood (2000).

233 See Ogilvie (1965) 7-17 for portraits of Macer, Antias and Tubero; cf. Luce (1977) 165-169; Oakley, (1997) 89 - 94.

234 Many editors of Livy's text include a passage at 29.22.10, which suggests Livy also used Clodius Licinus directly, e.g. Weissenborn (1868); Moore (1949); and François (1994). Oakley (1992) convincingly argues that Livy was not the author of this passage.

235 For more detailed analysis of the state of scholarship on Livy's sources see Walsh (1970 [1961]) 110-137; Walsh (1974) 13-16; Ogilvie (1971) 7-12; Luce (1977) 139-184; Oakley (1997) 3-108.

236 Luce (1977) 147.

237 Luce (1977) 72-3, Briscoe in his review of Luce's book (1978) finds this one of the few things with which he can agree.

238 Luce (1977) 148. For a discussion of perversions of the truth by Livy's sources see Oakley (1997) 89-100.

what he may have written. It may never be possible to discern directly from where his literary vision of battle arose. It is possible however to identify the influence of other more extant writers on Livy's rhetoric of combat. Though Livy received a vast amount of information from Polybius' battle narratives, there are enough variations to suggest that Polybius' account was adapted where passages failed to complement Livy's own literary vision of battle. Lendon suggests that a Latin rhetorical tradition of battle narratives existed, which differed from the Greek and, if this were the case, Livy may well have been influenced by that.[239] Of Livy's predecessors, Caesar is the most well preserved military author writing in Latin, and as we shall see an analysis of his work reveals some interesting similarities, but also some differences, between the two writers' visions of combat.

In this section it has been proposed that Livy used a larger number of sources and more conscientiously than is often suggested. He was not restricted to just the Sullan annalists, but may also have used second-century historians such as Pictor and Cato directly. For each section of his work, Livy tended to employ one main source which he followed closely. Where he saw problems with this source, he would use other works and his own assumptions to correct, adapt and explain these points. He was not restricted to, nor blindly followed his main source: various corrections or explanations suggest that he worked conscientiously and thoughtfully with his sources. As will be demonstrated in later chapters, Livy's battle descriptions conform to a standard formula throughout the extant books. This formula reflects Livy's literary vision of infantry battle and his understanding of close combat in general. Many of Livy's sources only survive as fragments and so it is difficult to trace where this vision came from. Nevertheless an analysis of the methods Polybius and Caesar use to describe battle may reveal the influence on Livy of these two authors, or at least the two literary traditions which they represent.

## 5. Livy's influences

### *The influence of Polybius*

Polybius is an obvious choice of author to represent the Greek tradition of battle narration. Not only was he one of Livy's most important sources for the mid-Republican Roman army, he was also an experienced cavalry officer in the Achaean league and wrote a now lost handbook on *Tactics*. As one of a thousand Achaeans held in Rome for sixteen years after Pydna he became friends with noble Romans and in particular Scipio Aemilianus. In 151 he accompanied Scipio to Spain and to the siege Carthage as a military advisor. Through these experiences he would have been acquainted with the Roman army and had access to experienced officers and soldiers. His main work examining the rise of the Roman state was written for a Greek audience to explain this dominance. For this reason his battle narratives usually conform to Greek conventions, but also periodically include more specific descriptions and analyses of Roman battle mechanics.[240]

*The battle of Cynoscephalae: an example of Polybius' battle narratives*

The battle of Cynoscephalae, fought in Thessaly in 197BC between the Romans under T. Quinctius Flamininus and the Macedonians under Philip V, was the decisive battle of the Second Macedonian War. The two armies had encamped with a range of hills between them known as Cynoscephalae, so that neither knew the other's position. On the following morning a mist made visibility difficult, which led the two scouting parties to stumble on to each other and begin skirmishing. This skirmish eventually encouraged both commanders to commit their full force and after some initial success by the right wing of Philip's phalanx, the Macedonians were defeated when a tribune attacked the rear of Macedonian phalanx with twenty maniples from the Roman right. Polybius records this battle in detail, celebrating it as the archetypal example of legionary and phalanx warfare. His digression on the superiority of the legion over the phalanx immediately follows this account and demonstrates the fundamental differences between the two forms of combat. This digression demonstrates Polybius' awareness that the Romans fought in a very different way to the Macedonians, yet as we shall see in his account of the battle he describes the fighting of both formations in a similar way.

The Roman reconnaissance force sent to occupy the heights was made up of "ten squadrons of horse and about a thousand light-armed infantry" (18.21.1). The composition of the Macedonian covering force is not given, but was presumably of comparable size and strength. The two forces met in an initial skirmish, and the 'Romans began to be *overpowered* and to suffer losses at the hands of the Macedonian reserve'.[241] Polybius describes this fighting with the term κατεβαρoῦντο. Καταβαρεω means 'to weigh down or overload', but in the passive it can mean 'to be crushed', or 'to be pressed down with weight or physical force'.[242] For Polybius it is the 'weight' of the Macedonian light infantry which crushes the Romans.

In response to this loss Flamininus sent forward a further "five hundred horse and two thousand foot" (18.21.5) to support his reconnaissance force. Again these troops were light infantry.[243] The Macedonians "were in their turn pressed hard, and upon being completely overmastered, fled to the summits" (Paton, 1926).[244] In this passage it is

[239] Lendon (1999).

[240] On Polybius in general and as a military expert: Walbank (1957-79), (1972), (1979), (2002); Marsden (1973); Derow (1979); Davidson (1991); etc.

[241] 18.21.4: οἱ Ῥωμαῖοι κατεβαροῦντο καὶ κακῶς ἔπασχον ὑπὸ τῆς τῶν Μακεδόνων ἐφεδρείας.

[242] LSJ s.v. 1

[243] Walbank (1967) 580.

[244] 18.21.8: οἱ δὲ Μακεδόνες ἠμύνοντο μὲν γενναίως, πιεζούμενοι δὲ πάλιν οὗτοι καὶ καταβαρούμενοι τοῖς ὅλοις προσέφυγον πρὸς τοὺς ἄκρους

the Macedonian forces which are being crushed (καταβαρεω) by the 'weight' of the Roman light infantry and cavalry. Polybius also uses πιέζω to describe the combat, which Paton translates as 'press hard'; the term can also have the connotation of squeezing or pressing down of a heavy weight.[245] Light infantry do not fight in massed formation, but rather tend to skirmish back and forth with missile weapons and intermittent hand-to-hand combat, but Polybius is able to use 'pushing' and 'weighing' metaphors to describe this form of combat and even that of the cavalry.[246]

When Philip received word of this reversal, he dispatched his Thessalian and Macedonian horse together with "all the mercenaries except those from Thrace" (18.22.2). After the arrival of Philip's mercenaries, "the Macedonians, having received such a *large reinforcement*, *pressed hard* on the enemy and in their turn began to *drive* the Romans from the heights" (Paton, 1926).[247] Livy claims that these mercenaries numbered 2,000 Illyrians and 1,500 other mercenaries (33.4.4-5). These would also be lighter armed troops than members of the phalanx. For the third time Polybius uses metaphors of pushing and weight to describe the combat of light-armed troops. He calls the mercenaries and cavalry 'a heavy band' (βαρύς χειρ), their attack is described by the verb ἔγκειμαι, suggesting that the light infantry were 'pressing upon' the Romans, and were able to 'drive' (ἐλαύνω) them from the field. The term ἐνκειμαι can have the sense of metaphorical pressing, as in pressing on a retreating enemy and could mean close pursuit rather than physical pressing.[248] Ἐλαυνω generally means to drive, but can also have the sense of setting something in motion.[249] Polybius' terms can be taken figuratively, meaning the Romans were not being 'pushed' away from the heights by physical weight of the Macedonians, but rather were driven away by the imposing presence of a much larger force.[250] In either case Polybius' literary formula of battle narration involves the use of 'pushing' and 'weighing' metaphors to describe combat, even for that of cavalry and light infantry.

Polybius uses similar metaphors to describe the heavy infantry and in particular the Macedonian phalanx. The attack of the Phalanx at 18.25.4 is expressed by the term ἐφοδος, which Paton translates as "charge" for the Loeb edition, but should perhaps be translated with a more neutral term such as "onset".[251] Initially the Romans could not withstand this attack of Philip's right wing because "they were attacking from higher ground and were superior in the *weight of their formation*" (Paton, 1926).[252] It is the weight (τῷ βάρει τῆς συντάξεως) of the formation that leads to the Macedonian success. Later the reason given for the success of this same attack is again explained "by their weight forcing back the Roman left" (πιεζοῦντα τῷ βάρει) at 18.26.3. Here, as with his description of the Roman light infantry, Polybius uses the term πιέζω to give the impression of pressing down and in this case he is even more explicit by combining it with βάρος.

Polybius' use of such metaphors to describe the attack of the Macedonian heavy infantry is easier to understand than for the light infantry. In his digression on the legion and phalanx after his account of Cynoscephalae Polybius explains the nature of the phalanx. It is a close-order formation in which the first five ranks lower their spears as an offensive weapon. The rear ranks (eleven in the sixteen deep formation described by Polybius) are there in part to defend against missile fire with their spears acting as a sort of umbrella, but primarily they were there to add weight to the formation. Polybius writes that "these men by the sheer pressure of their body weight in the charge add to its force, and it is quite impossible for the first ranks to face about" (Paton, 1926).[253] In this description, the phalanx used the weight of its formation to push back the opposition forces physically, making his use of such physical metaphors understandable.

There are two opposing hypotheses explaining why phalanx fighting was described in this way. Hanson follows Polybius, and believes that "the real importance of these men in the rear (of the phalanx) was simply to push those in front with their shields".[254] If this were the

[245] LSJ s.v. 1 (squeezing, etc), though 2 notes the pressing of a victorious army.

[246] On light infantry tactics see Polybius 11.22.9-10.

[247] 18.22.3: Καὶ προσγενομένης τοῖς Μακεδόσι βαρείας χειρός, ἐνέκειντο τοῖς πολεμίοις· καὶ πάλιν οὗτοι τοὺς Ῥωμαίους ἤλαυνον ἐκ μεταβολῆς ἀπὸ τῶν ἄκρων.

[248] LSJ s.v. II; e.g. Thucydides 1.49.7.

[249] LSJ s.v. 3; examples of this sense include a shepherd driving his flock (Odyssey 9.237); or a commander sending more cowardly soldiers into the middle of his battle-line (Iliad. 4.299).

[250] Krentz (1985b) 51-56 and Van Wees (2004) 189, believe that all similar Greek metaphors of weight' and pushing should only ever be taken figuratively.

[251] Ἐφοδος is used three times in Polybius' theoretical discussion of the phalanx (18.29.1, 30.1, and 30.11). In this digression, Polybius describes the phalanx as a close order formation: "each man, with his arms, occupies a space of three feet in breadth" (18.29.2), and, due to his measurements of the pikes (18.29.2-6), three feet from chest front to chest front in depth. For such a large body of men, in such a close order, carrying a pike of about six metres in length, it would be unlikely that they could attack at a run without some men falling over disrupting the whole formation. Rather the ἐφοδος of the phalanx is likely to have been a slow, almost irresistible attack, with the entire formation moving as one unit. Therefore 'charge' is an unsuitable translation for ἐφοδος. The term ἐφοδος seems to be a Greek equivalent to the Latin *impetus*, in that it appears to have no specific speed connotation and it can also be used to describe various types of onset. These include naval attacks (Pol. 1.36.11, 3.25.4); attacks on fortified camps (Dionysius of Halicarnassus 4.51.4); phalanx attacks; and the attacks of much more open formations like the Romans (Dionysius of Halicarnassus. 3.4.2) and the Illyrians (Thucydides 4.126.5).

[252] 18.25.2: ἅτε καὶ τὴν ἔφοδον ἐξ ὑπερδεξίου ποιούμενον καὶ τῷ βάρει τῆς συντάξεως ὑπέρεχον.

[253] 18.30.4: αὐτῷ γε μὴν τῷ τοῦ σώματος βάρει κατὰ τὴν ἐπαγωγὴν πιεζοῦντες οὗτοι τοὺς προηγουμένους βιαίαν μὲν ποιοῦσι τὴν ἔφοδον, ἀδύνατον δὲ τοῖς πρωτοστάταις τὴν εἰς τοὔπισθεν μεταβολήν.

[254] Hanson (1989) 172, cf 171-184. It should be noted that he is discussing a hoplite rather than a pike phalanx, which is only half as deep as Polybius' phalanx.

case, battles between phalanxes would have literally involved pushing and a literary tradition may have arisen to reflect the nature of the combat. On the other side, some argue that hoplite battle was never a huge pushing match.[255] Pritchett suggests that these metaphors were common in Homer and would have been used by later writers for stylistic reasons, leading to a tradition where phalanx battle was described with archaic metaphors which did not reflect the reality of the combat.[256]

Cynoscephalae was an unusual battle for the Romans because sustained combat between the opposing heavy infantry only occurred at one point, the Roman left, where they were driven back by the Phalanx. This wing had been successful earlier in the battle against the Macedonian light infantry and so at that point there are some clues as to how Polybius describes Roman heavy infantry combat. After the initial skirmish, Flamininus brought forward his left wing and, after being reinforced by the heavy infantry, this combined force "fell upon their foes" (ἐνέκειντο τοῖς ὑπεναντίοις, 18.23.8). Similar to the description of the Macedonian skirmishers, Polybius here employs the term ἔγκειμαι, implying that the Roman infantry were 'pressing upon' the Macedonians. Later this same attack is described as the Romans "*pressing heavily* on the enemy [they] killed many of them".[257] Again Polybius uses a metaphor of weighing to describe Roman heavy infantry combat. His phrase βαρέως ἐπέκειντο suggests that the Romans were successful because they pressed upon the Macedonians with their weight, a strange description for the more open style of Roman infantry combat.

In his theoretical comparison of the phalanx and the legion, Polybius is very much aware that the Romans fought in an open formation unsuitable for massed pushing:

> "each soldier with his arms occupies a space of three feet in breadth, but as in their mode of fighting each man must move separately, as he has to cover his person with his shield, turning to meet each expected blow, and as he uses his sword for both cutting and thrusting it is obvious that a looser order is required, and each man must be at a distance of at least three feet from the man next to him in the same rank and those in front of and behind him, if they are to be of proper use".[258]

The Roman formation was much more open than that of the phalanx and the style of combat involved cutting and thrusting with swords rather than using weight to push the enemy back. The three-line system of the Romans also demonstrates that the advantage of their fighting style was not in its combined weight. Polybius chose to place his discussion of the two combat systems immediately after his narrative of Cynoscephalae because this battle exemplified how both systems fought in actual practice.[259] It follows then that the Roman legion fought at Cynoscephalae in the open style and with the hand-to-hand fighting described in his digression, rather than the *othismos* implied by Polybius' metaphors. In this case at least the metaphors within the battle narrative should be taken figuratively rather than literally. The battle account of Cynoscephalae reveals that Polybius could describe the Roman form of attack with metaphors of weight and pushing despite being aware that this description did not reflect their actual combat.

In this short analysis it has been demonstrated that Polybius was able to employ metaphors of weight to describe the combat of the Macedonian heavy infantry, perhaps reflecting the massed advance of that formation, but he was also able to use similar terms to illustrate the scattered skirmishing of both Macedonian and Roman light infantry and cavalry. Stranger still is his description of the mechanics of the Roman heavy infantry. In his digression after the battle Polybius paints a picture of the legion fighting individually with swords in an open formation allowing them room to turn in any direction. Nevertheless he describes the combat of legion with the same physical metaphors he used for the Macedonian phalanx. Livy used Polybius as one of his main sources for the fourth and fifth decades of his work but his method of describing battle is different. Livy's involves more specific and dynamic terms like compounds of *currere*, *impetus* and *inferre*, rather than Latin equivalents of Polybius' metaphors. He seems to have imposed his own literary vision of combat on to his source in order to reflect better the fighting of the Roman legion. Later in this study, after Livy's combat vocabulary has been examined in more detail, the parallel battle accounts of these two authors will be compared to see just how far their visions differ.

### *The influence of Caesar*

No mid-Republican Latin histories survive in more than mere fragments and so necessarily a late-Republican writer will have to represent a possible Latin tradition of battle narration. Caesar has been chosen over Sallust because of his extended focus on combat and his vast military experience. Caesar's *commentarii* are not impartial history, if such a thing could ever exist, but rather calculated political propaganda justifying himself, his officers and men. The renowned military theorist John Keegan used Caesar as almost an archetypal example of unrealistic battle narration and in many ways he is correct. Caesar's battle accounts generally do focus too much on his own role relegating both the enemy and the legionaries to automata, with a uniformity of behaviour and simplified motivations.[260] Nevertheless the methodological approach which will be taken in the following chapters, focussing not on individual battle accounts but analysing the vocabulary used to describe

[255] Krentz (1985b) and (1994); Goldsworthy (1997), etc.
[256] Pritchett (1985) 29.
[257] 18.24.5: βαρέως ἐπέκειντο τοῖς πολεμίοις καὶ πολλοὺς αὐτῶν ἔκτεινον.
[258] 18.30.7-8.
[259] 18.28.1.
[260] Keegan (1976) 63-4.

attacks and its context, can offer glimpses of the mechanics of combat. Caesar's battle descriptions tend to be less formulaic than Livy's but a similar fundamental rhetoric can still be seen based around *impetum facere*.[261]

It is generally accepted that Livy had read Caesar's works and it is likely that he was influenced by them, but unfortunately the only evidence is indirect. The most convincing is the similarity of their descriptions of Gaul. Livy writes that "while Tarquinius Priscus reigned at Rome, the Celts, who made up one of three divisions of Gaul, were under the domination of the Bituriges".[262] This seems to have come almost directly from the famous first line of the *Gallic Wars*: "Gaul is a whole divided into three parts, one of which is inhabited by the Belgae, another by the Aquitani, and a third by a people called in their own language Celts, in the Latin Gauls".[263] As Ogilvie notes, Caesar and Livy are the only ancient writers to use the term *Celtae* for the inhabitants of the central area of Gaul. In other writers the terms 'Gaul' and 'Celt' are used indiscriminately to describe all the members of the ethnic group as a whole.[264] Further evidence includes some linguistic parallels and other similar passages.[265] While no individual piece is conclusive, the weight of the evidence as a whole makes it likely that Livy read and was influenced by Caesar's works. It is logical that Livy would look to Caesar, arguably the most famous general during his lifetime, for instruction on how to compose a battle account. But how far can it plausibly be suggested that Caesar had a direct influence on Livy's literary vision of combat?

Caesar's descriptions of Roman infantry attacks, like Livy's, are predominantly described with *impetus* which the enemy had to try to withstand (*sustinere*). At Bibracte in 58BC fighting lasted from the seventh hour until evening, when the Helvetii could no longer hold out against the Roman attacks, part of their forces fled while others tried to defend the baggage carts.[266] This passage exemplifies Caesar's view that *impetus* was something that the enemy must sustain to avoid a rout. The fighting in this battle lasted for many hours, making it unlikely that the *impetus* Caesar describes was a single assault, as the physical and psychological strain of fighting within the 'killing zone' for that length of time would be impossible to endure. Caesar's use of the plural form of the term *impetus* also suggests that the fighting consisted of many distinct attacks. Caesar's *impetus* seems to have been a series of attacks, probably punctuated with lulls in the fighting to allow the soldiers to recover, and to remove casualties from the frontline. This passage resembles the theoretical model of the dynamic standoff and also, as will be demonstrated in the coming chapters, Livy's descriptions of infantry combat.

There are also some direct stylistic similarities between Caesar's battle descriptions and the formula of Livy's vision of combat. At 28.15.10 Livy describes the Roman infantry fighting with such spirit that 'their attack could not easily be sustained' (*nec facile impetus sustineri posset*), which is noticeably similar to Caesar's *sustinere... impetus... non possent*.[267] Again at 38.22.9, where the Romans were fighting the Galatians, Livy describes the attack as *nec diutius impetum Romanorum sustinuerunt*. Throughout the works of both Caesar and Livy there are many examples of twinning the words *impetus* and *sustinere*, which may suggest that Livy had been influenced by Caesar's battle accounts. In the Greek literary tradition, attacks are described with pushing metaphors in which infantry, and even light infantry and cavalry, weigh on the enemy and push back their line, giving the impression of a giant rugby scrum.[268] Caesar envisages a Roman *impetus* as a force designed to break the enemy battle-line, which in turn must withstand this force or fall into disorder. As will be demonstrated in this study in Livy's battle formula attacks described with the term *impetus* are also intended specifically to disrupt the enemy battle-line.

During the withdrawal in contact from Aduatica the Roman infantry fought a hard battle against the Gauls. Caesar writes that whenever a Roman cohort dashed out of their line to attack the enemy, a large number of the enemy were killed at that point. The Gallic chief Ambiorix noticed this and ordered his men to give way wherever the Romans made an attack, and when the Romans retired back to their standards his men should pursue in their turn.[269] This combat description is again similar to the dynamic stand-off model: the Romans attack out of their line, cross the safety distance, and cut down the enemy at the particular point against which the attack was aimed. The enemy give way to the Roman *impetus* and, as the attackers return to their standards, the Gauls pursue the Romans. This shows the fluid nature of the stand-off, the battle-lines could move back and forth depending on which side was attacking. The Roman *impetus* is not a massed attack, but a series of attacks against localised points along the enemy battle-line.

As will be demonstrated in the coming chapters, Livy conceived of Roman infantry combat in a similar way and employed a similar vocabulary to describe battle. The most important term of this formula, like Caesar's, is *impetus*. Caesar, or at least a wider Latin tradition,

---

[261] Caesar's life and career: Gelzer (1968 [1921]); Meier (1995 [1982]). His works: among many, Carter (1991), (1993); Batstone and Damon (2006); Rice Holmes (1914); Eden (1962); Gotoff (1984). Political propaganda: Collins (1972); Henderson (1996); Batstone (1990), (1991); Goldsworthy (1998); Welch and Powell (1998); Riggsby (2006). Combat rhetoric: Lendon (1999).

[262] 5.34.1: *Prisco Tarquinio Romae regnante Celtarum quae pars tertia Galliae est, penes Bituriges summa imperii fuit.*

[263] *B Gall.* 1.1.1: *Gallia est omnis divisa in partes tres, quarum unam incolunt Belgae, aliam Aquitani, tertiam qui ipsorum lingua Celtae, nostra Galli appellantur.*

[264] Ogilvie (1965) 707.

[265] Klotz (1953) 62-67. See Walsh (1970 [1961]) 43, 203, for some influences of Caesar on how Livy makes his battle narratives more dramatic.

[266] *B Gall.* 1.26.1: *diutius cum sustinere nostrorum impetus non possent.*

[267] *B Gall.* 1.26.1.

[268] On this see chapter 6 below. Cf. Lendon (1999).

[269] *B Gall.* 5.34.3-4: *quotiens quaeque cohors procurrerat, ab ea parte magnus numerus hostium cadebat ...Ambiorix ... iubet... quam in partem Romani impetum fecerint cedant...rursus se ad signa recipientes insequantur.*

appears to have been an important influence on how Livy understood and described battle. This influence will be examined in more detail later in this study.

***The influence of the fragmentary historians***

Much has been written about the influences of the earlier Roman historians used by Livy as his sources.[270]These early source include Fabius Pictor, Coelius Antipater, Cato, Calpurnius Piso, and the later annalists, Valerius Antias, Claudius Quadrigarius, C. Licinius Macer and Q. Aelius Tubero. The extent of their influence on Livy's literary vision of battle is impossible to judge given the fragmentary nature of the surviving material. Throughout the entire corpus of the fragmentary historians the term *impetus* occurs three times, once in Cato to describe mercenaries making an attack on their general; once in Claudius Quadrigarius, during single combat between Titus Manlius and the Gaul; and once finally in Sisenna, in which the Romans are driven back by an *impetus* and then pursued.[271] Occurrences of the term *inferre* are even sparser, with just one fragment, from Sisenna, stating that the Romans came to deal destruction.[272] None of these fragments describe an attack of the Roman heavy infantry in a pitched battle, and so it is impossible to judge how far Livy's descriptions of combat were influenced by his Roman sources from the extant fragments.

**6. Greek and Latin traditions of combat rhetoric**

Having looked briefly at the specific influence of some of Livy's predecessors, it is worth now discussing the Greek and Latin literary traditions in general. Lendon claims that each culture possesses an inherited rhetoric of combat used to describe the experience of battle, though in all cases it is arbitrary and unreal. "What is described in a battle description depends on unconscious cultural and conscious intellectual decisions about what it is important to describe".[273] He suggests that the Greek tradition's rhetoric of combat focuses on formation, the dangers of disorder and uses physical metaphors of weight and pushing to describe battle. These metaphors were drawn from the Greek experience of classical phalanx fighting, and therefore the Greeks conceived combat between sets of troops in terms of weight and pushing.[274] As we have seen from Polybius' account of Cynoscephalae, it is not just phalanxes which 'push' and 'weigh', but also light armed troops and even the Roman heavy infantry.

Lendon suggests that "a set of metaphors drawn from experience has been elaborated into a physical theory of battle".[275] Peter Krentz disagrees suggesting that these metaphors were instead handed down through the Greek tradition from Homer. In the *Iliad* the formations tend to be loose, with men disengaging from their line and moving about the battlefield. There are few massed collisions of infantrymen and yet Homer often describes the combat with 'pushing' metaphors. Krentz believes that in most cases these metaphors should be taken figuratively rather than literally, and even when they describe actual pushing, such as Thucydides' account of the battle of Delion (4.96.2), they need not imply a massed shove or shock tactic.[276] Further, Walbank claims that Polybius emphasises "the historical importance of the individual, the general in command, as opposed to the ordinary soldier".[277] So these generic metaphors may be an attempt to relegate the ordinary soldier to just a part of the mass.

Lendon further suggests that Caesar adapted the Greek tradition to his experiences of Roman battle, but his method of describing battle was different. "Unlike the Greeks, Caesar tends to envisage the fundamental mechanics of battle not as the pushing of a weight but as the crash of one moving force, an *impetus*, against a stationary one, which must sustain (*sustinere*, *G* 1.24, 26, 4.37) or bear (*ferre*, *G* 5.21, *C* 2.25) that force".[278] Lendon hypothesises a Latin tradition of combat rhetoric in which heavy infantry do not 'push' and 'weigh', but are far more dynamic, attempting to disrupt the enemy line with *impetus*. We have already seen this style of combat description in Caesar's narratives. Although most of the Latin battle descriptions before Caesar have not survived antiquity, it seems likely that Caesar was part of a wider tradition and that this Latin tradition would certainly have influenced Livy's narrative style.[279]

We have seen that Polybius was influenced by the Greek tradition in his descriptions of infantry battle. His cultural language and conceptual 'stock' allowed him to describe battle in this way despite being aware that it did not accurately reflect Roman combat. These terms for pushing and weighing are simply metaphors and should be taken figuratively. They do not imply a massed charge, but describe the same form of open and individualistic combat for which the Latin tradition would use a term such as *impetus*. This explains the differences we shall see in chapter 6 between Livy's and Polybius' battle

[270] A few examples include: Ogilvie (1965) 5-17, Walsh (1970 [1961]) 20-45, Briscoe (1973) 1-12, Luce (1977) 139-183, Oakley (1997) 13-109.

[271] Cato (frag. 79 (Peter) = Gell. 5, 21, 17): '*Compluriens eorum milites mercennarii inter se multi alteri alteros in castris occidere, compluriens multi simul ad hostis transfugere, compluriens in imperatorem impetum facere*'.
Claudius Quadrigarius (frag 10b (Peter) = Gell. 9.13.4): '*...eo pacto ei sub Gallicum gladium successit atque Hispanico pectus hausit; deinde continuo umerum dextrum eodum successu incidit neque recessit usquam, donec subvertit, ne Gallus impetum in ictu haberet.*'
Sisenna, *Historiarum libro III*: '*Romanos inpetu* [*impetu*] *suo protelant, protelatos persecuntur*'.

[272] Sisenna, *Historiarum libro VI* (=Gell. 9.14.12): '*Romanos inferendae pernicii causa venisse*'.

[273] Lendon (1999) 275.

[274] Cf. Pritchett (1985) 65-68.

[275] Lendon (1999) 285.

[276] Krentz (1985b) 55-56.

[277] Walbank (2002) 22.

[278] Lendon (1999) 287.

[279] Cf. Walsh (1970 [1961]). 43: "The sole possible link with his [Livy's] predecessors [Caesar, Sallust and Asinius Pollio] lies in considerations of style. Of these predecessors, Caesar exercises the most direct influence. Livy learned a great deal from the narrative of the Gallic and Civil Wars; the influence of the *Commentarii* may be noted in Livy's method of describing troop dispositions and certain other techniques of military narration".

narratives and strengthens the claim that Livy is a 'worthwhile' military historian. Livy does make some mistakes, but his battle descriptions fall within a tradition combining Greek theories of order and disorder, and Roman, especially Caesar's, military experience of more dynamic combat. Where he avoids Greek metaphors he attempts to explain the details of Roman battle with terms such as *impetus* and *inferre* [*signa*] which have specific meanings in the context of infantry combat. Livy synthesises the two literary traditions in a thoughtful way and produces his own formula for describing infantry fighting. In order to understand Livy's vision of battle fully, and perhaps to improve our knowledge of mid-Republican infantry combat, it is necessary to examine the different ways he used these terms to discover the form of combat he envisaged.

## 7. Conclusion

This short introduction to mid- to late-Republican battle narratives has tried to defend Livy against the charge of military ignorance and demonstrate that he was a careful and diligent historian attempting to recreate an authentic image of Roman combat as far as this is possible in a battle narrative. This chapter has also shown that there are important differences between the Greek and Latin tradition of battle narratives. Both methods are arbitrary and neither can fully express the reality of an individual battle, but an analysis of the descriptions in general can offer insight into the mechanics of the combat which archaeology and theory alone can not provide.

In the following three chapters it will be demonstrated that Livy's rhetorical toolbox for describing battles is similar to Caesar's, but, as will be established through a comparison of their methods in chapter 7, it differs in some important ways. These differences may reflect changes in the form of combat from the mid to the late Republic which Livy tries to express. In chapter 6 there will be an analysis of the parallel battle descriptions found in Livy and Polybius' narratives, which will demonstrate that Livy was also influenced by the Greek tradition of battle description and Polybius in particular. In this study as a whole it will be proposed that Livy takes aspects from both traditions and combines them with his own understanding of infantry combat to create his particular method of narrating battle. The similarities between Livy's and other writers' battle descriptions and the consistency of his approach underlines the essential accuracy of his method. Livy may have been mistaken about the specific events of a particular battle, but the overall impression given by his narratives of Roman combat is a reliable reflection of reality. Although each of the three methods for describing combat is a literary construction, the similarities between them may have some basis in a historical reality. It is through a close analysis of these battle accounts that it will be possible to derive a new more realistic model of mid-Republican heavy infantry battle.

## Chapter 4: Livy's use of the compounds of *currere*

In the previous chapter it was proposed that Livy's battle narratives offer a credible description of mid-Republican infantry combat. Even a cursory glance at these narratives reveals certain terms which occur with a frequency suggesting more than mere chance. If Livy's battle narratives were simply literary set pieces, with no attempt to reflect the reality of the combat, one would expect a much wider variety of combat terms to entertain his audience, to display his skill as a writer and to conform to the literary convention of *variatio*.[280] The consistency and limited range of Livy's vocabulary suggests that, in a military context, these terms have specific meanings. Though they are not technical terms, which tend to be avoided by Livy and the annalists,[281] it seems that Livy imagined specific forms of attack when he used this combat rhetoric. It is my contention that an analysis of this vocabulary and the contexts in which these words can be found will enable us to gain an understanding of Livy's literary vision of infantry combat. When combined with the archaeological evidence and the theoretical parameters discussed in the first chapter, this will allow us to derive a new and more convincing model of Roman legionary fighting.

The most frequently occurring term used by Livy to describe an attack is *impetus*, and the next most common is the verb *inferre*, often with *signa*. These terms will be analysed in the fourth and fifth chapters. In addition to these two main terms, compounds of *currere* are also often employed by Livy in military contexts. The forms which occur most regularly are *concurrere*, *incurrere*, *procurrere* and *decurrere*. Livy frequently uses these to describe both cavalry and infantry attacks. The morphology of these terms, derived as they are from *currere*, the Latin word 'to run', suggests that Livy may have used these words to describe high speed attacks. Although their use is understandable in the context of a cavalry assault, the archaeological evidence indicates that a Roman legionary would not usually have run in to attack. It is important then to analyse closely how Livy used these terms and to consider the part they played in his vision of combat and ultimately how this should affect our model of infantry battle.

To achieve this end I have systematically scrutinised each occurrence of these terms in the extant books of Livy, and examined the context in which it was found and how Livy used the term. The full results of this research take the form of appendices at the back of the book. These appendices should be referred to for supporting evidence of the hypotheses proposed throughout this study. In this chapter and for the remainder of the work, I have grouped the terms by meaning and limited the discussion only to the most interesting and illustrative examples, while offering corroborating references in the footnotes, which can be examined in the relevant appendix. The current chapter examines the results of the analysis of each of the four main compounds of *currere*.

### 1. The occurrences of *concurrere*

In the extant books of Livy, the term *concurrere* is the most frequently used of the four compounds of *currere* discussed in this chapter, with 170 occurrences. It often denotes the coming together of infantry formations in battle, and is important for understanding how Livy conceived the initial stages of combat. The analysis of *concurrere* in the *OLD* offers six main nuances, which are reflected in Livy's use of the term. Four of these are particularly important for our understanding of how Livy applied the term in a military context. These are: 1. to assemble at a run or in haste, hurry together; 2. to come in large numbers to a person or a place for some purpose; b) to arm oneself hastily, stand to arms; 3. (of opponents in battle) to run together, charge; b) to engage in battle, fight, (poet., of a battle) to be joined; c) (transf.) to engage in a combat, strive, contend, fight; 4. to knock together violently, collide; c) (transf., of arguments, interests, etc) to be at a variance, conflict, clash.[282]

The noun *concursus*, derived from the verb, also has the meaning of 'the gathering of a crowd, a violent encounter or a coming together'.[283] Livy uses the term in each of these senses and they each reflect an aspect of how he seems to have envisaged the coming together of battle lines. The following section explores each of the various senses in which the term is used and the impacts on our understanding of Roman infantry combat.

#### Concurrere *meaning to rush to a point*

Livy often uses the term *concurrere* to describe the movement of a group of people towards a point. As this verb is a compound of *currere*, it implies some form of running or speed and, when it is used in this way as a main verb, it can often be translated as 'a *rushes towards* b'. For example, at 2.59.4, Livy says that legates and tribunes rushed towards / hurried around Appius Claudius (*concurrunt ad eum legati tribunique*). The noun *concursus* can be used impersonally to offer a similar meaning when combined with verbs such as *fieri*. At 5.7.6, Livy states that the people rushed to the curia (*ad curiam concursus fit plebis*). *Concurrere* is used in this way twenty-eight times within the extant books of Livy and in each case it suggests some form of hurried movement towards a point.[284]

---

[280] It is worth noting that in Livy's speeches there is a "constant search for variety" (Oakley (1997) 119) which is not found in his battle narratives, apart from the standard motifs discussed in the previous chapter (above pp. 77-81).

[281] Oakley (1997) 148. On Livy's use of technical terms see Kraus (1994) 19; Roth (2006) 56.

[282] *OLD* s.v. 1a and b, 2a, 3a, b and c, 4a and c.

[283] *OLD* s.v. 1 and 2

[284] Rushing to a point: 1.48.2, 2.12.8, 2.19.6, 2.24.7, 2.27.2, 2.56.14, 2.59.4, 5.7.6, 5.18.11, 6.28.3, 8.28.7, 9.13.1, 10.25.1, 22.20.11, 22.42.2, 24.29.8, 26.5.7, 27.50.9, 28.26.12, 29.9.4, 29.9.5, 30.24.10, 35.42.5, 36.24.2, 37.44.4, 37.32.7, 38.33.9, 38.40.11.

### *Concurrere meaning the coming together of a crowd*

In a similar way the term is used to describe the gathering or formation of a crowd. As a noun at 3.26.12 it is used to describe a huge crowd of people,[285] and as a verb, at 42.16.2, after Livy describes the attempt on King Eumenes' life, he uses it to describe the gathering of the king's friends, courtiers and slaves around his body.[286] The term is used in this way thirty-six times.[287] Although the contexts of the terms do not necessarily suggest speed, the use of a compound of *currere* may imply haste in the formation of the crowd.

### Concurrere *meaning a rush to arms*

On twenty-one occasions the term *concurrere* is used to describe the hasty gathering of arms or a rush towards a point for the purpose of defence.[288] At 2.25.1, the Volsci attacked the Roman camp and after the signal had been given, the soldiers rushed to arms.[289] During the siege of Haliartus, at 42.63.6, the townsfolk rush to defend against an attack on their wall.[290] In each of these cases the movement is an attempt to defend against an attack. The contexts of these occurrences suggest movements at speed, which is reinforced by the use of the verb *concurrere*.

### Concurrere *meaning an argument*

On three occasions the term is used to signify an argument, such as at 40.13.6, where a stubborn contest and argument angered Perseus.[291] This use does not have implications of speed or a massed movement but is rather the metaphorical clash of opinions.

### Concurrere *applied to naval battle*

On fifteen occasions the term is used to denote combat between ships.[292] Within the context of naval battle the term has a number of meanings. It has the specific meaning of a collision between two ships.[293] More generally it can be used to describe the coming together of two ships in combat, such as at 26.39.14, when the Romans encountered the Tarentines, Livy states that "conspicuous, however, among all the rest was the battle between the two ships which had encountered each other at the head of the columns" (Moore,1943).[294] Here, the term neither implies speed nor a massed attack, but is rather a general term for the coming together of two things, in this case ships, within a battle situation. The term can also be used to describe the attack of fleets, such as at 22.19.12, where two Carthaginian ships had been taken and four sunk in the first attack;[295] or at 25.27.11, where the Roman and Carthaginian fleets "lay on this side and that of the promontory of Pachynum, ready to engage as soon as calm weather should enable them to put to sea" (Moore, 1940).[296] In both these examples the term is used in a general way to describe the coming together of two fleets in an attack. Although the term used is *concurrere*, as they are made by ships these attacks do not involve running. In fact, it seems that the term need not imply that an attack was particularly quick or massed in nature. Instead the term *concurrere* seems to have been used as a general word to describe naval battle or the coming together of two fleets.

### Concurrere *and heavy infantry combat*[297]

The term is used on fifty-nine occasions to describe fighting of the heavy infantry.[298] The implications of the evidence so far would suggest that an infantry attack described with the term *concurrere* took the form of a massed movement at speed. This form of attack would support the traditional model of Roman combat. Some of the examples in Livy seem to bear this out, such as:

> "Indeed **it is said** that on that day from the third hour to the eighth the outcome was so much in doubt, that there was never a second cheer after that which was once given when the armies **rushed together**; nor were the standards either moved forward or withdrawn; nor did the combatants anywhere give ground. Facing each other with every man squarely in his place, **they pressed forward with their shields** and fought without stopping to breathe or to look behind" (Foster, 1926).[299]

This passage describes Roman combat against the Samnites, and gives the impression of a massed collision of the two opposing forces leading to an *othismos* style pushing match, which lasted for five hours. In chapter

---

[285] *Plebis concursus ingens fuit.*

[286] *Ad corpus regis primo amici, deinde satellites ac serui concurrerunt.*

[287] A gathering crowd: 1.7.9, 1.14.2, 1.41.1, 2.18.2, 3.26.12, 3.44.7, 3.50.4, 4.34.7, 4.35.3, 4.50.4, 4.60.1, 5.27.10, 9.30.10, 21.12.8, 22.19.4, 22.7.6, 26.13.1, 26.15.7, 27.7.1, 27.21.1, 27.45.6, 28.37.2, 29.26.7, 30.25.3, 33.48.3, 33.48.9, 35.36.3, 36.30.1, 36.34.5, 37.29.4, 39.53.7, 42.16.2, 44.44.4, 45.36.7, 45.39.7, 45.44.5.

[288] A rush to arms: 1.1.5, 2.25.1, 5.37.5, 9.38.7, 25.30.9, 25.39.9, 26.5.7, 27.3.5, 29.9.5, 32.13.11, 32.23.7, 32.24.4, 36.24.4, 38.2.13, 38.3.5, 38.25.15, 41.10.3, 42.53.9, 42.54.4, 42.63.6, 44.30.9.

[289] *Signo dato concursum est ad arma.*

[290] *Concursu aduersus se oppidanorum facto.*

[291] *Pertinaci certamine et concursu iratum te efficere.* An argument: 40.13.2, 40.13.6, 40.46.10.

[292] Naval battle: 22.19.12, 25.27.11, 26.39.9, 26.39.12, 26.39.14, 29.27.11, 29.27.6, 36.44.7, 36.44.10, 37.23.9, 37.24.2, 37.24.9, 37.30.4, 37.30.5, 44.42.5.

[293] 26.39.12: *cum rostris concurrissent.*

[294] *Insignis tamen inter ceteras pugna fuit duarum quae primae agminum concurrerant inter se.*

[295] *Duae tamen primo concursu captae erant Punicae naves, quattuor suppressae.*

[296] *duae classes infestae circa promunturium Pachynum stabant, ubi prima tranquillitas maris in altum euexisset, concursurae.*

[297] Cf. *TLL* IV.109.77ff.

[298] 1.25.3, 1.25.4, 2.11.9, 3.4.8, 3.61.8, 4.37.8, 5.32.3, 5.38.3, 5.49.5, 6.7.6, 6.24.1, 7.26.9, 8.7.9, 8.8.15, 8.23.8, 8.38.10, 9.13.2, 9.25.8, 9.32.7, 9.40.8, 10.14.8, 10.19.15 (twice), 10.27.11, 10.40.13, 21.55.4, 21.57.12, 21.59.3, 21.59.8, 22.24.11, 23.29.9, 23.44.4, 23.44.8, 24.15.7, 25.6.20, 25.18.13, 26.51.4, 27.48.8, 28.14.6, 29.18.10, 30.8.7, 30.34.1, 31.33.8, 32.30.11, 33.37.8, 34.14.7, 34.28.11, 35.1.6, 35.5.1, 37.41.12, 40.6.5, 40.6.6, 40.39.10, 42.59.4, 44.4.4, 44.35.21, 44.37.10, 44.38.11, 44.41.9.

[299] 8.38.10-11: *Et hercule illo die ab hora diei tertia ad octavam ita anceps* ***dicitur*** *certamen stetisse, ut neque clamor, ut* ***primo semel concursu est*** *sublatus, iteratus sit, neque signa promota loco retrove recepta, neque recursum ab ulla sit parte. In suo quisque gradu obnixi,* ***urgentes scutis****, sine respirationes ac respectu pugnabant*

one it was proposed that the Roman panoply would make running very difficult and that the Roman shield boss would have made this form of pushing match impossible or at least cripplingly uncomfortable for those pushed forward by the man behind. This form of combat would correspond better to the fighting of a phalanx formation than the three-line system of the mid-Republican Romans, whose advantage was psychological, keeping the majority of troops in reserve, rather than physical, adding weight to a push. The final argument against such a type of combat is that when a similar form was used, such as during the hoplite period in Greece, *othismos* battles could last only short periods of time, and certainly not the five hours noted by Livy.[300]

Oakley, in his discussion of this passage, comments that Livy's use of *dicitur* "draws attention to the unusual fighting, and perhaps suggests that L. does not vouch for the detail which he records", and he states further that the narrative of this campaign is "almost certainly fictitious".[301] The fighting in this passage is unusual, and Livy's use of the term *dicitur* may suggest that he has taken the passage straight from his source. Instead of imposing his own vision of battle on to his source, as we have seen was his tendency with Polybius' account, he may have taken it *verbatim*. In the second chapter it was proposed that Livy wrote history by collecting and synthesising his sources. His use of *dicitur* may suggest he believed the source was rather dubious, but was forced to include it for want of anything better.

Even if this account is Livian, Foster's translation is slightly misleading and is based on traditional assumptions about infantry combat. Livy describes the fighting as *urgentes scutis*. This need not denote massed pushing with shields but rather the use of the shield boss to 'punch' the enemy.[302] The employment of the term *concurrere* itself is also ambiguous. As we have seen in situations outside infantry battle, it could simply mean a general coming together of two groups or a general engagement in combat and need not imply any form of running. This passage shows the importance of looking closely at the words Livy actually employs and the way they are utilized throughout his work. In fact, as we shall see shortly, Livy's use of *concurrere* to describe infantry battle typically reflects a different form of combat than that implied by Foster's translation. This highlights the circular nature of translation, which will be important throughout this study. A translator necessarily has to put the original language into target language using the conceptual tools at his disposal. The predominant model of combat will influence a translation, but we should limit how much a translation influences the model of combat

Other occurrences of *concurrere* suggest Livy envisioned a different form Roman infantry combat. For example, in Livy's description of Aquilonia in 293:

> "before the first shout and engagement, a rashly thrown javelin struck the chicken-keeper [who had been stationed in the front rank by the consul] and he fell before the standards".[303]

This passage may suggest a period of stand-off before infantry engagement, involving missile exchange. It was during this period that the chicken-keeper was killed. However, Livy's use of *temere* (rashly, blindly) might imply the opposite, that the javelin was quite random and that this period before engagement rarely involved missile combat. Livy's description of the fighting at Hibera in 216 supports the former proposition that missile combat did precede infantry attacks:

> "[the Celtiberians were not keen to fight] therefore at the first clash, when they had scarcely thrown their *pila*, the centre of the line fell back, and as the Romans advanced with great vigour, they turned their backs [and fled]".[304]

Here the Romans threw their *pila*, to disrupt the enemy line, before they came together in close combat. This is further supported by Livy's description of the Romans fighting in Samnium in 320:

> The Romans, stirred up by a previous humiliation, were avid for battle, "[so the infantry] went forward in to battle, urging on the standard bearers; and, that there might be no delay in coming together while they were discharging their *pila* and drawing their swords, they threw away their *pila*, as if a signal had been given them, and, sword in hand, they came together quickly".[305]

The implications of this passage are that in Livy's vision infantry battle usually began with missile exchange and was followed by some form of attack involving hand-to-hand combat with swords, rather than pushing with shields.[306] In the following chapter there will be a more detailed discussion of the type of fighting involved in Livy's vision of infantry combat, since the occurrences of the term *concurrere* only offer this limited but tantalising evidence.

[300] See, for example, Hanson (1985) 191, where he proposes that "battle quickly exhausted those in the phalanx, both physically and psychologically – perhaps in little less than an hour's time."

[301] Oakley (1998) 765.

[302] Note 9.41.18-19: "They did their work more with shields than with swords, swinging them from the shoulder and knocking down their enemies with the bosses" (Foster, 1926) (*scutis magis quam gladiis geritur res; umbonibus incussaque ala sternuntur hostes*) Cf. 4.37.10, 30.34.3, 34.46.10, etc.

[303] 10.40.13: *Priusquam clamor tolleretur concurreretur que, emisso temere pilo ictus pullarius ante signa cecidit.*

[304] 23.29.9: *Primo igitur concursu, cum uix pila coniecta essent, rettulit pedem media acies inferentibusque se magno impetu Romanis uertit terga.*

[305] 9.13.2: *Vadunt igitur in proelium urgentes signiferos et, ne mora in concursu pilis emittendis stringendisque inde gladiis esset, pila uelut dato ad id signo abiciunt strictisque gladiis cursu in hostem feruntur.*

[306] For the abandonment of *pila* see Oakley on Livy 6.12.8. For fighting with swords, cf. Livy's account of the mythical battle between the Horatii and the Curiatii, at 1.25.4: *Ut primo statim concursu increpuere arma micantesque fulsere gladii.*

*Concurrere* is used most frequently by Livy as a general term to signify the coming together of two bodies, whether infantry lines, cavalry formations or fleets of ships, rather than a specific term to describe the nature of the engagement. For example, at 9.40.8, the Romans fought the Samnites, and this fighting in general is described with the term *concurrere*: "from the moment of contact, there was a huge struggle with the enemy".[307] This use of the term to describe an infantry engagement in general can be seen at 23.44.8, where Livy says that "Hannibal's and Marcellus' armies engaged on the plain around Nola".[308] Again, after a skirmish between the Romans and the Macedonians on the previous day, Livy states that now "their tempers had been roused for the next day, a more savage clash of larger forces occurred".[309] In each of these three examples Livy uses the term *concurrere* as a general word for engagement, or coming together of bodies in conflict, in these cases infantry lines, rather than as a specific term to describe the form which the attack took. The term is used in this way on fifty-eight occasions, the majority involving infantry combat, but also including the attacks of cavalry, light infantry and ships.[310] Although this term is a compound of *currere*, it does not necessarily imply that engagements described with *concurrere* were particularly at speed, or necessarily massed and coordinated movements, though in specific contexts it can describe hurried movement and large numbers of participants. Rather, *concurrere* is predominantly used as a generic term to describe the coming together of objects, and these tend to be troops in a military context. The term therefore only offers limited evidence for the nature of infantry combat.[311]

## 2. The occurrences of *incurrere*

The term *incurrere* is used far less frequently than *concurrere*, appearing only twenty-five times in the extant books. Nevertheless it is very important for the purposes of this study as, in the majority of cases, it is used as a specific term to describe the attacks of infantry and cavalry. This is reflected in the analysis of the term found in the *OLD*, that, when used in a military situation, *incurrere* primarily has the meaning of rushing or charging at, or making an attack on, the enemy. This sense is also given in the analysis of the *Thesaurus Linguae Latinae*, which links the term in this context with *impetus*.[312] Nine of the occurrences involve the attacks of cavalry, with a further two describing cavalry fighting in conjunction with infantry and once with light infantry. On six occasions *incurrere* is used to describe an attack of heavy infantry.[313] The following section will discuss the use of the term to describe these attacks of the cavalry and infantry, and consider how this might affect our understanding of Livy's literary vision of Roman infantry combat.

### **Incurrere** ***as an attack of the cavalry***

On nine occasions Livy uses the term *incurrere* to describe attacks of the cavalry alone, twice more where the cavalry attack with heavy infantry and once with the light infantry. Nine of these twelve cavalry attacks are made by the Romans. In the following chapter there will be a more detailed discussion of Roman cavalry tactics, since they are more frequently described with the term *impetus*. Nevertheless, these twelve attacks described with *incurrere* offer some clues as to how cavalry may have fought in battle. Livy's use of the term, describing a specific attack rather than engagements in general, seems to imply that these attacks were at speed. This is understandable. A cavalry attack would normally be at a run, and so it is possible that Livy used the term *incurrere* to represent particularly fast attacks. This can be borne out by the evidence. Eight of the twelve occurrences of *incurrere* for cavalry combat, describe attacks against the flanks or rear of enemy formations.[314] In his description of the fighting between the Romans and Samnites in 305, Livy says that the Roman cavalry charged into the enemy flanks.[315] During the Battle of Zama, while the infantry lines were engaged in combat, Livy states that:

> "after pursuing the routed cavalry for a considerable distance, at the right moment Laelius and Masinnissa, returned and attacked the rear of the enemy's line".[316]

In the following chapter the mechanics of cavalry attacks will be considered and it will be proposed that only rarely, if ever, did cavalry crash into the enemy. Instead a cavalry attack was predominantly psychological, with the purpose of terrifying the enemy into flight. An infantry formation is strongest against frontal attacks, while attacks on its flanks or rear are particularly effective as they usually occur during unexpected points in the battle and are aimed against troops who are unprepared for this dangerous new development.[317] The fear that arises in those initially engaged would spread quickly along the line and is magnified in those in the middle of the battle

---

[307] *Simul est concursum, ingens fuit cum hoste certamen.*

[308] *Eo spatio - et sunt omnia campi circa Nolam - concurrerunt.*

[309] 44.4.4: *inritatis in posterum diem animis maioribus copiis atque infestius concursum est.*

[310] A general term for engagement: 1.25.3, 1.25.4, 3.4.8, 3.61.8, 4.37.8, 5.32.3, 5.38.3, 5.49.5, 6.7.6, 6.24.1, 7.26.9, 8.23.8, 9.13.2, 9.32.7, 9.40.8, 10.14.8, 10.19.15 (twice), 10.27.11, 10.40.13, 21.5.14, 21.55.4, 21.57.12, 21.59.3, 21.59.8, 22.24.11, 22.47.1, 22.47.2, 23.29.9, 23.44.4, 23.44.8, 25.6.20, 25.41.6, 26.51.4, 27.48.8, 28.14.6, 29.18.10, 30.8.7, 30.34.1, 32.30.11, 33.12.9, 33.37.8, 34.14.7, 34.28.11, 35.1.6, 35.5.1, 37.41.12, 40.6.5, 40.6.6, 40.39.10, 42.59.1, 42.59.4, 44.4.4, 44.9.7, 44.35.21, 44.37.10, 44.38.11, 44.41.9.

[311] Livy sometimes uses terms in conjunction with *concurrere*, such as *iustum proelium*, to signify that the fighting was 'regular battle', such as 10.14.8, 26.51.4, 34.28.11, 37.41.12, 40.6.5, etc. But the term is still only used to describe generic engagements.

[312] *OLD* s.v. 1a; *TLL* VII.1.1085.52ff.

[313] The term is also used three times to describe light infantry attacks (22.17.6, 26.4.7, 28.33.5), once the spontaneous attack of townspeople (9.21.4), once as a general word describing Aetolian raids into Macedonia (26.25.7) and twice metaphorically meaning to fall violently upon something (5.11.4, 9.21.4).

[314] Flank attacks: 1.37.3, 9.40.12, 10.29.9, 27.18.15, 28.14.20, 30.35.1, 37.21.3, 39.31.7.

[315] 9.40.12: *in transuersa latera hostium incurrunt.*

[316] 30.35.1: *In tempore Laelius ac Masinissa pulsos per aliquantum spatii secuti equites, reuertentes in auersam hostium aciem incurrere.*

[317] Sabin (1996) 75-6, (2007b) 432-3.

formation, who can not see the enemy at their rear but only hear the panic of their fellow soldiers.[318] Owing to the weakness of infantry formations on the flanks and rear, the cavalrymen, attacking one of these points, would have a psychological advantage and could charge with more vigour and speed than when attacking the front of an infantry line. For similar reasons, cavalry attacks against disordered troops could also be unusually fast and decisive.[319] The implications of this are that when Livy used the term *incurrere* to describe cavalry attacks, he was intentionally highlighting the unusually fast nature of these attacks. In most cases Livy explains this unusual speed with reference to the fact that the attacks were made against the rear or flanks of enemy formations, or against disordered troops.[320]

### Incurrere *as an attack of the infantry*

The evidence suggests Livy used the term in a similar way when describing infantry attacks. In two of the eight occurrences of *incurrere*, Livy's descriptions offer some insight into how he saw the mechanics of infantry combat. Livy describes the fighting between the Romans and the Macedonians at the battle of Pydna:

> "[The Macedonian phalanx is weak when attacked at many points.] Such was the case on this occasion, when the phalanx was compelled to meet the Romans who were attacking in groups, while the Macedonian line was broken at many points. The Romans for their part kept infiltrating their units wherever gaps presented themselves. If they had attacked frontally in solid line against an orderly phalanx, as happened to the Paelignians who at the beginning of the battle recklessly met the light infantry, the Romans would have spitted themselves on the spears and would not have withstood the solid line" (Schlesinger, 1951).[321]

This passage reveals how Livy envisioned the mechanics of Roman infantry combat. The Roman assault is described with the phrase *catervatim incurrentes*, which implies that the Romans were not attacking as a massed line (*universa acie*), but rather in small groups against localised points along the enemy line. This form of attack corresponds closely to that proposed by the dynamic stand-off model of infantry combat and, as we shall see in the following chapter, is similar to the type of fighting Livy describes with the term *impetus*. That these attacks are not described with *impetus* but with *incurrere* perhaps suggests that they were at unusual speed. Nevertheless, the form of combat remains consistent with the type of attack Livy usually describes with *impetus*: a small-scale localised flurry of hand-to-hand combat.

The fighting between the Romans and the Umbrians described at 9.41.18 suggests a similar form of attack:

> The Romans were inspired by the words of Fabius Maximus Rullianus: "before the command could be given, they hurled themselves – to the blare of the horns – with the wildest abandon against the enemy. They fought not as though their opponents had been men and armed; but – marvellous to relate – began with tearing the standards out of the bearers' hands, and then fell to dragging the bearers themselves before the consul and to bringing armed men over from the other line to their own; wherever they met with resistance, they did their work more with shields than with swords, swinging them from the shoulder and knocking down their enemies with the bosses" (Foster, 1926).[322]

The picture presented here is that of two battle formations separated by some distance, with the Roman soldiers repeatedly moving out of their own line and attacking localised points along the enemy line in an attempt to drag back enemy soldiers. This image of Roman combat corresponds again with that proposed by the dynamic stand-off model: a series of small-scale localised attacks.[323] Livy appears to use the term *incurrere* to give the further impression that this fighting was unusually ferocious, owing to the agitation caused by the Consul's words. This attack is unusually fast, but, as with the previous passage, the form of the attack is consistent with Livy's vision of 'normal' Roman infantry combat, which is usually described with the term *impetus*.

It was proposed earlier that the unusual speed of cavalry attacks described with *incurrere* could have had a psychological explanation. A similar explanation can be seen in Livy's description of infantry attacks, such as his account of the fighting in 212. Even though this describes the defence of a camp, it suggests that Livy imagined soldiers being driven to attack more ferociously by external influences.

> A Roman garrison had lost its commanders and the soldiers were struck with grief. The centurions tried to rouse their men, and Marcius upbraided them for their 'womanish' ways and inspired them to not allow their commanders' deaths to go unavenged.

[318] Cf. Sabin (1996) 76; Goldsworthy (1996) 219; Daly (2002) 193.

[319] At 28.13.6, a Carthaginian cavalry attack against men working on fortification would have been successful had not the Roman cavalry attacked from an ambush and charged them unexpectedly in their disorder. (*ni abditi post tumulum opportune ad id positum ab Scipione equites improviso in effusos incurrissent*).

[320] Three other unusually fast cavalry attacks: 27.32.5, 42.7.6 (possibly a flank attack) and 42.59.2 (possibly a flank attack: *in dextrum cornu*).

[321] 44.41.8-9: *Sicut tum adversus catervatim incurrentes Romanos et interrupta multifariam acie obviam ire cogebantur; et Romani, quacumque data intervalla essent, insinuabant ordines suos. Qui si universa acie in frontem adversus instructam phalangem concurrissent, quod Paelignis principio pugnae incaute congressis adversus caetratos evenit, induissent se hastis nec confertam aciem sustinuissent*

[322] 9.41.17-18: *Ante imperium deinde concentu tubarum ac cornuum cursu effuso in hostem feruntur. Non tamquam in uiros aut armatos incurrunt; mirabilia dictu, signa primo eripi coepta signiferis, deinde ipsi signiferi trahi ad consulem armatique milites ex acie in aciem transferri et, sicubi est certamen, scutis magis quam gladiis geritur res; umbonibus incussaque ala sternuntur hostes.* On trumpets and horns ordering an attack and for variant readings of this passage see Oakley *ad loc*.

[323] The offensive use of shields to 'punch' at the enemy, highlighted in this passage, has already been discussed.

> When the Carthaginians approached, the sound of trumpets was heard. "With that, their grief instantly changing to anger, they rushed to arms. As they swiftly manned the gates, they seemed to burn with frenzy, and flew at the enemy, who were advancing carelessly and in disorder".[324]

This attack is excessively fierce because of the unusual anger which the deaths of their commanders inspired in the Romans. Livy describes them as aroused by madness (*uelut accensi rabie*). The circumstances surrounding this attack were particularly unusual and Livy seems to have used the term *incurrere* to express further the extraordinary nature of the assault. The psychological explanation for the unusual speed involved in this infantry attack can also be seen in two further examples: at 5.49.5, the Gauls attack with great anger (*iraque magis quam consilio in Romanos incurrunt*), and at 38.21.8, it is the fear and panic of the Gauls which cause them to run into each other like wounded animals (*uelut ferae transfixae in suos temere incurrunt*).

For similar reasons to those discussed above, infantry attacks, like those of cavalry, would be especially devastating against the flanks or rear of an enemy formation. Livy's awareness of this can be seen in his description of the Roman flank attack at the River Metaurus in 207:

> "[Claudius] drew off a number of cohorts from the right wing, where he saw that they would be standing idly by instead of fighting. He led them round behind the [Roman] battle-line, and to the surprise not only of the enemy, but also his own troops, charged into the enemy's right flank. And such was his speed that soon after showing themselves on the flank, they were already attacking the rear" (Moore, 1943).[325]

Here it is the surprise of the attack that offered the Romans an advantage. This allowed them to attack unusually quickly. This uncommon speed is underlined not only with Livy's use of the term *incurrere*, but also the phrase *tantaque celeritas fuit*.[326]

From this short analysis, it appears that Livy used the term *incurrere* to signify the unusually fast nature of an attack.[327] The evidence also suggests that the reason for this uncommon speed tended to be psychological. For Livy, soldiers were able to overcome their natural fear and reluctance to attack if external influences, such as the death of a commander, changed the group's psychological state or if they were offered a psychological advantage over their enemy, such as making an attack on the flank or rear. In Livy's vision of combat attacks at speed were unusual and he signifies this by describing them with *incurrere* rather than simply as *impetus*. Nevertheless, these unusual attacks still took the typical form of Roman infantry combat as described by Livy: small-scale localised flurries of hand-to-hand fighting. As will be shown in the next chapter, it is this type of attack that forms the primary phase of Livy's literary vision of infantry combat.

### 3. The occurrences of *procurrere*

The *OLD* offers three main classifications of this term each involving some aspect of rushing or running. Within a military context it has the sense of running forward to attack.[328] It occurs within Livy's corpus more frequently than *incurrere*, with forty incidences, but is typically used in a similar fashion. The *TLL* likens both terms, when used in a military context, to phrase *impetum facere*, which will be examined in the next chapter.[329] This military form is the most frequent of Livy's uses of the term. In other contexts it is used on eight occasions with the meaning of 'rushing out', as of people rushing out of their houses into the streets.[330] It is used to describe a skirmish, rather than pitched battle, on eleven occasions and five times it describes the attack of cavalry.[331] For the purpose of this study the most important aspect of *procurrere* is Livy's use of it to describe heavy infantry attacks. The following section will focus on term within this context and assess the affect of this usage on our understanding of Livy's vision of Roman battle.

#### **Procurrere *as an attack of the infantry***

The term *procurrere* is used by Livy on thirteen occasions to describe attacks of the heavy infantry.[332] The term is used in a similar way to *incurrere*, describing attacks of unusual speed. In three instances this unusual speed can be explained by psychological factors. In his description of fighting against the Latins in 386, Livy states that the aged Camillus advanced in person against the enemy. As the infantry saw this, they gave a cheer and charged forward shouting 'follow the General'. At this the general ordered the standard to be thrown into the enemy line to incite the men of the front rank to recover it.[333] In this case, not only were the soldiers inspired by

[324] 25.37.11: *inde uerso repente in iram luctu discurrunt ad arma ac uelut accensi rabie discurrunt ad portas et in hostem neglegenter atque incomposite uenientem incurrunt.*

[325] 27.48.13-14: *cohortes aliquot subductas e dextro cornu, ubi stationem magis segnem quam pugnam futuram cernebat, post aciem circumducit, et non hostibus modo sed etiam suis inopinantibus in sinistrum <euectus in dextrum> hostium latus incurrit; tantaque celeritas fuit ut cum ostendissent se ab latere mox in terga iam pugnarent.*

[326] Two further examples of flank and rear attacks, described with *incurrere*, can be seen at 27.18.15 and 37.21.7.

[327] This hypothesis is further supported by Livy's use of the term three times to describe the high speed attacks of light infantry (22.17.6, 26.4.7, 28.33.5).

[328] *OLD* s.v. 1b.

[329] *TLL* X.2.X 1588.33ff; VII.1.1085.52ff.

[330] Rush out: 4.40.3, 10.14.10, 24.21.8, 34.2.9, 34.3.6, 34.39.3, 44.9.7, 44.10.5.

[331] Skirmish: 3.61.13, 5.19.9, 21.8.6, 22.41.1, 23.40.9, 27.2.11, 27.41.5, 28.33.3, 33.7.6, 42.64.6, 44.4.6. Cavalry: 22.16.2, 22.44.5, 25.9.7, 25.39.6, 40.30.5.

[332] Infantry combat: 6.8.2, 6.12.8, 7.14.4, 10.36.5 (twice), 25.11.3, 25.21.5, 27.42.3, 28.14.3, 34.15.4, 35.5.2, 38.26.7, 42.65.8.

[333] 6.8.2: *Quod ubi uidere, ipsum Camillum, iam ad munera corporis senecta inualidum, uadentem in hostes, procurrunt pariter omnes clamore sublato 'sequere imperatorem' pro se quisque clamantes.*

the bravery of their commander, but also were impelled to attack quickly to protect the general and save the standard. In 359, a Gaul drove off some cattle that were grazing outside the stockade. Roman soldiers took the cattle from him, and were stoned to death by the rest of the Gauls.

> "Following this a shout rose from the Roman outpost, and men ran forward from both sides. And now the skirmish was likely to end in regular battle, had the centurions not quickly parted the combatants".[334]

Though not describing a pitched battle, it shows that Livy chose to describe such an infantry attack with the term *procurrere*. His purpose seems to have been to highlight the abnormal speed involved, sparked off as it was by the stoning. In 193, the Romans were eager to fight the Gauls, who, on the previous night, had tried to ambush them. The consul stayed with the leading standards, holding the legions back in reserve, "lest in their enthusiasm for the battle they should rush forward before the signal was given".[335] Here in their eagerness, the troops would have advanced in a particularly rapid attack. In each of these examples there are specific reasons for the soldiers desire to rush forward. These are unusually fast attacks and Livy seems to have chosen the term *procurrere* to highlight this.

As well as describing abnormally rapid attacks, some of the occurrences of *procurrere* also offer small clues as to how Livy envisaged the mechanics of Roman infantry combat. In his description of Camillus' advance against the Latins, mentioned above, Camillus grabs the nearest standard-bearer and advances with him. Those around the general, seeing his attack, quickly pursue, shouting for others to follow the commander. Finally, Camillus orders the standard to be thrown into the enemy formation to stir up his troops. It is at the point where the standard is hurled that the enemy line breaks. As Livy states, "here the Antiates were first repulsed, and the panic spread not only through the front ranks but also into the reserves".[336] Livy explains this success:

> "[the break in the enemy line] was due not only to the efforts of the troops, stimulated as they were by the presence of their general, but also to the terror which Camillus' actual appearance inspired in the Volscians, to whom he was a special object of dread. Thus, wherever he advanced he carried certain victory with him".[337]

This passage describes a small-scale localised attack. Livy's use of *signum* in the singular implies that Camillus advances with one standard-bearer and throws only one standard forward. Each maniple had two standards, so it is likely that Livy means a century, about sixty troops, when he mentions the men immediately surrounding Camillus' standard. Even if the calls of these men brought others with them, the size of the attacking force would have been relatively small and certainly not the entire battle-line. This small scale attack also appears localised, as it was aimed at the specific point where the standard had been thrown. This is reinforced by Livy's use of *ibi primum pulsum Antiatem*, after *emissum etiam signum Camilli iussu in hostium aciem ferunt*, to show that it was at this specific point that the enemy were broken.

Oakley correctly suggests that this passage, "as also the others from L's first decade, has no value as evidence for the nature of fighting in the fourth century, and represents only the plausible reconstruction of L. or an annalist".[338] Though this passage reveals little about the specifics of this fourth century battle, it nevertheless reflects Livy's own literary vision of combat. Battle narratives may never offer reliable testimony of specific events in specific battles due to the difficulties of describing combat accurately, but they can reveal the way in which the author imagined the conflict. Livy's vision of combat remains consistent throughout the extant work and offers a convincing, and possibly realistic, image of mid-Republican infantry fighting. The passage suggests that Livy's vision involved small-scale localised attacks, which could lead to wide-spread disruption of the enemy line. Livy's use of both the terms *incurrere* and *procurrere* suggest ordinary infantry attacks made at unusual speed. The *TLL* draws a direct parallel between these terms and *impetum facere*, which fits Livy's usage. In the following chapter it will be argued that when Livy employed the term *impetus*, it was this type of small-scale localised attack he envisaged and that this form of attack is fundamental to his vision of infantry combat.[339]

**4. The occurrences of *decurrere***

The term *decurrere* is more straightforward than the previous compounds of *currere*, with the basic meaning 'to run down'. The *OLD*'s analysis offers a variety of uses, many of which can be seen within Livy's text.

*Emissum etiam signum Camilli iussu in hostium aciem ferunt idque ut repeteretur concitatos antesignanos*

334 7.14.4: *iumenta forte pascentia extra uallum Gallo abigenti duo milites Romani ademerunt. In eos saxa coniecta a Gallis; deinde ab Romana statione clamor ortus ac procursum utrimque est. Iamque haud procul iusto proelio res erat, ni celeriter diremptum certamen per centuriones esset.*

335 35.5.2: *nouus consul nunc ad prima signa erat, nunc legiones continebat in subsidiis, ne certaminis studio prius procurrerent quam datum signum esset.*

336 6.8.4: *ibi primum pulsum Antiatem, terroremque non in primam tantum aciem sed etiam ad subsidiarios perlatum.*

337 6.8.5-6: *Nec uis tantum militum mouebat, excitata praesentia ducis, sed quod Volscorum animis nihil terribilius erat quam ipsius Camilli forte oblata species; ita quocumque se intulisset uictoriam secum haud dubiam trahebat.*

338 Oakley (1998) 766.

339 Other occurrences of *procurrere* may also offer some supporting evidence for this form of combat. The attack at 10.36.5 appears to be a small-scale isolated flurry of fighting. The passages at 6.12.8, 34.15.4, 38.26.7 and 42.65.8 all seem to suggest attacks involving movement out of the line rather than a massed advance of the line as a whole.

Livy's uses of the term range from the simple meaning of running/rushing/hurrying down from a height, to the flow of a river down stream or of a ship travelling shoreward, and to carrying out military exercises or going through a drill.

### Decurrere *as the movement of rivers and ships*[340]

On three occasions Livy uses the term *decurrere* to describe the flow of rivers. He states that the River Rhone flows into the sea through several mouths and that the River Meander flows through the middle of Celaenae.[341] A river rises in the highlands and flows down to the sea, thus *decurrere* is suitable term to describe this motion. It is also used to describe the movement of ships sailing into port. At 24.36.4, fifty-five ships under Bomilcar sail from the sea into the large harbour in Syracuse.[342] In ancient thought the sea as something which one climbed up on to, when sailing away from shore. Sailing back into shore from the sea, the movement then is downwards, making *decurrere* suitable again to describe this motion.

### Decurrere *as a military exercise*[343]

Livy also uses the term to describe military exercises, such as marching in full gear or practice in following the standards. This can be seen, for example, in the passage describing the training of Scipio's troops:

> 'On the first day the legions, fully equipped, marched over a space of four miles; the second day was employed in cleaning and sharpening their weapons in front of their tents; the third day they engaged in the mode of regular battle, practicing with wooden swords and javelins, the points of which were muffled with balls of cork or lead; the fourth day they rested, and on the fifth they were again marched under arms.'[344]

In this passage *decurrere* is used twice to describe a training march under arms, while *concurrere* is used, as discussed above, as a generic word for the coming together of battle-lines. In 215, Tiberius Sempronius ordered his men on frequent manoeuvres so that the new recruits could learn to follow the standards and recognise their own ranks in the battle-line.[345] The term *decurrere* is used in this way eleven times within the extant books of Livy and highlights the importance of military training.[346] These exercises suggest that, as with modern armies, fitness and the ability to follow the correct standards was important. The ability to recognise one's own ranks, which Sempronius tried to teach his new recruits, would be extremely important under a system of combat similar to the dynamic stand-off, where troops regularly left their line to attack the enemy and, after the clash, would need to return to their original positions. Scipio's training also suggests the importance of practicing with, and taking care of, weapons. This passage highlights the primacy of the sword and *pila* over the shield as offensive weapons.

### Decurrere *as rushing downhill*[347]

The most straightforward use of *decurrere* simply means 'to run down from a height'. For example, Livy's description of a deserter's plan to take the city of Sora in 314: after posting ten Romans on the citadel with a large supply of missiles, he then ran down from there making as much noise as possible, to panic the citizens.[348] In 211, 1,200 Numidian deserters from the Carthaginian army were ordered to move from the Aventine hill through the centre of the Esquiline. When men on the Capitoline saw them riding down the public hill, they believed the Aventine had been captured.[349] Both of these examples involve running down from a hill, with *decurrere* used to describe this movement; the term is used eleven times in this way.[350]

### Decurrere *as a downhill attack*[351]

In an extension of the previous connotation, the term can also be used to describe attacks from high ground. This use of the term can be seen at 1.12.8, where Livy states that Mettius Curtius had run down from the citadel in front of the Sabines and driven the Romans into flight.[352] In a speech in 321, looking back to 390, Lucius Lentulus urges the Romans to run down from the Capitoline against the Gauls.[353] In 218, the Carthaginians needed to get through a pass which the Gauls guarded by day. Hannibal left his baggage, cavalry and most of the infantry in the valley at night and took some of the light infantry to occupy the heights. At dawn his main army decamped and were attacked by the Gauls. Hannibal then 'ran down from higher ground and routed the enemy by the vigour of the attack'.[354] In each of these cases an attack is launched from high ground onto an enemy below, in these examples Livy states the attacks were *ab arce*, *ex Capitolio* and *ex superiore loco*. *Decurrere* is

[340] *OLD* s.v. 2, 4a and b.
[341] Rhone: 21.26.4 *Pluribus enim divisus amnis in mare decurrit*; Meander: 38.13.7 *Media urbe decurrens*; and 21.31.4 describes the flow of both the Rhone and the Isara.
[342] 24.36.4: *sub idem fere tempus et naues longae quinque et quinquaginta Carthaginiensium cum Bomilcare in magnum portum Syracusas ex alto decurrere.*
[343] *OLD* s.v. 7.
[344] 26.51.4-5: *Primo die legiones in armis quattuor milium spatio* ***decurrerunt***; *secundo die arma curare et tergere ante tentoria iussi; tertio die rudibus inter se in modum iustae pugnae concurrerunt praepilatisque missilibus iaculati sunt; quarto die quies data; quinto iterum in armis* ***decursum*** *est.*
[345] 23.35.6: *Ibi quia otiosa statiua erant, crebro decurrere milites cogebat ut tirones—ea maxima pars uolonum erant—adsuescerent signa sequi et in acie agnoscere ordines suos.*
[346] Military exercises: 23.35.6, 24.48.11, 25.17.5, 26.51.4, 26.51.5, 26.51.8, 29.22.2, 35.35.9, 40.6.5, 40.7.1, 40.47.8.
[347] *OLD* s.v. 1a and b
[348] 9.24.9: *decurrit inde, quanto maxime poterat cum tumultu.*
[349] 26.10.6: *quos cum ex arce Capitolioque clivo Publicio in equis decurrentes quidam uidissent, captum Auentinum conclamauerunt.*
[350] Rush down from a height: 2.10.3, 2.50.6, 3.11.1, 4.50.5, 9.24.9, 24.27.9, 26.10.6, 33.17.12, 39.13.12, 41.2.8, 45.1.8.
[351] For *decurrere* in a military context: *TLL* V.1.229.37ff.
[352] 1.12.8: *Mettius Curtius ab Sabinis princeps* ***ab arce*** *decucurrerat et effusos egerat Romanos toto quantum foro spatium est.*
[353] 9.4.9: *illis ut decurrere* ***ex Capitolio*** *armatis in hostem licuit.*
[354] 21.33.4: *decurrit* ***ex superiore loco*** *et cum impetu ipso fudisset hostem.*

used in this way by Livy on ten occasions.[355] An attack from higher ground would have more speed, and perhaps more force, than a normal attack on level ground. This extra speed may explain Livy's use of the term *decurrere* to describe such attacks, rather than his regular term for infantry combat, *impetus*.

**5. Conclusion**

Many of the ways Livy uses the main compounds of *currere* have been examined in this chapter to develop our understanding of his literary vision of infantry combat. The most frequently occurring of these terms, *concurrere*, is used in various ways, and thus it was important to identify each of the meanings Livy ascribes to the term. In a non-military context *concurrere* appears to imply massed movement such as the gathering of a crowd, and speed when moving towards a point. In a military context, the term is predominantly employed as a generic word for engagement or the coming together of two formations. When used in this way, *concurrere* implies nothing about the mechanics of the engagement. It is not possible to judge whether the conflict was massed in nature or at notable speed with *concurrere* used in this abstract form, and consequently analysis of the term offers only limited insight for our understanding of Livy's vision of battle. Equally the term *decurrere* is useful in only a limited capacity for this study, as it was used specifically to describe attacks from high ground. This technical use of the term implies little about the mechanics of the attack, other than that aggressor moved from higher to lower ground. The *currere* component of the verb may suggest that the attack was at a run, but this could be explained by the peculiar circumstances of the specific attack, it was from high ground, rather than suggesting a universal element of generic infantry combat.

On the other hand, the terms *incurrere* and *procurrere* both offer some clues to how Livy envisioned infantry combat in general. The contexts in which the terms are found and the morphology of the verb suggests that Livy employed these words to describe attacks carried out at unusually high speeds. Livy's use of these terms to describe infantry attacks represents exceptions to the normal form of Roman combat. The unusual speed of these attacks may represent Livy's attempt to portray responses to both positive and negative psychological influences. Attacking the flanks or rear of the opposition formation gave the aggressors a psychological advantage over their enemy, allowing them to throw off their natural reluctance and attack more vigorously. The response to negative influences could have a similar effect. In response to the death of a commander or cruel treatment of their comrades, Livy describes soldiers becoming enraged and attacking without regard for their own safety. Livy tends to include such psychological details to add interest the monotony of his battle accounts. Whether these details are authentic elements of the battle or a rhetorical tool matters little to the present study. The purpose of this analysis is to attempt to understand the ways in which Livy uses his combat vocabulary and how this reflects his vision of combat. It seems that Livy employed a term such as *incurrere* or *procurrere* to highlight the unusual nature of an attack. It follows that when there were no unusual psychological influences Livy used a different word to describe a 'normal' attack. The frequency of its occurrence in the extant books suggests this term was *impetus*, and this is supported by the links made in the *TLL*'s analysis between these terms. Although the attacks described with *incurrere* and *procurrere* were at unusually high speeds, they still took the form of small-scale localised flurries of hand-to-hand combat with swords. The analysis of the term *impetus* in the following chapter will show that these small-scale attacks were the primary method of infantry fighting in Livy's vision of infantry combat.

[355] Attack from high ground: 1.12.8, 9.4.9, 21.33.4, 21.33.9, 24.39.4, 27.42.4, 28.20.5, 42.16.1. Attack on a camp from high ground: 40.31.2, 40.31.8.

## Chapter 5: Livy's use of the term *impetus*

Of the vocabulary comprising Livy's formula for describing battle, *impetus* is the most important term for this study, as it occurs most frequently throughout the work and is often used to describe heavy infantry combat.[356] For this reason it is important to understand its full range of meaning and the various ways it is used by Livy. The *OLD* offers a range of general meanings, the most useful for this study include: a violent onward movement or force; a hostile movement, onset or in a military context a charge or attack (with *facere*, to make such an attack); or a vigorous effort or action.[357] These all offer aspects of what is a rather flexible term. *Impetus* is often associated with the movement of natural forces, implying a large violent and/or continuous movement.[358] Tacitus uses *impetus* to describe the movement of fire; Caesar uses it to describe the rushing of the river Rhine; and Seneca for the impulse of wind across the sea.[359] In each of these three examples *impetus* is used to denote a constant, continuous natural force or forward rush. At times, Livy uses *impetus* in this way, such as his descriptions of river currents.[360] Often, in a military context, 'charge' is offered as the closest approximation of the term in English. The English term 'charge' has a connotation of speed and this, coupled with the perception of *impetus* as a large continuous force, has had a major influence on our understanding of Roman heavy infantry attacks. Such translations of *impetus* give the false impression that Roman infantry attacks involved a massed advance at speed of the whole line. This view supports the traditional model of Roman infantry combat, which, as has been shown, would have been unlikely for archaeological, psychological and theoretical reasons. We must look closer at the term to gain a clearer picture of how it can be used and the impact this has on a model of Roman infantry combat.

In fact *impetus* can equally be used to describe a short, violent movement in isolation, such as the rush of a spring, described by Seneca as 'as brief as it is sudden', or even the force produced by a series of distinct motions, such as the waves of the sea pushing a ship off course.[361] A wave is an isolated movement with a force of its own, but the effect on the ship is caused by a combination of many such movements. Both of these two uses offer a different impression of *impetus*. Within a military context these forms would inspire a fundamentally different image of infantry combat than that of a massed charge.

*Impetus* is a complex term with many possible uses and thus many possible translations. It is better to translate *impetus* differently on different occasions, depending on the circumstances, or to employ a neutral term, such as 'attack', to avoid loaded English words which can carry false connotations. This chapter will examine Livy's use of the term within a military context to gain an understanding of the form these attacks took within his vision of battle and ultimately to derive from this a model of the mechanics of Roman heavy infantry combat.

In the surviving books the word *impetus* occurs three hundred and forty-eight times, with a myriad of meanings ranging from a generic 'attack' to an impulse, a land invasion to a naval engagement, or an assault on a city or camp.[362] Individually and in isolation these terms can be ambiguous, but the weight of the evidence as a whole offers interesting insights into Livy's use of the term and his vision of combat. This study will concentrate mainly on occurrences of the term *impetus* within an infantry context. It will be useful first however to examine Livy's use of the term within the context of cavalry combat, as this will go some way to dispelling the perception of *impetus* as a massed rush forward, in an attempt to relieve the burden of an initial massed charge and pave the way for a revised interpretation of the term.

### 1. *Impetus* and the Roman cavalry[363]

Based on the perception of *impetus* as a large-scale continuous movement, one would expect a cavalry attack to take the form of a massed rush forward and collision. There are forty-five occurrences (thirteen percent of the total) involving cavalry attacks and in nearly two thirds of these the Roman cavalry are the offensive arm. The following discussion will thus concentrate on the Roman

[356] Cf. *TLL* VII.1.606.54ff on the general uses of *impetus* in a military context.
[357] *OLD* s.v. 1a, 2, 4.
[358] *TLL* VII.1 604.28ff.
[359] Tacitus *Ann.* 15.38; Caesar *B.G.* 4.17; Seneca *Nat.* 5.1.1.
[360] On five occasions Livy describes the current of rivers as an *impetus*: 21.27.8, 21.28.2, 21.28.5, 21.47.5, 35.21.5. The current of a river is a continuous rush towards the sea.
[361] Seneca *Nat.* 6.7.2; Ovid. *Tr.* 1.4.15. Cf. *OLD* s.v. 1b.
[362] *Elephants five times:* 27.48.10, 30.33.3, 30.35.6, 37.42.5, 44.41.5. *Generic attack word twenty-five times:* 1.4.9, 1.5.7, 1.12.9, 1.23.3, 2.29.4, 2.34.4, 2.35.2, 2.52.6, 3.11.7, 3.14.3, 4.3.6, 4.44.6, 5.45.7, 6.15.8, 7.42.4, 10.2.10, 21.25.5, 23.16.9, 24.7.5, 24.26.12, 29.9.6, 36.5.4, 37.21.2, 39.21.10, 40.10.7.*Impulse eleven times:* 6.33.6, 7.39.16, 10.19.14, 22.50.12, 23.16.9, 25.21.5, 26.13.12, 26.19.1, 26.7.3, 36.29.1, 42.29.11. *Land invasion eleven times:* 1.5.4, 1.10.4, 2.51.4, 21.25.3, 26.25.16, 31.40.1, 31.40.5, 36.8.6, 40.1.3, 42.36.9, 42.67.4. *Naval attack five times:* 28.30.11, 30.10.9, 30.10.14, 30.25.8. *Attack on a city or camp eighty-eight times:* 1.10.5, 1.57.3, 2.10.3, 2.30.14, 2.31.3, 2.47.5, 3.5.1, 3.10.7, 3.22.7, 3.30.2, 5.6.7, 5.26.9, 5.39.6, 5.41.4, 5.41.5, 5.43.1, 6.2.12, 6.2.14, 6.4.9, 6.10.5, 6.15.8, 6.23.5, 6.33.6, 7.37.13, 9.4.14, 9.25.9, 9.26.2, 9.39.11, 10.32.9, 10.34.1, 10.43.2, 21.14.2, 24.2.10, 24.30.1, 24.32.4, 24.32.8, 24.33.9, 24.34.1, 24.40.4, 25.13.12, 25.25.8, 25.30.9, 25.31.1, 25.38.17, 26.6.5, 26.39.23, 26.46.6, 28.15.11, 29.6.12, 29.30.6, 30.12.5, 30.4.12, 31.16.4, 31.21.16, 31.26.3, 31.27.2, 32.13.11, 32.13.12, 32.16.15, 32.18.6, 32.18.9, 32.23.12, 32.24.4, 33.40.6, 34.15.7, 34.29.8, 34.39.12, 34.39.8, 35.11.5, 35.30.4, 36.13.3, 36.24.10, 36.24.11, 36.6.3, 36.9.11, 37.21.5, 37.31.2, 37.32.4, 37.43.11, 38.14.1, 38.5.8, 39.36.10, 40.49.3, 41.2.6, 41.2.9, 41.14.2, 42.67.7, 44.13.4.*Cavalry forty-five times:* 2.19.7, 3.61.8, 3.63.2, 4.19.2, 4.28.1, 4.38.5, 4.39.12, 6.29.3, 7.7.7, 8.30.6, 8.30.7, 8.38.12, 10.5.6, 10.14.12, 10.28.7, 10.28.11, 10.29.9, 10.29.11, 10.29.13, 10.41.9, 22.6.4, 23.16.12, 25.16.19, 25.16.21, 25.36.3, 27.27.5, 27.41.9, 28.33.3, 29.2.3, 29.34.13, 30.8.7, 30.35.2, 31.38.6, 31.41.14, 33.36.11, 35.5.4, 35.35.18, 37.38.3, 37.41.11, 37.42.2, 37.42.7, 38.13.12, 38.25.11, 38.25.15, 42.59.4. There are very few *impetus* involving light infantry; compounds of *currere* were usually used for this arm to denote the speed at which it fought. *Light infantry six times:* 21.33.9, 26.4.7, 27.18.2, 28.22.13, 31.35.3, 31.35.4. Interestingly two of the six (31.35.3 and 4) describe light infantry fighting in the 'style' of heavy infantry.
[363] On Roman republican cavalry in general see amongst others McCall (2002); Sidnell (2006) 149-252 and Sekunda (2007) 352-4.

form of combat, first examining cavalry versus cavalry engagements and then cavalry against infantry.

Captain Louis Nolan, an authority of cavalry tactics and a British cavalry officer at the charge of the light brigade, described nineteenth century cavalry engagements in following manner:

> "Cavalry seldom meet each other in a charge executed at speed; the one party generally turns before joining issue with the enemy, and this often happens when their line is still unbroken and no obstacles of any sort intervene. The fact is, every cavalry soldier approaching another at speed must feel that if they come in contact at that pace, they both go down and probably break every bone of their body...there is a natural repugnance to engage in deadly strife".[364]

This highlights the psychological nature of cavalry engagements and suggests that cavalry rarely came in to contact following a charge. Keegan concurs in his account of Waterloo, arguing that such a collision would have ended in a growing pile of injured men and horses.[365] The Roman cavalry would have been even more inclined to avoid a collision as they did not use stirrups.[366] If one can assume that in the majority of cases there was no collision, it appears the primary purpose of cavalry charges was psychological, an attempt to inspire fear in the enemy units and cause them to break ranks and flee. The unusual nature of the cavalry combat in his description of Cannae suggests Livy understood this:

> "the Gallic and Spanish horse which formed the left wing engaged with the Roman right in combat very unlike a cavalry action. For they had to charge front-to-front, there being no room to move out round the flank, for the river shut them in on one side the ranks of the infantry on the other" (Foster, 1929).[367]

The topography of the battlefield forced the cavalry to fight in this highly unusual frontal assault, which seems to imply shock tactics. It follows that Livy's descriptions of cavalry combat generally do not involve this form of assault. The Roman cavalry charge was, primarily, an attempt to inspire fear in the enemy units, causing them to flee. On a few occasions within Livy's battle accounts this objective was successfully achieved, such as at Magnesia in 190 when Antiochus' heavily armed Cataphracts were not able to withstand even the first *impetus* of the Roman cavalry.[368] However, as the hoped for disruption of the enemy rarely occurred, it is necessary to offer an explanation of how cavalry fought when the enemy stood their ground.

McCall has some interesting views on how the Roman cavalry fought in the middle Republic based on evidence such as Dionysius of Halicarnassus' description of the battle of Ausculum in 279:

> "The cavalry stationed upon both wings, knowing beforehand in what tactics they had the advantage over the enemy, resorted to those tactics, the Romans to a hand-to-hand, stationary combat, and the Greek horse to flanking and deploying manoeuvres. The Romans, when they were pursued by the Greek, would wheel their horses about, and checking them with the reins, would fight an infantry battle".[369]

McCall argues that the Romans employed two types of cavalry combat. In the first type, the Romans would ride up to the enemy and, instead of crashing into them, would halt and begin stationary, individual, hand-to-hand combat, followed swiftly by a reformation of the cavalry unit. The second Roman tactic involved the cavalry dismounting and attempting to fight on foot, as infantry.[370] McCall claims that both these styles of combat seem to be peculiar to the Roman cavalry.[371] It is possible that Livy may have made the assumption that the Roman form of cavalry combat, at least stationary mounted fighting, was the form generally used by all cavalry units.[372] For this reason, he is able to use the same term, whether *impetus* or a compound of *currere*, to describe both Roman and non-Roman cavalry attacks.

McCall suggests that in the vast majority of cases cavalry would only be able to charge an infantry formation that was in disorder. The purpose of cavalry attacks on disordered infantry formations was either to rout them

[364] Nolan (1853) 279

[365] Keegan (1976) 148

[366] Connolly, using Groenman-van Waateringe's work on the leather finds from Valkenburg and Vechten in the Netherlands (1967), reconstructed a Roman saddle. He claims that the pommels on this saddle perform the same function as stirrups, allowing the rider to regain his riding position in the saddle. The implication of this claim is that "the long accepted view that shock tactics were impossible before the introduction of the stirrup will have to be reconsidered" (Connolly (1987) 17). On this saddle and its experimental use see Connolly (1987) and (1990), and Hyland (1990) 130-134. This saddle would certainly allow the rider to wield a sword without being dragged down by his own momentum. Connolly's reconstruction is based on the sculptural evidence of first century AD tombstones and it is unclear whether the Republican cavalryman used a similar saddle. The sculptural evidence of the horsemen on the Aemillius Paullus monument and the altar of Ahenobarbus suggests that the cavalry did not use a saddle in this period (McCall (2002) 47-48).

[367] 22.47.1: *Deinde equitum Gallorum Hispanorumque laevum cornu cum dextro Romano concurrit, minime equestris more pugnae: frontibus enim adversis concurrendum erat quia nullo circa ad evagandum relicto spatio hinc amnis hinc peditum acies claudebant.*

[368] 37.42.2: *ne primum quidem impetum sustinuerunt*; cf. 3.61.8 (after infantry had attacked), 6.29.3, and 38.25.15.

[369] 20.2.1-2: οἱ μὲν ἱμμεῖς οἱ παρὰ ἀμφότερα τεταγμένοι τὰ κέρατα, προειδότες ἐν οἷς ἐπλεονέκτουν αὐτοὶ τῶν πολεμίων, εἰς ταῦτα κατέφευγον, Ῥωμαῖοι μὲν εἰς τὴν ἐκ χειρὸς καὶ σταδίαν μάχην, τὸ δὲ τῶν Ἑλλήνων ἱππικὸν εἰς τὰς περιελάσεις καὶ τοὺς ἐξελιγμούς. καὶ οἱ μὲν, ὁπότε διώκοιντο ὑπὸ τῶν Ἑλλήνων, ἐπιστρέψαντες τοὺς ἵππους καὶ τοὺς χαλινοὺς κατασχόντες ἐπεζομάχουν.

[370] For the Roman cavalry fighting as infantry see: Livy 2.20.10-11, 3.62.8, 4.38.2-4, 4.38.12, 6.24.10, 7.7.8, 25.16.19 etc. Cf. the Ticinus, Pol. 3.65.3, Liv. 21.46.6-7; and Cannae, Pol. 3.115, Liv. 22.47.3, which show that Polybius also thought this form of fighting was possible. Oakley (1997) 597-598, discusses this regular battle motif in greater detail.

[371] McCall (2002) 62-73.

[372] We have seen Livy's tendency towards this type of assumption in chapter two.

through the psychological force of the charge, or at least further disrupt the formation by breaking into the gaps already opened up in the line. Generally in mid-Republican battles, the infantry would engage the enemy, trying to disrupt their line before the cavalry decisively attacked their rear or flanks, as can be seen in Livy's account of the battle of Zama.[373] Cavalry would attack the flanks or rear, rather than the front, as an infantry formation offered a much less formidable defence at these vulnerable points.[374] Although the Roman cavalry may have carried missile weapons, they generally engaged infantry in close-combat.[375]

McCall states that "there is no explicit evidence of a cavalry charge in the Republic ending in collision", from this he has proposed an interesting model of cavalry tactics.[376] This suggests that against cavalry the Roman horsemen preferred stationary hand-to-hand combat or dismounted combat. Against infantry they attempted to rout the enemy by the psychological force of the charge, and shock tactics could be used only against the infantry flanks or against a disordered formation. Finally, if the infantry were not routed through fear of the charge then the cavalry preferred close-combat rather than missile fire.

Livy's descriptions of cavalry combat appear to support McCall's model. Cavalry attacks described with the term *impetus* seem not to be a single decisive charge, but rather a series of attacks.[377] Such as his description of the Romans fighting the Hernici in 362; the outcome of the battle was at first in some doubt with the frequent Roman cavalry attacks having little effect.[378] In these cases there must have been some attempt at reforming the cavalry line after an initial attack, and before the cavalry could attack again. If these attacks involved a massed collision, it would be very difficult to reform the cavalry unit for further assaults. In McCall's model the Roman cavalry would ride up to the enemy, but instead of crashing in with shock tactics, they would halt and fight hand-to-hand for a short period of time. Whichever side came off worse in the skirmish would pull back and reform before making another assault.

McCall's model suggests a form of cavalry combat similar in many ways to the dynamic infantry stand-off, proposed by Sabin. It includes a series of short, sporadic attacks of hand-to-hand fighting, resulting in one side pulling away from the enemy to regroup before making another attack. Similar cavalry attacks are described by Livy with the term *impetus*, or, if particularly fast, with a compound of *currere*. This form of combat does not fit with the common perception of *impetus* as a continuous force forward, but rather fits better with the idea of *impetus* as a short, violent motion in isolation, or within a series. Having taken the first step towards dispelling the common perception of *impetus*, it will now be possible to look closely at infantry attacks described with the term, to discover the type of combat involved in Livy's description of these attacks.

## 2. *Impetus* and the heavy infantry

It has been argued that an initial massed and coordinated charge of the whole line followed by an *othismos*-style shoving match is incompatible with the parameters of battle. In contrast, Sabin's theoretical dynamic stand-off model of combat does satisfy all of the parameters and appears to be the most convincing theoretical model of Roman infantry combat. This model involves the formations lining up with an interval between the two battle-lines. This interval is called the 'safety distance' and enables both sides to stand outside effective weapons range, or the 'killing zone', relieving some of the stress of combat. With the safety distance intact soldiers would be able to hurl missiles and insults against the enemy, while building up the psychological energy needed to launch an attack. From this default position attacks would consist of small groups of men, advancing out of their line and attacking across the safety distance at specific points along the enemy line. These are spontaneous attacks made by groups whose combined levels of nervous energy have reached a peak, erupting in a rush forward in response to the visual stimulus of, for example, a natural leader advancing out of the line. The initial force of this attack is psychological, with the purpose of intimidating enemy soldiers at the point of attack into flight. The psychological element of this attack is reinforced by the war cry and the elaborate decoration worn by the men.[379] A war-cry was "designed to make each soldier forget his own fear as he sent a message of terror to the enemy".[380] If the enemy did not immediately break ranks and run, the force of the attack becomes physical, consisting of hand-to-hand combat. As one side gets the worst of this fighting they would step back to reinstate the safety distance. In this model of battle, these small-scale localised flurries of hand-to-hand fighting would occur repeatedly all along the line, wherever pockets of men

[373] 30.32-35, cf. Pol. 15.9-14.

[374] Cf. Sabin (1996) 75-6, (2007b) 432-3; Goldsworthy (1996) 219.

[375] McCall (2002) 55-62.

[376] McCall (2002) 66; although the *impetus* in Livy 8.30.7, could be used as evidence against this assumption: The Roman cavalrymen "pulled the bridles off their horses and spurred them on so hotly that nothing could resist the shock, and arms and men went down before them over a wide front. The foot soldiers, following up the cavalry charge, advanced on the disordered enemy" (Foster, 1926). Here the cavalry attacked the front of the Samnite line, and appear to have collided with the enemy. Livy uses the term *perrumpere* at 8.30.6, 10.14.16, 10.41.9, etc., "breaking through" may suggest some form of collision. This could simply mean finding a way into the formation through gaps in the enemy line.

[377] Note the use of *primus*, meaning the first in a series of attacks, which implies that normally, when the battle is not won *primo impetu*, there is more than one *impetus*: 3.61.8, 6.29.3, 37.42.2, 38.25.15, etc.

[378] 7.7.7: *Primo stetit ambigua spe pugna nequiquam saepe conatis equitibus Romanis impetu turbare hostium aciem*; cf. a series of repeated attacks: 7.7.7, 8.30.6, 33.36.11, etc.

[379] *Impetus* involving some form of war-cry: 1.11.2: *clamor*; 2.65.5: *clamore renovato*; 6.13.2: *clamore*; 7.40.10: *clamor prius incipiet atque impetus*; 8.16.6: *clamore atque impetu primo fudisset*; 10.41.2: *clamorem atque impetum Romanorum*; 25.21.8: *clamorem quidem atque impetum*; 25.41.6: *clamor atque impetus*; and 38.41.7: *clamore impetu facto*. See Oakley (1998) 765-766, for a discussion of the Roman war-cry. On military decoration see Gilliver (2007).

[380] Hanson (1989) 149.

had built up enough psychological energy to launch an attack, until finally one side would break and turn in flight, leading directly to a rout.

Livy's description of the infantry combat at Pydna corresponds closely to this dynamic stand-off model:

> "[The Macedonian phalanx is weak when attacked at many points.] Such was the case on this occasion, when phalanx was compelled to meet the Romans who were attacking in groups, while the Macedonian line was broken at many points. The Romans for their part kept infiltrating their units wherever gaps presented themselves. If they had attacked frontally in solid line against an orderly phalanx, as happened to the Paelignians who at the beginning of the battle recklessly met the light infantry, the Romans would have spitted themselves on the spears and would not have withstood the solid line" (Schlesinger, 1951).[381]

Livy's vision of Roman infantry combat in this passage is consistent with the small-scale localised attacks of a dynamic stand-off. The examination of Polybius' digressions on the Roman legion and the archaeological parameters of Roman combat in chapter 1 demonstrated that it is likely these small-scale, localised attacks of hand-to-hand combat involved open-order fighting with swords using both cutting and stabbing strokes, rather than a close-order shield drive and *othismos*.

The proposals of this study are that Livy's literary formula for describing battle and his vision of infantry combat are similar in form to the combat predicted by the dynamic stand-off model, satisfy the archaeological and theoretical parameters of mid-Republican infantry battle and therefore reflect, as far as it is possible for any narrative account to do so, many of the realities of infantry fighting. It will be proposed in this section that where Livy uses the term *impetus* to describe heavy infantry combat, he appears often to be portraying a series of these small-scale, localised flurries of hand-to-hand fighting, or, on occasion, one such attack in isolation.

The term *impetus* is most frequently used by Livy to describe infantry combat, with one hundred and twenty-two occurrences, thirty-five percent of the total. Unfortunately, on thirty-six occasions he offers no further information about the mechanics of the attack than simply describing it as *impetus*.[382] There are also a number of occurrences where *impetus* simply means violence or vigour in general, rather than describing a specific attack.[383] But the remaining occurrences of the word, individually, offer small clues, either from the context of the term or with phrases describing the attack, which are suggestive of the type of infantry combat he imagined when using the term. Although in isolation these examples may only prove that one aspect of the dynamic stand-off model is present in a specific battle, by taking them in combination, the weight of the evidence as a whole offers a more accurate understanding of Livy's vision of Roman battle and a more convincing model of infantry combat than theory alone.

Many of these attacks involve non-Roman fighters and the use of the same vocabulary suggests that Livy conceptualised foreign infantry combat as similar to Roman. Arguably Livy is misinterpreting non-Roman warfare according to Roman models. Nevertheless, as argued in chapter 2, there is only a limited range of tactical variables in combat between similarly armed heavy infantry and so his (mis)interpretation should not adversely affect the overall hypothesis to a great extent. Whether or not an individual non-Roman force fought in this way does not refute the proposition that Livy understood and imagined infantry combat to take this form and that to some extend this vision reflects the realities of mid-Republican infantry battle.

### Impetus *against a localised area*

There are eight examples in Livy's work where an *impetus* appears aimed at a specific point or points in the enemy line. During a conflict with the Samnites in 306, the Romans attacked the enemy flank and burst through *at the point* where they attacked.[384] This attack was implemented by a second Roman army on an enemy already engaged. It suggests that an *impetus* could be made against a localised point in the enemy line, in this case the flank. The Romans are then able to break the line and advance through the middle of the enemy formation. In 212, the Carthaginians attacked the men surrounding the Roman general, Scipio, in a wedge formation.[385] Again, in 195, there is a successful attack in wedge formation, this time a Roman attack ordered by the consul Cato against Spanish troops.[386] An *impetus* in wedge formation, whether a series of small wedges, as one would expect of a Roman *quincunx*-style infantry formation, or one vast 'barbarian' wedge, is, by definition, an attack against a specific point along the enemy line. In 208, while the Romans were fighting the Macedonians, Philip attacked the Roman lines with his cavalry and fell from his horse. There followed a fierce skirmish as the Romans attempted to attack the king and his guards tried to protect him. Livy describes this small-scale, localised

[381] 44.41.8-9. For discussion of this passage see chapter 3 above.

[382] Eighteen Roman attacks: 1.27.10, 2.50.1, 2.64.6, 2.64.11, 4.47.3, 5.43.3, 6.24.11, 7.11.10, 22.23.10, 22.24.2, 25.11.2, 25.11.4, 25.37.14, 31.27.7, 31.39.12, 34.41.9, 40.48.6, and 44.35.7.
Eighteen non-Roman attacks: Veientes, 2.53.2; Volsci, 4.38.3, 6.24.4; Latins, 6.33.11; Gauls, 7.12.11, 31.2.8, 35.5.4; Etruscans, 10.4.12; Samnites, 10.29.9; Syracusans, 24.29.4; Carthaginians, 25.11.5, 26.2.11; Achaeans, 33.15.6, 33.16.9, 33.18.14, 35.29.5; Spartans, 39.36.15; and Mesenê, 39.49.3.

[383] For example: 2.14.6, 3.60.10, 4.32.12, 6.13.2, 27.16.1, 38.21.8.

[384] 9.43.15: *raptimque eductis in aciem militibus transuersam hostium aciem ...Qua impetum dederat, perrumpit aciemque per mediam in castra hostium tendit.*

[385] 25.34.11: *Cuneusque is hostium qui in confertos circa ducem impetum fecerat.*

[386] 34.15.2: *Nova acies facta; integri recentibus telis fatigatos adorti hostes primum acri impetu velut cuneo perculerunt, deinde dissipatos in fugam averterunt.*

attack, isolated from the rest of the battle as an *impetus*.[387] These four incidents are all examples of attacks against a specific, isolated point on the enemy line and show that Livy could use *impetus* to describe this form of small-scale localised combat.

In his description of a fighting against the Volsci in 385, Livy offers a more detailed account of his vision of heavy infantry combat:

> The Volsci's "bravery went no further than the battle-cry, the discharge of missiles, and the first violence of the battle; the play of swords, when foot met foot, and the glance of the foemen that darted out the fire of his spirit, they could not abide. Their frontline was driven back...next their ranks were broken at many points, and everything was disturbed, the line resembling surging waves"[388]

Here the battle began with a period in which both sides were psychologically buoyed, but the bravery of the Volsci only lasted for a period of missile fire and the initial violence of the fighting. They could not withstand the hand-to-hand fighting with swords nor the spirit of the Roman soldiers. This highlights the psychological nature of infantry combat and the importance of attacking with the sword rather than pushing with shields. The frontline of the Volsci is driven back (*impulsa frons prima*), this could be taken literally, meaning that they were physically driven back by Roman pushing, but this would seem unlikely given the predominance of sword play. It is possible they were psychologically driven back by their fear of the Romans, and that whenever the Romans advanced the enemy pulled back to reinstate a safety distance, until finally their line was broken at many points. Livy could plausibly be describing a massed attack of the whole line, which was successful at many points. But as the enemy line had been pushed back and was retreating, it is likely that such an attack by the Romans would have forced the whole enemy line into flight. Livy claims that the line was broken in many places (*rupti inde multis locis ordines*) and he uses a metaphor of wave-like undulations (*fluctuanti similis acies erat*). This is more consistent with a number of attacks against many specific points along the line than a massed advance.

During fighting in 212, when the Romans had abandoned their normal three-line system, adopting instead a single line of extended length, the tribunes feared that *wherever* the Carthaginians should make an attack they would pierce the line.[389] The use of *quacumque*, meaning 'at whatever point' or 'in whatever part', suggests that this potential *impetus*, would have involved attacks against a specific point or points along the enemy line.[390] Owing to the incompetence of the Roman commander and the disorganised formation, when the Carthaginian attack did come the Romans could not even stand their shout and first attack (*primus impetus*).[391]

In Livy's description of Ilipa, when the Romans had enjoyed much success from an unspecified form of attack, they began to realise that the advantage was shifting in their direction and that the Carthaginians were retreating. They became braver and began to attack everywhere along the line. Livy then states that this *impetus* was difficult to withstand.[392] Here, *undique inveherent* has been taken as 'everywhere along the line', rather than 'from all sides', as in this particular passage the Carthaginian line is formed opposite rather than surrounded by the Roman forces. After the Carthaginian line had been disrupted by an attack described with *impetus*, the Romans carried out a new and different form of attack, which finally led to a rout. The second phase attack, causing the rout, is described with the phrase *inferre signa*. In the following chapter it will be proposed that Livy used this phrase to describe an attack in the form of a massed advance of the standards against a disordered enemy formation. It is unlikely that the initial attacks leading to the disruption of the enemy line in the first phase, described as *impetus*, would have been a massed advance of the whole line. It is more likely that Livy is describing a series of small scale advances at various points along the enemy battle-line.

Finally, at Lake Trasimene, the Romans were surrounded by the enemy at their front and rear, and hemmed in by the mountains and the lake on their flanks. They attempt to make attacks against all parts of the enemy line, but fail to break through.[393] The use of *omnes* again, suggests a number of attacks against many individual points along the enemy line, rather than a massed advance against the enemy as a whole. Although this case is rather unusual as the soldiers were panicked and in chaos, it nevertheless reveals that Livy was happy to use the term *impetus* as a combat phase consisting of multiple separate attacks.

These eight examples show that Livy was able to use the term *impetus* to describe an attack made against a specific, localised area of the enemy line. These attacks, pin-pointing small sections along the enemy line, rather than an advance against the line as a whole, are consistent with a dynamic stand-off.

### Impetus *consisting of small groups*

Livy is able to use *impetus* to describe attacks upon isolated areas of the enemy battle-line, which would necessarily have been made by a relatively small group of soldiers. There are also a number of examples in Livy's work where he uses the term *impetus* to describe

[387] 27.32.5: *ab Romanis impetu in regem facto.*

[388] 6.13.2 : *Clamore tantum missilibusque telis et primo pugnae impetu ferox gladios et conlatum pedum et voltum hostis ardore animi micantem ferre non potuit. Impulsa frons prima...rupti inde multis locis ordines motaque omnia et fluctuanti similis acies erat.*

[389] 25.21.7: *Quacumque impetum fecisset hostis, perrupturos.*

[390] *OLD* s.v. 1c.

[391] 25.21.8: *Ergo ne clamorem quidem atque impetum primum eorum Romani sustinuere.*

[392] 28.15.7: *Sed cum eo ipso acrius, ubi inclinatum sensere rem, victores se undique inveherent, nec facile impetus sustineri posset.*

[393] 22.5.6: *Deinde, ubi omnes partes nequiquam impetus capti....*

specifically an attack carried out by a small group, or groups, of men.[394]

In 431, the Volscian soldier Messius led an *impetus*, composed of a group of courageous young men, which moved over the slain bodies of the enemy, and finally reached the Volscian camp to defend it from the Romans.[395] He was unsuccessful and the Romans took the camp. Livy's use of the superlative implies that this group consisted of a relatively small number of men. Even though the passage is mythical and should not be used as evidence for the specifics of this particular battle, it shows that Livy could use the term *impetus* to describe the battlefield movements of a small body of men.

A similar description can be seen in the mob violence of 189, where the Achaeans led an advanced force, consisting of armed men, ambassadors and exiles, to the gates of the Spartan camp to arrest some of the Spartans.

> "At first they assailed them with insults and then, as a quarrel broke out and their passions were aroused the most impetuous of the exiles attacked the Lacedaemonians" (Sage, 1936).[396]

The fighting involves Spartans on both sides, rather than Roman infantry and is not a regular battle, but the account reflects Livy's views on infantry combat in general. The fracas begins with a stand-off in which the exiles shout insults against their enemy, building up their anger and psychological energy. This stand-off is broken when the bravest of the exiles lead an attack against the Spartans. This is not a massed attack of the whole mob, but is made up only of the most spirited fighters (*ferocissimi*). Livy's use of the superlative suggests that this attack was executed by a relatively small group of men. This use of the term *impetus*, despite only describing mob violence, is consistent with the idea that small-scale attacks would be led by natural fighters advancing out from a group of less aggressive men.[397]

Livy describes attacks made by infantry formed into wedges (*cunei*). In 349, the Romans formed into wedges and burst through the middle of the Gallic line.[398] In 195, after the first Roman line grew weary, Cato formed up the second line of fresh troops, who with unused weapons attacked the enemy and first, with a violent attack in wedge formation, beat them down, then scattered them and put them to flight.[399] The Carthaginians also formed into wedges, in 212, when they made an attack on the Roman soldiers who surrounded the general Scipio.[400] This Carthaginian attack was focused on the relatively small number of troops who surrounded Scipio. This *impetus* was one attack, made up of a small number of men formed into a wedge, who advanced out of their battle-line to attack a specific, localised point on the enemy line, corresponding closely to the dynamic stand-off model. In general the Carthaginian infantry fought in a similar way to the Romans.[401] It is likely that when Livy describes infantry as fighting in 'wedge-formation', he means a similar type of attack, performed by a small group, perhaps the size of a century or maniple.

At times Livy uses the term *impetus* to describe attacks performed by relatively small groups of soldiers. These small-scale attacks are necessarily focused upon localised points along the enemy line, and in turn, the evidence for isolated and localised attacks in general must also refer to attacks made by small groups of men. Livy could specifically describe Roman infantry combat as small-scale attacks against isolated points along the enemy line. It is possible that more generally when he describes an attack with the term *impetus* it is this form of combat he imagined and tried to reflect in his narrative.

### **Impetus** ***as a series of attacks***

The combat proposed by the dynamic stand-off model took the form of a series of attacks rather than one massed effort. Livy's use of *impetus* also suggests that the attacks he describes were a series of assaults. In twenty-three cases an *impetus* phrase is qualified with adjectives such as *primus*.[402] This usage highlights the psychological nature of infantry attacks described by Livy. The purpose of the *primus impetus*, the first attack, appears to have been to break the nerve of the enemy and force them into premature flight, similar, as we have seen, to cavalry assaults, and often this was successful. But the use of a qualifying adjective also shows that this was not the case in all battles and implies that in general if the enemy were able to withstand the first assault, the aggressors would usually have to pull back from the engagement to regroup before launching a second or a third. While the phrase *primus impetus* is relatively common, *secundus impetus* is not.[403] Nevertheless the adjective, with its connotations of being first within a

[394] At 22.6.4 Flaminius is killed by Ducarius, an Insubrian horseman, who attacked through the crowd of enemies (*hostium turbam impetum facit*). Although this describes the attack of a cavalryman, the passage shows that Livy imagined an *impetus* could be made by an extremely small force, one man in this case.

[395] 4.29.1: *Messium impetus per stratos caede hostes cum globo fortissimorum iuvenum extulit ad castra Volscorum.*

[396] 38.33.6: *primo lacessere iurgiis, deinde, altercatione orta, cum accenderentur irae, ferocissimi exulum impetum in Lacedaemonios fecerunt.*

[397] This idea, that armies and crowds contain a majority of less aggressive men and a minority of natural fighters who may spur the others on, is proposed in Marshall (1947).

[398] 7.24.8: *Cuneis deinde in medium agmen perrumpunt.*

[399] 34.15.2: *Nova acies facta; integri recentibus telis fatigatos adorti hostes primum acri impetu velut cuneo perculerunt, deinde dissipatos in fugam averterunt.*

[400] 25.34.11: *Cuneusque is hostium qui in confertos circa ducem impetum fecerat.*

[401] Polybius states that Hannibal armed his troops with captured Roman equipment early in the Second Punic War (3.87.3, 114.1), which implies that they would have had a comparable fighting style for the majority, if not all, the land battles of the Punic Wars.

[402] *Primo impetu*: 1.11.2; *primus impetus*: 25.41.6; *inito... impetus*: 2.14.6; *eodem impetus*: 2.20.13; *primo impetus*: 2.65.2; *primum impetum*: 2.65.4, 10.41.2, 25.21.8, 30.11.11, 3035.8, 38.17.7, 38.27.1, 38.6.3; *primoque impetu*: 7.16.6; *impetus primo*: 8.16.6; *primo impetu*: 9.23.15, 9.27.9, 10.28.3, 23.44.4, 25.36.13, 26.46.9, 37.43.5, 41.10.4.

[403] It appears once at 33.36.11, describing repeated cavalry attacks.

series,[404] does at least suggest the possibility that infantry combat usually involved more than one attack.

Unfortunately, Livy tends to describe this phase of infantry combat simply with the term *impetus*, rather than offering more specific evidence about the nature of the attack. The limited evidence that is supplied tends to derive from unusual situations, which is often the reason Livy offers an explanation at all. Nevertheless, this evidence he does offer is consistent with a series of attacks. At times *impetus* is used in the plural, such as at 35.5.7, where the Gauls were able to withstand the attacks of the Romans.[405] The implications of the plural form suggest that the Roman assault was made up of a number of attacks. At Zama, the initial phase of Livy's combat description involved the Carthaginians making repeated attacks at high speed.[406] These attacks are not described as *impetus*, but they do suggest that for Livy infantry could fight in a series of small, repeated attacks. In 480 the Etruscans found themselves surrounded after entering the Roman camp and made several attacks, in an attempt to break out, but to no purpose.[407] Livy's use of *aliquotiens* reinforces the idea that there were several attempts made at different times, rather than one massed advance. Although not a pitched battle, it reinforces the hypothesis that Livy could use the term *impetus* to describe this form of attack. At Lake Trasimene a similar situation occurred, in which the Romans themselves were surrounded and attempted to break out with a series of assaults.[408] Although these are special cases, where an infantry line is surrounded, they do suggest Livy could imagine infantry fighting as a series of attacks. In 185, the Romans attacked the Celtiberians *alii super alios inferentes.* [409] Though this is described using the term *inferre*, it again reinforces the idea that the Roman infantry could attack successively. This limited amount of evidence, combined with Livy's frequent use of adjectives such as *primus*, offers some support to the assertion that attacks described with the term *impetus* could be made up of a series of assaults.

It has been proposed that it would be extremely difficult, for two battle-lines to separate following a massed collision. In this form of attack, the opposing lines, both over a mile in length, would lose their integrity and become inter-mingled to various extents, depending upon the relative strength of a particular position in the line. Amid this chaos, it would be difficult enough to hear the recall signal let alone be able to disengage from the enemy and retreat while maintaining a cohesive formation. A dynamic stand-off on the other hand would allow the lines to separate more easily. A number of small-scale localised attacks would only involve a relatively small proportion of troops at any one time. The majority of the line would remain with their formation intact, able to provide men for a second wave of attacks without the necessity of a massed and coordinated disengagement of combat and reformation of the line. In this model there would be no need to sound a recall order, in the same way that there was no need to order a specific attack. The small, autonomous group of men, making the attack in response to the visual stimulus of one of their unit advancing out of the line, would themselves be able to decide when to withdraw, and owing to their close proximity could signal this with visual signs. For these reasons this phase of Roman infantry combat seems likely to have been a series of small-scale, localised attacks at different points along the enemy line, rather than a massed collision of the whole infantry formation. Livy's use of adjectives to qualify the term *impetus* and his images of repeat attacks suggest he was attempting to describe a similar form of combat.

### **Impetus *and the safety distance***

In the dynamic stand-off model the default state of Roman infantry combat was a stand-off, with the two battle-lines separated by a small gap, called the safety distance. This interval was wide enough to keep the troops out of effective sword range but seems to have been within the range of missile weapons (about 30 yards for the Roman *pilum*). This division allowed the soldiers, in relative safety, to insult the enemy and, periodically, to move forward and throw missiles, while building up the nervous energy required to move, in a small group, out of the battle-line and attack the enemy. Livy's battle descriptions offer evidence that he knew the importance of this safety distance in heavy infantry combat and that it formed part of his literary vision of battle.

In 294, the Roman and Samnite lines approached each other, "and now there was but a little space between the armies, they halted, each waiting for the other to be the first to attack and the first to raise a shout".[410] Livy's description corresponds closely to idea of a safety distance, behind which men spurred each other on to make an attack. This passage gives an impression of the fear involved in battle, with neither army wishing to be the first to make an *impetus*, content instead to stay in the relative security of the crowd. Camillus' advice to his troops in 385, not to advance but to await the attack of the Volsci, again gives the impression that a period of stand-off was normal in Roman battle.[411] As we have seen, the description of the conflict between the Exiles and the Spartans also supports the idea of a 'safety distance'. Here, when the Exiles had advanced close to the Spartans, there was an initial period of stand-off, in which insults were exchanged and both sides worked themselves up into a frenzy, before the most spirited of the Exiles made

[404] *OLD* s.v. 3b and 9.

[405] *densis tamen ordinibus nunc alii in alios, nunc in scuta incumbentes sustinebant impetus Romanorum*

[406] 30.34.3: *Concursatio et uelocitas illinc maior quam uis.*

[407] 2.47.6: *Nam cum incursantes quacumque exitum ostenderet spes uano aliquotiens impetu issent.*

[408] 22.5.6.

[409] 39.31.10: *Renovatur ab omnibus clamor: impetus fit velut ex superiore loco. Haud secus ergo quam torrentis modo fundunt sternuntque perculsos, nec sustineri alii super alios inferentes sese possunt.*

[410] 10.36.2: *Iam exiguum inter duas acies erat spatium, et stabant exspectantes dum ab hostibus prius impetus prius clamor inciperet.*

[411] 6.12.8: *Ne procurri quidem ab acie velim, sed obnixos vos stabili gradu impetum hostium excipere.*

an attack.[412] This account describes exactly the psychological and emotional energy, which was built up within the crucible of this stand-off phase. When this energy reached a peak at any point along the line, it erupted into an *impetus*.[413]

A further battle description highlights the offensive advantage such a safety distance could offer the Roman infantry. In 198, the Romans faced a Macedonian phalanx, but as they were fighting between broken parts of a rampart, protecting the phalanx from flank attack, the Romans could not get past the Macedonian spears. Livy states that "nor was it possible either to retire or to attack from a distance, a manoeuvre which usually throws the ranks in to disorder".[414] This suggests that, at least against a phalanx, the Romans were able to disengage from the initial combat, retire over a distance and then launch *impetus* from across the safety distance. This form of attack was usually successful in disrupting the enemy ranks. In this passage the safety distance is described as *longum spatium*, while at 10.36.2 another safety distance is described with the phrase *exiguum spatium*. The use of these opposing adjectives suggests that the size of a safety distance could vary depending on the context of the battle. As Livy uses qualifying adjectives in both of these cases it suggests that they are exceptions and it follows that in most battles there would be a normal *spatium* between the two lines.

The safety distance could also be used to keep an enemy pinned down with missile fire. At 9.35.7, the Etruscans found themselves in difficulties because they had no missiles. The Romans could attack them from a distance while they, standing exposed to the *pila* fire, could not retaliate. At 38.21.8, the Gauls found themselves in a similar position, pinned down under heavy missile fire. The implication of these two descriptions is that Livy understood there often to be a gap between the opposing battle-lines, allowing for attacks from a distance.

There are a few more general descriptions of battle which appear to support the proposal that Livy's infantry combat involved a series of attacks and that the default state of battle was a stand-off. At Ilipa, in a skirmish a few days before the main battle, the Carthaginians retreated from the Roman infantry, but without breaking ranks. Until, finally, the Carthaginians scattered and were routed when the Roman cavalry fell on their rear and the attack could not be withstood.[415] It has been proposed that disengaging the enemy and retreating in formation would be difficult following a massed charge, as the two lines, on losing their cohesion, would have become too deeply intertwined to allow such a manoeuvre. With a form of combat involving a stand-off punctuated with small scale attacks, it would have been much easier for the Carthaginians to pull back without breaking ranks because only a relatively small number of troops would have been engaged.

At Cynoscephalae, the Roman light infantry were coming off worse in a skirmish. Flamininus brought up his left wing to help, and encouraged by the arrival of the general and the heavy infantry, 'they renewed the battle, attacked and turned back the enemy'.[416] Here again we see distinct periods within the battle, the initial attack, a break for an indeterminable time and then the renewal of the attack. This ebb and flow of combat, and the necessary mobility of the battle-lines, fits the dynamic stand-off model better than a massed infantry charge. In 193, Roman troops were not holding the Gallic attack, the second legion was brought in and after the irregular troops had been relieved the battle was restored. The Gauls, though tired from the sun, withstood the attacks of the Romans.[417] In order to allow enough time and space to relieve the exhausted troops there must necessarily have been a period of relative inactivity with the two lines at a safe distance from each other.

The implications of the evidence so far appear to support the hypothesis and suggest that the two opposing lines usually drew up with a 'safety distance' between them. The purpose of the safety distance was to keep the maximum number of troops out of the 'killing zone' for the longest possible time. The mid-Republican legion was a citizen militia; they would not have had the discipline nor the *esprit de corps*, to make an immediate combined attack of the whole line on the order of the commanding officer. The default position in Roman combat was this rest period, which allowed the men to build up the required nervous energy to make an attack. This stand-off was periodically disrupted by small-scale attacks on a localised area of the enemy line. These attacks would be led by the spontaneous advance of a particularly brave soldier, who would bring along in his wake a small group of men closest to him, perhaps a maniple, century or even smaller.[418] After a short flurry of close combat this autonomous group would make the decision to return to the safety of their line, in order to rebuild their expended energy. The purpose of this form of combat was to disrupt the enemy battle-line while allowing as many men as possible relief from psychological pressure of being in the 'killing zone'. This model offers a plausible system of combat for a citizen militia and corresponds well with Livy's descriptions of infantry combat.

### Impetus *and the Roman fighting style*

The examination of the archaeological and theoretical evidence for the Roman fighting style in the first chapter

[412] 38.33.6. Livy uses the phrase *accenderentur irae*, to describe this build up of nervous energy.

[413] Oakley (2005a) 417-418, discusses the standard motif in Livian battles that both sides watched each other but were reluctant to start the fight. This motif may reflect the realities of a dynamic stand-off.

[414] 32.17.15: *Nec ex longo spatio aut cedendum aut impetus faciendus erat, quae res turbare ordines solet.*

[415] 28.13.9: *Dein, postquam acrius ultimis incidebat Romanus neque sustineri impetus poterat.*

[416] 33.8.6: *Pugnam renovant impetuque facto rursus avertunt hostem.*

[417] 35.5.7: *Sustinebant impetus Romanorum.*

[418] At times Livy makes note of the leaders of such an attack: Messius, 4.29.1; Sextus Tullius, 7.16.5; Quintus Navius, 26.5.17; the most ferocious of the Spartan exiles, 38.33.6; etc.

demonstrated that it was more likely the heavy infantry fought in open-order, cutting and thrusting with swords, than an initial collision followed by close-order pushing with shields and stabbing with swords.

Ancient literary sources rarely express the mechanics of hand-to-hand combat. Their battle narratives tend to focus on the main sequence of events, and rarely describe in detail how individuals or small groups fought. They instead tend to resort to metaphors or generic statements to explain the situation of large sections of the battle-line. A more detailed description of close combat was often unnecessary as the majority of the audience would have had direct experience of a similar form of hand-to-hand fighting. A modern reader, without the benefit of such experience, has to try to reconstruct this form of combat by piecing together the periodic, more detailed descriptions scattered throughout the surviving material. These sporadic details found in Livy's battle narratives support the conclusions of our first chapter.

There are thirteen occurrences of the term *impetus*, which offer some insight in to the nature of the fighting involved in Livy's descriptions of heavy infantry combat. Six specifically mention the use of swords, revealing the dominance of this weapon.[419] There are other references to the style of Roman combat, which seem to suggest sword fighting rather than driving forward with shields. In four places Livy qualifies his description of an *impetus* with a form of *caedere*, implying the use of swords.[420] The verb *caedere* indicates cutting with the edge of the weapon as opposed to *pungere*, expressing a stabbing action. On one occasion *obtruncare* is used alongside *impetus* to describe the attack of the Aequi against the Romans. The meaning of this verb is to cut to pieces, again suggesting the use of swords.[421] Finally *percellere* is twice used with *impetus*, meaning 'to strike down with weapons'. [422] We have seen the primacy of swords in Roman combat in the accounts of Polybius and now Livy. It is likely that the weapons implied by the term *percellere* would have been swords. The archaeological and theoretical evidence, as well as the descriptions of Polybius, all indicate that Roman infantry attacks, and those fighting in a similar way, consisted of hand-to-hand combat with swords. The term *impetus* itself tends to denote the use of swords when used in a military context. Veith certainly was thinking in this way when he described the term *impetus* as "*Einbruch mit dem Schwert*".[423] It is very likely then that when Livy used the term *impetus* to describe heavy infantry combat it was this form of cut-and-thrust sword fighting he envisioned.

There are some incidences of *impetus* indicating the importance of missile warfare. In 310 the Etruscans made the mistake of throwing away their missiles in order to proceed straight to hand-to-hand combat.

> "The Romans, on the contrary, fell to pelting them, now with javelins and now with stones, of which later the ground itself provided a good supply and even Etruscans who were not wounded were confused by the blows that rattled down on their helmets and shields. It was not easy to get close enough for fighting hand-to-hand, and they had no javelins for long-range work. There they stood, exposed to the missiles, with no sort of adequate cover, and as some of them gave ground and the line began to waver and be unsteady the *hastati* and *principes*, after drawing their swords and renewing their war-cry attacked them. The Etruscans were unable to withstand this attack... ."[424]

This initial period of missile discharge was designed to break up the Etruscan battle-line and after the line "began to waver and be unsteady" the Roman infantry attacked sword in hand (*strictis gladiis*). Here *pila* and other missiles were used to disrupt the enemy line as a precursor to hand-to-hand combat with swords. Similarly, at Ibera in 216 (or 215), as the lines first engaged, the unreliable Spanish centre of the Carthaginian line fell back when the Romans had barely thrown their javelins. The Roman infantry then advanced with such an *impetus* that the enemy turned and ran.[425] This attack is described as *magnus impetus*, perhaps suggesting a larger-scale attack than usual. This would be understandable owing to the particular weakness in Spanish line, commented on directly by Livy, which would offer a psychological advantage to the aggressors. The use of such a qualifying adjective suggests that *impetus* were generally smaller in scale. In 209, after the Romans had merely thrown their *pila*, the Tarentines retreated almost before they came to hand-to-hand combat.[426] In 468, it is the Volsci who hurl missiles at the Romans during their first attack.[427] In each of these five examples missiles appears to have been used to disrupt the enemy line before the infantry move forward to engage in hand-to-hand combat. Two further examples, where Livy notes the lack of missile exchange, reinforce this idea, though the attacks are not directly

---

[419] 6.13.2: *ferox gladios*; 7.16.5: *stricto gladio*; 7.40.10: *strinxeritis ferrum*; 9.13.4: *strictisque gladiis*; 9.35.7: *strictis gladiis*; 9.39.9: *gladiis pugna coepit.*

[420] 5.28.13: *caedes inde fugientuium*; 28.3.12: *nec secus quam adversa acies caesi*; 28.22.14: *caede primorum*; 33.10.5: *primis caesis ceteri in fugam dissipate sunt.* Cf. *OLD* s.v. *caedere* 3 and 5; *caedes* 2 and 5.

[421] 4.46.5: *obtruncati.* Cf. *OLD* s.v. 2.

[422] 2.65.2: *Volscum primo impetus perculit*; 34.15.2 - *primum acri impetu velut cuneo perculerunt.* Cf. *OLD* 1330 (2); however, *percellere* can also mean to overcome more or less instantaneously, which fits well with Livy's use of *primus* and would not, therefore, specifically describe the use of swords.

[423] Kromayer and Veith (1928) 430.

[424] 9.35.5-7: *Romanus contra nunc tela, nunc saxa, quibus eos adfatim locus ipse armabat, ingerere. Igitur scuta galeaeque ictae cum etiam quos non uolnerauerant turbarent—neque subire erat facile ad propio rem pugnam neque missilia habebant quibus eminus rem gererent—stantes et expositos ad ictus cum iam satis nihil tegeret, quosdam etiam pedem referentes fluctuantemque et instabilem aciem redintegrato clamore strictis gladiis hastati et principes inuadunt. Eum impetum non tulerunt Etrusci.*

[425] 23.29.9: *Primo igitur concursu, cum vix pila coniecta essent, rettulit pedem media acies, inferentibusque se magno impetu Romanis vertit terga*

[426] 27.16.1: *igitur pilis tantum coniectis, prius paene quam consererent manus terga dederunt.*

[427] 2.65.4-5: *Volscus effusis ad primum impetum missilibus telis...*

described as *impetus*. In 320 the Romans were so anxious to engage at close quarters that they dropped their *pila* to the ground to avoid the normal delay taken in throwing them at the enemy and drawing their swords.[428] Again, at Lake Vadimonis in 310, the battle between the Romans and the Etruscans was contested with such rage that neither side threw a missile, fighting instead with swords.[429] This evidence shows that in Livy's vision of battle heavy infantry attacks tended to begin with a period of missile exchange, followed by an advance into hand-to-hand combat with swords.[430]

Zhmodikov's model of legionary combat, introduced in the first chapter, proposes that missile exchange was not confined to the start of a battle, but was rather a continuous feature.[431] He rightly dismisses the traditional notion that combat consisted of a volley of *pila* followed by a decisive massed charge, which fits neither the parameters of battle nor the evidence from Livy. But Zhmodikov's assertion that missile combat was the dominant form of Roman battle, with hand-to-hand combat relegated to a very minor role, contradicts both Polybius' and, as we have just seen, Livy's accounts. The problem can be overcome with a dynamic stand-off, which, as has been presented in this chapter, is compatible with the form of combat described by Livy. Within a dynamic stand-off, each small group of men could throw their *pila* at the localised point of attack, before advancing across the safety distance. This corresponds to the impression given in the literary sources, that missile discharge was a precursor to an infantry attack. As these attacks happened at various times from isolated points along the line and involved a minority of the total number of troops, those soldiers taking no part in these attacks would retain their *pila*, which could be used later in the battle. With an initial massed charge all of the *pila* of the front line would have to be thrown before or during the charge.[432] As Zhmodikov notes, this does not fit the literary evidence that missiles were regularly thrown throughout battles lasting many hours. Under the traditional model of combat this would be improbable, but under the dynamic stand-off model missiles would remain available throughout even the longest of conflicts.

### 3. *Impetus* and elephant attacks

On five occasions Livy uses the term *impetus* to describe the 'charge' of elephants.[433] The ferocious charge of elephants in battle appears to fit better with the perception of *impetus* as a large continuous, almost unstoppable, force, than with the proposed understanding of a series of sporadic, isolated, attacks. However, there are similarities between the proposed form of an infantry attack described by *impetus* and the charge of war elephants. Scullard suggests that "the purpose of an elephant in war was not only to destroy the enemy but first to terrify him: so they were given splendid trappings, as well as receiving on occasion a ration of fermented wine to stimulate their fury".[434] The primary purpose of an elephant *impetus* would be a psychological stimulus to cause the enemy to flee.[435] It has been shown that the attacks of both cavalry and infantry were fundamentally psychological. For this reason, the Roman legionary wore a long feather on top of his helmet in an attempt to seem taller and thus scare the enemy into flight.[436] The elephant too, and to a similar extent the horse, was equipped with crests, head-pieces, and even body armour, in order to strike a more imposing figure. An important part of this psychological warfare was the shout of the infantry while attacking. The trumpet of the elephant would have a similar effect upon enemy troops, and this could be enhanced with the use of a bell.[437]

Scullard describes the spacing of the elephants within a battle-line:

> "When in line the distance between individual animals would vary according to number and location, but 100 feet may have been a normal space, and half or less than that on occasion".[438]

Often these gaps would be filled with light infantry "to keep the elephants isolated from each other".[439] Elephants were not used in a pack to drive the enemy line back as a whole. They were instead used in isolation and at various intervals to puncture holes in the enemy formation, at the point where they attacked. In a similar way to an infantry attack described with the term *impetus*, the attack of the elephant attempted to disrupt the enemy line by focusing its energy on a particular, localised, point in the opposing formation. These isolated elephant attacks were violent but were not at particularly high speed. The *impetus* of elephants were no more massed charges than infantry *impetus*. The purpose of both was to disrupt the enemy line initially through fear, as Scullard suggests: "terror was their primary weapon, and its effect runs like a red thread through the history of elephant warfare, terror inflicted on men and horses".[440] If this terror did not have the desired effect, as with an infantry attack, a violent struggle ensued.

[428] 9.13.4: *et ne mora in concursu pilis emittendis stringendisque inde gladiis esset, pila velut dato ad id signo abiciunt.*

[429] 9.39.9: *tantoque irarum certamine gesta res est ut ab neutra parte emissa sint tela. Gladiis pugna coepit*.... On the abandonment of javelins see Oakley on Livy 6.12.8.

[430] This standard motif of Livian battle is discussed in more detail in Oakley (1997) 509-510.

[431] Zhmodikov (2000).

[432] It may have been possible to carry *pila* in a charge, either by strapping the javelin on the inside of the shield or by holding it against the shield with the left thumb. For discussion of this see chapter 1.

[433] *Impetus* of Elephants: 27.48.10, 30.33.3, 30.35.6, 37.42.5, 44.41.5.

[434] Scullard (1974) 238.

[435] Glover (1948) 3-4.

[436] On crested helmets see Oakley (2005a) 514-515. Cf. Gilliver (2007).

[437] Scullard (1974) 240; Glover (1948) 4.

[438] Scullard (1974) 246; cf. Glover (1948) 5-6, who believes that the best results would have been to use "mass attack of elephants in force", but notes that this "seems seldom to have been done", and offers no examples for it having been done at all.

[439] Scullard (1974) 246.

[440] Scullard (1974) 247.

## 4. Livy's description of the battle of Zama

So far it has been proposed that Livy's descriptions of Roman infantry combat took a similar form to that proposed by the dynamic stand-off model. An apparent exception to this is Livy's famous description of the combat between the *hastati* and the first Carthaginian line at Zama:

> "For the Romans [Zama was] a battle of little movement, as they *pressed on* into the enemy by *their own weight and that of their arms*; on the other side repeated charges at high speed but with less power. Consequently by the first attack the Romans at once dislodged the enemy's line. Then *beating back with their shoulders and the bosses of their shields*, being now in close contact with men forced from their position, they made considerable progress, as no one offered any resistance, while as soon as they saw that the enemy's line had given way, even the rear line *pressed upon the first*, a circumstance which of itself gave *them great force in repulsing the enemy*."[441] (Moore, 1949).

Sabin claims that this passage supports his model of infantry combat: "Livy's references to 'repeated charges' and to steady advances and withdrawals before the final rout accord well with the image of sporadic surges forward from a shifting stand-off position".[442] Certainly the repeated, high speed charges fit well with the dynamic stand-off model, but it is the Carthaginian mercenaries who surge forward in these small-scale flurries. The Roman attack was one of far less movement and speed: "a battle of little movement, as they pressed on into the enemy by their own weight and that of their arms" (*pugna Romana stabilis et suo et armorum pondere incumbentium in hostem*). Livy's language, such as *urgentibus* (physical pushing), *pellendum* (driving back), *incumbentium* (pressing with weight), etc, does not seem to correspond with the dynamic and flexible combat usually described by Livy. It is difficult to justify the proposed form of Roman combat against this description of a slow, grinding infantry attack. But this is the only use of *impetus* that seems to contradict the proposed model, and there is evidence that Livy may have included this unusual description because of a corrupted passage within his text of Polybius itself.

An assessment of Polybius' description of the mechanics of combat at Zama is affected by a strange sentence at 15.13.1: "As the whole battle was a hand-to-hand affair [the men using neither spears nor swords]..." (Πάσης δ᾽ οὔσης ἐκ χειρὸς καὶ ἄνδρα τῆς μάχης [διὰ τὸ μὴ δόρασι μηδὲ ξίφεσι χρῆσθαι τοὺς ἀγωνιζομένους]...). The phrase in brackets makes little sense and causes some serious difficulties in the rest of the account. For this reason modern scholars generally suppose it to be a corruption in the text. The text could easily be amended by changing it to either διὰ τὸ μὴ δόρασι **ἀλλὰ** ξίφεσι χρῆσθαι τοὺς ἀγωνιζομένους,[443] or διὰ τὸ μὴ δόρασι ξίφεσι χρῆσθαι τοὺς ἀγωνιζομένους.[444] These amendments would change the meaning of the sentence to, '...the men could not use their spears, only their swords'. Walbank suggests that even after these amendments the sentence remains flat, making a case for rejecting the whole phrase as a substantial corruption or a later addition to the text, as suggested by De Sanctis.[445]

The possibility of such a corruption occurring in the manuscript tradition of Polybius within such a relatively short period of time was discussed in chapter two. Similar differences between the two historians' texts were found, supporting the proposition that Livy may have read a corrupted version of Polybius' account of Zama. Livy's methodological approach has also been discussed, revealing that he generally followed his main source closely, in this case Polybius. When he discovered an error or an anomaly, instead of discarding this piece of information, he recorded it and tried to explain it using his own experiences and imagination or other minor sources, following his general practice of acceptance and elaboration. It is likely Livy's description of the battle of Zama is an example of this practice. He would have read the corrupted passage in his text of Polybius and found it strange; this much is clear from his attempted explanation of the phrase. Instead of discarding the anomaly and writing his own account of the infantry battle, his methodological process caused him to elaborate on this point. From his own imagination he created an image of an infantry battle where no swords or javelins could be used, while, at the same time, trying to synthesise this with his literary formula for describing battle. The account of Zama includes his standard vocabulary of combat rhetoric, but, fused with this, are descriptions of pushing with shoulders and shields. This form of combat described as *ala deinde et umbonibus pulsantes* does not necessarily represent a massed *othismos*, but could describe individual close combat with the Romans using their shields as an offensive weapon to punch their opponents, which is consistent with other Livian battle accounts. The unusual aspect of this passage is the repeated language of pushing and driving, which might imply massed movement, but this could well have been the result of a corruption in Livy's copy of Polybius. The passage remains elusive, but it does not necessarily imply that at Zama the Romans drove the Carthaginians back with a massed shield drive nor that this was the general form of Roman combat envisaged by Livy.

---

[441] 30.34.2-5: *Pugna Romana stabilis et suo et armorum pondere incumbentium in hostem, concursatio et uelocitas illinc maior quam uis. igitur primo impetu extemplo mouere loco hostium aciem Romani. ala deinde et umbonibus pulsantes in summotos gradu inlato aliquantum spatii uelut nullo resistente incessere, urgentibus et nouissimis primos ut semel motam aciem sensere, quod ipsum uim magnam ad pellendum hostem addebat.*

[442] Sabin (2000) 15.

[443] Walbank (1967) 459.

[444] Lazenby (1978) 221.

[445] Walbank (1967) 459. De Sanctis (1916) 2.607.

**5. Conclusion**

It is now possible to piece together a plausible model of the mechanics of Livy's vision of heavy infantry *impetus*. This will be further elaborated on in chapter 8, but here it will be useful to offer a short description of the form of combat Livy may have imagined when using the term. *Impetus* is used to describe both an isolated small-scale attack and a phase of battle, involving a series of these same types of attack. During what I will term the *impetus* phase, the initial phase of Roman combat, the two opposing armies would line up in a loose formation. The lines then would move slowly together until they were separated by a distance generally less than *pila* range. This is the 'safety distance' and from here the stand-off would begin. The stand-off was an indeterminate period of time in which the two armies would size each other up and hurl insults and missiles at one another. The purpose of the stand-off was to allow time for nervous energy to build up within the soldiers. When the energy levels were high enough one side would make an attack.

Such an attack could be sparked off by the bravest men bursting out of the line, bringing less brave men along in their wake. The attack would consist of a relatively small number of men in a group or a number of groups, who would advance from the safety of their line with a shout, cross the safety distance and begin a short flurry of hand-to-hand combat with swords, against a small section of the enemy line. The side which came out worse in this attack would step back to reinstate the safety distance. There would again be a further stand-off period, in which energy levels could once more build up, more missiles could be thrown and the wounded could be passed back through the line until another attack was made. Assuming that these small scale attacks were occurring along the whole line, and the loser kept pulling back to reinstate the safety distance, the battle-lines could shift forward and back over hundreds of yards. The stand-off punctuated with small-scale attacks would continue, with relatively few casualties, until one side's nerve gave up and the ranks began to break up. This description of a generic heavy infantry battle, based on Sabin's dynamic stand-off model satisfies the archaeological and theoretical parameters of mid-Republican battle addressed in chapter 1 and also corresponds well to Livy's use of the term *impetus*.

But this is not always the end of a Roman infantry battle. In the following chapter it will be proposed that Livy's formula for describing battle has two distinct phases, the initial, or *impetus* phase, followed by the secondary phase described with the term *inferre* [*signa*], which leads to a rout of the enemy. The purpose of the *impetus* phase was primarily to intimidate the enemy into flight, if this failed a series of small-scale attacks were aimed at the enemy line disrupting it enough to allow for the secondary phase of Roman combat. This secondary phase is not predicted by the dynamic stand-off model, but rather derives directly from analysis of Livy's battle descriptions. The following chapter will examine his use of the term *inferre* and determine the type of combat involved in this secondary phase.

### Chapter 6: Livy's use of the term *inferre* [*signa*]

The term *inferre* is the second most frequently used in Livy's combat vocabulary, occurring two hundred and eighty-two times within the extant books. The analysis of the *OLD* suggests a wide variety of meanings and this again is reflected in Livy's usage. It is often employed as a generic term with words like *bellum* to mean waging war.[446] Other uses include the carrying of objects forward, inspiring emotions such as fear, inflicting wounds or casualties, as well as a range of less common usages.[447] The most common sense of the term is to carry something forward with hostile intent. In a military context the term is often used in conjunction with *signa* to denote an infantry attack.[448] The selective examples provided by the *TLL* of Livy's use of *inferre* highlight this military sense, but are too limited to be able to differentiate properly his range of uses.[449] In this chapter Livy's various uses of *inferre* [*signa*] will be examined in an attempt to demonstrate the form of attack envisaged when he employed the term.

For this study the most important use of *inferre* [*signa*] is as a description of an infantry attack. As far as it can be used to describe a specific military manoeuvre, it tends to involve the heavy infantry, with none of the incidences describing light infantry alone and only five for cavalry.[450] To discover the form of combat Livy tried to express with this term it is useful to look first at part of his description of one of the most famous battles in Roman history, Cannae:

> "At first they were evenly matched in strength and courage, as long as the Gauls and Spaniards maintained their rank; but at last the Romans, after prolonged and frequent efforts, pushing forward with an even front and a dense line, beat back the wedge-like formation which projected from the enemy line, for it was too thin to be strong; and then, as the Gauls and the Spaniards gave way and fell back in confusion, pressed forward and without once stopping forced their way through the crowd of fleeing, panic-stricken foes" (Foster, 1929, with minor alterations).[451]

In this passage both lines fight, evenly matched, for an unspecified period of time. This Roman combat is described as *diu ac saepe conisi*.[452] Livy may have used *conitor* here rather than, as we might expect, *impetum facere*, to express the unusually dense formation the Romans were forced to adopt at Cannae owing to their very large numbers.[453] Though *conitor* perhaps suggests a continuous effort or force, Livy's use of *saepe* implies that this period of fighting involved a series of attacks. These attacks were more likely to have been the localised flurries Livy usually associates with infantry fighting, as argued in the previous chapter, than a massed and coordinated advance of the whole line, which would be very difficult to pull back and reform before advancing a second time. Although Livy does not specifically use the term *impetus* to describe this period of combat, it still resembles the initial or '*impetus*' phase of Roman infantry combat, through which the Romans would attempt to break-up the enemy's line. Livy isolates this phrase from the rest of the sentence by using the perfect participle of *conitor* prior to the main verb. This gives the sense that the 'prolonged and frequent' attacks were a separate phase of combat distinct from, and leading to, the attack that followed.[454] After the Romans had forced the Gauls and Spaniards back with a series of attacks, they then move into a secondary phase of assault. This is described as an advance with an even front and dense line (*aequa fronte acieque densa*). It is this assault that drove back the thin enemy line, pressing forward through the disordered enemy (*pauore fugientium agmen*) and finally causing a rout.

It has been proposed that when Livy used the term *impetus* in a military context he was describing a specific form of attack: a series of small-scale localised flurries of hand-to-hand combat. These attacks periodically erupting out from the relative safety of the crowd are very similar to those predicted by the dynamic stand-off model. In Sabin's model the stand-off would continue until one side's morale gave way and they turned in flight. This would lead directly to a rout in which the vast majority of the slaughter took place, due to the predominance of encirclement tactics and cavalry strength in this period. Livy's use of the term *impetus* within his battle narratives supports this theoretical model and in turn increases Livy's credibility as a military source. But Livy's literary vision of infantry combat goes further than the dynamic stand-off model. It will be proposed in this chapter that his vision of combat was in two phases, and that the second involved a separate and distinct form of combat, often described as *inferre* [*signa*]. The purpose of the first phase, or *impetus*-phase, was to intimidate the enemy into flight or failing that to physically disrupt their battle-line. On occasion this phase alone would be successful and

[446] *OLD* s.v. 9c. This sense of making war occurs 78 times, 28% of the total.

[447] Carry: 34 times, 12%, cf. *OLD* s.v. 1; fear: 21 times, 7%, cf. *OLD* s.v. 9b; wounds/casualties 22 times, 8 %.

[448] Attack: 75 times, 27% (60 times of the heavy infantry, 21%), cf. *OLD* s.v. 2a.

[449] *TLL* VII, 1.1377.53f; 1379.72; 1379.81ff.

[450] Cavalry: 3.5.7; 6.32.8; 9.27.10; 10.28.18; 28.33.6; with three further examples of cavalry fighting as infantry: 4.38.4, 4.39.2 and 7.8.3.

[451] 22.47.4-6: *Primo et viribus et animis par, dum constabant ordines Gallis Hispanisque; tandem Romani, diu ac saepe conisi, aequa fronte acieque densa impulere hostium cuneum nimis tenuem eoque parum validum, a cetera prominentum acie. Impulsis deinde ac trepide referentibus pedem institere ac tenore uno per praeceps pauore fugientium agmen in mediam primum inlati.*

[452] *Conisi* derives from the verb *conitor*, literally meaning 'to make a great physical effort'. Cf. *OLD* s.v. 1.

[453] Polybius (3.107 and 113) suggests 80,000 infantry troops. On this figure see Sabin (2007a) 184-5.

[454] In this phase of attack the Romans drive back (*impulere*) the *hostium cuneum*. In the previous chapter it was proposed that wedge formation generally consisted of several small wedges. Here, Livy's *hostium cuneum* is in the singular, describing one wedge. This denotes the peculiar crescent-shaped line of the Spanish at Cannae (cf. Pol. 3.113.8-9).

lead directly to a rout, as predicted by Sabin's model. But often in Livy's battle descriptions the *impetus*-phase only threw the enemy into disorder but was not enough to cause a rout. For Livy, if this initial phase failed to rout the enemy, a secondary phase would follow, consisting of a massed advance of the whole line against an enemy formation, which was broken and disordered by the initial combat. The two phase nature of the initial infantry combat at Cannae exemplifies this additional aspect of Livy's vision of Roman combat.

In the first part of this chapter it will be argued that heavy infantry advances described by Livy with the term *inferre* [*signa*] often take this secondary form of a massed attack against a disordered enemy. As with the other terms examined in this study, only few of the occurrences of the word offer insight into its specific meaning within a military context. Nevertheless, those incidences that do provide hints to Livy's intentions, through the specific use of the word within a phrase or the context in which it is found, generally conform to this hypothesis. In the remainder of the chapter, there will be an analysis of the conditions necessary for this form of massed advance to occur and, finally, an examination of some apparent anomalies.

### 1. *Inferre* as a massed infantry attack

The secondary phase of the Roman advance at Cannae is described as being performed *aequa fronte acieque densa*, suggesting an attack of the whole infantry line in massed formation. The *TLL* proposes that massed movement can be implied by the term and there are also specific attacks described Livy with *inferre* [*signa*] which suggest a massed infantry advance.[455] In 477 the Romans were surrounded by the Etruscans:

> "as the Etruscans drew together and the Romans were now fenced in by a continuous line of armed men, the harder the enemy pressed them the smaller was the space within which they themselves were forced to contract their circle" (Sage, 1919).[456]

Here the Romans are enclosed (*saepiri*) by a continuous line of armed soldiers (*continenti agmine armatorum*), and this massed formation, as a whole, was advancing (*inferebat*) against them. Here the term *inferre* does not describe a series of localised assaults, but a massed advance of the whole line.

The battle of Mutina in 193, against the Gauls, also highlights the two phase nature of Livy's battle descriptions. After the first legion had been defeated by the Gauls, a second legion was sent forward, the wounded troops were relieved and battle was renewed:

> "[The Gauls] in dense ranks, resting now on one another, now on their shields, they withstood the attacks of the Romans...
> [as the infantry attacks could not break the Gallic line, the cavalry are sent to attack]...
> ...this storm of horsemen at first threw the battle-line of the Gauls into confusion and disorder, then scattered it, but without causing a rout...
> [the Consul then] ordered the standard-bearers to advance. All joined in the effort and at last turned the enemy to flight" (Sage, 1935).[457]

There are two reasons to suppose that the Romans attacked initially with a series of assaults. The first, as was shown in the previous chapter, is that *impetus* is used in its plural form. The second is Livy's use of the imperfect form of *sustinere*, suggesting that the Gauls had repeatedly to withstand these *impetus*. This phase of the Roman attack did not break the enemy line, though perhaps the passage implies that such attacks would usually have been enough. Since the *impetus* phase of the attack was unsuccessful, the cavalry is sent in, eventually disrupting the enemy line. Following the cavalry attack, the standard bearers are ordered to advance, the whole line then joins the attack, finally causing a rout. This secondary phase of the infantry attack, described with *inferre...signa*, appears to have been a massed advance of the whole formation. Livy uses the plural of *vexillarius* and *signum*, implying that all the standard-bearers, or at least a number of them, advanced the standards and thus led a massed movement of the whole line. This is further supported by Livy's use of *omnis* in the plural, signifying that the advance involved all the infantry.

The fighting between the Romans and the Gauls in 196 again suggests that an attack described with the term *inferre* [*signa*] was a massed advance:

> "The Gauls, encouraged by the defiance of the Boii a few days before, engaged in battle while still in marching formation. They attacked so fiercely at first that they overthrew the Roman front line. When Marcellus observed this, fearing that once they had been broken they would be routed, he opposed them with a cohort of Marsi and sent in all the squadrons of Latin cavalry against the enemy. Their first and second attacks blunted the ferocious Gallic advance, and the rest of the Roman line, having been encouraged, at first resisted, then advanced their standards fiercely. The Gauls did not sustain the struggle any longer, but turned their backs and fled in various directions".[458]

---

[455] *TLL* VII.1.1381.15ff.

[456] 2.50.7: *Coeuntibusque Etruscis iam continenti agmine armatorum saepti, quo magis se hostis inferebat, cogebantur breviore spatio et ipsi orbem colligere.*

[457] 35.5.7-12: *Densis tamen ordinibus nunc alii in alios, nunc in scuta incumbents sustinebant impetus Romanorum...Haec procella equestris primo confudit et turbavit deinde dissipavit aciem Gallorum, non tamen ut terga darent...Inferre vexillarios iussit signa. Omnes conisi tandem averterunt hostem.*

[458] 33.36.9-12: *Galli, feroces Boiorum ante dies paucos pugna, in ipso itinere proelium committunt; et primo adeo acriter inuaserunt ut antesignanos impulerint. quod ubi Marcellus animaduertit, ueritus ne moti semel pellerentur, cohortem Marsorum cum opposuisset, equitum Latinorum omnes turmas in hostem emisit. quorum cum primus secundusque impetus rettudisset inferentem se ferociter hostem,*

In this passage the Gallic attack had caused the Roman line to break, allowing them to advance further. The Latin cavalry then made two attacks (*primus secundusque impetus*) that checked the Gallic advance and encouraged the Romans. The rest of the Roman line (*reliqua acies Romana*), the heavy infantry, were at first able to resist the enemy, then finally to advance as a massed formation (*signa acriter intulit*), which led to the Gallic flight. The massed nature of the attack is again reinforced by Livy's use of the plural of *signum*, suggesting an advance of the whole line, or at least a larger scale attack than those he tends to describe with *impetus*. When the term *inferre* is used in conjunction with *signa* it has the specific meaning of an advance of the standards in an attack, implying a massed movement.[459] The two words are frequently used together by Livy to describe infantry attacks, which imply some form of massed advances.[460]

These passages suggest, in a similar way to Livy's description of the fighting at Cannae, that heavy infantry battle could comprise two distinct forms of combat. The primary form being small-scale localised attacks, and the secondary, a massed advance of the whole infantry line, often described with *inferre* and frequently in conjunction with *signa*. This secondary phase of infantry battle is not explained by the dynamic stand-off model. The consistency of Livy's initial phase combat with the attacks predicted by the dynamic stand-off model demonstrates that his narratives offer a credible representation of mid-Republican infantry combat, fulfilling both the archaeological and theoretical parameters of mid-Republican infantry battle. In the next chapter it will also be argued that a similar two-phase depiction of Roman battle can be identified in Polybius' battle narratives. For these reasons Livy's descriptions of a secondary phase of infantry combat should not be discarded as not fitting the dynamic stand-off model, but rather the model should instead be adapted to incorporate this secondary combat-phase.

**2. Livy's pre-requisites for a massed infantry advance**

It has been proposed that, for archaeological, theoretical and psychological reasons, an initial massed infantry charge would have been unlikely, if not impossible. But Livy appears to depict a massed infantry advance when he uses the term *inferre* [*signa*]. Although this secondary phase is not a 'charge', since the term has no speed connotation, the attack is still a massed advance of the whole line. Such an advance was dismissed as the primary method of infantry combat for two main reasons. The first was the mechanical difficulty of coordinating a series of attacks in a massed formation. It would be difficult for an entire line to disengage the enemy as one unit, pull back while maintaining formation and regroup, before making the second of many attacks during a battle lasting hours.

The second reason for dismissing a massed movement was the psychological difficulty of getting a battle-line to attack in unison at all. While advancing on the enemy, the line would naturally lose some of its cohesion as the morale of individuals and small groups would differ within the formation. The men with the highest morale, at that moment the bravest, would move to the front, while those with lowest morale would naturally hang back as far as they could. Each man's morale within the line would fit somewhere along this spectrum. The resultant attack, which to be effective would need to be united, would end up at best as a multitude of weak assaults and at worst, chaos, from which there could be no recall of the line. In order for a massed advance to be effective, it would need to occur at a time when the majority of the men had similarly high morale and at a point in the battle where the one attack would be both devastating and decisive. These two pre-requisites can be observed in Livy's descriptions of his secondary phase of combat.

Livy's depiction of a Volscian attack against the Romans offers insight into the conditions needed for such a massed advance of the whole line.

> "The battle-cries were the first intimation how the affair was likely to go, for the enemy's was louder and fuller, that of the Romans dissonant and uneven and, dragging more with each repetition, betrayed the faintness of their hearts. This caused the enemy to attack the more boldly, thrusting with shields and making play with swords. On the Roman side helmets nodded, as their wearers looked this way and that for help, and irresolute soldiers made falteringly for the nearest group; at one moment the standards would be left behind by the retreat of the front-rankers, at the next they would be falling back among their proper maniples. **It was not yet a definite flight, not yet a victory**; the Romans sought rather to protect themselves than to fight; the Volscians **advanced [their standards]** and bore hard against the Roman line, but saw more of their enemies killed than running away." (Foster, 1922).[461]

This passage reinforces the picture presented so far of Livy's vision of Roman combat. In the initial stand-off battle-cries are raised by both sides. The Romans' cry was inferior and betrayed their fear, while the Volscian cheer was louder and fuller. This psychological

*confirmata et* ***reliqua acies*** *Romana restitit primo, deinde* ***signa acriter intulit****; nec ultra sustinuere certamen Galli quin terga uerterent atque effuse fugerent.*

[459] *OLD* s.v. 2a.

[460] *Signa inferre*: 3.60.8, 3.60.9, 3.62.8, 3.70.10, 4.18.5, 4.37.11, 4.47.2, 8.30.7, 9.32.6, 10.5.9, 10.29.9, 10.36.10, 22.29.6, 26.5.15, 26.6.1, 27.14.11, 27.42.10, 28.15.10, 28.22.15, 30.18.2, 30.30.17, 35.5.12, 37.42.4, 39.31.9, 41.4.1.

[461] 4.37. 9-11: *Clamor indicium primum fuit quo res inclinatura esset, excitatior crebriorque ab hoste sublatus: ab Romanis dissonus, impar, segnius saepe iteratus prodidit pavorem animorum. Eo ferocior inlatus hostis urgere scutis, micare gladiis. Altera ex parte nutant circumspectantibus galeae, et incerti trepidant applicantque se turbae; signa nunc resistentia deseruntur ab antesignanis, nunc inter suos manipulos recipiuntur.* ***Nondum fuga certa, nondum victoria erat****; tegi magis Romanus quam pugnare; Volscus* ***inferre signa****, urgere aciem plus caedis hostium videre quam fugae.*

advantage allowed the Volscians to attack more boldly, punching the enemy with their shield-bosses and cutting them down with their swords. The purpose of this initial phase of combat was to disrupt the enemy line and gain a psychological advantage. In this battle, the Volsci had gained this advantage immediately, and so were able to attack straight away with a massed advance of the line. On the other side, the Romans, having lost the psychological advantage, immediately fell into disorder, which Livy recounts in detail. He describes the Volscian attack with the phrase *inferre signa*, expressing the massed nature of the advance. The Volsci were able to advance immediately in massed formation precisely because the Romans were in disorder and they had already gained a psychological advantage during the initial period of stand-off. Livy is often interested in describing the psychology of troops. It is generally held that he did this to add interest to his rather repetitive battle descriptions, but it may also be due to his awareness of the importance this factor played on the battlefield.

In nearly half of the heavy infantry attacks described with *inferre [signa]* Livy specifically notes that it was aimed against a formation in some form of disorder or confusion. It seems that in Livy's mind a massed infantry advance would only have been possible against an enemy whose line had been disrupted, a condition satisfying both the pre-requisites advanced above. Examples of this include: Cincinnatus' speech to Sempronius in 380, that '[he] will attack them [the Latins] when they are in disorder and confusion'.[462] In 325, the Roman infantry advanced in massed formation against the Samnites, who had fallen into disorder after a cavalry attack; [463] again, in 322, after the Samnite standards had become disordered and their line began to waver, the Romans, with a fresh cheer, advanced their ranks.[464] In 209, when the Carthaginian elephants had thrown their own infantry line into confusion, the Roman infantry advanced their standards and, with no great struggle, made the scattered and wavering enemy line retreat.[465] In 190 Antiochus' whole left flank had wavered and the panic spread to the phalanx, as soon as the ranks were thrown into disorder the Romans advanced.[466] There are many other examples of massed attacks, described by Livy with the term *inferre [signa]*, against enemy formations in general disorder, fleeing, not in proper formation or showing so much fear that the opponent gained a psychological advantage.[467] The weight of this evidence suggests that for Livy a massed advance of the infantry was only possible when the enemy were in some form of disorder. It is likely then that where Livy uses the term *inferre* [signa] to describe an infantry attack, even when not specifically mentioned, some state of disorder was implied.

The implications of the argument advanced so far in this chapter are that an attack described with the term *inferre [signa]* was a massed advance and that such an advance was only possible against a disordered or broken enemy. Previously in this study it has been proposed that psychological factors affected the ability of soldiers to attack with more ferocity than normal. In a dynamic stand-off, the default rest state allowed the men to build up their nervous energy and when this peaked an attack would be launched. While the enemy was in a cohesive formation, which is strong against frontal attack, the majority of soldiers would naturally remain reluctant to attack, explaining the default rest state. Sabin suggests that natural leaders within the units of the line would slowly stir up the nervous energy of their neighbouring troops until this pocket of men exploded into an attack. After this energy was dissipated the two sides once again step back to re-impose the safety distance.[468] In the third chapter it was proposed that soldiers would be more willing to attack an enemy formation on the flank or rear as this form of attack offered the aggressors a psychological and physical advantage. The unusual speed and ferocity of this form of attack is highlighted by Livy with his use of terms such as *incurrere* and *procurrere*. When making a frontal attack on an enemy formation in disorder and confusion, the psychological advantage for the aggressors would be even greater. The visual and aural indications of the disorder and fear of the enemy would be apparent to all the members of the attacking line, especially those experienced in battle. Each man would sense victory. At this point their natural fear and nervous energy would change to something more like a 'blood lust'.[469] Owing to the indications of the enemy's confusion, perhaps seeing them turn their backs or dropping the standards, or hearing cries of fear and pain, the aggressors would be willing to cast aside their natural tendency for caution and to attack with far more aggression than normal. For the first time in the battle, the majority of the men would simultaneously have a will to fight, and it is because of this change that a massed infantry advance would be possible. Such an advance could occur naturally as the more successful side begins to sense victory or, alternatively, it could be created by commanders ordering an advance of the standards at a key point in the battle. During regular combat the casualty rates of both sides would appear to have been

[462] 6.29.2: *Ego cum legionibus in turbatos trepidantesque **inferam signa**.*
[463] 8.30.7: *turbatis hostibus intulit signa.* C.f 4.47.2: *Itaque primo statim proelio cum dictator equitatu immisso antesignanos hostium turbasset, legionum inde **signa inferri** propere iussit.*
[464] 8.39.5: *turbataque signa et fluctuantem aciem... novato clamore **signa inferuntur**.*
[465] 27.14.11: *In perturbatam transcursu beluarum aciem **signa inferunt** Romani pedites et haud magno certamine dissupatos trepidantesque avertunt.*
[466] 37.42.4: *Ibi simul perturbati ordines et impeditus intercursu suorum usus prealongarum hastarum - sarisas Macedones vocant - **intulere signa** Romanae legiones et pila in perturbatos.*
[467] General disorder: 9.27.12: *victorem hostem signa in perculsos inferentem*; 10.33.4; 30.34.3: *velut nullo resistente incessere*; 33.36.12. Fleeing: 7.24.6, 10.5.9, 23.29.9 and 28.15.10. Not in formation: 3.60.9 and 10.36.10 : *suis paucos et ordinibus inconpositis effuse venire hostes.* Fear: 2.30.13: *velut stupentibus metu intulissent Romanis;* 3.18.8: *Trepidantibus inferunt signa Romani sociique*; 4.37.10; 9.40.13: *ad terrorem hostium legions Romanae redintegrato clamore intulissent gradum.*
[468] Sabin (1996) 72-3 and (2000) 14-15.
[469] On the psychology of killing in battle see Marshall (1947); Holmes (2003 [1985]) 176-203; and Grossman (1998).

mutually low. The disproportionate final casualty figures suggest that it was in this final stage, when the enemy formation had been broken and the whole offensive line had a will to fight, that the enemy sustained its heaviest casualties.[470]

Livy's combat vocabulary reflects the different forms of attack he believed made up infantry combat. The term *impetus* seems to describe the 'normal' form of infantry fighting, periodic small-scale localised attacks. Terms like *incurrere* are used to describe unusually vigorous or fast attacks, though often in form the same as *impetus*. The reason for the unusual nature of these attacks frequently appears to have been external influences on the psychological state of the soldiers. The third form of attack, described with the term *inferre* [*signa*] is distinct from the previous two involving as it does a massed infantry advance. The frequent references to disruption and disorder within the enemy ranks before such an advance highlight the unusual nature of this form of attack. It differs from the 'normal' mode of infantry combat, which could be used at any point within a battle, in that it can only be performed under specific circumstances.

### 3. Exceptions

Now that the general trend in Livy's use of the term *inferre* [*signa*] has been examined, it is necessary to analyse the few passages that at first sight do not appear to fit this interpretation. On four occasions the term *inferre* appears to describe the initial attack of a battle, each performed by non-Roman infantry.[471] Given the proposal that the term *inferre* [*signa*] is used to describe a massed infantry advance on a disrupted enemy, it is possible that Livy used the term in these cases to signify a different style of combat than one normally encompassed by his vision of infantry battle; more like the attack of a phalanx than of a legion. On the other hand, it is possible that Livy imagined, though did not state explicitly, that the aggressors in these four cases had somehow gained a psychological advantage which allowed for a massed advance, similar to the Volscian attack at 4.37.9-11, discussed above.

In two further cases, the Romans appear to make an initial advance described with *inferre signa*. At 4.18.5 the Roman dictator advanced on the right, against the Faliscans, and Q. Capitolinus on the left, to meet the Veientes.[472] At first glance, this appears to be a Roman massed attack at the beginning of a battle; but, Livy proceeds: "for a brief moment all was hushed and still, since the Etruscans were resolved not to begin fighting unless they were forced" (Foster, 1922).[473] Here, the phrase *inferre signa* does not describe an initial massed attack but rather an advance towards the enemy to gain position. Livy uses the connotations of massed movement implied in the phrase to signify the massed advance of the line towards the enemy. The actual Roman infantry attack is described later at 4.13.8 with the term *impetus*, as we might expect.[474]

The second case does seem to depict a Roman force making an initial attack described by the term *inferre* [*signa*]. In 315:

> The dictator makes a speech to rouse his soldiers' spirits. "[His] words, pointing to the dire necessity to which they were reduced, produced intense excitement, and rendered desperate by the sight of the burning camp - although the dictator had only ordered some spots nearest to them to be set on fire - they attacked like madmen, and at the first onset threw the enemy into confusion".[475]

This passage suggests that the first attack was a massed advance of the infantry, implied by the use of *inferre signa*. The same attack is also described with the term *impetus*. It seems Livy is using *impetus* in an abstract form, meaning assault in general rather than a more specific form of attack, while *inferre signa* reveals the nature of the advance.[476] Before the battle the dictator had employed a ruse: he burnt the Roman tents, allowing his men to believe that this had been done by the enemy. This ruse and the Dictator's speech fired up the Roman troops and Livy states that they 'attacked like madmen' (*velut vecordes*). Livy appears to have used *inferre signa* to underline the mental state of the Romans and highlight the unusual nature of the initial attack caused by this. The aggravation fuelled by the ruse stirred the Romans so much they were able to overcome their natural reluctance for attacking an organised enemy, advancing like madmen, everyone with a similar will to fight. It is Livy's departure form his general use of the phrase *inferre signa*, as an attack normally on a defeated enemy, which makes this passage so explicit, highlighting the madness of the men.

There is one final difficult passage which at first seems not to correspond to the proposed understanding of the terms *impetus* and *inferre*:

> "After the dictator had attacked with his cavalry and had thrown the enemy's front ranks into confusion, he ordered the legions to advance rapidly and when one

[470] An example of how a rout was more slaughter than fighting can be seen in Livy's description at 22.48.1-6.

[471] Etruscans (2.14.6; 9.32.6), the Tartesii (23.27.6) and the Volsci (6.12.9).

[472] 4.18.5: *Dictator dextro cornu adversus Faliscos, sinistro contra Veientem Capitolinus Quinctius intulit signa.*

[473] 4.18.6: *Parumper silentium et quies fuit, nec Etruscis nisi cogerentur pugnam inituris.*

[474] 4.18.8: *Nulla parte legiones Etruscae sustinuere impetum Romanorum.*

[475] 9.23.15: *et oratione dictatoris, quae necessitatis ultimae index erat, milites accensi uadunt in hostem, et respectus ipse ardentium castrorum, quamquam proximis tantum—ita enim iusserat dictator—ignis est subditus, haud paruum fuit inritamentum. Itaque uelut uecordes inlati signa primo impetu hostium turbant.*

[476] A similar example of *inferre* and *impetus* used in this way can be seen at 4.38.4.

of the standard bearers hesitated, he cut him down. The ardour for battle was so much that the Aequi could not withstand the attack, and when, defeated in the field, they had withdrawn to their camp in disordered flight [the camp was then stormed]".[477]

Here, Livy seems to use both *impetus* and *inferre* to describe the same attack, but there are two plausible explanations for this apparent discrepancy. The first, in a similar way to the previous passage, is that Livy used the term *inferre* to illustrate the unusually vigorous nature of the attack also described with *impetus*. Certainly the attack is unusual; a standard-bearer is killed by his own general and the infantry attack with uncommon vigour (*tantus ardor ad dimicandum fuit*). Although not stated specifically, there appears, by the very mention of the standard-bearer's death, to be an implied link between these two events: that it was due to this death that the ardour for battle was so great. Alternatively, the killing of the standard-bearer acts as a break in the narrative and perhaps expresses two different forms of attack. The original attack ordered by the dictator was *intended* to be a massed advance of the standards, described with *inferre signa*, while the *actual* attack was only made by a few small groups, described as *impetus*.

Frontinus offers some support for this explanation. The killing of the standard-bearer in Livy's work appears to be a rather insignificant event which he glosses over with one line. In Frontinus, who also records this incident, or at least a suspiciously similar one,[478] the same event is very much more serious:

> "The dictator Servilius Priscus, having given the command to carry the standards of the legions against the hostile Faliscans, ordered the standard-bearer to be executed for hesitating to obey. The rest, cowed by this example, advanced against the foe" (Bennett, 1925).[479]

Frontinus implies that the standard-bearer's hesitation caused the whole line to halt and only after the execution was the line inspired to attack. Another reading of the passage may suggest that the whole battle-line was unwilling to carry out the order to advance in massed formation and that the dictator used the standard-bearer as a scapegoat to quell the rebellion and force the soldiers to attack. The similarity of the two passages suggests that they were derived from the same source or at least a similar tradition. Although it is possible that Frontinus took the story from Livy and elaborated upon it, his claim that the attack was against the Faliscans rather than the Aequi makes this less likely. If, then, the two stories are derived from the same source, it is possible that the original source was closer to Frontinus' account, in which the order is not carried out, the line does not advance, the standard-bearer is killed and only then is an attack made. If this were the case, it is plausible that Livy's source used two different terms to describe the two different forms of attack, the one ordered and the one actually carried out, as does Frontinus. Livy's account and his use of two different attack terms may reflect his source, while for some reason he chose to gloss over the serious nature of the disobeyed order and subsequent execution. Such a contraction of the events in the story may explain the confusion and suggests that *inferre* and *impetus* denote two distinct attacks, the one potential, but not performed, and one actual attack.

## 4. Conclusion

This analysis of Livy's use of the term *inferre* [*signa*] suggests that it in a military context it was used mainly to denote a massed advance of the infantry against a broken or disordered enemy battle-line. Livy's vision of Roman infantry battle involved two combat phases. The primary phase, often described with *impetus*, was the regular form of infantry combat, involving a series of small-scale localised flurries of hand-to-hand combat with swords. The purpose of this phase was fundamentally to intimidate the enemy into flight, but if unsuccessful it could continue, interspersed with rest periods, until the enemy line was thrown into disorder. Only after this disruption had been achieved was it possible for the second (*inferre* [*signa*]) phase of the attack to be launched. This involved a massed advance of the whole line against the disordered enemy and led to the rout. On occasion the *impetus* phase could not disrupt the enemy line sufficiently to allow for a massed advance. In these cases another arm, such as the cavalry, was sent against the enemy infantry for the purpose. This two phase pattern can often be seen in Livy's battle narratives and it constitutes Livy's literary vision of Roman infantry battle.[480] Now that it has been elucidated it will be useful in the next two chapters to compare Livy's vision of combat with the Greek and Latin traditions of battle narration, represented by the works of Polybius and Caesar.

---

[477] 4.47.2-3: *Itaque primo statim proelio cum dictator equitatu immisso antesignanos hostium turbasset, legionum inde signa inferri propere iussit signiferumque ex suis unum cunctantem occidit. Tantus ardor ad dimicandum fuit ut impetum Aequi non tulerint; victique acie cum fuga effusa petissent castra.*

[478] He claims that it occurred against the Faliscans rather than the Aequi.

[479] *Strat.* 2.8.8: *Servilius Priscus dictator, cum signa legionum ferri in hostis Faliscos iussisset, signiferum cunctantem occidi imperavit; quo exemplo perterriti hostem invaserunt.*

[480] *Impetus* of heavy infantry to disrupt the enemy line, followed by an attack described with the term *inferre*: 22.47.6, 25.5.17-6.1, 28.15.7-10, 30.34.3-6 (both discussed further in following chapter), 33.36.9-12, 35.5.7-12, etc. Cavalry attack to disrupt, followed by *inferre*: 4.33.11: *dictator exclamat Quinctium legatum et suos ab tergo hostem adortos; ipse redintegrato clamore infert acrius signa.* Cf. 8.30.7, 9.40.13, 10.29.9, 33.36.12 and 35.5.7-12.

## Chapter 7: Polybian parallels to Livy's use of *impetus* and *inferre*

So far in this study it has been proposed that where Livy used the terms *impetus* and *inferre* to describe heavy infantry combat, he envisaged specific types of attack: a series of small scale flurries of hand-to-hand fighting against specific points along the enemy line, followed by a large scale massed advanced of the infantry against a disordered enemy formation. It has already been demonstrated that Livy relied heavily on Polybius' *Histories* as a source for the third and fourth decade of his own narrative. In addition, from the analysis of Polybius' account of Cynoscephalae in chapter 2, two hypotheses were developed concerning Polybius' literary vision of Roman battle and Livy's use of the Greek historian as a main source.

The first is that Polybius' battle narratives are part of a Greek rhetorical tradition which used metaphors of weight and pushing to describe battle. This proposition was based on Lendon's claim that each culture possesses an inherited rhetoric of combat used to describe the experience of battle. The Greek combat vocabulary was drawn from their experience of classical phalanx fighting, and perhaps ultimately derived from Homer. This inherited literary practice caused the Greeks to conceive combat between sets of troops in terms of weight and pushing. This general premise needs qualifying. Polybius seems to have been aware that the Roman fighting style differed from the Greek style and at times reflects this in his combat descriptions. Polybius is certainly part of this Greek rhetorical tradition, but he is not necessarily trapped in it.

The second hypothesis is that Livy was influenced by Polybius, and relied on him as his main source for the details of many mid-Republican battles. But while Polybius' literary vision of battle fluctuates, Livy's remains consistent. Where Polybius describes combat with pushing metaphors, Livy tends to impose his own literary vision upon his source, causing stylistic differences between their accounts. Conversely, where Polybius detaches himself from his usual metaphors and attempts to offer a realistic image of Roman infantry combat the two authors' battle descriptions correspond closely.

To investigate the plausibility of these two propositions the combat descriptions of the both authors will be evaluated. Rather than examining all of the battle accounts in both authors, the study will focus on occurrences of *impetus* and *inferre* in Livy's battle narratives where there are parallel accounts in Polybius.

There are nineteen battles for which parallel narratives survive from both Polybius and Livy, including some of the major engagements within the mid-Republican period (c.295 – 146 BC).[481] Many of these battles are treated only briefly by these two writers, leaving a rather limited amount of data from which to draw a comparison between their respective visions of infantry combat: Livy makes use of the term *impetus* nineteen times and *inferre* seven times in these nineteen battle narratives. In nine out of the nineteen Livian battle narratives neither of the terms appears. Five of these nine comprise the shortest accounts in the sample and their brevity and superficiality makes the absence of specific combat terms unsurprising.[482] On eight further occasions there is no direct parallel between Livy's use of this combat vocabulary and Polybius' narratives.[483] Although the occurrences of these words remain a relatively small data set, a study of eighteen direct parallels within fourteen or even nineteen battles remains significant and produces interesting results.

### 1. Polybius' physical metaphors and the imposition of Livy's literary vision

In order to determine the validity of these hypotheses, it is necessary first to examine the passages in which Livy chose to impose his own combat rhetoric on to attacks that Polybius originally expressed using pushing metaphors.

In his account of the battle of Ilipa in 206 Livy uses the term *impetus* on two occasions for which there is parallel vocabulary in Polybius. At 28.13.9, in a skirmish days before the battle, part of the Carthaginian cavalry were put to flight by the Roman cavalry, the rest fought hard until they finally turned about face and retreated from the Roman infantry, but without breaking ranks. The Romans fell more fiercely on their rear and the attack could not be withstood, so the Carthaginians scattered and were routed.[484] In Polybius' account it is the Roman horse who dismount (11.21.4: καταβαινόντων ἐν τοῖς Ῥωμαϊκοῖς ἱππεῦσιν) and force back the Carthaginians. "At first they retired in good order, but when the Romans pressed them hard, the squadrons broke up and they took refuge under their own camp" (Paton, 1976).[485] Here, where Livy uses *impetus*, Polybius employs ἔγκειμαι,

[481] Camerinum 295 (L. 10.26 (7-11), P. 2.19(5)), Sentinum 295 (L. 10.26 (14) – 29, P. 2.19 (6)), R. Rhodanus 218 (L. 21.26 (3-5) and 27-29, P. 3.42-45), Trebia 218 (L. 21.54 -56, P. 3.71-74), Cissis 218 (L. 21.60 (5-9), P. 3.76 (5-6)), Iberus 217 (L.22. 19-20 (1-3), P. 3.95-96 (6)), L. Trasimenus 217 (L. 22.4-7 (1-5), P. 3.83-85), Callicula 217 (L. 22.15-18 (4), P. 3.92-94 (6)), Gerunium 216 (L. 22.28-29, P. 3.104-5), Cannae 216 (L. 22.43(10) – 49, P. 3.110-117), New Carthage 209 (L.26.44(1-4), P.10.12), Baecula 208 (L.27.18, P. 10.38(6)), R. Metaurus 207 (L. 27.43-49, P. 11.1-3 (fragment)), Ilipa 206 (L. 28.12 (13) – 15, P. 11. 20-24), Utica 203 (L. 30.3(8) – 6, P. 14.4-5), Great Plains 203 (L. 30.8, P. 14.7(9) – 8), Zama 202 (L. 30.32-35, P. 15.9-14), Cynoscephalae 197 (L. 33.6-10, P. 18.19-26), and Ancyra 189 (L. 38.25, P. 21.39).

[482] These five short battle narratives are: Camerinum, Sentinum, Cissis, Iberus, and New Carthage.

[483] *Impetus*: 28.15.5, 28.15.11, 30.4.12, 30.35.6, 38.25.11, 38.25.15. *Inferre*: 22.28.12, 22.5.6.

[484] ...*terga haud dubie vertunt Poeni Numidaeque. Et primo turmatin abibant, nihil propter pavorem festinationemve confuses ordinibus; dein, postquam acrius ultimis incidebat Romanus neque sustineri impetus poterat.*

[485] 11.21.5: Καὶ τὸ μὲν πρῶτον ἐν τάξει τὴν ἀναχώρησιν ἐποιοῦντο, τῶν δὲ Ῥωμαίων ἐγκειμένων αὐτοῖς λύσαντες τὰς ἴλας κατέφυψον ὑπὸ τὴν αὐτῶν παρεμβολήν.

meaning "press hard, especially of troops *pressing upon* a defeated or retreating enemy".[486] Here Polybius uses a metaphor of pushing to describe an attack unlikely to have actually involved shoving at all. The Roman cavalrymen were armed with a round, or slightly oval, θυρεὸν (shield), a lance and a sword which was longer than the infantry *gladius*.[487] Unlike the infantry *scutum*, the round cavalry shield may have allowed the Roman horsemen to 'push' against the enemy when fighting on foot. But, in order to use their long swords effectively, they would have had to fight in an open formation, limiting their capacity for a massed drive forward. This form of combat is particularly unrealistic in this situation as it would involve men on foot pushing against retiring mounted cavalry. When Livy describes the same attack, using Polybius as his source, he decided to use the term *impetus*, instead of a similar metaphor in Latin, to represent the type of combat used by, in his case, the infantry. It has already been demonstrated from the archaeological evidence that the Romans were unlikely to have used their shields to push forward in massed formation. Polybius' metaphor does not reflect the reality of Roman combat and is misleading. On this occasion Livy can be seen to have corrected Polybius' account by using the more specific, and realistic, term *impetus*.

Livy's description at 28.15.7 involves combat between infantry on both sides. The Carthaginian line was retreating intact, 'but when the victors, on seeing that the tide of battle had turned, for that reason attacked with more spirit everywhere along the line, and this attack could not easily be sustained', this soon led to a general rout.[488] This *impetus* is a phase of attack against an ordered, though retreating, enemy. Here *undique inveherent* has been taken to mean that they attacked 'everywhere along the line', rather than 'from all sides'. This is justified because Livy tends to use *impetus* to describe localised attacks and because, in this particular passage, "from all sides" does not fit the context of the battle, in which the Carthaginian line is formed opposite rather than surrounded by the Roman forces. This fits better with the passage, implying many attacks against multiple points along the enemy line, in accord with Livy's usual meaning of *impetus*. Polybius describes this attack as follows: "At first Hasdrubal's men, yielding to the pressure, retired step by step..." (Paton, 1976).[489] Polybius' account is blander than Livy's and implies a constant pushing force forward, rather than the localised attacks apparently described by Livy.

In both of these passages, Livy employs *impetus* where Polybius had used a term such as ἔγκειμαι or πιέζω. Polybius describes these two attacks using a pushing metaphor, which one would not expect to describe the relatively open formation of a Roman infantry attack and certainly not the attack of dismounted horsemen against mounted Carthaginian cavalry. In both cases Livy does not offer a verbal 'translation' of ἔγκειμαι and πιέζω, but rather uses the term *impetus* to represent the nature of the attack. Livy's use of *impetus*, rather than a Latin equivalent of the pushing metaphor such as *urgere*, makes sense, as in neither case were the Roman troops literally 'pushing' the Carthaginians back. At 28.13.9 where the Roman infantry attack the rear of retreating cavalry squadrons, it is difficult to imagine foot-soldiers literally pressing upon retreating horse. At this point in Polybius' account ἔγκειμαι should be understood figuratively. Further, in the second passage of Livy, at 28.15.7, the Romans begin unspecified form of attack. When the troops realised this initial attack had caused the Carthaginians to make an ordered retreat, they began attacking more fiercely (*acrius*) everywhere along the line, and this *impetus* caused the enemy to become disordered and break up. Finally, after the Carthaginian line had been disrupted, the Romans carried out a massed attack, leading to a rout. The final phase, leading to the rout, is described by Livy with the phrase *inferre signa*, which, as argued in the previous chapter, took the form of a massed advance of the standards. The initial attack then, leading to the original disruption of the enemy line, was not a massed advance, but more likely to have been a series of small-scale attacks. Livy makes a distinction between the two phases of attack and chose to use *impetus* to describe this phase of the attack, rather than merely translating Polybius' metaphor. Here again he is imposing his own method of describing combat on his source.

Their descriptions of Cynoscephalae also highlight that Polybius' use of metaphors of 'pushing' and 'weight', while Livy remains consistent with his use of *impetus*. In Livy's account, at 33.8.6, there is a skirmish between the Roman and Macedonian light infantry. After initial difficulties, Flamininus brought up his left wing to help - encouraged by the arrival of the army and their general, 'they renewed the battle, attacked and turned back the enemy'.[490] This passage reveals the ebb and flow of battle, similar to a dynamic stand-off, where one side could receive the worst from the initial skirmishes, forcing them to retreat. Then, with either physical or psychological encouragement, they are able to rally, attack, and cause the enemy to retreat. Polybius describes the same attack: "the advanced force of the Romans thus supported by the infantry of the Legions now turned and fell upon their foes" (Paton, 1960).[491] Again, the term used by Polybius is ἔγκειμαι, which could be translated as "press hard", rather than "fall upon" as in Paton's translation.[492] There is no mention of the enemy retreating, unless the use of

[486] LSJ s.v. II.

[487] Goldsworthy (2000) 45, suggests that the cavalrymen used swords with blades longer than 50.5 cm.

[488] *Sed cum eo ipso acrius, ubi inclinatam sensere rem, victores se undique inveherent, nec facile impetus sustineri posset*

[489] 11.24.7: τὰς μὲν οὖν ἀρχὰς οἱ περὶ τὸν Ἀσδρούβαν κατὰ πόδα πιεζούμενοι τὴν ἀναχώρησιν ἐποιοῦντο. For discussion of similar organised withdrawals see Walbank *ad loc.*

[490] *Qui adventu exercitus imperatorisque pugnam renovant impetuque facto rursus avertunt hostem.*

[491] 18.23.8: οἱ δὲ προκινδυνεύοντες τῶν Ῥωμαίων, προσλαβόντες τὴν τῶν πεζῶν στρατοπέδων ἐφεδρείαν, ἐκ μεταβολῆς ἐνέκειντο τοῖς ὑπεναντίοις.

[492] LSJ s.v.

ἔγκειμαι itself suggests that the attack caused the enemy to retreat. This may explain why Livy added *rursus avertunt hostem* to the *impetus*, which simply describes an attack and does not have the extra implication of causing a retreat. In this case, Polybius is again describing a Roman attack with a pushing metaphor. Such pushing metaphors appear throughout his description of this battle, such as in the later description of the same attack of the Roman left wing: "for when the heavy-armed Roman infantry had joined the light infantry, as I said, and gave them their support, they availed themselves of the additional help thus thrown into the scale, and *pressing heavily* on the enemy killed many of them" (Paton, 1960). [493] Whereas Livy has: 'the Macedonians who turned their backs were being cut down, and they had no chance of survival unless they received support'.[494] Here, the Macedonians are not being "pressed heavily", as in Polybius, but are being cut down with swords. One would expect a pushing metaphor to be used to describe Macedonian phalanx at Cynoscephalae,[495] but not the more open formation of the Roman legion. This passage again highlights the difference between the two historians: Polybius uses metaphors which do not reflect the mechanics of Roman infantry combat; while Livy, perhaps because of this, imposes his own literary vision of battle and more realistic combat vocabulary onto his Greek source.

This pattern continues in longer parallel passages where Livy describes attacks with the term *inferre*. Such as his description of the fighting at Cannae in 216:

> "At first they were evenly matched in strength and courage, as long as the Gauls and Spaniards maintained their rank; but at last the Romans, after prolonged and frequent efforts, pushing forward with an even front and a dense line, beat back the wedge-like formation which projected from the enemy line, for it was too thin to be strong; and then, as the Gauls and the Spaniards gave way and fell back in confusion, pressed forward and without once stopping forced their way through the crowd of fleeing, panic-stricken foes" (Foster, 1929, with minor alterations).[496]

This passage was examined in the previous chapter where it was used to highlight the two-phase nature of Livy's vision of infantry combat. Polybius' description of the same Roman advance at Cannae is similar to Livy's:

> "For a time the Spaniards and Celts kept their ranks and struggled bravely with the Romans, but soon, borne down by the weight of the legions, they gave way and fell back, breaking up the crescent. The Roman maniples, pursuing them furiously, easily penetrated the enemy's front, since the Celts were deployed in a thin line while they themselves had crowded up from the wings to the centre where the fighting was going on." (Paton, 1922).[497]

Here again the Roman advance is in two phases. At first, while the Celts and Gauls held their line, the two sides struggled with each other (διεμάχοντο), before the Romans broke up the enemy line; this corresponds to the first phase of combat. After the enemy had become disrupted, it was easy to advance through the line, because the Romans were densely packed together (πυκνόω). This passage highlights the two-phase nature of Roman infantry combat, and corresponds closely to our understanding of Livy's secondary phase of combat, a massed advance against disordered or fleeing troops.

The two descriptions of the initial combat phase differ slightly. In both accounts there is an unspecified period of time in which both sides are evenly matched and fight bravely. In Livy this phase involved a long period of frequent attacks causing the enemy to break their ranks and fall into disarray. In Polybius, while the two sides fought (διεμάχοντο), the Spaniards and Celts were pressed down by the weight of the legions (τῷ βάρει θλιβόμενοι), which disrupted their line. Both authors agree that there were two phases of fighting, that the first phase lasted for some time and led to the breakdown of the enemy formation, but they disagree on the mechanics of combat within this phase: Polybius appears to describe an *othismos*-style attack, with the Romans weighing down upon the enemy, whereas Livy seems to depict a series of localised attacks.

The accounts of the fighting at the battle of Ilipa reveal a similar divergence between the two authors. As we have seen above, at 28.15.7-10, Scipio attempted to drag out the day in order to tire the Carthaginians:

> "Weakened therefore in body and spirit the Carthaginians retreated, but keeping their formation, as if the line was giving way intact by order of the general. But when the victors, on seeing that the tide of the battle had turned, for that reason attacked with more spirit everywhere along the line, and this attack could not easily be sustained, although Hasdrubal

[493] 18.24.5: προσγενομένων γὰρ τοῖς τῶν Ῥωμαίων εὐζώνοις τῶν ἐν τοῖς βαρέσιν ὅπλοις ἀνδρῶν, καθάπερ ἀρτίως εἶπα, καὶ συνεργούντων κατὰ τὴν μάχην, προσλαβόντες οἷον εἰ σήκωμα τὴν τούτων χρείαν, βαρέως ἐπέκειντο τοῖς πολεμίοις καὶ πολλοὺς αὐτῶν ἔκτεινον.

[494] 33.8.8: *praeterquam quod caedebantur auersi nec nisi defenderentur seruari poterant.*,

[495] As we do in fact find, e.g. 18.25.2: the superior weight of the Macedonian formation (τῷ βάρει τῆς συντάξεως ὑπέρεχον).

[496] 22.47.4-6.

[497] 3.115.5-6: ἐπὶ βραχὺ μὲν οὖν τῶν Ἰβήρων καὶ τῶν Κελτῶν ἔμενον αἱ τάξεις καὶ διεμάχοντο τοῖς Ῥωμαίοις γενναίως· μετὰ δὲ ταῦτα τῷ βάρει θλιβόμενοι κλίνοντες ὑπεχώρουν εἰς τοὐπίσω, λύσαντες τὸν μηνίσκον. αἱ δὲ τῶν Ῥωμαίων σπεῖραι κατὰ τὴν ἐκθυμίαν ἑπόμεναι τούτοις διέκοψαν ῥᾳδίως τὴν τῶν ὑπεναντίων τάξιν, ἅτε δὴ τῶν μὲν Κελτῶν ἐπὶ λεπτὸν ἐκτεταγμένων, αὐτοὶ δὲ πεπυκνωκότες ἀπὸ τῶν κεράτων ἐπὶ τὰ μέσα καὶ τὸν κινδυνεύοντα τόπον. On the various discussions of this withdrawal see Walbank *ad loc.*

tried to hold his men back... Nevertheless, as fear overcame their respect for him and those nearest to the enemy were falling, at once they faced about and all took flight. At first the standard-bearers began to halt at the foot of the hills and to call the soldiers back into ranks, hesitating to encourage the Roman line up the hill. Then when the enemy saw that standards were being advanced quickly, they were driven panic-stricken into renewed flight to the camp."[498]

This passage, as with previous examples, corresponds closely with the proposed understanding of the terms *impetus* and *inferre*. The weaker force in body and spirit, the Carthaginians, begin to retreat *while maintaining their ranks*. Given the phrase *ubi inclinatam sensere rem*, we may assume that some sort of combat forced this withdrawal. This perhaps suggests a dynamic stand-off, which more easily allowed this form of ordered retreat.

While the Carthaginians withdraw, the Romans advance, presumably maintaining a safety distance. As the Romans began to realise that the advantage was shifting in their direction, they became more fierce (*acrius*) and began to attack everywhere along the line (*undique inveherent*). This *impetus* was difficult to withstand. Apparently, Livy is describing an *impetus*, made up of a series of attacks, against various points along the enemy line, carried out by psychologically buoyed troops, enabling the Romans to disrupt the previously ordered Carthaginian battle-line and cause them to take flight. After they 'faced about and all took flight', the standards are actively advanced (*inferri inpigre signa*), and the Carthaginians are driven panic-stricken into their camp. This again highlights the two-phase nature of Livy's combat descriptions.

Polybius provides a parallel account:

> "The wings [where the Romans were engaged], however, kept up a gallant struggle for some time, as each side was aware that all depended on the result of this battle. But when the heat of the day was at its height, the Carthaginians grew faint, as they had not left their camp on their own initiative and had been prevented from preparing themselves properly, while the Romans began to exhibit superior strength and spirit, chiefly because, owing to the foresight of their commander, their choicest troops encountered here the least efficient of the enemy. At first Hasdrubal's men, yielding to the pressure, retired step by step, but later they gave way in a body and retreated to the foot of the hill, and when the Romans pushed their attack home with more violence they fled in rout to their camp" (Paton, 1976).[499]

Polybius' account also suggests a two-phase model of battle. For some time there was a struggle between the two lines (διαγωνίζομαι), echoing Livy's *impetus* phase. There is no mention of the type of combat employed in this struggle, but as it lasted for some time (χρόνον...τινα) and the Carthaginians were able at first to withdraw with their line intact (κατὰ πόδα πιεζούμενοι τὴν ἀναχώρησιν ἐποιοῦντο), the combat seems consistent with a dynamic stand-off model.

When it is clear that the Romans had the advantage, the Carthaginians became disordered and turned in flight. Like Livy, Polybius stresses that the advantage in this initial phase of battle is both physical and psychological, factors fundamental to the dynamic stand-off model. Finally, as the Carthaginians fled, the Romans 'pushed their attack home with more violence' (ἐγκειμένων δὲ τῶν Ῥωμαίων βιαιότερον), routing the enemy. This again corresponds to Livy's final phase of combat: a massed attack against disordered or fleeing enemy.

In this passage Polybius uses pushing metaphors to describe both phases of the Roman attack. The use of ἐγκειμαι describing the final phase of the attack may denote the massed nature of the Roman advance. The use of πιεζω to describe the attack which forced the initial retreat, paralleling Livy's *impetus*, does not appear to correspond with the reality of Roman infantry combat.[500] Both authors represent the same Roman advance as a similar two phase attack, but describe these attacks using different combat rhetoric.

One further example, though not a direct parallel between the two authors, reinforces the proposed understanding of the secondary phase of infantry combat. In Livy's account of Gerunium in 216, Minucius' troops were being routed by Hannibal, until Fabius arrived and checked their retreat. He made them face the enemy and formed the defeated army and his own fresh troops into one line, ready to advance against the Carthaginians.[501] This passage describes the reforming of a broken and fleeing

---

[498] 28.15.7-10: *Fessi igitur corporibus animisque rettulere pedem, ordines tamen seruantes, haud secus quam si imperio ducis cederet integra acies. Sed cum eo ipso acrius, ubi inclinatam sensere rem, uictores se undique inueherent, nec facile impetus sustineri posset, quamquam retinebat obsistebatque cedentibus Hasdrubal... tamen uincente metu uerecundiam, cum proximus quisque hostem cederet, terga extemplo data, atque in fugam sese omnes effuderunt. Ac primo consistere signa in radicibus collium ac reuocare in ordines militem coeperant cunctantibus in aduersum collem erigere aciem Romanis; deinde, ut inferri impigre signa uiderunt, integrata fuga in castra pauidi compelluntur.*

[499] 11.24.4-7: οὐ μήν *ἀλλὰ χρόνον μέν τινα διηγωνίζοντο* τὰ κέρατα γενναίως διὰ τὸ περὶ τῶν ὅλων ἑκατέροις συνεστάναι τὸν κίνδυνον. ἤδη δὲ τοῦ καύματος ἐφεστῶτος κατὰ τὴν ἀκμήν, οἱ μὲν Καρχηδόνιοι παρελύοντο διὰ τὸ μὴ πεποιῆσθαι τὴν ἔξοδον κατὰ τὴν ἰδίαν προαίρεσιν, κεκωλῦσθαι δὲ τῆς ἁρμοζούσης παρασκευῆς, οἱ δὲ Ῥωμαῖοι καὶ τῇ δυνάμει καὶ ταῖς εὐψυχίαις καθυπερεῖχον, καὶ μάλιστα τῷ τοῖς χρησιμωτάτοις πρὸς τοὺς ἀχρειοτάτους τῶν πολεμίων συμβεβληκέναι διὰ τὴν τοῦ στρατηγοῦ πρόνοιαν. τὰς μὲν οὖν ἀρχὰς οἱ περὶ τὸν Ἀσδρούβαν *κατὰ πόδα πιεζόμενοι τὴν ἀναχώρησιν ἐποιοῦντο*, μετὰ δὲ ταῦτα κλίναντες ἁθρόοι πρὸς τὴν παρώρειαν ἀπεχώρουν; *ἐγκειμένων δὲ τῶν Ῥωμαίων βιαιότερον* ἔφευγον εἰς τὸν χάρακα προτροπάδην.

[500] LSJ s.v. πιεζω, 1: 'to squeeze, crush' etc.

[501] 22.29.6: *...ac iam prope una acies facta erat victi atque integri exercitus inferebantque signa in hostem.*

legion, something which some theorists claim was impossible. Culham states that: "if one or more of his [a commander's] units succumbed to entropy, it was not possible to rally them back to a standard in good order. At the most crucial moments of every set-piece battle, the role of command decision and even intent was drastically limited in this way." [502] Livy's battle descriptions contradict Culham and show that, at least in his opinion, broken units could be reformed.[503] Culham's conclusions are adversely affected by her insistence on an *othismos* model for both Greek and Roman battle, but such a reformation of the line would be possible with a dynamic standoff. This further underlines the fundamental need for change in the traditional model of combat.

So, after the arrival of Fabius and his fresh troops, Minucius' troops joined the reinforcing army and were ready to make a counter attack. Livy describes the hypothetical attack of this composite legion as an advance of the standards (*inferebant signa*) in one line (*una acies*); implying a massed advance of the heavy infantry similar to the final phase of our model. Polybius offers a slightly different account: Minucius's army is being defeated until Fabius comes to their aid. "On his approach the Romans again plucked up courage, although they had now entirely broken their ranks, and collecting round the standards retreated and took refuge under cover of Fabius' force" (Paton, 1922),[504] until Hannibal, fearing the fresh Roman legions, withdrew. In Polybius' account there is no mention of a potential attack by Fabius' legions and so there is no direct parallel with Livy's use of the term *inferre*. However Polybius' passage does have some of the same features as Livy's, reinforcing our understanding of his use of *inferre*: that a broken legion could be reformed, that the ability to attack depends on morale and that there was a massing together behind the standards.

The passages discussed in this section support the hypotheses proposed at the beginning of the chapter. Polybius appears to have been influenced by a Greek rhetorical tradition of battle description. His conceptual stock of language allows him not only to describe the advance of the Macedonian phalanx with physical metaphors but also the attacks of light infantry, cavalry and the open formation of the Roman heavy infantry. The metaphors used to describe Roman infantry attacks include terms implying weight, such as βάρος at 3.115.5, and pushing, such as πιέζω at 11.24.7, and ἔγκειμαι: 11.21.4, 11.24.7 and 18.23.8. It has already been argued that Roman heavy infantry combat would not have involved massed pushing. Indeed, Polybius' own digression after his account of Cynoscephalae on the different fighting styles of the phalanx and the legion support this proposition. Polybius states that the Romans fought in a more open formation than the Macedonians, fighting hand-to-hand with swords as individuals or in small groups, rather than the often irresistible massed advance of the phalanx. [505] It is apparent that Polybius was aware Roman combat did not involve pushing and yet, in his own mind, he was still justified in using physical metaphors to describe it. The reason for this may be that Polybius is caught within a cultural context of battle description. Greek historians and poets had always used such metaphors to describe battle and so Polybius, as part of this literary tradition, used the same vocabulary to describe Roman battle, even though he was aware of the peculiar nature of the Roman fighting style. For this reason Polybius' metaphorical descriptions of Roman combat can be misleading and should only be taken figuratively.[506]

These parallel passages also support the second hypothesis. Livy is not entirely reliant upon his main source nor is he merely translating Polybius' Greek. Where Polybius describes a Roman attack with a physical metaphor, Livy does not simply employ a similar Latin term. Instead he uses his own combat vocabulary which is employed consistently throughout his work. This vocabulary has been analysed throughout this study and reveals an appreciation of the more open and flexible style of Roman combat. Livy's literary vision of battle, and the accompanying combat vocabulary, offers a more realistic description of Roman fighting than Polybius'. This may have been the reason Livy chose to impose his own vision of combat onto Polybius' account.

### 2. Polybius' attempt to reflect the realities of Roman combat mechanics and Livy's response

Part of the initial hypotheses of this chapter proposed that Polybius was not only aware how the Roman infantry fought, but also periodically attempted to reflect this form of combat in his battle narratives. It was further suggested that when Polybius tries to express a more realistic view of Roman battle, Livy's descriptions are far closer to these accounts than the passages where generic physical metaphors are used.

In his account of Lake Trasimene, Livy uses the term *impetus* to describe the fatal attack on Flaminius. Here, Ducarius, an Insubrian horseman 'attacked through the crowd of enemies' and transfixed the Roman Consul.[507] Although this describes single cavalry combat, the use of the term is compatible with our perception of an *impetus*: a small group (or in this case one horseman) advancing out of the line to attack a specific point in the enemy formation with hand-to-hand weapons (here, a spear). Polybius' report of this incident differs slightly from Livy's: Flaminius was "attacked and slain by certain

[502] Culham (1989) 198.

[503] Cf. for example the broken and subsequently reformed Roman line at Magnesia (Livy, 37. 42-3).

[504] 3.105.6: ταχυ δε συνεγγισαντος αὐτου, παλιν ἀναθαρρησαντες οἱ Ῥωμαιοι, καιπερ λελυκοτες ἠδη την ὁλην ταξιν, αὐθις ἁθροιζομενοι περι τας σημαιας ἀνεχωρουν και κατεφευγον ὑπο την τουτων ἀσφαλειαν.

[505] 18.30.6-7

[506] Krentz (1985b) 55-56, and Van Wees (2004) 189, believe that the pushing metaphors used to describe Greek phalanx fighting should also only be taken figuratively.

[507] 22.6.4: *hostium turbam impetum facit*.

Celts" (Paton, 1922).[508] In Polybius' account it is a small number of Celts (τινὲς τῶν Κελτῶν) who killed the general, rather than Livy's horseman. Polybius uses προσπίπτω to describe the attack. It has many meanings including 'fall upon', 'strike against', 'attack', 'assault', and also 'embrace'.[509] In this context, it corresponds to our definition of *impetus*: the small group of Celts come out of their line, attack a specific point on the Roman line (Flaminius) and kill the commander.[510]

After their accounts of the battle of Zama both writers discuss Hannibal's use of his mercenaries. Livy states that he placed them in the frontline so "that at the same time as they met the first fiery attack of the enemy, they might exhaust them, and if they could do no more, might blunt the enemy's swords by their wounds" (Moore, 1976).[511] While Polybius writes: "he had placed the mercenaries in advance with the Carthaginians behind them in order that the Romans [before the final engagement] might be fatigued by their exertions and that their swords might lose their edge owing to the great slaughter" (Paton, 1976).[512] Polybius uses a verb to describe the Roman infantry attack, while Livy uses *impetus*, so there is no direct parallel vocabulary; Paton's translation has "exertions". Polybius' phrase προεκλῦσαι μὲν τῷ κόπῳ τὰ σώματα τῶν πολεμίων, means literally 'wearied early by [their] blows on the bodies of the enemy'. So he is describing an attack in which the Roman legionaries individually are hitting the bodies of the enemy, not 'pressing' or 'pushing them back. The following line is also interesting: ἀχρειῶσαι δὲ τὰς ἀκμὰς τῶν ὅπλων διὰ τὸ πλῆθος τῶν φονευομένων. Here, the soldiers lose the edges of their weapons because of the many people slain. This shows that the Romans were hitting the enemy with their swords. If ἀκμη can be translated as edge rather than point this further supports the archaeological evidence that the Roman *gladius* was both a cutting and a thrusting weapon.[513]

Polybius describes Roman soldiers attacking the enemy by cutting them down with swords rather than pushing them back, corresponding closely to the proposed understanding of the term *impetus* and contradicting the method of fighting implied by his frequent physical metaphors. When Livy uses Polybius' account to describe this same event he simply employs the term *impetus* to describe the attack, with *hebetare* to indicate a blunting of the Roman swords. The implications of this strengthen the proposition that Livy's view Roman heavy infantry combat was a flurry of hand-to-hand fighting and that this was the type of combat that he envisaged when using the term *impetus*.

As both authors place this passage in a digression on Hannibal's leadership, it could be argued that the passage does not reflect the reality of battle. But, in their descriptions of the battle proper, the Romans did cut down the mercenaries, and had more trouble with the Carthaginian veterans (possibly because they were exhausted and had lost the edges of their weapons). It is reasonable to assume that in this passage Polybius is trying to describe the reality of the battle as he imagined it. Even if this does not reflect what actually happened in the battle, something which is impossible to know anyway, the implication of the passage is that Polybius believed that a generic Roman infantry attack involved this form of individual hand-to-hand combat.

The account of the Roman attack on surrendering Macedonian pike-men after Cynoscephalae also suggests that Polybius, for all his pushing metaphors, really conceived Roman infantry combat as hand-to-hand fighting with swords. In Livy's account the Roman infantry, ignorant of the Macedonian custom of raising their spears in surrender, attacked their enemy, cut down the first and put the rest to flight.[514] Here, the enemy are "cut down" (*caedere*), confirming that the *impetus* involved sword-fighting. Polybius' account is similar: "some of the Romans who had advanced further fell on them from above and began to cut them down" (Paton, 1960).[515] Rather than a pushing metaphor Polybius uses πίπτω, which has the sense of falling on something violently or attacking.[516] The term τὰς χεῖρας may also suggest some sort of hand-to-hand combat similar to Livy's use of *impetus*.

Some of Polybius' descriptions of cavalry combat also correspond closely to Livy's use of the term *impetus*. In Livy's account of the battle of Zama, Laelius attacks the rear of the Carthaginian infantry: "...[Laelius and his cavalry] returned and attacked the rear of the enemy's line. That attack of the cavalry finally overpowered the enemy".[517] Polybius has: "when they fell on Hannibal's army from the rear, most of the men were cut down in their ranks" (Paton, 1976).[518] This cavalry attack is described by Livy using *incurrere* and *impetus*, while Polybius uses προσπίπτω, meaning to fall upon or

[508] 3.84.6: προσπεσόντες τινὲς τῶν Κελτῶν ἀπέκτειναν

[509] LSJ s.v. 1, 2 and 4.

[510] ἀποκτείνω meaning "to slay", presumably with swords.

[511] 30.35.8: *...simul primum ardorem atque impetum hostium excipientes fatigarent ac, si nihil aliud, vulneribus suis ferrum hostium hebetarent.*

[512] 15.16.3: τοὺς δὲ μισθοφόρους προέταξε καὶ τοὺς καρχηδονίους ἔθηκε μετὰ τούτους ἕνεκα τοῦ προεκλῦσαι μὲν τῷ κόπῳ τὰ σώματα τῶν πολεμίων, ἀχρειῶσαι δὲ τὰς ἀκμὰς τῶν ὅπλων διὰ τὸ πλῆθος τῶν φονευομένων.

[513] *LSJ* s.v. 1, as in ἐπι ξυρου ἀκμης, 'on the razor's edge'. Pol. 6.23.7 uses κενεμα for the point of a sword. The evidence for the *gladius* being used both as a thrusting and cutting weapon has been discussed above in chapter one.

[514] 33.10.5: *Impetus in eos est factus et primis caesis ceteri in fugam dissipati sunt.*

[515] 18.26.12: ἀκμὴν δὲ τοῦ Τίτου ταῦτα διανοουμένου τῶν προηγουμένων τινὲς ἐπιπεσόντες αὐτοῖς ἐξ ὑπερδεξίου προσέφερον τὰς χεῖρας.

[516] LSJ s.v. B. I.

[517] 30.35.2: *revertentes in aversum hostium aciem incurrere. Is demum equitum impetus perculit hostem.*

[518] 15.14.8 ὧν προσπεσόντων τοῖς περὶ τὸν Ἀννίβαν κατόπιν οἱ μὲν πλεῖστοι κατεκόπησαν ἐν τῇ τάξει.

attack violently. In neither case are pushing metaphors used to describe the combat. Polybius' use of κατακόπτω, meaning 'to cut down or cut into pieces', shows that this attack was carried out individually with edged weapons and supports the claim that Livy generally used *impetus* to describe this form of combat.

During Livy's description of the Great Plains in 203, both armies lined up with their infantry in the centre and their cavalry on the wings. "In this formation they clashed. By the first attack both wings, Numidians and Carthaginians alike, were beaten back at the same time" (Moore, 1971).[519] Polybius describes the same attack: "at the first encounter the Numidians gave way before the Italian horse and the Carthaginians before Massinissa" (Paton, 1976).[520] Here there is a direct parallel between *primus impetus* and πρώτος ἔφοδος. Although this passage describes the attack of the cavalry, it suggests that Livy relied heavily on Polybius and that when he read πρώτος ἔφοδος he was satisfied to translate it as *primus impetus*. The implications of this suggest that Polybius, in a similar way to Livy, at times envisaged battle as a series of attacks. The use of a term such as πρώτος, suggesting the first in a series, indicates that a 'normal' Roman attack was not a massed cavalry collision, as this would make it very difficult to pull back from in order to launch a second attack. There is a comparable passage at Livy 30.33.3, involving the attack of the Carthaginian elephants (*impetum elephantorum*) for which there is a direct parallel with Polybius (15.9.10: τῶν θηρίων ἔφοδον); here again ἔφοδος has been 'translated' as *impetus* by Livy.[521]

In Livy's description of Baecula in 208, the Romans made an attack on a Carthaginian outpost. After a march and before they chose a site to camp, the Roman light infantry and the vanguard of the heavy infantry, attacked the cavalry outposts of Hasdrubal's army.[522] This is an example of Livy's frequent use of *impetus* to describe an attack on an outpost, camp or city. Polybius describes the same attack: The *velites* and a picked group of foot were ordered "to throw themselves on the ridge and attack the enemy's covering force" (Paton, 1976).[523] In this example, Polybius uses a verb, καταπειράζω ('to make an attempt on'), to describe the assault on the outpost, for which Livy is content to use *impetus*. Following this attack on Hasdrubal's cavalry outposts stationed in front of the camp, Livy states that "The horsemen were forced into the camp in alarm and flight, and the Roman standards were all but carried inside the very gates" (Moore, 1943).[524] The initial attack on the cavalry outposts is described by Livy with *impetum fecerunt*. This attack caused the panicked flight of the cavalry and allowed the Roman standards to be advanced (*signaque...inlata*). Although this attack was against a cavalry outpost, it again corresponds well with the proposed understanding of the two terms. An *impetus* is made against an organised enemy, to disrupt them and force them into flight, while *inferre signa* describes a massed advance against a disordered foe.

Polybius does not have the cavalry retreating inside the camp, but rather has this attack as the initial skirmish leading to the battle, while for Livy the battle proper began the following day. In Polybius, Hasdrubal sees that his troops were being pressed hard because of the spirit of the Romans (10.39.2: διὰ τὴν τόλμαν τῶν Ῥωμαίων τοὺς παρ᾽ αὑτῶν πιεζομένους), and therefore moves in with the rest of his army.[525] Unfortunately, for this reason there is no direct parallel between the two accounts, but Livy's passage does reinforce the proposed understanding that the terms *impetus* and *inferre* [*signa*] are used to describe two distinct phases of battle.

Polybius' account of Zama again demonstrates that he could move away from pushing metaphors to describe Roman infantry combat with more realism. Livy's description of the fighting was examined in chapter 4 and it was suggested that it may have been based on a corrupted Polybian account.[526] The passage remains useful in general as, despite the unusual combat, it is still possible to identify a familiar two-phase battle formula. The Carthaginian line was disrupted at the first attack with an *impetus*, for which Livy provides no detail; this is the initial phase of combat (in this case very short as the line is broken on the first attack). In the proposed model, after the enemy line is broken, the infantry are able to advance *en masse* causing the enemy to flee or be routed. One would expect a term such as *inferre* to describe this phase of attack and Livy supplies it in the second sentence (*in summotos gradu inlato*). The pushing and the pressing of the rear line against the first is a

[519] 30.8.7: *Ita instructi concurrunt. Primo impetu simul utraque cornua, et Numidae et Carthaginienses, pulsi.*

[520] 14.8.8: ἅμα δὲ τῷ γενέσθαι τὴν πρώτην ἔφοδον εὐθέως οἱ Νομάδες ἐνέκλιναν τοὺς Ἰταλικοὺς ἱππεῖς οἵ τε Καρχηδόνιοι τοὺς περὶ τὸν Μασαννάσαν.

[521] ἔφοδος, like the Latin term *impetus*, is an attack word with many possible translations. LSJ (s.v. II) offers the general meaning of an attack or onslaught. Polybius' use within a military context tends to be an advance, such as 5.52.13, where men are started out of their sleep by a supposed advance on their camp (τὴν τῶν προσιόντων ἔφοδον); an advance of an infantry formation, such as the advance of a phalanx (18.30.1: τῆς ὅλης φάλαγγος ἔφοδον καὶ προβολήν) or the advance of the Roman line up to a distance of four stades at Ilipa (11.22.11); a war of aggression or an invasion, such as the Persian war against Greece (2.35.7); an expedition (5.79.1); or military intervention 9.39.1. ἔφοδος appears to be used as a general term for troop advancement or attack. Livy is able to use *impetus* as a Latin equivalent twice, but unfortunately as neither describes heavy infantry combat, the term is only of limited use for our purposes.

[522] 27.18.2: *Pro castris equitum stationes habant. In eas velites antisignanique et qui primi agminis erant advenientes ex itinere, priusquam castris locum caperent, adeo contemptim impetum fecerunt.*

[523] 10.39.1: προσβάλλειν πρὸς τὴν ὀφπὺν καὶ καταπειράζειν τῆς τῶν πολεμίων ἐφεδρείας [ἐφεδρεία can simply mean outpost, matching Livy's cavalry outposts].

[524] 27.18.3: *In castra trepida fuga conpulsi equites sunt, signaque Romana portis prope ipsis inlata.*

[525] Here again we see πιέζω, a 'pushing' metaphor, used to describe the attack of Roman infantry, against an outpost or covering force (possibly cavalry, as in Livy, though Polybius offers no detail about the composition of this force).

[526] 30.34.2-5

description corresponding to the secondary-phase massed advance against a broken enemy, offering little or no resistance.

Polybius' description of the same point in the battle is shorter and less detailed than Livy's:

> "As the battle was a hand-to-hand affair [the men using neither spears nor swords], the mercenaries at first prevailed by their courage and skill, wounding many of the Romans, but the latter still continued to advance, relying on their admirable order and on the superiority of their arms. The rear ranks of the Romans followed close on their comrades, cheering them on, but the Carthaginians behaved like cowards, never coming near their mercenaries nor attempting to back them up, so that finally the barbarians gave way" (Paton, 1976).[527]

After amending the bracketed corruption to: 'the men could not use their spears, only their swords'; the battle appears to have begun with a period of hand-to-hand combat, using swords rather than javelins.[528] This corresponds to the proposed initial phase of Roman infantry combat. Contrary to Livy's description, it is the Carthaginian mercenaries who were the more successful. The Romans are able to advance because of their order and the superiority of their weapons, rather than any advantage in weight as we might have expected from other Polybian battle narratives. In this account the Roman rear ranks do not press against the front rank, as they would have done in an *othismos*, but rather follow closely and offer their support.

While Livy's account describes two distinct phases consistent, Polybius seems only to describe the first phase. For Polybius, this period of the battle involved hand-to-hand fighting with swords, not pushing with shields, and the advantage switches from one side to the other. The Romans are able finally to advance and disrupt the enemy line because of their superior weapons and order. In many ways Polybius' account corresponds to a dynamic stand-off, with hand-to-hand fighting in which superior weapons and morale, allowing the men to keep order under the enormous stress of battle, would be a distinct advantage. While Livy imposes his two phase formula of battle, in Polybius the Romans are successful purely with the first phase of combat, involving hand-to-hand fighting with swords and not massed pushing with shields.

One further example of Polybius' more realistic descriptions of Roman combat occurs in the account of Cynoscephalae. In Livy, the Macedonian left flank is in disorder, and so "Quinctius, although he saw his men retreating on the right [the Roman left], first sending his elephants against the enemy, attacked, thinking that the defeat of a part would involve the rest" (Sage, 1935).[529] Polybius says that, on the right flank, "[Flamininus] observing that those of the enemy who were next to the actual combatants were idle, and that some of the rest were still descending to meet him from the summits and others had halted on the heights, placed his elephants in front and led on his legions to the attack" (Paton, 1960).[530] The phrase προσῆγε τὰς σημαίας τοῖς πολεμίοις means to bring up the standards towards the enemy. This is not a pushing metaphor but rather describes an advance of the whole right wing against a disordered foe.[531] It is striking that Livy describes this same attack with the term *impetus* rather than *inferre*, which would be more consistent with Polybius' account. Even with this discrepancy, the Polybian passage itself supports the general hypothesis that he was able to move out of his cultural context and offer more specific descriptions of Roman attacks.

The evidence put forward in this section supports the claim that Polybius was not trapped in the Greek tradition of battle description. He was in fact aware of the Roman combat style and, periodically, attempted to reflect this form of battle with more specific terms and phrases than the traditional Greek metaphors. At times, rather than using a metaphor, Polybius uses a general term for fighting, such as διαμάχομαι at 3.115.5 or διαγωνίζομαι at 11.24.4.[532] But in other descriptions he employs much more specific vocabulary, including the terms προσπίπτω (3.84.6 and 15.14.8 with κατακόπτω) and πίπτω (18.26.12 with ἐξ ὑπερδεξιου προσεφερον τας χειρας), meaning "to attack". These attacks, when combined with terms such as "cut down" (κατακόπτω) or ἡ χείρ, seem to have involved hand-to-hand combat with swords. The attack described with προσπίπτω at 3.84.6, consisted of a small group of men advancing out of their battle-line against a specific point along the enemy line, and cutting down their opponents with swords. This corresponds exactly with the proposed initial phase of infantry combat, as derived from the analysis of *impetus* in Livy. Finally, Polybius, at times, uses phrases which describe in detail

[527] 15.13.1-4: Πάσης δ᾽ οὔσης ἐκ χειρὸς καὶ ἄνδρα τῆς μάχης [διὰ τὸ μὴ δόρασι μηδὲ ξίφεσι χρῆσθαι τοὺς ἀγωνιζομένους], τῇ μὲν εὐχερείᾳ καὶ τόλμῃ προεῖχον οἱ μισθοφόροι τὰς ἀρχάς, καὶ πολλοὺς κατετραυμάτιζον τῶν Ῥωμαίων, τῷ δὲ τῆς συντάξεως ἀκριβεῖ καὶ τῷ καθοπλισμῷ πιστεύοντες οἱ Ῥωμαῖοι μᾶλλον ἐπέβαινον εἰς τὸ πρόσθεν. ἅμα δὲ τοῖς μὲν Ῥωμαίοις ἑπομένων καὶ παρακαλούντων τῶν κατόπιν, τοῖς δὲ μισθοφόροις τῶν Καρχηδονίων οὐ συνεγγιζόντων οὐδὲ παραβοηθούντων, ἀλλ᾽ ἀποδειλιώντων ταῖς ψυχαῖς, πέρας ἐνέκλιναν οἱ βάρβαροι...

[528] See chapter four above.

[529] 33.9.6: *In hos incompositos Quinctius, quamquam pedem referentes in dextro cornu suos cernebat, elephantis prius in hostem actis impetum facit, ratus partem profligatam cetera tracturam.*

[530] 18.25.5: καὶ συνθεασάμενος [τῆς] τῶν πολεμίων τὰ μὲν συνεχῆ τοῖς διαγωνιζομένοις ..., τὰ δ᾽ ἐκ τῶν ἄκρων ἀκμὴν ἐπικαταβαίνοντα, τὰ δ᾽ ἔτι τοῖς ἄκροις ἐφεστῶτα, προθέμενος τὰ θηρία προσῆγε τὰς σημαίας τοῖς πολεμίοις.

[531] The Macedonians were unable to form their phalanx owing to the difficulty of the ground and because many men were still in marching order (Pol. 18.25.6).

[532] διαμάχομαι: LSJ s.v. 1: 'to fight, contend', similar to the Latin *depugnare*. διαγωνίζομαι: LSJ s.v. 1: 'to struggle against'.

the form of combat used within an attack. He describes the attack at 18.25.5 as προσῆγε τὰς σημαίας τοῖς πολεμίοις, depicting a massed advance of the standards against a broken line. At 15.16.3, Polybius describes the Roman combat as τῷ κόπῳ τὰ σώματα τῶν πολεμίων. This is a description of individual hand-to-hand fighting which Livy was able to express by simply substituting the term *impetus*. In his account of Zama Polybius' phrase πάσης δ' οὔσης ἐκ χειρὸς καὶ ἄνδρα τῆς μάχης implies that the battle was fought hand-to-hand. While the corrupted passage, after emendation, suggests that this hand-to-hand combat involved sword fighting: διὰ τὸ μὴ δόρασι **ἀλλὰ** ξίφεσι χρῆσθαι τοὺς ἀγωνιζομένους. These more specific terms and phrases support the hypothesis that Polybius was aware of the Roman fighting style and periodically tried to reflect it in his narratives.

Livy's battle descriptions remain consistent throughout the work and reflect a form of battle much closer to Polybius' more specific accounts than his general metaphors. As has been proposed, Livy's literary vision of battle represents a two phase model. These two phases can be seen in Polybius' more specific battle terminology and, certainly the first phase, is reflected in his digressions on the legion. It is possible that these more specific descriptions and digressions on Roman combat influenced Livy's own literary vision of battle. Even if Livy's vision of battle was in place before he 'found' Polybius as a source, though it is likely he read Polybius before he began constructing his history, the similarity between Livy's vision and Polybius' further strengthens the claim that Livy's combat descriptions are an attempt to reflect a generic reality of mid-Republican battle.

### 3. Conclusion

Polybius' history was written within a Greek cultural context in which combat is described using physical metaphors. Nevertheless he still shows an awareness that the Romans did not fight in this way. This can be seen especially in his comparison of the legion and the phalanx after the battle of Cynoscephalae, the first time the Roman and Greek fighting systems came into contact. From time to time he attempts to give a more realistic impression of Roman combat by using specific phrases and terms implying sword-fighting in an open formation or small-scale attacks. He is not therefore trapped within this Greek rhetorical tradition, but he does remain part of it and is able to use, with equal validity in his own mind, these pushing metaphors. This study has shown that such metaphors make no sense in a Roman military context and Polybius' use of them can be misleading. A possible explanation for this variation within Polybius' battle accounts could be his audience. Polybius is writing for a Greek audience and so uses these metaphors, the Greek way of describing battle, despite being aware that they do not realistically reflect the Roman form of combat. The digressions on the legion and the more specific phrases found in his narratives may have been an attempt to educate his audience, many of whom would have been ignorant of Roman battle mechanics. The more specific phrases could also be explained by the failure of this Greek literary construction to encompass fully the Roman fighting system. Greek physical metaphors do not reflect the reality of Roman combat, as the literary construction used by Polybius was not designed for and not able to cope with describing Roman infantry fighting. To some extent this standard Greek description of battle, although not realistic, was suitable for the type of history he intended to write and so generally formed Polybius' conceptual toolbox. But at times Polybius found it necessary to insert more specific terms, allowing him to reflect better the reality of Roman combat, in order to enhance his explanation of certain aspects of his battles.

Livy, on the other hand, imposes his own rhetorical vocabulary onto Polybius' battle narratives and does not simply translate the Greek metaphors. He is trying to reproduce his own consistent vision of Roman combat throughout his work by the use of specific and repeated terms within his battle narratives. These specific terms are similar to the terms and phrases employed by Polybius himself on the few occasions where he offers a more realistic image of Roman fighting. The similarity on these occasions reinforces the claim that Livy's combat vocabulary reflects the realities of Roman mid-Republican infantry combat. The different methods of composing battle-scenes explain why Livy uses a few terms consistently throughout his accounts, while Polybius utilises a wide-ranging vocabulary. As do the different audiences. Polybius was writing for Greeks and so used the Greek method of describing combat with a few more specific descriptions where this fell short. Livy, on the other hand, was writing for a Roman audience with direct experience of similar close-combat in the time of Augustus and so used more specific and realistic terms to depict his mid-Republican battles. Although Polybius is often thought to be more experienced militarily than Livy, the consistency of Livy's terminology and the influence of the Greek tradition on many of Polybius' battle accounts, suggests that Livy's narratives are often more realistic descriptions of Roman infantry combat in general.

This chapter has shown that there are differences between Livy's and Polybius' methods of describing battle. It has also suggested that Polybius' vision of Roman combat, though frequently masked by metaphors, is consistent with that of Livy. It is thus plausible to suggest that, where there are parallel accounts, the two authors are describing, not only, the same attack, but also that they perceived the mechanics of the attack in a similar way. It seems that Livy's literary vision of combat may have been influenced by the occasional realistic Roman battle descriptions which occur in Polybius, but his methodology for constructing battle-scenes and his vocabulary were not derived from Polybius. It is necessary to investigate whether Livy drew on a Latin literary tradition of battle description for this by comparing his combat vocabulary with that of Caesar.

## Chapter 8: Caesar's combat vocabulary

It was proposed earlier that Livy was directly influenced in constructing his battle narratives by Caesar's writings. To assess the nature of this influence, Caesar's use of our main terms will be compared with the earlier analysis of Livy's combat terminology. A spreadsheet noting each occurrence of these terms can be found in appendix 2, and should be used in a similar way as appendix 1, to provide supporting evidence of the claims made within the chapter. This spreadsheet was constructed using Merguet's *Lexikon*.[533] While Merguet includes references to the pseudo-Caesarean texts, only those confidently ascribed to Caesar, the *Gallic War* and the *Civil War*, will be used here. Similar to that of Livy, this analysis discusses only the most important occurrences of each of the terms, while offering further corroborating references, in order to gain an understanding of how Caesar utilised this vocabulary. Such an analysis offers interesting results and supports many of the claims made so far in this study.[534]

### 1. The occurrences of the compounds of *currere* in Caesar's *Commentarii*

#### *Concurrere*

Like Livy, Caesar employs the verb *concurrere* in a variety of ways. On fifteen occasions the term is used to describe the gathering of a crowd.[535] Such as at *B Gall.* V. 40, where Q. Cicero is persuaded to spare himself by the protests of his soldiers as they crowd round him.[536] In this passage, as was seen in the earlier analysis of Livy's use of the term, a compound of *currere* appears to imply a certain amount of speed in the formation of the crowd. Further examples of an implicit speed connotation of the verb *concurrere* can be seen in Caesar's use of the term to describe the rushing of men to a specific point and the rushing of a defensive force to arms. At *B Gall.* V. 55, Caesar describes the hurrying of ambassadors to Indutiomarus: as he had gained such great authority in Gaul that deputations rushed to him from everywhere, seeking favours and friendship for their states or themselves.[537] The term *concurrere* is used six times in this way, in each case suggesting some form of haste.[538] On five occasions Caesar utilises the term to describe a rush to arms to defend against an attack.[539] An example of this can be seen at *B Gall.* V. 39, where the enemy [Eburones, Nervii and Aduatuci] attacked their camp and the Roman troops quickly ran to arms and mounted the rampart.[540] In this passage it is worth noting that Caesar qualifies the verb with the term *celeriter*, suggesting that *concurrere* alone need not necessarily imply speed, or that this was a particularly fast rush to arms.

Similar to Livy, Caesar uses the term to describe the collision of ships. There are three such occurrences in the *commentarii*, and although the term may suggest the convergence of the ships at speed, they certainly do not imply that the word necessitates some form of running.[541] An example of this use of the term can be seen at *B Gall.* V.10, where, owing to a storm on the previous night, the collision of Roman ships had caused great damage.[542]

The final common use of the term in Caesar is as a general word for the coming together of infantry (or cavalry) formations. At *BC* III.72, Caesar discusses the reasons for the over confidence of the Pompeian troops. One of the reasons is that they failed to consider that they had not fought in a sharp encounter or a pitched battle.[543] Here *concursu acri* describes a generic encounter rather than a specific form of attack. Although the term is used in this way less frequently in Caesar than in Livy, the nine occurrences with this sense suggest, as with Livy, that the term *concurrere* is rarely used to describe specific forms of attack.[544]

#### *Incurrere*

It was earlier proposed that Livy often used this term to represent unusually fast attacks, caused by either external or internal psychological influences. Caesar's application of the term appears quite different. It occurs only eight times in the *commentarii*, and in each case it is the noun *incursus* that is used. Twice the term describes cavalry attacks with the other six generally involving infantry.[545] Five of these six occurrences are rather different to the small-scale, high-speed infantry attacks within a pitched battle that Livy denotes with the term.[546] At *B Gall.* VII.36, Caesar writes that he built a defensive position at Gergovia which allowed even single soldiers to pass through in safety from enemy attack.[547] The attack here took the form of a surprise assault on a position or an ambush, rather than infantry attacks within a pitched battle. A further three occurrences of the term in Caesar reflect a similar usage.[548]

---

533 Merguet (1961 [1886]) and also Meusel (1887).

534 For introductions to Caesar's narrative style in general see Batstone and Damon (2006); Eden (1962); Gotoff (1984); Carter (1991) 21-28. On his rhetoric of combat see Lendon (2000). For his battle descriptions in general see Kagan (2006).

535 Crowd: *B Gall.* I.8, I.48, II.33, IV.14, V.40, VI.13, VII.28, VII.48, VII.79, VIII.23, VIII. 38; *B Civ.* I.3, I.53, I.76, III.106, III.106.

536 *Ut* (Cicero) *ultro militum concursu ac vocibus sibi parcere cogeretur.*

537 *Ac tantam sibi iam his rebus in Gallia auctoritatem comparaverat ut undique ad eum legationes concurrerent, gratiam atque amicitiam publice privatimque peterent.*

538 Rush to a point: *B Gall.* V.55, VII.3, VII.24, VII.38, VII.43; *B Civ.* I.71.

539 Rush to arms: *B Gall.* II.20, III.22, V.39, VII.4; *B Civ.* III. 80.

540 *Nostri celeriter ad arma concurrunt, vallum conscendunt.*

541 Collision of ships: *B Gall.* V.10; *B Civ.* II.6, II.22.

542 *Itaque ex eo concursu navium magnum esse incommodum acceptum.*

543 *Non ad haec addebant non concursu acri facto, non proelio dimicatum.*

544 General word for engagement: *B Gall.* VI.8, VII.62, VII.84; *B Civ.* II.25, III.72, III.86, III.89, III.92, III.93.

545 Cavalry attacks: *B Gall.* VIII.18; *B Civ.* I.75.

546 The only occurrence used in a similar way to Livy is found in his description of the fighting at Pharsalus (*B Civ.* III.93) and will be discussed below.

547 *Ut tuto ab repentino hostium incursu etiam singuli commeare possent.*

548 *B Civ.* I.25, I.41 and II. 8.

The term is used once to describe infantry movement in a battle at *BC* I.82. Here, the Romans were preparing for combat against the Afranians:

> "The two camps were separated by a distance of two thousand paces. The two battle-lines took up two thirds of this space, while the remaining third was left empty for the approach and attack of the troops."[549]

In this passage, there is a gap of some six hundred paces between the two battle-lines. This gap was needed for the *incursum atque impetum militum*. The term *impetus* is used to denote the attack of the soldiers, while *incursus* merely describes the advance of both sides towards each other. Caesar's use of a derivative of *currere* may suggest that this approach was at speed, but, the term *incursus* does not, here, describe an infantry attack. Overall, Caesar's use of the term *incurrere* differs to that of Livy.

***Procurrere***

Livy uses the terms *procurrere* and *incurrere* equally to describe small-scale localised attacks, carried out at unusually high speeds because of psychological influences. The term *procurrere* occurs twenty times in Caesar's works, eleven of which describe infantry attacks, and appears to have been used in a similar way.[550] At the battle of Pharsalus, Crastinus, the previous year's first centurion, led the following attack:

> "Crastinus ran forward first from the right wing, and about one hundred and twenty picked soldiers from the same cohort as volunteers followed him."[551]

In this passage the ex-centurion ran out of the battle-line to attack the enemy, pulling along a group of one hundred and twenty soldiers in his wake. Caesar calls these men *electi milites*. Such "'picked men' were, depending upon the situation, either habitually-risk-taking 'front fighters' known to their commanders as such, or volunteers who were 'picked' based on their high morale and fighting spirit at one crucial point in time."[552] These 'picked men' (*dilecti* or *electi*) were not an elite unit literally picked out above others, rather the term suggests more about the status of the men as brave fighters than the constitution of the group itself. In this case, it appears that it was the front rankers surrounding Crastinus, who had high enough morale to follow him into the attack. This attack corresponds closely with the form of Roman infantry combat proposed in this study. The assault was not a massed advance of the whole line, nor even the advance of a single cohort. Rather it was made by a relatively small group of men led by a man of known bravery and experience and consisted of a small-scale localised attack, similar to those depicted by Livy.

The use of *procurrere* implies speed. We are told that Crastinus announced to Caesar that "today, General, I will give you occasion to thank me alive or dead".[553] This is a particularly emotive scene within the narrative and Caesar's use of the term may be an attempt to underline the outstanding bravery of the attack.[554]

A similar use of the term is reflected in the Gallic response to the individual attack of Pullo:

> "Pullo, after baiting Vorenus, moved out of the rampart and ran to the part of the enemy nearest to the entrenchment...then, at close range, he threw his *pilum* at the enemy, and hit one man who had run forward from the crowd...Pullo is himself hit by enemy javelins, one pushing his scabbard out of place which delayed his right hand from drawing his sword."[555]

Here, Pullo runs out of the entrenchments to attack the Gauls. At least one of the enemy moved out of their battle-line to meet his challenge (*unum ex multitudine procurrentem*), and was hit by Pullo's *pilum*. This passage again highlights that the use of the term *procurrere* is similar in both writers. Caesar and Livy both use the term to describe small-scale attacks advancing out of the main battle-line at unusual speed. This hypothesis is supported by five further occurrences of the term used to describe infantry attacks, in each case involving cohorts or small groups rather than the whole battle-line.[556] It is not possible to tell from the contexts of the remaining six occurrences whether they also involved small-scale attacks.

***Decurrere***

The term *decurrere* occurs only seven times in the *Gallic* and *Civil Wars*, but is again used in a similar way to Livy. In both writers the term simply describes a movement from higher to lower ground. On four occasions Caesar uses *decurrere* to describe rushing down from high ground.[557] At *B Gall.* VIII.41 the townsfolk of Uxellodunum run down from the higher ground before attacking the Romans and wounding many.[558] Here, the

[549] *Non enim amplius pedum milibus duobus ab castris castra distabant; hinc duas partes acies occupabant duae; tertia vacabat ad incursum atque impetum militum relicta.*

[550] Infantry attacks: *B Gall.* I.52, V.34, V.44, VIII.10; *B Civ.* I.44, I.44, II.8, II.41, II.41, III.91, III. 93.

[551] *B Civ.* III.91: *primus ex dextro cornu procucurrit, atque eum electi milites circiter CXX voluntarii eiusdem cohortis [MSS. Centuriae] sunt prosecuti.*

[552] Levithan (2006). These 'front fighters' were similar to Homeric *promakhoi*; see van Wees (1997).

[553] 3.91.3: *Hodie, imperator, ut aut vivo mihi aut mortuo gratias agas.*

[554] On Crastinus: Brown (1999) 349-352, Batstone and Damon (2006) 135-6, Carter (1993) 213 and Henderson (1996) 281.

[555] *B Gall.* V.44: *procedit extra munitiones quaque pars hostium confertissima est visa irrumpit... Mediocri spatio relicto Pullo pilum in hostes immittit atque unum ex multitudine procurrentem traicit... Transfigitur scutum Pulloni et verutum in balteo defigitur. Avertit hic casus vaginam et gladium educere conanti dextram moratur manum.*

[556] Individual, small group or cohortal attacks *B Gall.* V. 34, V.44, VIII.10; *B Civ.* I.44, II.41.

[557] Rush down: *B Gall.* II.19, II.21, VIII. 41; *B Civ.* I.28.

[558] *Oppidani enim loco superiore decurrunt et eminus sine periculo proeliantur multosque pertinaciter succedentes vulnerant.*

term has the straightforward meaning of running down from the *locus superior*.

In Livy *decurrere* often describes an attack from high ground, and a similar usage can be seen on two occasions in Caesar.[559] At *B Gall.* III.2 the Seduni and Veragri held the high ground above Galba's legion. They believed that they would be successful since they themselves would charge down from the heights into the valley and throw their missiles, so that it would not be possible to withstand their first attack.[560] In this passage *decurrere* describes an attack in which the enemy run down from the hills into a valley (*ex montibus in vallem decurrerent*). The extra force gained by attacking from higher ground led the Seduni and Veragri to believe that the Romans would be unable to withstand their first attack. The phrase *primum impetum* in this case indicates that, although the attack described with the term *decurrere* was at speed, it was not necessarily massed in nature. As has been suggested earlier, it would be very difficult to carry out a series of attacks when the first involved a massed charge of the whole line downhill.

The compounds of *currere* are generally used by Caesar in a similar way to Livy. *Concurrere* denotes the coming together of a crowd, running towards a specific point or a rush to arms, or more generally as a generic term for the convergence of formations. The term *decurrere* is also used in a similar way, describing movement from high ground. Similarly, the term *procurrere* is used to describe small-scale, localised attacks at particularly high speeds. Only Caesar's use of the term *incurrere* differs to that of Livy. In Livy *incurrere* was analogous to *procurrere*, denoting high speed, small-scale attacks in a pitched battle. Caesar tends to use the noun *incursus* to denote ambush attacks and skirmishes.

## 2. The occurrences of *impetus* in Caesar's *Commentarii*

The analysis of Livy's use of *impetus* revealed that it was employed in various ways. Similarly, Caesar's use of the term includes the movement of winds and rivers, a general term for attack, and more specific attacks on camps or by the cavalry.[561] For the purposes of this study the most important usage of the term involves attacks of the heavy infantry. Like Livy, Caesar often described infantry assaults with no further description of the mechanics of the combat than simply using the term *impetus*. Nonetheless, a few of his battle descriptions offer insight into Roman infantry combat.

Caesar's description of the fighting against the German tribes reveals much about his literary vision of infantry combat and his use of the term *impetus*:

> "Our troops, when the signal had been given, attacked the enemy so sharply and the enemy moved forward so suddenly and quickly, that there was no space to discharge javelins upon them. The javelins were thrown aside, and it was a fight with swords. But the Germans, according to their custom, quickly massed together to form a phalanx, and received the attack of the swords. There were many Roman soldiers brave enough to jump into the phalanx, rip away shields and deal a wound from above."[562]

This passage offers a vivid image of the mechanics of Roman infantry combat. The Romans, on a given signal, attacked the enemy with unusual vigour. The phrase *impetum facere* describes the Roman attack, in conjunction with the term *acriter*, highlighting the unusual enthusiasm involved in the assault. The Germans too attacked with uncommon speed, which is underlined by Caesar's phrase *itaque hostes repente celeriterque procurrerunt*. The use of *procurrere* for the German attack, while the Roman assault is described with *impetus*, may underline the extra speed of the German advance. Certainly the qualifying terms in both attack phrases suggest that assaults were unusually vigorous.

Owing to the unusual nature of the initial attacks there was no time for the Romans to discharge their *pila*. The implication is that the Roman infantry often began a normal battle with a period of missile exchange. This could either take the form of a short volley to disrupt the enemy followed by an infantry attack, or a prolonged, but indeterminable, period of exchange, resembling the default stand-off position suggested in the analysis of Livy's vocabulary. Caesar writes *ut spatium pila in hostes coniciendi non daretur*, which corresponds well to the safety distance of a dynamic stand-off, allowing missiles to be thrown throughout the battle. In this particular case, because of the unusual speed and vigour of the attack, there was no period of stand-off or missile exchange, straight away the fighting was hand-to-hand with swords.

The Germans, as was their custom, quickly massed together into a phalanx to receive the Roman sword-attack (*at Germani celeriter ex consuetudine sua phalange facta impetus gladiorum exceperunt*).[563] Caesar's statement that they became a phalanx suggests that Germans gathered into a massed formation and in

[559] *B Gall.* III.2, III.4. The seventh occurrence of *decurrere* can be found at *B Civ.* I.5, and is used in a metaphorical sense to denote the flowing of opinion.

[560] *Cum ipsi ex montibus in vallem decurrerent et tela coicerent, ne primum quidem impetum suum posse sustineri existimabant.*

[561] Winds: *B Gall.* III.13. Rivers: *B Gall.* IV.17. Rush: *B Gall.* VII.28. Adverbial use: *B Gall.* II.6, *B Gall.* V.18, *B Civ.* III.36. General word for attack: *B Gall.* I.24, I.44, V.47, VII.10, VIII.30, VIII.35; *B Civ.* I.25, I.26, II.26, III.21. Naval battle: *B Civ.* I.58, II.6, II.32, III.24, III.26, III.101. Attacks on a camp or city: *B Gall.* I.22, V.21, VI.37, VI.40, VII.46, VIII.24; *B Civ.* I.27, III.9, III.111 (twice). Cavalry attacks: *B Gall.* I.46, II.11, II.19, .II.24, IV.12, V.18 (with infantry), VI.37, VII.13, VII.80, VII.80, VIII.18, VIII.48; *B Civ.* I.40 (with infantry), I.70, II.25, II.34, II.41, III.37, III.37, III.84, III.93.

[562] *B Gall.* I. 52.3-6: *Ita nostri acriter in hostes signo dato impetum fecerunt itaque hostes repente celeriterque procurrerunt, ut spatium pila in hostes coniciendi non daretur. Relictis pilis comminus gladiis pugnatum est. At Germani celeriter ex consuetudine sua phalange facta impetus gladiorum exceperunt. Reperti sunt complures nostri qui in phalangas insilirent et scuta manibus revellerent et desuper vulnerarent.*

[563] For this formation see Rice Holmes *ad loc.*

turn implies that the Romans were not in massed formation, but were attacking in small groups or individually. This is supported by the succeeding line, where many of the Roman soldiers jumped into the phalanx, trying to rip away the enemy shields. This passage reveals that Caesar used the term *impetus* to describe a form of Roman infantry combat very similar to that described by Livy: small-scale localised flurries of hand-to-hand fighting with swords or even individual wrestling. Neither Caesar nor Livy use the term to denote a massed infantry charge.

The fighting during the withdrawal in contact from Aduatica (*B Gall.* V. 34.3-4) reveals both a similar use of the term *impetus* and a similar form of infantry combat:

> "as often as each cohort dashed forward a great number of the enemy would fall in that quarter. Noticing this, Ambiorix ordered the command to be given that his men should discharge their missiles at long range and not approach too near, and give way where the Romans made an *impetus*, for that by reason of the lightness of their armament and their daily training no harm could be done to them, and when the enemy retired upon their standards they were to pursue in their turn." (Edwards, 1917).[564]

This passage was discussed earlier in the second chapter. It was shown that the description of combat corresponds to the dynamic stand-off model: the Romans attacked out of their battle-line, crossed the safety distance, and cut down the enemy at the particular point against which the attack was aimed. The passage adds support to the hypothesis that the *impetus* could be used to denote localised attacks of hand-to-hand fighting. The enemy gave way to the Roman *impetus*, and while the attackers returned across the safety distance to their standards, the Gauls, in turn, pursued the Romans. Such ebb and flow reflects the fluid nature of a stand-off, where the battle-lines could move back and forth depending on which side is attacking. The Roman *impetus* was not a massed attack, but rather a series of attacks against particular points along the enemy battle-line. In this case, the individual assaults in Caesar's *impetus*-phase are described as *cohors procurrerat*, suggesting that the Roman attacks were at speed and made by whole cohorts. This is not the massed charge of the whole battle-line proposed in the traditional model of Roman infantry combat. Livy's use of the term suggests that his *impetus* were carried out by small groups, numbering anywhere from one man to a whole maniple. In this passage of Caesar, the attacks are made by an entire cohort, roughly five hundred men. Caesar's *impetus* attacks are larger than Livy's, but much smaller than a massed charge of the whole line.

Caesar continues, describing how Ambiorix's plan worked against the Roman attacks:

> "The Gauls followed Ambiorix's order: when any cohort came out from the mass and made an attack, the enemy would quickly run back. Meanwhile that group of men was left exposed, and a volley of missiles was received on their flank. When they attempted to return to the place in the line which they had left, they were often surrounded by those who had retreated and those of the enemy who were nearest to them. If, however, they decided to hold their ground, there was no room left for bravery, and in close formation they could not avoid the missiles thrown by such a large crowd."[565]

This passage further supports the claim that Caesar's term *impetus* represents attacks involving groups advancing out of the rest of the line to attack the enemy. In this case, Caesar uses the phrase *cohors ex orbe excesserat atque impetum fecerat* to describe this attack. This phrase denotes a cohort advancing out of the crowd to attack. Again Caesar's *impetus* are larger attacks than Livy's, but smaller than a advance of the whole line. The passage reveals that such groups could be surrounded and isolated from the rest of the Roman battle-line, reinforcing the idea that the attack was not made by the whole line. The fighting in the passage again reflects the fluid nature of a dynamic stand-off, and suggests, at least for the Gauls, that missile fire was not limited to a short volley before an advance, but was rather a continuous feature of infantry battle.

In a similar way to the previous passages, the fighting described at *BC* II.41 suggests that the form of Roman infantry combat described by Caesar with *impetus* was similar to Livy's use of the term:

> "The enemy cavalry began to surround our line on either wing and began to trample us in the rear. Whenever cohorts came out of the line and charged, the Numidians by their swiftness fled unhurt from the attack of our men, and as the Romans returned again to their own ranks, the Numidians would surround them and cut them off from the battle-line. Thus it did not seem safe either to hold their ground and maintain the ranks or to rush out and endure danger."[566]

---

[564] *B Gall.* V.34.2-4: *Et quotiens quaeque cohors procurrerat, ab ea parte magnus numerus hostium cadebat. Qua re animadversa Ambiorix pronuntiari iubet ut procul tela coniciant neu propius accedant, et quam in partem Romani impetum fecerint, cedant (levitate armorum et cotidiana exercitatione nihil eis noceri posse), rursus se ad signa recipientes insequantur.*

[565] *B Gall.* V.35.1-5: *Quo praecepto ab eis diligentissime observato, cum quaepiam cohors ex orbe excesserat atque impetum fecerat, hostes velocissime refugiebant. Interim eam partem nudari necesse erat et ab latere aperto tela recipi. Rursus cum in eum locum unde erant egressi reverti coeperant, et ab eis qui cesserant et ab eis qui proximi steterant circumveniebantur; sin autem locum tenere vellent, nec virtuti locus relinquebatur, neque ab tanta multitudine coniecta tela conferti vitare poterant.*

[566] *B Civ.* II. 41.6: *Cum cohortes ex acie procucurrissent, Numidae integri celeritate impetum nostrorum effugiebant rursusque ad ordines suos se recipientes circuibant et ab acie excludebant. Sic neque in loco manere ordinesque servare neque procurrere et casum subire tutum videbatur.*

Although the Numidian enemy were on horseback, the Roman force was infantry. Caesar states that the Romans attacked as individual cohorts, advancing out of the battle-line to assault the enemy (*cohortes ex acie*). Caesar describes the individual advances with the term *procurrere*, suggesting again that these assaults could be at speed. The attack phase as a whole is described with *impetus*. This is similar to Livy's use of *impetus*, which could be used to describe individual small-scale isolated attacks, or a phase of combat involving a series of such attacks.

This brief examination of the more detailed occurrences of the term *impetus* highlights some important similarities between the two writers' battle narratives. Firstly, the attacks Caesar describes with *impetus* were not performed by the whole battle-line, but rather by smaller groups, often based around the cohort.[567] Secondly, as has been shown for Livy's combat narratives, an attack described with the term *impetus* took the form of a series of isolated flurries. Further, there are a number of occasions in which Caesar qualifies his use of the term with an adjective such as *primus*, implying that the term normally denoted an attack consisting of a series of assaults.[568] On five occasions Caesar employs the term within battle descriptions corresponding closely to the combat mechanics predicted by the dynamic stand-off model.[569] Finally, there are five examples where Caesar specifically describes an *impetus* attack as involving swords and (or) *pila*.[570] It is worth noting that though there are not several examples of the use of swords or *pila* within attacks described as *impetus*, no *impetus*-attacks describe fighting involving large-scale pushing with shields.[571] In addition to this evidence, the term *gladius* appears twenty-two times and the term *pilum* eighteen times in the works of Caesar, while *scutum* appears only thirteen times and in none of these passages are shields used as an offensive weapon.[572] It seems clear that, as with Livy, the Roman infantry attacks described by Caesar as *impetus* involved hand-to-hand fighting with swords rather than pushing with shields. These five features of Caesar's heavy infantry *impetus* correspond to the use of the term in Livy's work. The similarity between the two authors' use of the term suggests that Livy may have been influenced by Caesar's battle accounts and tried to imitate his combat vocabulary, or that both writers were influenced by a Latin tradition which described battle in this way. These similarities between the two writers' method of describing infantry fighting reinforces the overall plausibility of Livy's vision of infantry combat.

The main difference between Livy's and Caesar's use of the term can be found in the relative size of the infantry attacks. Caesar's *impetus* are usually, though not always, performed by cohorts, while Livy's tend to be carried out by smaller groups, such as maniples or centuries. The late Republican legion was distributed into ten cohortal units, while the mid-Republican legion consisted of thirty maniples or sixty centuries. It is possible that this divergence between the two writers was Livy's attempt to reflect the smaller scale of mid-Republican battle, while retaining the generally understood sense of the term.

### 3. The occurrences of *inferre* in Caesar's *Commentarii*

The term *inferre* occurs sixty-seven times in the *Gallic* and *Civil Wars*. As with Livy's use of the term it has a wide variety of meanings. The most common sense is a generic expression 'to wage war' usually in combination with *bellum*. It can also denote the movement of objects; in an abstract sense, the bringing of hope, fear and danger or it can also mean to inflict wounds.[573] All these connotations of the word can be seen, to varying extents, in Livy's use of the term. Caesar tends not to employ *inferre* in Livy's more specific sense, describing a massed advance against a disordered enemy. The evidence provided by the *TLL* is inconclusive as to whether the use of *inferre* with *signa* is markedly different in Caesar and Livy.[574] Nevertheless an analysis of the terms show that on only nine occasions is *signa* used in conjunction with *inferre* to denote a massed movement of the battle-line, and predominantly this phrase describes a defensive manoeuvre.

At *B Gall.* I.25.7, after retreating for about a mile, the rearguard of the Gallic force, the Boii and the Tulingi, began attacking the exposed Roman right flank and enveloping them. Seeing this success, the Helvetii, who had previously retired to higher ground, renewed their attack.

> "The Romans wheeled and advanced the standards in two divisions, the first and second line to oppose the part of the enemy which had been defeated and driven off, the third to face the fresh assault".[575]

The advance of the two divisions, described with *inferre signa*, is a massed movement of troops. The attack is not however an assault on a disordered enemy formation within a pitched battle, but is rather a response to being

[567] Small groups/cohorts/localised: *B Gall.* I.52, II.25, V. 34, V.35; *B Civ.* I.70, II.41, III.52, II.41.

[568] *Primus* or evidence of a series of attacks: *B Gall.* I.26, I.52, II. 24 (cav), III.2, III.19, V.28, VI.8, VI.37 (cav), VIII.19; *B Civ* I.40, I.44, II.25 (cav), II.26, II.32 (ships), II.34 (cav), II.41, III.24 (ships), III.69, III.111 (on a city).

[569] Stand-off: *B Gall.* V.34, V.35; *B Civ* I.46, I.82, III.93.

[570] Swords and/or *pila*: *B Gall.* I. 25, I. 52, II.25; *B Civ.* I.46, III.93.

[571] The only example where the term *scutum* appears with the term *impetus* is at *B Gall.* I. 52, where Romans attempt to wrestle the enemy shields away.

[572] *Gladius*: *B Gall.* I.25 (twice), I.52 (twice), II.23, II.25, V.42, V.44 (twice), VII.12, VII.88, VIII.23 (twice); *B Civ.* I.46 (twice), I.47, I.72, I.75, II.35, III.93 (twice), III.99.
*Pilum*: *B Gall.* I.25 (twice), I.52, II.23, II.27, II.52, V.40, V.44, VI.8, VII.82, VII.88; *B Civ.* I.57, II.15, III.46, III.92, III.93 (thrice).
*Scutum*: *B Gall.* I.25 (twice), I.52, II.21, II.25 (twice), II.27, II.33, V.44 (twice); B *Civ.* II.35, III.53 (twice).

[573] Hope, fear or danger: *B Gall.*III. 25, V.16, V.43, VII.8, VII.77, VIII.76, VIII.52; *B Civ.* II.2, III.27, III.72, III.80. Inflict wounds: *B Gall.* I.50, V.28; *B Civ.* II.6.

[574] *TLL* VII,1.1377.48ff.

[575] *Romani conversa signa bipertito intulerunt: prima et secunda acies, ut victis ac submotis resisteret, tertia, ut venientes sustineret.*

attacked from two sides. A similar use of the term can be seen in a famous scene at the battle of the Sabis[576]:

> Caesar came to his Twelfth Legion and saw that many men were injured and that the rear ranks were beginning to withdraw. "The enemy were not ceasing to move upwards in front from the lower ground, and were pressing hard on either flank. The condition of affairs, as he saw, was critical indeed, and there was no support that could be sent up. Taking therefore a shield from a soldier of the rearmost ranks, as he himself was come thither without a shield, he went forward into the first line, and calling on the centurions by name, and cheering on the rank and file, he bade them advance and extend the companies, that they might ply swords more easily" (Edwards, 1917).[577]

Here, again, the phrase *inferre signa* is used to describe a massed advance of the battle-line in response to an attack. Caesar found his men in a desperate position and was compelled to take extreme action to force the legions into a formation defensible from all sides.[578] This action involved going himself to the front ranks and, through encouragement, urging all his men to advance or be defeated. The use of *inferre signa* to describe massed advances arising from critical defensive situations is the most frequent sense of the phrase in Caesar, occurring five times.[579] Though Livy predominantly describes decisive attacks against broken enemy when using the phrase, he too was able to employ the term to describe a massed advance out of a desperate situation. As can be seen in his description of Luceria[580]:

> After a failed cavalry attack, there "began a flight that spread to the whole Roman army...[the consul] threatened the men himself, and stopped them as they made in disorder for the camp...the Samnites did not press their advantage, and he had time to reverse his standards and change his front from the camp to the enemy... the centurions snatched the standards from the standard-bearers and carried them forward" (Foster, 1926).[581]

This type of desperate defensive manoeuvre differs from the decisive offensive advance Livy usually describes using the phrase, though fundamentally they are similar actions. Both involve a massed advance made possible because of psychological pressures on the soldiers, positive in the case of an attack on a broken enemy and negative when out of a critical position. These similarities may explain the use of the same phrase in both cases.

Only once does Caesar use the term *inferre signa* to describe an attack similar to those seen in Livy's narratives. At *B Gall.* VII.62.3-7, the Romans were fighting the Gauls led by Camulagenus, a lieutenant of Vercingetorix.

> 'During the first engagement on the right wing, where the Seventh Legion was positioned, the enemy were defeated and thrown into flight; on the left, which was held by the Twelfth Legion, though the first ranks of the enemy had fallen pierced by the missiles, the rest resisted fiercely, and not a man gave the suspicion of flight. The leader of the enemy, Camulogenus, was present in person to urge on his men. Victory, however, was still uncertain; but when the tribunes of the Seventh Legion were told what was happening on the left wing, they brought out their legion behind the rear of the enemy and advanced the standards. Not even then did any man yield his position, but all were surrounded and slain'.[582]

This passage describes a massed attack similar to those seen in Livy. A massed advance of the whole infantry line would only take place if all men had a comparable level of morale, owing to the influence of psychological conditions. As has been shown, a massed advance would have been possible against a disrupted enemy line because the panic of the opposing forces gave the attackers a psychological advantage. It is also conceivable that a massed advance was possible in response to a critical situation, as seen in some of the passages above. The common fear of death and an outside influence such as the arrival of the general, could also offer a psychological advantage over the enemy, though deriving from desperation rather than confidence. In this passage, the Romans were able to advance as a whole line because they were attacking the enemy rear, which would offer a similar psychological advantage and allow them to overcome their natural tendency for caution.

Caesar uses the term *inferre* to describe infantry attacks less frequently than Livy and only rarely employs the

---

[576] On Caesar's narrative of this battle see Brown (1999) 329-42.

[577] *B Gall.* II.25.1-2: *hostes neque a fronte ex inferiore loco subeuntes intermittere et ab utroque latere instare et rem esse in angusto vidit, neque ullum esse subsidium quod submitti posset, scuto ab novissimis [uni] militi detracto, quod ipse eo sine scuto venerat, in primam aciem processit centurionibusque nominatim appellatis reliquos cohortatus milites signa inferre et manipulos laxare iussit, quo facilius gladiis uti possent.*

[578] On this formation see Rice Holmes *ad loc.* For *signa* used to rally troops in both Livy and Caesar see Oakley on Liv. 6.8.1-4.

[579] 'Defensive' use of *inferre signa*: *B Gall.* I.25, II.25, II.26, VII.67; *B Civ.* I.64 (an advance against harassing cavalry during a march); with three further uses of the phrase to describe general movement of the standards rather than an attack: *B Civ.* I.82, II.42, II.67.

[580] On Livy's narrative of this battle see Oakley (2005b) 362-72.

[581] Livy 10.36.10: *hinc fuga coepta totam avertit aciem Romanam...haec ipse minitans obstitit profuse tendentibus suis in castra...non institerunt Samnits spatiumque circumagendi signa vertendique aciem a castris in hostem fuit...centuriones ab signiferis rapta signa inferre.* Further examples of this include: 7.17.5, 10.33.4, 22.29.6, 39.31.9, etc.

[582] *Primo concursu ab dextro cornu, ubi septima legio constiterat, hostes pelluntur atque in fugam coniciuntur; ab sinistro, quem locum duodecima legio tenebat, cum primi ordines hostium transfixi telis concidissent, tamen acerrime reliqui resistebant, nec dabat suspicionem fugae quisquam. Ipse dux hostium Camulogenus suis aderat atque eos cohortabatur. Incerto nunc etiam exitu victoriae, cum septimae legionis tribunis esset nuntiatum quae in sinistro cornu gererentur, post tergum hostium legionem ostenderunt signaque intulerunt. Ne eo quidem tempore quisquam loco cessit, sed circumventi omnes interfectique sunt.*

phrase *inferre* [*signa*]. Where he does use the phrase he tends, like Livy, to describe a massed advance of the whole line, but, in Caesar, these movements are generally in response to a critical situation rather than a decisive assault on a disordered enemy. The reason for this variation may be the differences between a cohortal and manipular legion. Livy's manipular legion attacks with smaller scale assaults than Caesar's cohortal legion. The *impetus* of a cohortal legion would generally be more devastating than the *impetus* of a manipular legion, and would more often lead directly to a rout of the enemy. The smaller size of Livy's *impetus* tends to require a second phase of attack to generate a rout, which Livy describes with the phrase *inferre signa*. It is possible then that Livy, needing a term to describe this second phase, used Caesar's, or simply the Latin, term for a massed infantry advance, to depict such a large-scale attack on disordered troops. This is supported by the single similar Caesarean use of the term, to describe the attack of the Seventh Legion on the Gallic rear. This form of massed attack was less usual for Caesar's cohortal army, which is reflected by the relatively frequency of this specific use of the term in the two writers.

### 4. The attack at Pharsalus: an initial massed charge?

Caesar's famous account of the fighting at Pharsalus, the culmination of his *Civil War*, is a good example of how assumptions about combat can affect the reading of a battle narrative.[583] Peskett's translation of Caesar's battle-scene is as follows:

> "Between the two lines there was only as much space left as was necessary for the **charge** of each army. But Pompeius had previously ordered his men to await Caesar's **attack** without moving from their position, and to allow his line to fall into disorder. He is said to have done this on the advice of Gaius Triarius, in order that the **first charge** and impetus of the troops might be broken and their line spread out, and that so the Pompeians marshalled in their proper ranks might attack a scattered foe. He hoped, too, that the javelins would fall with less effect if the men were kept in their place than if they themselves discharged their javelins and advanced; also that by having a double distance to run Caesar's soldiers would be breathless and overdone with fatigue...
> [there follows a condemnation of Pompey for using such a tactic]
> ...But when our men, on the giving of the signal, had **run forward** with javelins levelled and had observed that the Pompeians were not advancing against them, profiting by the experience they had gained in former battles, they spontaneously checked their speed and halted in about the middle of the space, so that they might not approach the foe with their vigour exhausted; and after a brief interval, again renewing their rapid advance, they discharged their javelins and quickly drew their swords, according to Caesar's directions. Nor indeed did the Pompeians fail to meet the emergency. For they parried the shower of missiles and withstood the **attack** of the legions without breaking their ranks, and after discharging their javelins had recourse to their swords." (Peskett, 1951).[584]

Peskett has chosen to depict the attack of Caesar's men as an initial massed charge.[585] This reading is not based entirely on the text itself, but is influenced by the translator's own assumptions about Roman infantry battle. It is possible, using the proposed understanding of Caesar's combat vocabulary, to offer a different reading of the passage.

In this passage Caesar employs the terms *impetus* (twice), *concursus*, *incursus* and *procurrere* to describe the fighting. The first combat word is *concursus*, which Peskett translates with the rather loaded term 'charge'. Presumably, his intention was to put across the *currere* aspect of Caesar's term, but as we have seen, though the term *concurrere* does imply some form of speed in certain senses, when used in a battle account it tends to mean a generic 'convergence of battle-lines', and so it can be misleading to translate the term as 'charge'. Caesar next describes the advance of his own army with *impetus*. This term tends to be used by Caesar to describe attacks made by individual cohorts rather than the whole line. The same attack is described, hypothetically, with the phrase *primus incursus*. Caesar only uses the term *incursus* eight times in his works and only on this occasion to describe an attack in a pitched battle. From Livy's use of *incurrere*, however, it seems the term, when used in such a context, could describe high-speed, small-scale attacks. That Caesar is using it here in a similar way is supported by the qualifying adjective *primus*, implying that this attack would have been the first in a series and so unlikely to have involved a massed advance of the whole line. In a similar way, the attack of Caesar's men is described with the term *procurrere*. This again implies speed, but *procurrere* tends to describe groups smaller than a whole battle-line. Finally, the Pompeian troops receive the attack of Caesar's legions, which is again described with the term *impetus*. Here, *impetus* is used in the singular form, in a broad sense to describe the phase

[583] On this battle see Carter *ad loc*; Brown (1999) 343-57.

[584] 3.92-93: *Inter duas acies tantum erat relictum spatii, ut satis esset ad* ***concursum*** *utriusque exercitus. Sed Pompeius suis praedixerat, ut Caesaris* ***impetum*** *exciperent neve se loco moverent aciemque eius distrahi paterentur; idque admonitu C. Triarii fecisse dicebatur, ut* ***primus incursus*** *visque militum infringeretur aciesque distenderetur, atque in suis ordinibus dispositi dispersos adorirentur; leviusque casura pila sperabat in loco retentis militibus, quam si ipsi immissis telis occurrissent, simul fore, ut duplicato cursu Caesaris milites exanimarentur et lassitudine conficerentur...*
*...Sed nostri milites dato signo cum infestis pilis* ***procucurrissent*** *atque animum advertissent non concurri a Pompeianis, usu periti ac superioribus pugnis exercitati sua sponte cursum represserunt et ad medium fere spatium constiterunt, ne consumptis viribus appropinquarent, parvoque intermisso temporis spatio ac rursus renovato cursu pila miserunt celeriterque, ut erat praeceptum a Caesare, gladios strinxerunt. Neque vero Pompeiani huic rei defuerunt. Nam et tela missa exceperunt et* ***impetum legionum*** *tulerunt et ordines suos servarunt pilisque missis ad gladios redierunt.*

[585] Connolly (2000) 46 and Lendon (1999) 279-81 both agree that this passage supports a model of combat involving an initial massed charge.

of attack in general, as has been seen in Livy's use of the word, rather than one specific attack.

Reading the terms of the passage in this way, rather than following Peskett's translation, suggests that Caesar's men attacked with a series of small-scale, localised, high-speed attacks, rather than an initial massed charge of the whole line. There is further specific evidence supporting this hypothesis.

Firstly, Livy uses the terms *incurrere* and *procurrere* to describe *impetus*-like attacks at high speed. The reason for this unusual speed appears to have been psychological influences which stirred up the troops. The hypothesis proposed here is that Caesar also intended these terms to denote similar small-scale, high-speed attacks. One would expect Caesar's soldiers to have been particularly well motivated at the time of the attack and Caesar specifically mentions his men's high morale:

> "After delivering this speech, the soldiers clamouring for action and burning with zeal for the fight, he [Caesar] gave the signal with a trumpet" (Peskett, 1951).[586]

This may be rhetorical flag waving, but it fits well with the hypothesis that these terms denote attacks at unusual speed.

More specific evidence can be seen in Caesar's description of one individual assault which formed part of this phase of battle: Crastinus' attack. Immediately prior to his general account of the battle Caesar describes the specific attack of an ex-centurion Crastinus. The attack, inspired by a natural fighter, advancing out of the battle-line to attack the enemy, brought one hundred and twenty men in its wake. This is an excellent example of the small-scale, localised attacks proposed in this study. Caesar describes this particular attack with the term *procurrere*, reflecting the unusually high morale and vigour of the attackers, who burned with enthusiasm for the fight and were attempting to prove themselves in front of their general. The attack of Caesar's troops at Pharsalus would have been made up of many similar small-scale attacks all along the battle-line. Caesar portrays Crastinus' as an example of these smaller scale attacks to represent the specific form of fighting used by his men, which, when described on the grand tactical level, could only be illustrated with broad strokes. This idea is further supported by Caesar's statement that, owing to his men's vast experience, they were able to stop the attack and re-organise themselves on seeing the failure of Pompey's troops to advance. It is unlikely that even the most well trained army, attacking in a massed charge with a battle-line over a mile long, would be able to carry out such a manoeuvre. It would be possible however if the attack involved a series of small groups of men, as the majority of the troops would remain in their battle-line.

This reading of the attack at Pharsalus is supported by Appian's account of Pompey's decision:

> "When Pompey learned of this he ordered his infantry not to make any further rushes forward, or to run out from the battle-line, or to throw their javelins, but to maintain their ranks with their weapons ready and to ward off the enemy hand-to-hand with their spears. Some people praise Pompey for this tactic as the best where one is attacked in the flank, but Caesar condemns it in his letters."[587]

Appian's narrative of the battle is confused and, as Carter states, seems "to be a mixture of authentic detail and colourful invention". [588] This passage describing Pompey's tactic does not appear at the beginning of the battle account, as in Caesar's narrative, but after the fighting had begun and Pompey's infantry were surrounded by the enemy. Appian's belief that Pompey's men should ward off the advancing enemy with spears (δόρασι), surely meaning *pila*, seems unlikely as the late-Republican *pilum* was designed as a throwing rather than thrusting weapon, though it is certainly not impossible that they were used in this way. [589] His mention of Caesar's condemnation in his letters on the other hand does suggests that Appian is describing the same phase of battle as Caesar (III.92), and seems to imply that his account was derived from Caesar to some extent.

Appian claims that Pompey ordered his men not to rush forward (ἐπεκθεῖν) or run out *from the battle-line* (ἐκτρέχειν **ἐκ τῆς φάλαγγος**) or to throw their *pila*. This passage does not describe a Roman advance as a massed charge, rather the rushes forward out of the battle-line correspond better with the small-scale attacks proposed in our reading of Caesar's account. Appian's passage specifically describes Pompey's forces, but the account reflects Appian's general understanding of Roman infantry fighting and so Caesar's attack may have been similar. Peskett, because of his assumptions about Roman infantry fighting, translated Caesar's account depicting a Roman massed charge of the whole line. Appian, having read the same account, because of his own, different, assumptions depicts Roman combat in terms resembling a dynamic stand-off. Every reader understandings passages like this in their own way, based on their own vision of Roman infantry combat. It is

---

[586] *B Civ.* III.90: *Hac habita oratione ecentibus militibus et studio pugnae ardentibus tuba signum dedit.*

[587] *Civil Wars* 2.79: Πομπήιος δὲ πυθόμενος ἐκέλευε τοῖς πεζοῖς μήτ᾽ ἐπεκθεῖν ἔτι μήτ᾽ ἐκτρέχειν ἐκ τῆς φάλαγγος μηδ᾽ ἀκοντίζειν, ἀλλ᾽ ἐν προβολῇ διαστάντας ἀμύνεσθαι διὰ χειρὸς τοῖς δόρασι τοὺς ἐπιόντας. καὶ τόδε τινὲς αὐτοῦ τὸ στρατήγημα ἐπαινοῦσιν ὡς ἄριστον ἐν περικυκλώσει, ὁ δὲ Καῖσαρ ἐν ταῖς ἐπιστολαῖς καταμέμφεται.

[588] Carter (1996) 374 note 126.

[589] Arrian's *Ectaxis contra Alanos* (11-31) suggests that the Roman infantry used thrusting spears as well as javelins. As Wheeler states, "[Arrian's *acies* was] a compact mass deployed eight deep and combining the thrust of the *hasta* (κοντός) with the range of the *lancea* (λόγχη)" (1979) 311. Appian's battle-line at Pharsalus may in some way be reflecting the infantry fighting of his own day. Cf. Plutarch, *Pompey* 69.2.

important to be aware of this tendency when reading any battle narrative and to look closely at the words the author uses, in what way they are employed and how they fit in with one's own understanding of combat mechanics. In my view, which has been expressed throughout this study, Caesar's description of the attack at Pharsalus should be read as a series of localised, small-scale attacks advancing out of the battle-line, rather than as an initial massed charge.

## 5. Conclusion

This brief examination of Caesar's usage of the combat terms found in Livy has shown that both writers employed them in similar ways within a military context. The compounds of *currere* are equivalent; with *concurrere* used mainly as a generic term for engagement; *decurrere* for attacks down hill; and *procurrere* for small-scale, high-speed attacks. Caesar uses the term *incurrere* much less frequently than Livy, and tends to use it to describe ambushes rather than attacks in pitched battle. The term *impetus* is the most important and most common word in both works for infantry attacks. Both writers use the word predominantly to describe attacks made by groups of men advancing out of the battle-line and fighting in a flurry of hand-to-hand combat with swords, rather than a massed advance of the whole line. It seems that Caesar's *impetus* denote larger-scale attacks than Livy's, based around a cohort rather than a maniple or century. Yet at times Caesar's attacks could also be carried out by a smaller body of men. In both cases the phrase *inferre* [*signa*] describes massed advances of the whole battle-line. In Livy the term usually describes a decisive advance against a broken or disordered enemy, whereas Caesar uses the term to describe a massed advance much less frequently and then usually only to describe movement in response to a critical defensive situation.

From this analysis it is possible to raise some plausible points about the influence of Caesar on Livy's rhetorical formula for describing battle. It seems likely that Livy was influenced by Caesar's combat vocabulary or perhaps a larger Latin literary tradition of battle description, of which only Caesar, and to a lesser extent Sallust, survives extant. When constructing his battle accounts Livy may have consciously chosen to mimic Caesar's terminology, or more likely, the cultural context in which wrote compelled him to describe battle in a similar way. Simply, this was the means by which battles were described in Latin. He was aware that the combat mechanics of the mid-republican legion differed somewhat to those of the late-Republican legion, and he was able skilfully to adapt this vocabulary to reflect these differences.[590] The most obvious example of this can be seen in the two authors' use of the term *impetus*. Caesar's legion consisted of ten cohorts of heavy infantry, whereas Livy's was made up of thirty maniples including twelve-hundred light infantry. The legion of the late Republic was a bigger, heavier and more organised force than the citizen militia of the mid-Republic. These differences are reflected in the two writer's battle descriptions. Livy's infantry attacked in small groups, with localised and sporadic *impetus*, with which, if the enemy did not immediately turn in flight, they attempted to disrupt their opponents enough, and raise their own morale enough, to allow a decisive massed advance of the whole line. Caesar's infantry had sufficient discipline or *esprit de corps* to enable them to attack in larger groups, often a whole cohort. Such attacks, owing to their larger size and force, had a more devastating physical and psychological effect on the enemy line, leading directly to a rout. A massed advance of the whole line, often required for Livy's army to rout the enemy, was only needed in Caesar's narratives at times of particular crisis. The army described by Livy fought differently to Caesar's and so he used his vocabulary in a slightly different way. His battle narratives follow a wider Latin literary tradition and whether or not he was directly influenced by Caesar, his battle accounts offer a plausible impression of Roman mid-Republican infantry combat.

[590] Similarly, Roth (2006) 51, argues that Livy was aware Roman siege-craft had a history of its own and that he attempted to reflect this by avoiding mention of elements typical of sieges in his own day in his accounts of earlier sieges.

## Chapter 9: A model derived from Livy's literary vision of infantry combat

Any model of ancient battle must be based firmly on the surviving sources. Though no literary source can ever fully describe the reality of ancient combat, it can offer an authentic reflection of that reality, by reproducing a consistently realistic image of the fighting. The details of any particular battle-account may not reproduce the actual events of the engagement, but by analysing the battle-narratives within the sources, it is possible to reconstruct a realistic image of ancient battle in general. In this study Livy's literary vision of infantry battle has been reconstructed by analysing his combat vocabulary and a combat-model can now be derived from this literary construction.

### 1. Livy's credibility as a source for mid-Republican infantry combat

The consistency and limited range of Livy's vocabulary suggests that, in a military context, the terms we have examined have specific meanings. It seems that Livy imagined particular forms of attack when he employed his combat rhetoric. Owing to the collective military experience and knowledge of his Roman audience, his battle narratives would have had to be at least plausible representations of reality in order for them to have been accepted by an aristocratic elite raised on a fundamental military ethos. It is likely then that Livy's vision of combat, illustrated through his use of this combat terminology, reflected some realities Roman infantry combat in general.

The mechanics of Livy's accounts correspond closely to Polybius' digressions on the legion and the few specific descriptions of Roman fighting found in his battle-accounts. Where Polybius uses pushing metaphors, which make little sense for Roman combat, Livy does not simply translate the Greek, but imposes his own model for describing Roman fighting on to his source. In addition, this same vocabulary is used in a similar way by Caesar, underlining the credibility of Livy's accounts. But Livy is not simply interpreting mid-Republican combat using late-Republican models. There are some specific differences which demonstrate that Livy may have been trying to reflect the realities of mid-Republican combat, rather than simply imitating late-Republican battle-scenes. This vision of combat also satisfies both the archaeological and theoretical parameters of mid-republican infantry combat, further supporting this proposition. Livy's battle narratives can be seen as real attempts to describe mid-Republican infantry combat authentically rather than merely imposing a late-Republican literary tradition on to his sources.

Livy's literary vision of combat seems to be a synthesis of Polybius and Caesar, either directly or at least the Greek and Latin literary traditions they represent. Though he uses elements from both traditions, Livy's rhetoric of combat is his own, and represents his attempt to reflect the reality of mid-Republican battle within his narratives. The similarities between Livy's accounts and those writers thought to be more militarily experienced, Polybius and Caesar, suggest that a great deal of his combat description is realistic. Yes he made the occasionally mistake and, like any individual account of a battle, should not be relied upon of specific details of the conflict, but his general vision of combat is reliable and is actually a more realistic reflection of Roman infantry combat than many of Polybius' battle-scenes. Livy understood how the Roman infantry fought and so he should not be dismissed as a source for mid-Republican battle, but rather should be used as the basis of a model of infantry combat.

### 2. A model of Roman heavy infantry combat

There follows a general interpretation of how Livy's vision of combat would work during a battle. This description assumes a similarly armed and trained enemy, though, with slight variation, the model would work equally well against a Macedonian pike phalanx or a Gallic army.

The Romans would advance towards the enemy in their chequer-board formation, while banging and rattling their weapons. Such a spectacle would be intended to intimidate the enemy into immediate flight, thus winning a 'tearless victory'. If the enemy did not immediately flee, the advance would slow and stop just short of contact, allowing a small gap between the two lines. From behind this safety distance the soldiers would try to intimidate the enemy and throw missiles, while working themselves up by cheering and shouting encouragement to each another. With so many thousands of missiles being thrown, some would hit their mark, killing or wounding the victim and disrupting the line, but most would be deflected by shields and armour. When the physical and psychological energy levels of individual sections along the line reached a peak, natural leaders, those more aggressive than the rest, would break out of the line and cross the safety distance. This advance would stimulate a small number of men, those surrounding the leader, into an assault. This group would attack a localised point along the enemy line and, often, the men at this point would advance to meet the challenge. There followed a short burst of hand-to-hand fighting with swords and punching with shields, perhaps for as little as just a few minutes. This would take the form of loose, individual close-combat, rather than a clash of the two groups in formation. When one of the groups realised that they were receiving the worst in the fighting, they would step back to restore the safety distance. Owing to their close proximity, the withdrawal could be signalled using visual signs. This form of attack would take place spontaneously in many places all along the line that would fluctuate and resemble a wave, depending on which side was successful at various points. In an attack of such a small group, leaders, often centurions, would be the stimulus for the advance and would also be able to call for a retreat. The general's role was to order the phases of combat, not the individual attacks, and to decide the appropriate time for the reserve ranks to be deployed.

The first attack, the *primus impetus*, was an attempt to intimidate the enemy into flight and could involve a large number of these small attack-groups, as morale would often be highest at that point. If the enemy did not run, the battle would continue as a tentative stand-off punctuated with periodic and spontaneous localised attacks to disrupt the enemy line. The battle could last for many hours in this form with only minimal mutual casualties, as the majority of troops would not be engaged at any one moment. Over time, the frequency of the attacks would be reduced as morale dropped and the battle would become a stalemate. It is here that the Roman three-line system reveals its importance. The second line could advance into the intervals between the maniples of the first. In some cases the *principes* would fight alongside the *hastati*, to increase the intensity of the attacks. At others, the first line, if it had received the worst of the combat, could retreat into the gaps of the second and away from the fighting, to rest and re-organise. In particularly intense battles the *triarii* would also be needed to take over some of the fighting.

This series of small-scale attacks is the primary phase of Roman infantry combat, which could last many hours. Often, this phase of attack would be enough to break the enemy line, at which point, the morale of the enemy troops would drop, their nervous energy would turn to panic and they would turn in flight. There would follow a rout in which the enemy would suffer tremendous casualties. But at times, the primary phase would not directly cause a rout, but merely disorder and confusion in the enemy line, and a secondary phase was needed. At this point, the centurions, higher officers and even the soldiers would recognise the signs of such confusion in the enemy and the morale levels of all the Roman troops would increase greatly. The order to advance the standards would be given and the whole line would attack, routing the enemy.[591]

### 3. The model and the parameters of battle

This two-phase model derived from Livy's battle narratives, corresponds very well to the psychological, archaeological and theoretical parameters of mid-Republican infantry combat.

#### *Psychological parameters*

An initial massed assault was dismissed as the primary method of infantry attack for two main reasons. The first was the mechanical difficulty of a line to make more than one attack as a massed formation. The second was the psychological difficulty of getting a battle-line to attack in unison at all. The Roman army in this period was a citizen militia. Legionaries could not march in step and would have experienced varying responses to fear and danger. While advancing upon the enemy, even over a short distance, the line would naturally lose some of its cohesion as the men with the highest morale, at that moment the bravest, would move to the front, while those with lowest morale would shrink to the back as far as they could. Each man's morale within the line would fit somewhere along this spectrum. The resultant attack would end up as many weak assaults or in some cases complete chaos.

Psychological factors play a important role in the ability of soldiers to attack. In the primary phase of combat, the default rest-state allowed the men to build up their nervous energy before launching an attack. While the enemy was in a cohesive formation, which was strong against a frontal assault, the majority of soldiers would naturally remain reluctant to attack. This reluctance explains the tentative nature of the primary attack-phase. Soldiers would be more willing to attack an enemy formation on its flank or rear as this form of attack offered the aggressors a psychological and physical advantage. When making a frontal attack on an enemy formation in disorder and confusion, the psychological advantage for the aggressors would be even greater. The disorder and fear of the enemy line would be signalled by visual signs such as seeing the backs of the enemy, or their standards dropping, or hearing their cries of fear. These would be apparent to all of the members of the attacking force, especially those experienced in battle. At this point their natural fear and adrenaline would change to something more like a 'blood lust'. The aggressors would be willing to cast aside their natural tendency for caution and to attack with far more aggression than normal. For the first time in the battle, the majority of the men would simultaneously have a will to fight, and it is because of this change that the secondary phase of attack would be possible. Disruption of an infantry line could be triggered by many factors, including fatigue, a death of an officer or well-respected file leader, or surprise attacks on the flanks or rear. Whatever the trigger, similar characteristics of panic and distress would develop leading to a rout.[592]

The model of battle proposed above is more realistic than the traditional massed charge theory. The primary phase, involving a tentative stand-off interspersed with isolated flurries of combat, avoids the psychological problems of an initial massed charge. This form of combat depends on the varying morale of individuals and small groups along the battle-line. Where morale and energy levels are high, an attacking force would burst out of the line to assault the localised area in front of the particular attacking group. This could be in response to aggressive stimuli within the group themselves, such as the encouragement of a centurion, or the attack would be in response to signs of weakness in a particular section of the enemy formation. Areas along the line with low morale or energy levels need not attack, but could watch the fighting, while building up the confidence to make their own assault. Under this model, although the soldiers

[591] For an extended analysis of the experience of Roman combat based on this model see Koon (forthcoming).

[592] On a rout and factors leading to it: Sabin (1996)77; (2007b) 429-33.

would still feel combat stress and nervous panic, this would be less than under the traditional model, as the majority of the Roman formation would remain outside the killing-zone of the enemy, where psychological pressures are greatest. For this reason battle could continue for long periods of time without the combatants suffering complete physical and psychological exhaustion. Under the peculiar circumstances needed for the secondary phase of combat, the noticeable disorder and confusion within the enemy line would raise the mutual morale of the entire attacking formation, enabling them to advance as a cohesive unit in a devastating and decisive attack.

***Archaeological parameters***

The examination of the rather limited archaeological evidence uncovered a number of restrictions in the use of Roman weaponry. The horizontal handgrip allowed the shield to be wielded above the head to deflect missiles, and across the body to parry blows from hand-held weapons. But this same handgrip and the long oval shape of the shield made it very difficult to place bodyweight behind the shield. The Roman shield could not be used in a collision at speed without the real possibility of injury to the bearer. The metal shield-boss or wooden spine could be used as an offensive weapon to 'punch' individual enemies during close combat but not to push against the backs of those in the proceeding ranks during an *othismos*-type shield drive. The two forms of combat advocated by the traditional model are the massed charge and collision, followed by communal pushing forward by the whole front line. The mid-Republican shield, as it is depicted on sculptural evidence and as reconstructed from the find at Kasr el-Harit does not allow either of these forms of combat. In the model proposed here, the shield would be used to deflect missiles and blows from swords, as Polybius' describes it, but would not be used in a collision of troops.[593] During the close hand-to-hand combat the shield could be used to punch or push back individual enemies, but would not be used in a massed shield drive.

The shape of the shield would also restrict the legionaries' ability to run into combat. When wielded in front of the body at a run the lower rim of the shield would strike the knees and shins of the bearer. The Roman infantryman may have worn greaves to protect the lower legs, but these too would make it difficult to run. The weight of the shield and the panoply as a whole would further restrict movement. In the traditional model the Roman infantry attack at the run, charging into the enemy. In the model proposed here both the small-scale attacks of the primary phase and the massed advance of the secondary would not need to be at high speed as there are no massed collisions. At times these attacks could be made at unusually high speeds, but such attacks were relatively rare and tended to be triggered by particularly intense psychological pressures.

There is both literary and archaeological evidence to suggest that the Roman sword was both a cutting and a thrusting weapon. Under the traditional model the *gladius* was used predominantly to stab at the enemy from behind the shield, though it could conceivably be used in both ways when formation had been lost and soldiers fought individually during a rout. In the model proposed here, with its small-group and individual hand-to-hand combat, the infantryman would necessarily need the adaptability of a cutting and thrusting sword.

In the traditional model the hurling of *pila* is limited to a short burst before the massed charge. The extremely restricted time-frame for such a manoeuvre has led some to claim that only one *pilum* was carried into battle by each soldier. The implications of this are that there would be volleys of *pila* in a battle, as each man in the first two lines would need to release their weapon before attacking. The literary evidence suggests that the hurling of missiles occurred with a greater regularity than suggested by this traditional consensus. In the model proposed here, since there is no massed charge, the majority of soldiers would be able to retain their *pila*, which could be thrown in the course of an attack or from behind the safety distance during the frequent intervals between assaults, and would be a continual feature of battle.

***Theoretical parameters***

Sabin proposed four theoretical parameters of Roman heavy infantry combat: the duration of battle, which could last many hours; the relative asymmetry of the casualty figures, suggesting low casualty rates during the main combat and high rates in a rout; the mobility of the two battle lines, which could move back and forth over hundreds of yards; and the role of reserve ranks behind those initially engaged, to explain the Roman reliance on line-relief rather than depth. The primary phase of infantry combat in the model proposed above is fundamentally a dynamic stand-off, and as such corresponds well with these theoretical parameters from which Sabin's model was originally derived.

This dynamic stand-off is consistent with Livy's primary *impetus*-phase of combat and explains how battles could last for many hours without the troops becoming physically and psychologically exhausted. Throughout most of the battle the majority of Roman troops would remain outside the killing-zone. For this same reason, these long battles would produce only relatively low mutual casualties. The hand-to-hand fighting would only occur sporadically, while the majority of the missiles launched could be deflected by the shield. Therefore, before the rout, this phase of battle would yield mutually low casualty rates on either side, which corresponds better to the surviving evidence of casualty figures than an initial massed charge. Livy's secondary phase of combat, not predicted by the dynamic stand-off model, a massed advance against a disordered formation, would break the enemy and force a rout. It is in this period that the majority of casualties would occur, leading to the asymmetrical casualty figures found in our sources.

[593] Pol. 6.23.5

This model would also explain how battle-lines could move backwards and forwards over hundreds of metres without breaking. If one side repeatedly came off worse in the small-scale localised exchanges and were forced to step back to re-instate the safety distance, over time, the line would be 'pushed' back over great distances. With the traditional model this would be difficult, if not impossible, as the two lines would continually be engaged during each attack. The Roman sub-units of centuries and maniples would offer the ideal basis for the small-scale flurries of localised combat of the primary *impetus*-phase. Further, an advocate of a massed charge model must invent ways to convert the manipular chequer-board legion into a narrow phalanx. Whereas the primary phase of the model derived from Livy, during which there would be long pauses in the fighting, would allow gaps in the Roman lines to remain throughout the battle. It would also enable the second line to move up between the maniples of the first to fight either along side, or take over the combat from, the *hastati*, as the front-line would not constantly be engaged.

## 4. The model and the debates on line mechanics[594]

For many years there has been fierce debate over the line-spacing of the legion, whether the *quincunx* system remained in battle and how the line relief system worked in practice. By employing a model of battle derived from Livy's own descriptions of combat, these issues can be better understood, without the need for inventing manoeuvres for which there is no evidence in our sources.

The weakness of Vegetius as a source for the mid-Republican legion makes it necessary to discard his three foot line-spacing and to use instead the six foot spacing of Polybius. This larger spacing has been questioned by scholars because of their assumption that Roman battle began with a massed charge. By using a model of battle which casts off the burden of the massed charge, Polybius' statement makes more sense. During the default rest-state of battle, each infantryman would need to occupy a reasonably large space to allow him to wield his shield effectively and to cast his javelin. While attacking the enemy at close range, the larger spacing would allow each man to fight with his sword, using both cutting and thrusting blows. On occasion troops may have bunched together or spread further out depending on the circumstances of the battle, their morale at a particular moment and the topography of the ground. Polybius' spacing should only be taken as a guideline.

This study has shown that Livy understood how the Roman infantry fought in a battle, and as such, his descriptions of the *quincunx* formation and the line relief system are credible, though not without their problems. The chequer-board formation would have made it easier for the Roman *triplex acies* to march in formation towards the enemy. As even on level ground it is difficult for large bodies of men to march in a straight line, the intervals between the maniples would have provided the units enough space to move without throwing their neighbouring units, and eventually the whole line, off course. None of the ancient writers imply that this system was used only in the approach towards the enemy and that the intervals were filled before contact. Modern reconstructions of this manoeuvre, for which there is no evidence in the sources, often fall apart under close scrutiny and such a change of formation would have been dangerous in front of an enemy. It is more likely that the intervals remained during the battle. The separation of the maniples would provide the basis for the small-scale attacks described with *impetus* and the tentative nature of the primary phase would mean that the individual unit would not have been surrounded by the attacking enemy.

Many problems remain with Livy's account of the Roman line relief system at 8.8., but it is the only account of the manoeuvre and as such any modern description of the process should match Livy's account as much as possible.[595] It is likely that Livy's description would have been perceived as credible by his readers, since in order for literature to be convincing it must operate within the limits of what its audience were prepared to accept. So Livy's description would have at least been plausible to be accepted by his audience, most of whom would have been aware of how the late-Republican relief system operated in battle and so his account may reflect to some extent the mid-Republican manoeuvre. Under a system of battle derived from Livy's own accounts, this line relief operation makes sense. When the Romans were advancing successfully, the *principes* could move into the intervals between the *hastati*. The two lines fighting alongside one another would increase the intensity of primary attack phase, increasing the likelihood of the enemy line buckling. If the *hastati* had already created disruption in the enemy formation, the two lines could attack in combination using the secondary phase of attack (*inferre signa*). If the front ranks were receiving the worst of the fighting, the *hastati* could retreat, while maintaining their order, through the intervals in the *principes*, who would then take over the combat. The tentative nature of the primary phase of fighting would allow this type of relief manoeuvre to be achieved successfully without the units being enveloped by a charging enemy. Livy's account of how the *triarii* take over the fighting is more difficult, but if the *hastati* retreated through the *principes* and filtered around the maniples of the *triarii*, the third line could then advance unimpeded into the intervals between the *principes*. Again, the nature of the dynamic stand-off would allow this type of movement and decrease the chances of the units being surrounded by the enemy. Unfortunately, there is no evidence against which to test this hypothesis, but, fundamentally, Livy's account is credible and makes more sense in the context of the proposed model.

[594] These debates deserve substantial work in their own right and the discussion here will be limited simply to assessing how the model corresponds to them.

[595] On the difficulties of this account: Rawson (1971) 26-31; Oakley (1998) 451-466

**5. Conclusion**

This study has shown that literary sources can, and should, be used as direct evidence for the mechanics ancient infantry combat, when used in combination with the archaeological evidence and theoretical parameters of battle. Specific details of any particular battle may have been exaggerated or even invented to liven up the narrative, but the impression of battle imparted by the literary accounts in general can reflect some of the realities of combat. A model derived from Livy's literary vision of infantry battle is not only credible, but also fulfils all the parameters of mid-Republican battle. Though it is not possible to have a perfect literary model of ancient combat, Livy's is realistic and corresponds better with the surviving evidence for Roman mid-Republican infantry combat than many modern models. Livy should not be dismissed as a military source, but deserves to be ranked alongside Polybius and Caesar. It is through the close study of these writers' combat vocabulary that we will gain a greater understanding of mechanics of infantry combat. If this study has brought together the divergent literary, archaeological and theoretical approaches to battle even a little, it has been worthwhile.

## Appendix 1.1: the occurrences of *concurrere* in Livy

| *Date* | *Reference* | *Offensive Army* | *Defensive Army* | *Attacking Arm* | *Defensive Arm* | *Notes* | *Comments* |
|---|---|---|---|---|---|---|---|
| >753 | 1.1.5 | | | | | King Latinus and the Aborigines rush from the town and the fields to repel the Trojans. (*Ex urbe atque agris concurrunt*). | Rush to arms. |
| 753 | 1.7.9 | | | | | A crowd of shepherds (*Concursu pastorum*). | Gathering crowd. |
| 753-17 | 1.14.2 | | | | | A mob came together to kill Titus. (*Concursu facto interficitur*). | Gathering crowd. |
| 672-40 | 1.25.3 | | | | | The signal was given and with weapons drawn the six youths came together bearing the spirits of an army. (*Datur signum infestisque armis velut acies terni iuvenes magnorum exercituum animos gerentes concurrunt*). | General word for infantry engagement. |
| 672-40 | 1.25.4 | | | | | Straight away at the first clash there was a rattle of arms and a flash of glittering swords. (*Ut primo statim concursu increpuere arma micantesque fulsere gladii*). | General word for infantry engagement. |
| 616-578 | 1.41.1 | | | | | A crowd of people (*Concursusque populi*). | Gathering crowd. |
| 578-34 | 1.48.2 | | | | | People rush into the Curia. (*Concursus populi fiebat in curiam*) | Rush together to a point. |
| 509 | 2.6.9 | Arruns Tarquinius | Brutus | Cavalry | Cavalry | Tarquinius had seen Brutus in the crowd and charged for him (on horse). "They rushed at one another with such desperation, neither of them taking thought for his own defence if only he might wound his adversary, that each was pierced right through his shield by the other's thrust, and, impaled upon the two spears, they fell dying from their horses" (Sage, 1919). (*adeoque infestis animis concurrerunt, neuter dum hostem uolneraret sui protegendi corporis memor, ut contrario ictu per parmam uterque transfixus duabus haerentes hastis moribundi ex equis lapsi sint*). | Rush together |
| 508 | 2.11.9 | Romans | Etruscans | Infantry | Infantry | "Herminius had no sooner perceived that the skirmish had begun than he rushed in from his ambush and fell upon the Etruscans' rear" (Sage, 1919). (*Herminius ubi tumultum sensit, concurrit ex insidiis, uersisque in Lucretium Etruscis terga caedit*). | Infantry ambush attack. |
| 505 | 2.12.8 | | | | | Mucius killed the royal secretary by mistake, the royal guards came running and dragged him back before the King's tribunal. (*Cum concursu ad clamorem facto comprehensum regii satellites retraxissent*). | Rush together to a point. |
| 501 | 2.18.2 | | | | | Sabine youths abduct Roman prostitutes, but men gathered hastily (*concursu hominum*) and a brawl ensued. | Gathering crowd. |
| 499 | 2.19.6 | Tarquinius Superbus | Postumius | Cavalry | Cavalry | Superbus charged Postumius, but received a blow in the side, and 'his followers rushed in and rescued him'. (*Ictusque ab latere concursu suorum receptus in tutum est*). | Rush together to a point. |
| 495 | 2.24.7 | | | | | Debtors rush into the forum to take the military oath. (*Concursus in forum, ut sacramento dicerent, fieri*). | Rush together to a point. |
| 495 | 2.25.1 | Volsci | Romans | | | The Volsci attacked a Roman camp, but the soldiers, with the signal being given, rush to arms. (*Signo dato concursum est ad arma*). | Rush to arms. |
| 495 | 2.27.2 | | | | | A crowd rushes to the house of Servilius. (*Concursus ad Servilium fiebat*). | Rush together to a point. |
| 471 | 2.56.14 | | | | | Men rush to the forum. (*Concursus hominum in forum...fieret*). | Rush together to a point. |
| 471 | 2.59.4 | | | | | Legates and tribunes hurry to Appius. (*Concurrunt ad eum legati tribunique*). | Rush together to a point. |
| 464 | 3.4.8 | Hernici | Romans | Infantry | Infantry | Spurius Furius was repulsed at the first assault and withdrew to his camp. (*Primo concursu pulsus se intra castra recepit*). | General word for infantry engagement. |
| 458 | 3.26.12 | | | | | The Plebeans gather in great numbers. (*Et plebis concursus ingens fuit*). | Gathering crowd. |
| 449 | 3.44.7 | | | | | A gathering crowd (*fit concursus*). | Gathering crowd. |
| 449 | 3.50.4 | | | | | The bustle and confusion of a Roman gathering. (*Ex trepidatione concurrentium turba constitit*). | Bustle of a crowd |
| 449 | 3.61.8 | | | | | The Roman consul Valerius encouraged his cavalry by claiming that the 'infantry had forced back the enemy at the first encounter'. (*Primo concursu pedes movit hostem*). | General word for infantry engagement. |
| 426 | 4.34.7 | | | | | A few ships assembled near Fidenae. (*Navium concursum*). | Gathering crowd. |
| 424 | 4.35.3 | | | | | The Roman games were attended by a crowd of neighbouring peoples. (*Finitimorum concursu fecere*). | Gathering crowd. |
| 423 | 4.37.8 | Romans | Volsci | Infantry | Infantry | Sempronius entered the first battle without caution or deliberation when the fighting began. (*Primo proelio, quod ab Sempronio incaute inconsulteque* | General word for infantry engagement. |

| | | | | | | | |
|---|---|---|---|---|---|---|---|
| | | | | | | *commissum est, non subsidiis firmata acie, non equite apte locato concursum est*). | |
| 414 | 4.50.4 | | | | | A crowd gathered round men about to be executed. (*Concursu facto*). | Gathering crowd. |
| 406 | 4.60.1 | | | | | Crowds gather at the Curia (*concursum ... ad curiam*). | Gathering crowd. |
| 403 | 5.7.6 | | | | | The people rush to the Curia. (*Ad curiam concursus fit plebis*). | Rush together to a point. |
| 396 | 5.18.11 | | | | | A rush to the walls of Rome. (*Concursumque in muros est*). | Rush together to a point. |
| 394 | 5.27.10 | | | | | A gathering of people to see a spectacle. (*Ad quod spectaculum concursu populi primum facto*). | Gathering crowd. |
| 391 | 5.32.3 | Romans | Volsci | Infantry | Infantry | The Volscian line broke at the first clash. (*Fusa primo concursu acies*). | General word for infantry engagement. |
| 390 | 5.37.5 | | | | | The Gauls march towards terrified cities, the citizens rush to arms. (*Cum ex territae urbes ad arma concurrerent*). | Rush to arms. |
| 390 | 5.38.3 | Gauls | Romans | Infantry | Infantry | The Romans placed their reserves on a small hill to the right. Brennus, the Gallic chief, although outnumbering the Romans, feared a stratagem. Believing the Romans had captured the higher ground to attack the Gallic flanks when the Gauls had made a frontal attack on the legions.' (*Ratus ad id captum superiorem locum ut ubi Galli cum acie legionum recta fronte concucurrissent subsidia in auersos transuersosque impetum darent*). | Non-Roman infantry attack. |
| 390 | 5.49.5 | Romans | Gauls | Infantry | Infantry | At the first clash the Gauls were routed with as little effort as they themselves had made to conquer the Allia. (*Igitur primo concursu haud maiore momento fusi Galli sunt quam ad Alliam vicerent*). | Roman infantry attack |
| 386 | 6.7.6 | Romans | Volsci | Infantry | Infantry | In a speech by Camillus: "As soon as you have joined battle, every man will do what he has learned and has become accustomed to: you will conquer, they will run away" (Foster, 1924). (*Simul concurreritis, quod quisque didicit ac consuevit faciet: vos vincetis, illi fugient*). | General word for infantry engagement. |
| 381 | 6.24.1 | Romans | Volsci | Infantry | Infantry | "At the very instant of the first clash of arms the enemy gave ground, not out of fear, but guile" (Foster, 1924). (*Simul primo concursu concrepuere arma, hostis dolo non metu pedem rettulit*). | General word for infantry engagement. |
| 380 | 6.28.3 | | | | | Men run to walls and gates of Rome. (*Concursumque in muros adque portas est*). | Rush together to a point. |
| 348 | 7.26.9 | Marcus Valerius | A Gaul | | | Single combat between Valerius and a Gaul, when the Gaul is killed, both Romans and Gauls are pulled into the fight. 'Between those who began the fight, and by their conflict drew in others, there was a fierce battle'.(*Inter primos, quorum concursus alios exciverat, atrox proelium fuit*). | General word for engagement. |
| 340 | 8.7.9 | Titus Manlius | Maecius | Cavalry | Cavalry | Single combat between Titus Manlius and Maecius. On horseback, 'they rushed together with lances pointed'. (*Cum infestis cuspidibus concurrissent*). | Rush together (cavalry) |
| 340 | 8.8.15 | Latins | Romans | Infantry | Infantry | "[The Latins] knew that not only must section meet in battle with section, the *hastati* with *hastati*, *principes* with *principes*, but even if the companies were not disordered - centurion with centurion." (Foster, 1926). (*Nec uexilla cum uexillis tantum, uniuersi hastati cum hastatis, principes cum principibus, sed centurio quoque cum centurione, si ordines turbati non essent, concurrendum sibi esse sciebat*). | General word for infantry engagement |
| 326 | 8.23.8 | Samnites | Romans | Infantry | Infantry | A Samnite claims that their differences will be settled by the Campanian plain 'where they must meet in battle, by arms and the common chance of war.' (*Sed campus Campanus, in quo concurrendum est, et arma communis Mars belli decernet*). | General word for infantry engagement |
| 326 | 8.28.7 | | | | | A crowd, angry over the whipping of a boy, rushed down to the Forum and from there, in a mob, to the Curia. (*In forum atque inde agmine facto ad Curiam concurrit*). | Rush together to a point. |
| 322 | 8.38.10 | Romans | Samnites | Infantry | Infantry | "Indeed it is said that on that day from the third hour to the eighth the outcome was so much in doubt, that there was never a second cheer after that which was once given when the armies rushed together; nor were the standards either moved forward or withdrawn; nor did the combatants anywhere give ground. Facing each other with every man squarely in his place, they pressed forward with their shields and fought without stopping to breathe or to look behind" (Foster, 1926). (*et hercule illo die ab hora diei tertia ad octauam ita anceps dicitur certamen stetisse ut neque clamor, ut primo semel concursu est sublatus, iteratus sit neque signa promota loco retroue recepta neque recursum ab ulla sit parte. in suo quisque gradu obnixi, urgentes scutis, sine respiratione ac respectu pugnabant*). | Roman infantry attack. |
| 320 | 9.13.1 | | | | | Roman soldiers hurry to the *praetorium* for an | Rush together |

| | | | | | | | |
|---|---|---|---|---|---|---|---|
| | | | | | | assembly. (*Ad praetorium concursum est*). | to a point. |
| 320 | 9.13.2 | Romans | Samnites | Infantry | Infantry | The Romans, stirred up by a previous humiliation, were avid for battle "[so the infantry] went forward into battle, urging on their standard bearers; and, that there might be no delay in coming to grips while they were discharging their javelins, as if a signal had been given them, and, sword in hand, pushed forward at the double" (Foster, 1926). (*Vadunt igitur in proelium urgentes signiferos, et ne mora in concursu pilis emittendis stringendisque inde gladiis cursu in hostem feruntur*). | General word for infantry engagement. |
| 314 | 9.25.8 | Samnites | Romans | | | Samnite soldiers snuck into the city and at the same time gave the signal to their armed colleagues to rush in from their places of ambush. (*Simul datum signum armatis, ut ex insidiis concurrerent*). | Ambush attack |
| 311 | 9.30.10 | | | | | A crowd of people. (*Concusus populi factus*). | Gathering crowd. |
| 311 | 9.32.7 | Etruscans | Romans | Infantry | Infantry | After waiting all day, the two lines finally came together with enraged minds, the enemy having superiority in numbers, the Romans in courage. (*Concurrunt infensis animis, numero hostis, virtute Romanus superat*). | General word for infantry engagement. |
| 310 | 9.38.7 | Samnites | Romans | | | Samnites rush to bring all arms and strength in order to destroy the consul G. Marcius. (*Itaque armis virisque ad opprimendum C. Marcium consulem concurrunt*). | Rush to arms. |
| 305 | 9.40.8 | Romans | Samnites | Infantry | Infantry | 'From the moment of contact, there was a huge struggle with the enemy'. (*Simul est concursum, ingens fuit cum hoste certamen*). | General word for infantry engagement. |
| 297 | 10.14.8 | Samnites | Romans | Infantry | Infantry | The Samnites, themselves, "preferred to fight a regular engagement" (Foster, 1926). (*Et ipsi acie iusta malverunt concurrere*). | General word for infantry engagement. |
| 296 | 10.19.15 | Romans | Etruscans and Samnites | Infantry | Infantry | "Voluminius was engaged before Appius came within range of the enemy and the line of attack was accordingly uneven" (Foster, 1926). (*Prius concurrit Volumnius, quam Appius ad hostem perveniret itaque fronte inaequali concursum est*). | General word for infantry engagement. |
| 295 | 10.25.1 | | | | | Nearly all the young men rush to the Consul. (*Concursus inde ad consulem factus omnium ferme iuniorum*). | Rush together to a point. |
| 295 | 10.27.11 | Romans | Gauls and Samnites | Infantry | Infantry | At the first attack the things done by men on both sides was equal… (*Primo concursu adeo aequis viribus gesta res est*). | General word for infantry engagement. |
| 293 | 10.40.13 | Samnites | Romans | Infantry | Infantry | "Before the first shout and clash of arms, a random javelin struck the chicken-keeper [who had been stationed in the front rank by the consul] and he fell before the standards" (Foster, 1926). (*Priusquam clamor tolleretur concurreretur que, emisso temere pilo ictus pullarius ante signa cecidit*). | General word for infantry engagement. |
| 221 | 21.5.14 | Carthaginians | Vaccaei | Cavalry | Infantry | The Vaccaei infantry attempted to cross the river Tagus, Hannibal sent his Cavalry against them and the "meeting in mid-channel was no equal conflict" (Foster, 1929). (*Medioque alveo haudquaquam pari certamine concursum*). | General word for engagement. |
| 219 | 21.12.8 | | | | | A crowd of all types of men. (*Concursus omnis generis hominum esset factus*). | Gathering crowd. |
| 218 | 21.55.4 | Romans | Carthaginians | Infantry | Infantry | After a description of the battle dispositions Livy states that "these were the contending forces" (Foster, 1929) or 'there was a 'coming together' by these forces'. (*Iis copiis concursum est*). | General word for infantry engagement. |
| 218 | 21.57.12 | Carthaginians | People of Victumulae | Infantry | Infantry | The people of Victumulae went out to meet Hannibal, 'more like marching columns than battle lines, they engaged on the road'. (*Magis agmina quam acies in via concurrerunt*). | General word for infantry engagement. |
| 217 | 21.59.3 | Romans | Carthaginians | Infantry | Infantry | "At the first encounter the Romans had so far the best of it that not only were they victorious in the battle, but they pursued the beaten enemy to his camp, and were soon attacking the camp itself" (Foster, 1929). (*Primo concursu adeo res Romana superior fuit ut non acie vicerent solum sed pulsos hostes in castra persequerentur, mox castra quoque oppugnarent*). | General word for infantry engagement. |
| 217 | 21.59.8 | Romans | Carthaginians | Infantry | Infantry | A late battle would have been terrible if the light allowed it to carry on. Instead, "the fury of the combatants was consequently greater than the carnage, and as the battle was practically a drawn one, so were the losses equal when the opposing forces separated" (Foster, 1929). (*Itaque acrior concursus fuit quam caedes, et sicut aequata ferme pugna erat, ita clade pari discessum est*). | General word for engagement. |
| 217 | 22.7.6 | | | | | News of Lake Trasimene brought the Roman people into the forum in a frightened and tumultuous crowd. (*Romae ad primum nuntium cladis eius cum ingenti terrore ac tumultu concursus in forum populi est factus*). | Gathering crowd. |
| 217 | 22.19.4 | | | | | Collection of auxiliaries by the Carthaginians. (*Deinde minus terra propter ingentum famam novorum auxiliorum concurrere ausus*) | Gathering crowd |

| | | | | | | | |
|---|---|---|---|---|---|---|---|
| 217 | 22.19.12 | Romans | Carthaginians | Navy | Navy | Two Carthaginian ships had been taken and four sunk in the first attack. (*Duae tamen primo concursu captae erant Punicae naves, quattuor suppessae*). | Naval battle. |
| 217 | 22.20.11 | | | | | Ambassadors flock to the fleet from the furthest parts of Spain.(*Ultimae Hispaniae legati concurrerunt*). | Rush together to a point. |
| 217 | 22.24.11 | Romans | Carthaginians | Infantry | Infantry | The Carthaginians fled to their camp at the first encounter (*primo concursu*). | General word for infantry engagement. |
| 216 | 22.42.2 | | | | | A crowd rushes to the consuls' headquarters. (*Concursus fit ad praetoria conculum*). | Rush together to a point. |
| 216 | 22.47.1 | Gauls and Spanish | Romans | Cavalry | Cavalry | "With a shout the auxiliaries rushed forward and the battle began between the light-armed troops. Then the Gallic and Spanish horse which formed the left wing engaged with the Roman right in combat very unlike a cavalry action..." (Foster, 1929). (*Clamore sublato procursum ab auxiliis et pugna leuibus primum armis commissa; deinde equitum Gallorum Hispanorumque laeuum cornu cum dextro Romano concurrit, minime equestris more pugnae*...) | Non-Roman cavalry attack |
| 216 | 22.47.2 | Gauls and Spanish | Romans | Cavalry | Cavalry | "...for they had to charge front-to-front, there being no room to move out round the flank, for the river shut them in on one side the ranks of the infantry on the other" (Foster, 1929). (*... frontibus enim aduersis concurrendum erat, quia nullo circa ad euagandum relicto spatio hinc amnis, hinc peditum acies claudebant*). | Non-Roman cavalry attack |
| 216 | 23.29.9 | Romans | Spanish | Infantry | Infantry | The Spanish were not keen to fight, 'therefore at the first clash, when they had barely thrown their *pila*, the centre of the line fell back, and as the Romans advanced with a great vigour they turned their backs [and fled]'. (*Primo igitur concursu, cum uix pila coniecta essent, rettulit pedem media acies inferentibusque se magno impetu Romanis uertit terga*). | General word for infantry engagement. |
| 215 | 23.44.4 | Romans | Carthaginians | Infantry | Infantry | At Nola Marcellus sent out a sally from the town. 'Many were frightened and cut down at the first attack. Then when they had engaged the enemy and brought up equal numbers, the battle began to be fierce'. (*Aliquot primo impetu perculsi caesique sunt; dein concursu ad pugnantis facto aequatisque viribus atrox esse coepit pugnae*). | Roman infantry attack |
| 215 | 23.44.8 | Carthaginians | Romans | Infantry | Infantry | Hannibal's and Marcellus' armies clashed on the plain around Nola. (*Eo spatio - et sunt omnia campi cirac Nolam - concurrerunt*). | General word for infantry engagement. |
| 214 | 24.15.7 | Romans | Numidians | Cavalry | Cavalry | The Roman cavalry attacked the enemy. "Since the Numidians met this charge gallantly and the cavalry battle was no less spirited than that of the infantry, the issue was for the second time made doubtful" (Moore, 1940). (*Et eques etiam in hostes emissus; quibus cum impigre Numidae concurrissent nec segnior equitum quam peditum pugna esset, iterum in dubium adducta res*). | Cavalry attack. |
| 214 | 24.29.8 | | | | | Men flock to Syracuse (*Syracusas concursum sit*). | Rush together to a point. |
| 212 | 25.6.20 | | | | | A letter from M. Marcellus to the Senate: '...lines of infantry and cavalry clash'. (*Peditum, equitum acies concurrunt*). | General word for infantry engagement. |
| 212 | 25.18.13 | Badius | Crispinus | Cavalry | Cavalry | Badius, the Campanian, duels Crispinus, they clash on horseback. (*Infestis equis concurrerunt*). | Rush together (cavalry) |
| 212 | 25.27.11 | Romans | Carthaginians | Navy | Navy | The two fleets "lay on this side and that of the promontary of Pachynum, ready to engage as soon as calm weather should enable them to put to sea" (Moore, 1940). (*duae classes infestae circa promunturium Pachynum stabant, ubi prima tranquillitas maris in altum euexisset, concursurae*). | Naval battle. |
| 212 | 25.30.9 | Romans | City of Achradina | | | 'Columns of armed men from Nasus, leaving their posts, united in haste, to ward off the violent attack of the Roman'. (*Sed ab Naso etiam agmina armatorum concurrerent relictis stationibus suis ad vim et impetum Romanorum arcendum*) | Rush to arms. |
| 212 | 25.39.9 | Romans | Carthaginians | | | The Romans attacked the Carthaginian camp, when "inside the gates there was a rush from every part of the camp at the first shouting and commotion, and a fierce battle began" (Moore, 1940). (*Intra portas concursu ex totis castris ad primum clamorem et tumultum facto atrox proelium oritur*). | Rush to arms. |
| 212 | 25.41.6 | Romans | Carthaginians | Infantry | Infantry | The Numidians desert the Carthaginians, and during this 'coming together' they remained motionless on the wings. (*Numidae cum in concursu quiete stetissent in cornibus*), | General word for infantry engagement |
| 211 | 26.5.7 | | | | | Hannibal attacked a Roman camp. "The Romans in their alarm, so as not to leave one point undefended by rushing in the same direction, divided their forces among them" (Moore, 1943). (*Romani ut in re trepida, ne ad unam concurrendo partem aliquid indefensi relinquerent, ita inter sese copias partiti sunt*). | Rushing together to a point |

| | | | | | | | |
|---|---|---|---|---|---|---|---|
| 211 | 26.13.1 | | | | | A crowd of people before the Curia. (*Concursus ad Curiam populi*). | Gathering crowd |
| 211 | 26.15.7 | | | | | Fulvius entered Teanum with his cavalry. At the entry of this cavalry a crowd gathered. (*Concursusque ad primum equitum ingressum facto*). | Gathering crowd |
| 210 | 26.39.9 | Romans | Tarentines | Navy | Navy | "Seldom have regular fleets ever clashed with such spirit, since they were fighting for a greater issue than themselves" (Moore, 1943). (*Raro alias tantis animis iustae concurrerunt classes, quippe cum in maioris discrimen rei quam ipsae erant pugnarent*). | Naval battle |
| 210 | 26.39.12 | | | | | Collision of ships (*Cum rostris concurrissent*). | Naval battle |
| 210 | 26.39.14 | Romans | Tarentines | Navy | Navy | "Conspicuous, however, among all the rest was the battle between the two ships which had encountered each other at the head of the columns" (Moore, 1943). (*Insignis tamen inter ceteras pugna fuit duarum quae primae agminum concurrerant inter se*). | Naval battle |
| 210 | 26.51.4 | | | | | Scipio trains his army: on the third day with wooden swords they engaged each other after the manner of a regular battle and hurled missiles tipped with a button. (*Tertio die rudibus inter se in modum iustae pugnae concurrerunt praepilatisque missilibus iaculati sunt*). | General word for infantry engagement |
| 210 | 27.3.5 | | | | | 170 Capuans plan to burn Romans shelters, but the plan is exposed and 'when the soldiers had rushed to arms on a given signal (*cum ad arma signo dato milites concurrissent*) all the conspirators were arrested and killed. | Rush to arms. |
| 210 | 27.7.1 | | | | | Laelius entered Rome to a great crowd of people. (*Magnum concursum hominum fecit*). | Gathering crowd. |
| 209 | 27.21.1 | | | | | Assembly of the commons and all classes. (*Ingenti concursu plebisque et Omniun ordinum*). | Gathering crowd. |
| 207 | 27.45.6 | | | | | A gathering crowd (*concursu*). | Gathering crowd. |
| 207 | 27.48.8 | Romans | Carthaginians | Infantry | Infantry | That part of the front held by the Spanish clashed with the left wing of the Romans, the whole right line extended beyond the battle and had nothing to do'. (*Ea frons quam Hispani tenebant cum sinistro Romanorum cornu concurrit; dextra omnis acies extra proelium eminens cessabat*). | General word for infantry engagement. |
| 207 | 27.50.9 | | | | | People rush to the doors of the Curia. (*Populi ad fores curiae concursum est*). | Rush together to a point. |
| 206 | 28.14.6 | Romans | Carthaginians | Infantry | Infantry | The centre of the Roman and Carthaginian battle lines, between whom was the cause of the war, would clash equal in strength of spirit and arms. (*Medias acies, Romanum Poenumque, quos inter belli causa esset, pari robore animorum armorumque concursuros*). | General word for engagement. |
| 206 | 28.26.12 | | | | | "The men who had arrived the day before, on being summoned to an assembly, rushed fiercely into the open space and up to the general's platform" (Moore, 1949). (*Vocati deinde ad contionem qui pridie venerant, ferociter in forum ad tribunal imperatoris...concurrunt*). | Rush together to a point. |
| 206 | 28.37.2 | | | | | The gates of Gades were closed by a mob. (*Purgantibus iis multitudinis concursu factum*) | Gathering crowd. |
| 206 | 28.38.8 | | | | | The Roman people "flocked in large numbers both to his [Publius Scipio's] house and to him on the Capitol as he was sacrificing""(Moore, 1971). (*Concurrebantque et domum frequentes et in Capitolium ad immolantem eum*). | Rushing together to a point |
| 205 | 28.42.10 | | | | | There was competition between Syphax and Massinissa, but "show them Roman arms and a foreign-born army, and now they will rush, as it were, to put out a fire that concerns them all" (Moore, 1971). (*Ostende Romana arma et exercitum alienigenam; iam uelut ad commune restinguendum incendium concurrent*). | Rushing together to a point |
| 205 | 29.9.4 | | | | | The soldiers of Pleminius were beaten and ran to him with angry shouts and displaying bloody wounds. (*Victi Plemini milites cum ad Pleminium, cruorem ac volnera ostentantes, non sine vociferationes atque indigatione concurrissent*). | Rush together to a point. |
| 205 | 29.9.5 | | | | | Pleminius tried to whip two military tribunes. But their supporters "flushed by their recent victory [over P's men], came running from every quarter, just as if there had been a call to arms against the enemy" (Moore, 1971). (*Repente milites feroces recenti uictoria ex omnibus locis, uelut aduersus hostes ad arma conclamatum esset, concurrerunt*). | Rush together to a point. |
| 204 | 29.18.10 | Romans | Romans | Infantry | Infantry | Two factions within the Roman army [one under Pleminius, the other under two tribunes] "clashed with each other in actual battle" (Moore, 1971). (*Aliquotiens iam inter se signis conlatis concucurrerunt [concurrerunt]*). | General word for infantryengage ment |
| 204 | 29.26.7 | | | | | A crowd flocked to the harbour to see Scipio leave for Africa. (*Concurrerat ad spectaculum in portum* | Gathering crowd. |

| | | | | | | | |
|---|---|---|---|---|---|---|---|
| | | | | | | *omnis turba*) | |
| 204 | 29.27.11 | | | | | Scipio lays anchor at night so that his ships might not collide nor drift to the shore. (*Concurrerent naves aut terrae inferrentur*). | Coming together of ships |
| 204 | 29.27.6 | | | | | Collisions of ships in the fog. (*Concursus navium*). | Coming together of ships |
| 203 | 30.8.7 | Romans | Carthaginians | Cavalry and infantry | Cavalry and infantry | The Romans drew up their battle-line in the normal way, with cavalry on both wings, Hasdrubal opposed the Roman infantry with his Celtiberians and placed cavalry on both his wings. 'In this formation they clashed. By the first attack both wings, both the Numidians and Carthaginians, were at the same time beaten back'. (*Ita instructi concurrunt. Primo impetu simul utraque cornua, et Numidae et Carthaginienses, pulsi*). | General word for infantry engagement. |
| 203 | 30.24.10 | | | | | People run to the forum (*in forum concursum est*). | Rush together to a point. |
| 203 | 30.25.3 | | | | | A crowd (*concursu*). | Gathering crowd. |
| 202 | 30.34.1 | Romans | Carthaginians | Infantry | Infantry | On both sides the Carthaginian line had been stripped of their cavalry when the infantry clashed. (*Utrimque nudata equite erat Punica acies, cum pedes concurrit*). | General word for infantry engagement. |
| 200 | 31.33.8 | Romans | Macedonians | Cavalry | Cavalry | "Before they [the two forces of cavalry] came in sight of one another, they prepared horses and arms for battle, nor was there any delay in charging as soon as the enemy came in sight" (Sage, 1935). (*Itaque priusquam in conspectum venirent, equos armaque expedierant; nec mora, ubi primum hostem videre, concurrendi facta est*). | Rush together |
| 198 | 32.13.11 | Aetolians | People of Megalopolis | | | The townsmen gathered to defend their walls and drove back the Aetolians. (*Concursu oppidanorum ad tuenda moenia facto repulsi sunt*). | Rush to arms. |
| 198 | 32.23.7 | Romans | Macedonians | | | The Romans attacked the walls of Corinth, Macedonians rushed to the wall to defend it. (*Protegendum armis cum Macedones concurrerent*). | Rush to arms. |
| 198 | 32.24.4 | Romans | People of Elatia | | | The Romans destroy a section of the wall and attack through it. The guards from all parts of the city rush to the place endangered by the enemy attack. (*Qui premebatur impetu hostium locum concurrerunt*). | Rush to arms. |
| 197 | 32.30.11 | Romans | Insubres | Infantry | Infantry | The consul vowed a temple to Juno Sospita if the enemy were routed that day. "The soldiers shouted that they would bring about the fulfilment of the consul's vow and the attack on the enemy began. The Insubres broke at the first assault" (Sage, 1935). (*A militibus clamor sublatus compotem voti consulem se facturos, et impetus in hostes est factus. Non tulerunt Insubres primum concursum*). | Roman infantry attack. |
| 197 | 33.12.9 | | | | | In general, 'an armed enemy ought to be met with hostile spirits'. (*Cum armato hoste infestis animis concurri debere*). | General word for infantry engagement |
| 196 | 33.37.8 | Boii | Romans | Infantry | Infantry | The Boii ambush the Romans and "a battle began, more sudden and furious than if they had clashed with minds prepared to fight at a predetermined time and place" (Sage, 1935). (*Proelium celerius acriusque commissum quam si tempore locoque ad certamen destinato praeparatis animis concurrissent*). | General use meaning a coming together of troops. |
| 195 | 33.48.3 | | | | | A crowd gathers to pay their respects to Hannibal. (*Concursus salutantium esset factus*). | Gathering crowd. |
| 195 | 33.48.9 | | | | | A crowd gathered at the door of Hannibal's house. (*Concursus ad vestibulum aedium est factus*). | Gathering crowd. |
| 195 | 34.14.7 | Romans | Celtiberians | Infantry | Infantry | After the cavalry had been repulsed the consul ordered "two picked cohorts to march around the right flank of the enemy and to show themselves in the rear before the infantry masses clashed" (Sage, 1935). (*Duas cohortes delectas ab dextro latere hostium circumduci iubet et ab tergo se ostendere priusquam concurrerent peditum acies*). | General word for infantry engagement. |
| 195 | 34.28.11 | Romans | Spartans | Infantry | Infantry | The soldiers of Nabis attack the Roman marching column in the rear, but Appius Claudius was prepared for this, and made his men turn about to face the enemy. 'So, as if straight/organised battle-lines had met, there was a regular battle for some time'. (*Itaque, velut rectae acies concurrissent, iustum aliquamdiu proelium fuit*). | General word for infantry engagement. |
| 193 | 35.1.6 | Romans | Lusitani | Infantry | Infantry | Publius Cornelius Scipio, with his troops in a compact body, "had clashed with a column long drawn out and hindered by the great number of its pack animals, and he fought with fresh troops against an enemy worn out by a long march" (Sage, 1935). (*Nam et acie frequenti armatis adversus longum et impeditum turba pecorum agmen et recenti milite adversus fessos longo itinere concurrerat*). | Roman infantry attack |
| 193 | 35.5.1 | | | Infantry | Infantry | At the second hour battle began'. (*Hora secunda ferme concursum est*). | General word for infantry |

| | | | | | | | |
|---|---|---|---|---|---|---|---|
| | | | | | | | engagement. |
| 192 | 35.36.3 | | | | | After Nabis had been murdered, his guards gathered around the body. (*Concurrunt ad relictum tyranni corpus*). | Gathering crowd. |
| 192 | 35.42.5 | | | | | There would be a rush to the (Greek) shores to see Antiochus. (*Concursum ad littora futurum*...) | Rush together to a point. |
| 191 | 36.24.2 | | | | | During a Roman night attack the Aetolians would rush to the point where they heard a noise. (*Unde clamor exaudiretur, haud dubie ratus hostes concursuros*). | Rush together to a point. |
| 191 | 36.24.4 | | | | | At the siege of Heraclea, the Aetolians rushed from all sides to bring help against the Romans attempting to get over the walls. (*Adversus quos undique ad opem ferendam concurrunt*). | Rush to arms. |
| 191 | 36.30.1 | | | | | Aetolians assembled at Naupactus. (*Naupactum concurrisse Aetolos*). | Gathering crowd. |
| 191 | 36.34.5 | | | | | Men from all quarters rushed to the walls to welcome Quinctius. (*Itaque concursu facto undique in muros*...) | Gathering crowd. |
| 191 | 36.44.7 | Romans | Antiochus | Navy | Navy | "The one which was fighting in equal combat, when it saw that the other ship was taken, fled to the fleet before it could be surrounded by three". (*Una, quae pari Marte concurrerat, postquam captam alteram navem vidit, priusquam ab tribus simul circumveniretur, retro ad classem refugit*). | Naval battle |
| 191 | 36.44.10 | Romans | Antiochus | Navy | Navy | 'Now the fleets clashed everywhere'. (*Et iam classes quoque undique concurrerant*) | Naval battle |
| 190 | 37.23.9 | Rhodians | Antiochus | Navy | Navy | "Eudamus [the Rhodian fleet commander] saw the enemy arrayed and ready to engage" (Sage, 1935). (*Eudamus postquam hostium aciem instructam et paratam ad concurrendum vidit*). | Naval battle |
| 190 | 37.24.2 | Rhodians | Antiochus | Navy | Navy | "If a ship clashed head on with a ship of the enemy, it either crushed its prow or broke off its oars or, passing through the open intervals between the files, it attacked the stern" (Sage, 1935). (*Si qua concurrerat rostro cum hostium naue, aut proram lacerabat, aut remos detergebat, aut libero inter ordines discursu praeteruecta in puppim impetum dabat*). | Naval battle |
| 190 | 37.24.4 | Carthaginians | Eudemus | Navy | Navy | "All the ships which had been victorious on the right flank had hurried off to bear aid to their comrades" (Sage, 1935). (*Omnes quae in dextro cornu uicerant naues ad opem ferendam suis concurrissent*). | Rush together to a point. |
| 190 | 37.24.9 | | | | | Hannibal towed a captured seven bank ship back to Eudamus, which had been struck at the first clash. (*Ad Eudamum revecti hepterem captam, quae primo concursu icta erat*). | Naval battle. |
| 190 | 37.29.4 | | | | | Men assembled at the ships (*concursum ad Naves est*) | Gathering crowd. |
| 190 | 37.30.4 | | | | | Antiochus' ships swerve to avoid a collision of their prows. (*Ne prorae concurrerent*). | Naval battle |
| 190 | 37.30.5 | Romans | Antiochus | Navy | Navy | If one ship did clash it was covered by flames pouring upon it. (*Si qua concurrerat, obruebatur infuso igni*). | Naval battle |
| 190 | 37.32.7 | | | | | The *Praetor* ordered the recall of his troops, and "when the fighting stopped, not even then did they turn to rest, but rushed in every direction to build and repair what had been laid to ruins" (Sage, 1935). (*Dirempto proelio, ne tum quidem ad quietem uersi, sed undique omnes ad munienda et obmolienda, quae ruinis strata erant, concurrerunt*). | Rush together to a point. |
| 190 | 37.41.12 | Romans | Selucids | Infantry | Infantry | "Then at length the signal was given on both sides and the clash of regular battle began" (Sage, 1935). (*Tum demum ad iustum proelium signo utrimque dato concursum est*). | General word for infantry engagement. |
| 189 | 38.2.13 | Athamanians and Aetolians | Macedonians | Infantry | Infantry | The Athamanians and the Aetolians came together from all sides (*undique concurrerunt*) to destroy Xeno and his 1,000 Macedonians. | Coming together. |
| 189 | 38.3.5 | | | | | The Dolopians at first rushed to arms for Philip. (*Hi primo ad arma concurrerunt*). | Rush to arms. |
| 189 | 38.25.15 | | | | | Roman cavalry rout Gallic cavalry, and then the foragers run in from the fields to face them. (*Et primo impetu fusi Galli sunt, et ex agris concurrebant pabulatores*). | Rushing together to a point |
| 189 | 38.33.9 | | | | | After the Spartan exiles had attacked the Spartans the Achaeans rushed up to see the sight. (*Et Archaei ad spectaculum primo concurrebant*). | Rushing together to a point |
| 188 | 38.40.11 | | | | | A Thracian ambush of the Roman army as they marched through a defile. When the noise reached the front and rear of the column there was a rush from both directions to the centre. (*Utrimque in medium concurritur*). | Rush together to a point. |
| 183 | 39.53.7 | | | | | Philip was displeased by the crowds of Macedonians who visited his son. (*Offendebatur interdum concursu Macedonum ad eum*). | Gathering crowd. |
| 182 | 40.6.5 | Macedonians | Macedonians | Infantry | Infantry | A mock battle, but "they came together just as if it were a struggle for the throne, and many wounds | General word for infantry |

| | | | | | | | |
|---|---|---|---|---|---|---|---|
| | | | | | | were dealt by the pointless weapons, nor was anything but iron wanting to make it look like a regular battle" (Schlesinger, 1938). (*Ceterum non imago fuit pugnae, sed tamquam de regno dimicaretur, ita concurrerunt, multaque vulnera rudibus facta, nec praeter ferrum quicquam defuit ad iustam belli speciem*). | engagement. |
| 182 | 40.6.6 | Macedonians | Macedonians | | | Macedonian ritual of splitting the army into two and having them clash in a sham battle. (*Mos erat lustrationis sacro peracto decurrere exercitum, et divisas bifariam duas acies concurrere ad simulacrum pugnae*). | Non-Roman infantry battle |
| 182 | 40.13.2 | | | | | Demetrius states that Perseus claims that he (Demetrius) wished to kill Perseus after they clashed. (*Volui... cum concurrimus... occidere*). | Argument |
| 182 | 40.13.6 | | | | | A stubborn contest and clash argument made Perseus angry. (*Pertinaci certamine et concursu iratem te efficere*). | Argument |
| 180 | 40.39.10 | Celtiberians | Romans | Infantry | Infantry | The Celtiberians attacked the Romans on two sides. "The enemy was charging and on the extreme flanks the battle was already in progress. Then the battle lines clashed" (Schlesinger, 1938). (*Invehebant se hostes, et in partibus extremis iam pugnabatur. Deinde acies concurrerunt).* | General word for infantry engagement. |
| 179 | 40.46.10 | | | | | A speech by Q. Caecilius Metellus: "Titus Tatius and Romulus, in whose city they had clashed as enemies in battle in the middle of the Forum, reigned there in harmony" (Sage, 1938). (*T.Tatius et Romulus, in cuius urbis medio foro acie hostes concurrerant, ibi concordes regnarunt*). | Clash of two men |
| 177 | 41.10.3 | | | | | The young men of the Histrians rush together to form an army. (*Concursu ex omnibus populis iuventutis facto repentinus et tumultuarius exercitus...* ) | Rush to arms. |
| 172 | 42.16.2 | | | | | The King's friends, courtiers and slaves gathered around his body. (*Ad corpus regis primo amic, deinde satellites ac servi concurrerunt*). | Gathering crowd. |
| 171 | 42.53.9 | City of Cyretiae | Macedonians | | | Perseus beseiged Cyretiae, but was repulsed on the first day by a sharp rush of fighters to the gates. (*Primo die acri concursu ad portas armatorum est repulsus*). | Rush together to a point. |
| 171 | 42.54.4 | | | | | At the siege of Mylae, Macedonians attacked but the townsfolk rush to the gate to defend it. (*Ad portuam tuendam concurrunt*). | Rush to arms. |
| 171 | 42.59.1 | Macedonians | Romans | Light infantry | Light Infantry | "Drawn up in very nearly this fashion and with numbers of cavalry and light troops about even on both sides, the lines clashed, the battle beginning with the slingers and javelin throwers, who were in advance" (Schlesinger, 1938). (*In hunc modum maxime instructae acies, par ferme utrimque numerus equitum ac leuis armaturae, concurrunt, a funditoribus iaculatoribusque, qui praecesserant, proelio orto*). | General word for infantry engagement. |
| 171 | 42.59.4 | Macedonians | Romans | Infantry | Infantry | "The Thessalian cavalry, which had been in support, [was] away a short distance from the left wing and the melée..." (Schlesinger, 1938). (*Thessalorum equitatus, qui a laevo cornu brevi spatio diiunctus in subsidiis fuerat extra concursum*). | General word for infantry engagement. |
| 171 | 42.63.6 | | | | | At the assault of Haliartus, the townsfolk rally to defend against an attack on their wall. (*Concursu adversus se oppidanorum facto*). | Rush to arms. |
| 169 | 44.4.4 | Romans | Macedonians | Infantry | Infantry | Because of skirmishing on the previous day a more stubborn clash of larger forces occurred. (*Inritatis in posterum diem animis maioribus copiis atque infestius concursum est*). | General word for infantryengage ment. |
| 169 | 44.9.7 | | | | | Within a description of the *testudo*: two men would climb the tortoise and "they would then act as if skirmishing at the outer edges of the 'tortoise', now clash with each other in the centre, and leap about just as if they were on solid ground" (Schlesinger, 1951). (*Nunc uelut propugnantes per oras extremae testudinis, nunc in media inter se concurrentes, haud secus quam stabili solo persultabant*) | Clash of two infantrymen in an exercise. |
| 168 | 44.30.9 | | | | | A few scattered soldiers were killed by rallying farmers. (*Aliquot palati milites agrestium concursu interfecti sunt*). | Rush to arms. |
| 168 | 44.35.21 | Romans | Macedonians | Infantry | Infantry | Because of skirmishing on the previous day a more stubborn clash of larger forces occurred. (*Sole orto postero die irritatis certamine animis etiam acrius concursum est*). | General word for infantry engagement. |
| 168 | 44.37.10 | Romans | Macedonians | | | So great was the eagerness of both armies to engage. (*Tantus utrique ardor exercitui ad concurrendum fuerat*). | General word for infantry engagement. |
| 168 | 44.38.11 | | | | | Paulus' speech to his war council. The Romans "had to incur the hasty turmoil of drawing up our line and had to enter battle in disorder" (Schlesinger, 1951). (*Nobis tunc repente trepidandum in acie instruenda erat et incompositis concurrendum*) | General word for infantry engagement. |

| | | | | | | | |
|---|---|---|---|---|---|---|---|
| 168 | 44.41.9 | Romans | Macedonians | Infantry | Infantry | "If the Romans had attacked frontally in solid line against an orderly phalanx, as happened to the Paelignians who at the beginning of the battle recklessly met the peltasts, the Romans would have spitted themselves on the spears and would not have withstood the solid line" (Schlesinger, 1951). (*qui si uniuersa acie in frontem aduersus instructam phalangem concurrissent, quod Paelignis principio pugnae incaute congressis aduersus caetratos euenit, induissent se hastis nec confertam aciem sustinuissent*). | General word for infantry engagement. |
| 168 | 44.42.5 | | | | | Small boats gathered from all around the Roman fleet to kill the Macedonian survivers of Pydna. (*Et cum scaphas concurrere undique ab navibus cernerent*). | Gathering fleet. |
| 168 | 44.44.4 | | | | | Women gather at the temple of Diana. (*Concursusque matronarum in templum Dianae*). | Gathering crowd. |
| 167 | 45.36.7 | | | | | The leaders gather on the Capitol. (*Concursus in Capitolium principum civitatis factus est*). | Gathering crowd. |
| 167 | 45.39.7 | | | | | When Syphax had been captured he had drawn a crowd. (*Quos Syphax rex captus... concursus fecerit*). | Gathering crowd. |
| 167 | 45.44.5 | | | | | A crowd gathers around Prusias. *Concursuque undique facto*). | Gathering crowd. |

## Appendix 1.2: the occurrences of *incurrere* in Livy

| *Date* | *Reference* | *Offensive Army* | *Defensive Army* | *Attacking Arm* | *Defensive Arm* | *Notes* | *Comments* |
|---|---|---|---|---|---|---|---|
| 616-578 | 1.37.3 | Romans | Sabines | Cavalry | Infantry | The Roman cavalry attacked from both wings (*incurrisse ab lateribus ferunt*). | Cavalry attack. |
| 401 | 5.11.4 | | | | | P. Curatius, M. Metilius and M. Minucius prosecute Sergius and Verginius, the previous year's military tribunes. (*Prioris anni tribunos militares incurrunt*). | Metaphoricalus e: to fall violently on. |
| 390 | 5.49.5 | Gauls | Romans | Infantry | Infantry | Camillus drew up the Roman battle line and challenged the Gauls. In response the Gauls, with more anger than judgement, attacked the Romans. (*Iraque magis quam consilio in Romanos incurrunt*). | Infantry attack. |
| 325 | 8.31.7 | | | | | Metaphorical hurling oneself against "the head of their councils, upon their general". (*In caput consilii, in ducem incurrere*). | Metaphorical use |
| 316 | 9.21.3 | Saticulani | Romans | Armed townsfolk | Roman outposts | The Romans were laying siege to Saticula. The Saticulani arm themselves, then open their gates and charge quickly against the Roman outposts. (*Saticulani magno cum tumultu patefactis repente portis in stationes hostium incurrerunt*). | Spontaneous attack of townspeople. |
| 305 | 9.40.12 | Roman | Samnites | Cavalry | Infantry | The Roman cavalry, posted on the wings, charged into the enemy flanks. (*In transversa latera hostium incurrunt*). | Cavalry attack. |
| 308 | 9.41.18 | Roman | Umbrians | Infantry | Infantry | The Roman infantry attacked the enemy "not as though their opponents had been men and armed; but - marvellous to relate - began tearing the standards out of the bearers' hands, and then fell to dragging the bearers and to bringing armed men over from the other line to their own; wherever they met resistance, they did their work more with shields than with swords, swinging them from the shoulder and knocking down their enemies with the bosses" (Foster, 1926). (*Non tamquam in uiros aut armatos incurrunt; mirabilia dictu, signa primo eripi coepta signiferis, deinde ipsi signiferi trahi ad consulem armatique milites ex acie in aciem transferri et, sicubi est certamen, scutis magis quam gladiis geritur res; umbonibus incussaque ala sternuntur hostes*). | Infantry attack. |
| 295 | 10.29.9 | Romans | Samnites | Cavalry | Infantry | Fabius ordered the prefects "to lead their squadrons round the wings of the Samnites, that, on the signal being given, they might attack them in the flank with all possible vigour" (Foster, 1926). (*Praefectis equitum iussis ad latus Samnitium circumducere alas, ut signo dato in transuersos quanto maximo possent impetu incurrerent*). | Cavalry attack on flanks. |
| 217 | 22.17.6 | Romans | Carthaginians | Light infantry | Light infantry | The Roman troops, who were to hold the pass, after they had fled from Hannibal's burning cattle, 'also ran into some light armed Carthaginian troops'. (*Leui quoque armaturae hostium incurrere*). | Light infantry skirmish. |
| 212 | 25.37.11 | Romans | Carthaginians | Infantry | Infantry | Roman garrison feared the approaching Carthaginian army. Inspired by Marcius their grief turned to anger and they suddenly dash out and attack the disorganised Carthaginians. (*Inde uerso repente in iram luctu discurrunt ad arma ac uelut accensi rabie discurrunt ad portas et in hostem neglegenter atque incomposite uenientem incurrunt*). | Infantry attack. |
| 211 | 26.4.7 | Romans | Capuans | *Velites* | Cavalry | The Roman legions are forced to create new tactics: the swiftest of the legionaries were given seven small javelins and a small round shield. They were transported on the backs of the cavalry and rode out to face the Capuan cavalry. The *velites* then leapt down and dashed out of the cavalry and while attacking, hurled one javelin after another. (*Pedestris inde acies ex equitatu repente in hostium equites incurrit iaculaque cum impetu alia super alia emittunt*). | Light infantry attack. |
| 211 | 26.25.7 | Aetolians | Macedonians | | | Aetolia was in the habit of making raids into Macedonia. (*Incurrere ea gens in Macedoniam solita erat, ubi regem occupatum externo bello ac sine praesidio esse regnum sensisset*). | General term for attack. |
| 209 | 27.18.15 | Romans | Carthaginians | Infantry and Cavalry | Infantry | Carthaginians were driven to higher ground: 'Scipio ordered his victorious troops to go up facing the centre of the line, divided the rest of his forces with Laelius, and ordered him to circle round the right side of the hill. Scipio himself on the left, after a moderate circuit, charged into the flank of the enemy" (Moore, 1943). (*Inde Scipio iussis aduersus mediam euadere aciem uictoribus ceteras copias cum Laelio diuidit, atque eum parte dextra tumuli circumire ... iubet: ipse ab laeua, circuitu haud magno, in transuersos hostes incurrit*). | Infantry attack on the flanks |
| 208 | 27.32.5 | Achaean League | Romans | Cavalry | Infantry | The King [Philip V] also attacked a Roman cohort with his cavalry. (*Et ipse rex cum equitatu in cohortem Romanam incurrit*). | Cavalry attack. |

| 207 | 27.48.14 | Romans | Carthaginians | Infantry | Infantry | Claudius leads a few idle cohorts around the back of the Roman line and charges into the flank of the enemy. (*Post aciem circumducit, et non hostibus modo sed etiam suis inopinantibus in sinistrum <euectus in dextrum> hostium latus incurrit*). | Infantry attack on the flanks |
|---|---|---|---|---|---|---|---|
| 206 | 28.14.20 | Romans | Carthaginians | Cavalry and Light infantry | Infantry | The Cathaginian wings were pressed with a double attack, the Roman cavalry and light infantry with enclosing wings were attacking the flanks, while the heavy infantry attacked the front, trying to cut off the wings from the rest of the line. (*Cornua ancipiti proelio urgebantur; eques leuisque armatura <ac> uelites circumductis alis in latera incurrebant: cohortes a fronte urgebant ut abrumperent cornua a cetera acie*). | Cavalry and light infantry attack. |
| 206 | 28.33.5 | Romans | Spanish | Light Infantry | Infantry | The Roman light armed troops attacked the Spaniards busy with the cattle. (*Hispani in conspecta procul pecora, uelites in Hispanos praeda occupatos incurrere*). | Light infantry skirmish. |
| 206 | 28.13.6 | Romans | Carthaginians | Cavalry | Cavalry | Mago and Massinissa attack the Romans working on fortifications. Roman cavalry, earlier hidden by Scipio, unexpectedly charge this enemy and drive them off. (*Castra ponentes eos Mago et Masinissa cum omni equitatu adgressi sunt, turbassentque munientes ni abditi post tumulum opportune ad id positum ab Scipione equites improuiso in effusos incurrissent*). | Cavalry attack. |
| 202 | 30.35.1 | Romans | Carthaginians | Cavalry | Infantry | At Zama, Laelius and Massinissa return with their cavalry at an opportune moment and attacked the rear of the enemy line. (*In tempore Laelius ac Masinissa pulsos per aliquantum spatii secuti equites, reuertentes in auersam hostium aciem incurrere*). | Cavalry attack on rear |
| 190 | 37.21.3 | Achaeans | Seleucids | Infantry and Cavalry | Infantry | Diophanes and the Achaeans attacked the rear of the Seleucid troops, who were in marching order. (*deinde eodem, quo pridie, impetu in postremum agmen incurrit*). | Infantry attack |
| 189 | 38.21.8 | Gauls | Gauls | Infantry | Infantry | Romans kept the Gauls at a distance with missiles, with nowhere to run, "like wounded animals [the Gauls] rush headlong upon their friends" (Sage, 1936). (*Velut ferae transfixae in suos temere incurrunt*) | Panicked rush. |
| 185 | 39.31.7 | Romans | Celtiberians | Cavalry | Infantry | The Roman cavalry attacked the flank of the wedge of the enemy pressing on the centre. (*Ipse cum equitibus duarum legionum paulum circumuectus in cuneum hostium, qui mediam urgebat aciem, ab latere incurrit*). | Cavalry attack on flanks. |
| 173 | 42.7.6 | Romans | Ligurians | Cavalry | Infantry | "Then, when the consul saw that the Ligurian masses were nowhere shaken, he ordered the cavalry to mount their horses and to charge the enemy at three points at the same time and with all possible uproar." (Sage, 1938). (*Quod ubi consul uidit nulla parte moueri Ligurum signa, imperat equitibus, ut equos conscendant ac tribus simul partibus in hostis, quanto maximo possent tumultu, incurrant*). | Cavalry attack |
| 171 | 42.59.2 | Thracians | Romans | Cavalry | Cavalry | "First of all the Thracians, like beasts of prey long held behind bars, charged so vigorously with a great shout upon the Roman right wing, the Italian cavalry, that this people, courageous by nature and through experience in war, was thrown into confusion" (Sage, 1935). (*Primi omnium Thraces, haud secus quam diu claustris retentae ferae, ita concitati cum ingenti clamore in dextrum cornu, Italicos equites, incurrerunt, ut usu belli et ingenio inpauida gens turbaretur*). | Cavalry attack |
| 168 | 44.41.8 | Romans | Macedonians | Infantry | Infantry | Macedonians were compelled to go in various ways into a violent meeting with the Romans, who were attacking with speed in small groups and the Macedonian line was interrupted. (*Sicut tum aduersus cateruatim incurrentes Romanos et interrupta multifariam acie obuiam ire cogebantur*). Livy suggests: The Phalanx is irresistible, "but if attacked at several points you compel them to swing their spears about, unwieldy because of their length and weight, they become tangled in a haphazard mess... as was the case on this occasion"(44.41.7-8). | Infantry attack. |

## Appendix 1.3: the occurrences of *procurrere* in Livy

| *Date* | *Reference* | *Offensive Army* | *Defensive Army* | *Attacking Arm* | *Defensive Arm* | *Notes* | *Comments* |
|---|---|---|---|---|---|---|---|
| 449 | 3.61.13 | Romans | Samnites | Infantry | Infantry | Small Roman raids on the Samnites (*procursantes pauci*). | Infantry raids. |
| 423 | 4.40.3 | | | | | People run out of their houses into the streets (*procurreretur in vias*). | Run out |
| 396 | 5.19.9 | Romans | Veii | Infantry | Infantry | Frequent skirmishes between the Romans and Veii. (*et a procursationibus quae multae temere inter murum ac uallum fiebant, edicto ne quis iniussu pugnaret, ad opus milites traducti*) | Small skirmishes |
| 386 | 6.8.2 | Romans | Latins | Infantry | Infantry | An aged Camillus advanced in person against the enemy. The infantry saw this, gave a cheer, and charged forward shouting 'follow the General'. (*Procurrunt pariter omnes clamore sublato 'sequere imperatorem' pro se quisque clamantes*). | Infantry attack |
| 385 | 6.12.8 | Romans | Volscians | Infantry | Infantry | Roman dictator orders: "let us lay our javelins at our feet and arm our right hands with swords only. I would have none run out from the line, but all stand firmly planted and receive the onset of our enemies" (Foster, 1924). (*Pilis ante pedes positis gladiis tantum dextras armemus. ne procurri quidem ab acie uelim sed obnixos uos stabili gradu impetum hostium excipere.*). | Infantry attack |
| 359 | 7.14.4 | Romans | Gauls | Infantry | Infantry | A Gaul drove off some cattle that were grazing outside the stockade. Roman soldiers took the cattle from him, and were stoned to death by the Gauls. "Whereupon a shout arose in the Roman outpost, and men ran forward from both sides. And now the melley was likely to end in regular battle, had not the centurions speedily parted the combatants" (Foster, 1924). (*Deinde ab Romana statione clamor ortus ac procursum utrimque est. Iamque haud procul iusto proelio res erat, ni celeriter diremptum certamen per centuriones esset*). | Infantry attack. |
| 340 | 8.9.14 | Romans | Latins | Light Infantry | Infantry | "The *rorarii* were running out between the *antipilani* and were joining their strength to that of the *hastati* and the *principes*, and the triarii, kneeling on the right knee, were waiting till the consul signed to them to rise" (Foster, 1924). (*Nam et rorarii procurrerant inter antepilanos addiderantque uires hastatis ac principibus et triarii genu dextro innixi nutum consulis ad consurgendum exspectabant*). | Light infantry rush forward. |
| 297 | 10.14.10 | Romans | Samnites | | | Fabius and two military tribunes, his son Maximus and Marcus Valerius, had rushed to the front line (*ad primum aciem procurrerat*). | Rush forward |
| 294 | 10.36.5 | Samnites | Romans | Infantry | Infantry | Roman cavalry charge, but are unhorsed. There is then a rush forward on the part of the Samnites to kill the fallen and on the part of the Romans to save their men. (*Et a Samnitium acie ad opprimendos eos qui ceciderant et ad suos tuendos ab Romanis procursum est*). | Infantry attack. |
| 294 | 10.36.5 | Samnites | Romans | Infantry | Infantry | The Samnites charged forward to kill fallen Roman cavalry more quickly and in greater numbers (*aliquanto et impigre magis et plures procurrerant Samnites*) than the Romans coming to save their men. | Infantry attack. |
| 219 | 21.8.6 | Carthaginians | Saguntines | Infantry | Infantry | The wall of the town is breached and both sides rushed through the gap to attack. (*ita utrimque in pugnam procursum est*). | Infantry attack. |
| 217 | 22.16.2 | Carthaginians | Romans | Cavalry and Light Infantry | Infantry | Carthaginian cavalry and light infantry attack in cycles, charging up then retreating. (*Carptim Poeni et procursando recipiendoque sese pugnauere*) | Cavalry and light infantry attack. |
| 216 | 22.41.1 | Romans | Carthaginians | Infantry | Infantry | "The repulse of a foraging party had led to a general melee, which had come about from the soldiers rushing forward to attack the enemy, rather than any plan or orders on the part of the generals" (Foster, 1929). (*Quod in prohibendis praedatoribus tumultuario proelio ac procursu magis militum quam ex praeparato aut iussu imperatorum*). | Infantry attack. |
| 216 | 22.44.5 | Carthaginians | Romans | Numidian Cavalry | Infantry | Hannibal wanted to draw the Romans into battle by using his Numidian cavalry to attack and provoke the enemy. (*Lacessitque Numidarum procursatione hostes*). | Cavalry attack. |
| 216 | 22.47.1 | Carthaginians | Romans | Light infantry | Light infantry | With a shout the auxiliaries charged forward and battle began between the light infantry. (*Clamore sublato procursum ab auxiliis et pugna leuibus primum armis commissa*). | Light infantry attack. |
| 215 | 23.40.9 | Romans | Carthaginians | Light infantry or infantry | Light infantry or infantry. | 'Charges led to skirmishes with varying results. Finally they went into battle. With standards against standards they fought a regular engagement'. (*per procursationes leuia certamina uario euentu inita; postremo descensum in aciem. Signis conlatis iusto proelio per quattuor horas pugnatum*). | Infantry attack |
| 214 | 24.21.8 | | | | | A crowd of people runs out into the street (*multitudo pars procurrit in vias*). | Run out. |

| | | | | | | | |
|---|---|---|---|---|---|---|---|
| 212 | 25.9.7 | Carthaginians | Romans | Numidian Cavalry | Roman Farms | Numidian raids on farms (*procursatio Numidarum*). | Cavalry raids. |
| 212 | 25.11.3 | Romans | Carthaginians | Infantry | Infantry | Hannibal, unable to take the citadel near Tarentum by siege, decided to protect the Tarentines by separating the city from the citadel with an earthwork. He hoped that if they should make a ferocious attack the garrison's strength would be depleted'. (*Si ferocius procucurrissent, magna caede ita attenuari praesidii uires ut facile per se ipsi Tarentini urbem ab iis tueri possent*). | Possible infantry attack. |
| 212 | 25.21.5 | Romans | Carthaginians | Infantry | Infantry | Fulvius is drawn into battle by the impulse of his soldiers (*quam militum impetu fortuito tractus*). With this same recklessness the battle line was drawn up "according to the whim of the soldiers" (*acies ad libidinem militum*). "Who happened to dash forward and take their stand wherever their own fancy had carried them, and then capriciously or in fear abandoned their positions" (Moore, 1940). (*procurrentium consistentiumque quo loco ipsorum tulisset animus, deinde per libidinem aut metum deserentium locum*). | Infantry 'rushing forward'. |
| 212 | 25.39.6 | Romans | Carthaginians | Cavalry and Infantry | Infantry | Marcius planned to take a Carthaginian camp in Spain. He hid a cohort and a cavalry unit in a wood between the nearest Carthaginian camp and the other Carthaginians, stationed six miles away. The Romans set fire to the camp. In the panic the Carthaginians fled and ran towards the other Carthaginian forces. 'They were surrounded by the cohort and cavalry rushing out of their hiding place and were slain to the last man'. (*Ubi ab cohorte et equitibus ex occulto procurrentibus circumuenti caesique ad unum omnes sunt*). | Cavalry and infantry attack |
| 210 | 27.2.11 | Romans | Carthaginians | Cavalry and Infantry | Cavalry and Infantry | "Mixed cavalry and infantry engagements, rather skirmishes than important battles". (*Ibi per dies aliquot cum ab stationibus procursaretur, mixta equitum peditumque tumultuosa magis proelia quam magna*). | Skirmishes |
| 207 | 27.41.5 | Romans | Carthaginians | Light Infantry | Light Infantry | In the plain between the two armies, charges, starting from outposts brought on engagements not important enough to be mentioned. (*In medio campo ab stationibus procursantes certamina haud satis digna dictu serebant*) | Light infantry skirmishes. |
| 207 | 27.42.3 | Romans | Carthaginians | Cavalry and Infantry | Cavalry and Infantry | "Of the Roman infantry also the first legion and the right *ala* were coming into the battle. In disorder the enemy engaged, just as chance brought a man face to face with either a foot-soldier or a horse-man. The battle was enlarged by the reserves and increased by the numbers of men rushing into the fray" (Moore, 1943). (*Peditum etiam prima legio et dextra ala proelium inibat. incompositi hostes, ut quemque aut pediti aut equiti casus obtulit, ita conserunt manus. crescit pugna subsidiis et procurrentium ad certamen numero augetur*). | Infantry attack |
| 206 | 28.14.3 | Romans | Carthaginians | Infantry | Infantry | A standoff: "from neither side was there a charge, or a missile hurled, or any raising of a shout" (Moore, 1949). (*Ab neutra parte procursum telumue missum aut uox ulla orta*). | Infantry attack |
| 206 | 28.33.3 | Romans | Carthaginians | Light Infantry | Infantry | Scipio sent in his light infantry. When these had begun the battle with an attack (*a quibus ubi per procursationem commissa pugna esset*), he ordered the cavalry to attack. | Light infantry attack. |
| 203 | 30.10.6 | Romans | Carthaginians | | | Roman vessels dash out to attack the enemy (*qua procurrere speculatoriae naues in hostem*). | Naval attack. |
| 197 | 33.7.6 | | | | | The battle began at first with fighting between *skirmishers*'. (*Principio a paucis procurrentibus lacessita pugna est*). | Participle: those skirmishing. |
| 195 | 34.2.9 | | | | | Running into the streets (*in publicum procurrendi*). | Run out. |
| 195 | 34.3.6 | | | | | Matrons running into the streets (*matronae... procucurrerint in publicum*). | Run out. |
| 195 | 34.15.4 | Romans | Spanish | Infantry | Infantry | Cato ordered the second legion to attack the Spanish camp. 'If a soldier in too great eagerness went ahead of the rank, he himself rode up between the lines and struck him with a spear shaft' (*Si quis extra ordinem auidius procurrit, et ipse interequitans sparo percutit*). | Breaking ranks |
| 195 | 34.39.3 | Spartans | Romans | Infantry | Infantry | The Spartans, using missiles, were unable to hurl them on the run (*ad emittenda cum procursu*) on account of the limited space. | Run out. |
| 193 | 35.5.2 | Romans | Gauls | Infantry | Infantry | The new consul was now with the leading standards, holding the legions back in reserve, "lest in their ardour for the fight they should rush forward before the signal was given" (Sage, 1935). (*Nunc legiones continebat in subsidiis, ne certaminis studio prius procurrerent quam datum signum esset*). | Breaking ranks. |
| 189 | 38.26.7 | Gauls | Romans | Infantry | Infantry | "The discharge of a veritable cloud of light missiles overwhelmed the line of the Gauls. No one dared to rush forward from the ranks lest he expose his body | Breaking ranks. |

| | | | | | | | |
|---|---|---|---|---|---|---|---|
| | | | | | | to wounds from all sides, and, standing fast, the more closely they were crowded together the more wounds they recieved, the attackers aiming, so to speak, at a target" (Sage, 1936). (*Velut nubes leuium telorum coniecta obruit aciem Gallorum. Nec aut procurrere quisquam ab ordinibus suis, ne nudarent undique corpus ad ictus, audebant, et stantes, quo densiores erant, hoc plura, uelut destinatum petentibus, uulnera accipiebant*). | |
| 181 | 40.30.5 | Spanish | Romans | Cavalry | Cavalry | Marcus Fulvius took two troops of allied cavalry to reconnoitre the enemy camp. The enemy's cavalry rushed out of the camp (*ubi equitatus hostium castris procucurrisset*). | Cavalry attack from out of a camp. |
| 171 | 42.65.8 | Romans | Macedonians | Infantry | Infanty | Perseus had the Romans surrounded: 'whenever they broke ranks by charging forward, they were exposed to javelins and arrows'. (*Ingens Romanos terror circumstabat; nam neque conferti propellere eos, qui in tumulum conitebantur, poterant et, ubi ordines procursando soluissent, patebant iaculis sagittisque*). | Roman infantry attack. |
| 171 | 42.64.6 | Romans | Macedonians | Light infantry | Light infantry | A brief engagement between light armed troops and skirmishers (*breue certamen leuis armaturae maxime cum procursatoribus fuit*). | Participle: those skirmishing. |
| 169 | 44.9.7 | | | | | The *testudo*: the infantry lock shields so that they form a 'tortoise' sloped like a roof. Then two armed men rush out (*duo armati procurrebant*) and climb the tortoise. | Run out. |
| 169 | 44.10.5 | Thessalonicans | Romans | Infantry | Infantry | G. Marcius was successful against those who rushed out of the city (*procurrentes ab urbe*). | Run out. |
| 169 | 44.4.6 | Romans | Macedonians | Light Infantry | Light Infantry | The light infantry were able to charge forward over the ridge and engage the enemy light infantry in flanking attacks over favourable and unfavourable ground. (*Leuis armatura etiam per anfractus iugi procurrere et ab lateribus cum leui armatura conserere per iniqua atque aequa loca pugnam poterat*). | Light infantry attack. |

## Appendix 1.4: the occurrences of *decurrere* in Livy

| *Date* | *Reference* | *Offensive Army* | *Defensive Army* | *Attacking Arm* | *Defensive Arm* | *Notes* | *Comments* |
|---|---|---|---|---|---|---|---|
| 753 | 1.12.8 | Sabines | Romans | Infantry | Infantry | Sabines attack Romans from higher ground. (*Mettius Curtius ab Sabinis princeps ab arce decucurrerat et effusos egerat Romanos).* | Attack from high ground. |
| 672 - 640 | 1.27.10 | Albans | Fidenates | Infantry | Infantry | 'In case the Albans should suddenly charge down from the hills and cut them off from their town, they beat a retreat'. (*Itaque ne subito ex collibus decursu Albanorum intercluderentur ab oppido, terga vertunt*). | Attack from high ground. |
| 508 | 2.10.3 | Etruscans | Horatius Cocles | | | Cocles sees the enemy charge down. (*Inde citatos decurrere hostes uidisset* ). | Rushing down from high ground. |
| 477 | 2.50.6 | Fabii | Veii | Infantry | | The Fabii run down (*decurrerent*) to capture some sheep. | Rushing down from high ground. |
| 461 | 3.11.1 | | | | | The consuls held the levy and the tribunes rushed down to the place, drawing the crowd with them. (*Eo decurrunt tribuni contionemque secum trahunt*). | Rushing down from high ground. |
| 414 | 4.50.5 | | | | | Postumius orders savage punishments. A crowd gathers to interrupt the execution and Postumius, in a rage, ran down from his tribunal (*de tribunali decurrit*) to the crowd. | Rushing down from high ground. |
| 396 | 5.23.10 | | | | | "Camillus to pay in a tenth part of its value [his share of the spoils] to the public treasury". (*Decimae pretium partis in publicum deferret*). | Non-military use. |
| 384 | 6.19.3 | | | | | The Romans decide on a proposal which sounded milder than assasinating Marcus Manlius. (*Decurriter ad leniorem verbis sententiam*). | Metaphorical use meaning 'flowing' of opinion. |
| 368 | 6.38.3 | | | | | "When the tribes were summoned to vote, and the proposers of the measures would not yield to the vetoes of their colleagues, the frightened patricians were put to their two last shifts - the greatest office, and the greatest of the citizens" (Foster, 1924). (*Cum tribus uocarentur nec intercessio collegarum latoribus obstaret, trepidi patres ad duo ultima auxilia, summum imperium summumque ad ciuem decurrunt*). | Metaphorical use. |
| 321 | 9.4.9 | Romans | Gauls | Infantry | Infantry | Lucius Lentulus made a speech saying that it was in their power to charge down from the Capitoline against the enemy. (*Illis ut decurrere ex Capitolio armatis in hostem licuit*). | Attack from high ground. |
| 314 | 9.24.9 | | | | | A deserter from Sora had a plan to take the city. He posted ten Romans on the citadel, then running down from there he made as much noise as possible. (*Decurrit inde, quanto maxime poterat*). | Rushing down from high ground. |
| 295 | 10.27.8 | | | | | Between the battle-lines of the Romans and Gauls a hind is chased by a wolf. (*Inter duas acies decurrit*). | Rushing down. |
| 218 | 21.26.4 | | | | | The river Rhone flows into the sea through several mouths. (*Pluribus enim divisus amnis in mare decurrit*). | Flow of a river. |
| 218 | 21.31.4 | | | | | The flow of the rivers Isara and Rhone. (*Ibi Isara Rhodanusque amnes diuersis ex Alpibus decurrentes*). | Flow of a river. |
| 218 | 21.33.4 | Gauls | Carthaginians | Infantry | Infantry | The Gallic infantry rushed down from the cliffs on either side and attacked the Carthaginian army. (*Diversis rupibus iuxta inuia ac deuia adsueti decurrunt*). | Attack from high ground. |
| 218 | 21.33.9 | Carthaginians | Gauls | Light Infantry | Infantry | The Carthaginians needed to get through a pass which the Gauls guarded by day. Hannibal left his baggage, cavalry and most of the infantry in the valley at night and took some of the light infantry to occupy the heights. At dawn his main army decamped and were attacked by the Gauls. Then Hannibal 'charged down from higher ground and routed the enemy by the vigour of the attack'. (*Decurrit ex superiore loco et cum impetu ipso fudisset hostem*). | Attack from high ground. |
| 217 | 22.4.6 | Carthaginians | Romans | Infantry | Infantry | The Romans were hemmed in between the mountains and the lake, the Carthaginians attacked. "As they charged down, each at the nearest point, their onset was all the more sudden and unforeseen in as much as the mist from the lake lay less thickly on the heights than on the plain…" (Foster, 1929). (*Qui ubi, qua cuique proximum fuit, decucurrerunt, eo magis Romanis subita atque improuisa res fuit, quod orta ex lacu nebula campo quam montibus densior sederat*). | Attack from high ground. |
| 217 | 22.4.7 | Carthaginians | Romans | Infantry | Infantry | "…and the attacking columns had been clearly visible to one another from the various hills and had therefore delivered their charge at more nearly the same instant" (Foster, 1929). (*agminaque hostium ex pluribus collibus ipsa inter se satis conspecta eoque magis pariter decucurrerant*). | Attack from high ground. |
| 217 | 22.31.10 | | | | | "It was because the nation, appalled by their great disaster, could not put up with so long a delay that resort was had to the popular election of an acting dictator" (Foster, 1929). (*Quam moram quia exspectare territa iam clade ciuitas non poterat, eo decursum esse ut a populo crearetur qui pro dictatore esset*). | Non-military use. |
| 215 | 23.35.6 | | | | | Sempronius orders his soldiers on frequent manoeuvres so that the new recruits could learn to follow the standards and recognise their own ranks in the battle line. (*Ibi quia otiosa statiua erant, crebro decurrere milites cogebat ut tirones—ea maxima pars uolonum erant—adsuescerent signa sequi et in* | Military exercise. |

| | | | | | | | |
|---|---|---|---|---|---|---|---|
| | | | | | | *acie agnoscere ordines suos*). | |
| 214 | 24.27.9 | | | | | Syracusan mob rushed down to the waterfront in disorder to keep away invaders (*ac primo etiam tumultuose decurrerat multitudo ad prohibendos si in terram egrederentur*). | Rushing down from high ground. |
| 214 | 24.36.4 | | | | | Fifty-five Carthaginian ships under Bomilcar sail from the sea into the large harbour at Syracuse. (*Sub idem fere tempus et naues longae quinque et quinquaginta Carthaginiensium cum Bomilcare in magnum portum Syracusas ex alto decurrere*). | Sailing of ships. |
| 214 | 24.39.4 | Romans | People of Henna | | | The Hennensians held an assembly to get the keys of the city back from the Roman garrison commander. Roman soldiers take up position above the theatre, on an agreed signal the soldiers rush down and slaughter the men of Henna. (*Militesque intenti dudum ac parati alii superne in auersam contionem clamore sublato decurrunt, alii ad exitus theatri conferti obsistunt*). | Attack from high ground. |
| 213 | 24.48.11 | | | | | Quintus Satorius taught the Numidian infantry in the Roman style to follow standards and keep the ranks. (*Proxime morem Romanum instruendo et decurrendo signa sequi et seruare ordines docuit*). | Military exercises. |
| 212 | 25.17.5 | | | | | At Gracchus' funeral customary military exercises were performed. (*Armatum exercitum decucurisse cum tripudiis Hispanorum motibusque armorum et corporum suae cuique genti adsuetis*). | Military exercises. |
| 211 | 26.10.6 | | | | | Numidian deserters (from Carthaginians) were ordered to move from the Aventine through the centre of the Esquiline hill. When men on the Capitoline saw them riding down (*cliuo Publicio in equis decurrentes*), they believed the Aventine had been captured. | Rushing down from high ground. |
| 211 | 26.18.4 | | | | | Recourse to holding an election for pro-consul. (*Cum alii alium nominarent, postremum eo decursum est ut proconsuli creando in Hispaniam comitia haberentur*). | Non-military use. |
| 210 | 26.51.4 | | | | | Scipio trains his army: 'on the first day the legions would march for four miles under arms'. (*Primo die legiones in armis quattuor milium spatio decurrerent*). | Military exercise. |
| 210 | 26.51.5 | | | | | Scipio trains his army: on the fifth day they again run under arms. (*Quinto iterum in armis decursum est*). | Military exercise. |
| 210 | 26.51.8 | | | | | Scipio trains his army: he marches with his legions (*Nunc cum legionibus decurrebat*). | Military exercises. |
| 207 | 27.42.4 | Romans | Carthaginians | Infantry | Infantry | 'In disorder the enemy engage, just as chance brought a man face-to-face with either a foot-soldier or a horse-man. The battle was enlarged by the reserves and increased by the numbers of men rushing in. While his men were fighting, in spite of the uproar and the panic, Hannibal would have drawn them up - a difficult thing except in a veteran army and for a veteran commander - if from the rear the sound of the shouting cohorts and maniples, as they dashed down the hillsides, had not inspired the fear of being cut off from the camp'. (*incompositi hostes, ut quemque aut pediti aut equiti casus obtulit, ita conserunt manus. crescit pugna subsidiis et procurrentium ad certamen numero augetur; pugnantesque — quod nisi in uetere exercitu et duce ueteri haud facile est— inter tumultum ac terrorem instruxisset Hannibal, ni cohortium ac manipulorum decurrentium per colles clamor ab tergo auditus metum ne intercluderentur a castris iniecisset*). | Infantry rushing down from a hill. |
| 206 | 28.20.5 | Romans | City of Iliturgi | Light Infantry | | Roman light infantry attack the city of Iliturgi from a hill above the city. (*decurrunt cum clamore in urbem iam captam ab Romanis*). | Attack from high ground. |
| 204 | 29.22.2 | | | | | Practice battle of Scipio's Roman troops: ([*Exercitum*] *non instructos modo, sed hos decurrentes*). | Military exercises. |
| 204 | 29.27.13 | | | | | Scipio's fleet sails into port (*Eo classis decurrit*). | Sailing of ships. |
| 200 | 31.20.5 | | | | | It was proposed that Lentulus enter the city in ovation. (*decurrebatur tamen eo ut ouans urbem iniret*). | Non-military use. |
| 197 | 33.17.12 | Leucadians | Romans | Infantry | Infantry | The Romans breach Leucas and the Leucadians rush down from higher ground and draw up their line in the forum. (*Eos tamen ex superiore loco magno cum tumultu decurrentes acie in foro instructa iusto proelio aliquamdiu Leucadii sustinuerunt*). | Rushing down from high ground. |
| 196 | 33.26.9 | | | | | A wolf runs through the forum (*decurrisset*). | Running animal. |
| 192 | 35.35.9 | | | | | Advice to Nabis, that he should keep his troops trained and fit, he "should lead them out, force them to march under arms and at the same time stimulate their courage and train their bodies" (Sage, 1935). (*In armis decurrere cogeret, simul animos acueret et corpora exerceret*). | Military exercises. |
| 190 | 37.13.4 | | | | | The Roman fleet sailed into a Samian port. (*In eundum portum decurrit*). | Sailing of ships. |
| 189 | 38.8.3 | | | | | The opinions of all flowed in this direction - that peace should be sought, if possible on equal terms, if not, endurable terms'. (*Omnium eo sententiae decurrerunt, ut pax si posset aequis, si minus tolerandis condicionibus peteretur*). | Metaphorical use meaning 'flowing' of opinion. |
| 189 | 38.13.7 | | | | | The River Meander flowing through the centre of the city. (*Media urbe decurrens*). | Flow of a river |
| 186 | 39.13.12 | | | | | Women dressed as Bacchantes ran down to the Tiber in order to dip burning torches into the water. (*Matronas Baccharum habitu crinibus sparsis cum ardentibus facibus decurrere ad Tiberim*). | Rushing down from high ground. |

| 182 | 40.6.5 | | | | | Mock battle of Perseus and Demetrius: "it was the custom when the ceremony of purification was finished to manoeuvre the army and dividing it into battle-lines to clash in a sham battle" (Sage. 1938). (*Mos erat lustrationis sacro peracto decurrere exercitum, et diuisas bifariam [duas] acies concurrere ad simulacrum pugnae*). | Military exercises. |
|---|---|---|---|---|---|---|---|
| 182 | 40.7.1 | Macedonians | Macedonians | Cavalry and Infantry | Cavalry and Infantry | Perseus and Demetrius meet in a mock battle. (*Conuiuium eo die sodalium, qui simul decurrerant, uterque habuit, cum uocatus ad cenam ab Demetrio Perseus negasset*). | Military exercises. |
| 182 | 40.9.10 | | | | | Military exercises (*hesterno die in lustratione et decursu et simulacro ludicro pugnae*) | Military exercises. |
| 182 | 40.10.3 | | | | | Military exercises (*decursus militum*). | Military exercises. |
| 181 | 40.31.2 | Romans | Celtiberians | Cavalry and Infantry | | Roman cavalry and 6,000 auxiliary infantry marched around a hill behind the enemy camp. On a signal they were to attack the camp from the hill (*inde ubi clamorem audisset, decurrere ad castra eorum*), which was taken without a struggle. | Attack on a camp, from high ground. |
| 181 | 40.31.8 | Romans | Celtiberians | Cavalry and Infantry | | The Romans did not delay to rush down upon the camp as they had been ordered. (*Nec morati sunt quin decurrerent, sicut imperatum, ad castra*). | Attack on a camp, from high ground. |
| 179 | 40.47.8 | | | | | Gracchus orders the tribunes of the soldiers to command the Roman infantry and cavalry to march under arms in order to discourage Celtiberian ambassadors from sending aid to the besieged city of Certima. (*Tribunisque militum imperat, ut ornari omnes copias peditum equitumque et decurrere iubeant armatas*). | Military exercise. |
| 178 | 41.2.8 | | | | | In confusion Romans were drawn out of their camp and, some armed, but most unarmed, ran down to the sea. (*Pauci, armati alii, maior pars inermes, ad mare decurrunt*). | Rushing down from high ground. |
| 172 | 42.16.1 | | | | | Perseus hired Evander the Cretan and three Macedonians to assassinate Eumenes on his way to Delphi. From high ground they rolled down rocks which stunned the king. "The assassins might have made a short detour around the end of the wall and have run down to kill the wounded man" (*latrones, cum brevi circumitu maceriae decurrere ad conficiendum saucium possent*), but instead they ran away. | Rushing down from high ground. |
| 171 | 42.52.4 | | | | | Movement of troops, but not in regular manouvre (*non iusto decursu tamen*). | Military exercise. |
| 171 | 42.67.7 | | | | | The consul moves camp to Gonnus, as it offers a "sally-point" to Thessaly (Sage, 1938). (*In Thessaliam opportunum Macedonibus decursum*). | Meaning a point of attack. |
| 169 | 44.9.5 | | | | | The Romans perform military manoeuvres in an arena. (*Horum inductio ex parte simulacrum decurrentis exercitus erat, ex parte elegantioris [exercitus] quam militaris artis propiorque gladiatorium armorum usum. cum alios decursu edidissent motus*) | Military exercise. |
| 169 | 44.9.6 | | | | | The same exercises as above | Military exercise. |
| 168 | 45.1.8 | | | | | Gaius Licinius displays despatches from Macedonia after a chariot race in Rome. Seeing them the people rushed down into the arena. (*quibus conspectis repente inmemor spectaculi populus in medium decurrit*). | Rushing down from high ground. |

## Appendix 1.5: the occurrences of *impetus* in Livy

| *Date* | *Reference* | *Offensive Army* | *Defensive Army* | *Attacking Arm* | *Defensive Arm* | *Notes* | *Comments* |
|---|---|---|---|---|---|---|---|
| >753 | 1.4.9 | | | | | Romulus and Remus would attack robbers laden with booty. (*Sed in latrones praeda onustos impetus facere*). | General use of 'attack'. |
| >753 | 1.5.4 | Romans | Numitor | | | Romulus and Remus charged with making attacks on the lands of Numitor. (*Crimini maxime dabant in Numitoris agros ab iis impetus fieri*). | General use of 'attack'. |
| 753 | 1.5.7 | Romulus | King Amulius | | | Imaginary assault on the gates of the Roman camp (*impetum facit*) | Attack on camp |
| 753-717 | 1.10.4 | Caeninenses | Romans | | | The Caeninenses invade Roman territory. (*Ita per se ipsum nomen Caeninum in agrum Romanum impetum facit*). | General use of 'attack'. |
| 753-717 | 1.10.5 | Romans | Sabines | | | Romans captured the Sabine city in the first assault once their king had been killed. (*Duce hostium occiso urbem primo impetu capit*). | Attack on a city. |
| 753-717 | 1.11.2 | Romans | Antemnates | Infantry | Infantry | The Romans rout the Antemnates at the first attack. (*Fusi igitur primo impetu et clamor hostes*). | Roman infantry attack. |
| 753-717 | 1.12.9 | Romans | Sabines | | | Romulus led a band of youths in an attack on Mettius Curtius. (*Iuvenum Romulus impetum facit*). | General use of 'attack' |
| 753-717 | 1.13.1 | Sabines | Romans | Sabine women | | The Sabine women move into the battle to part the hostile forces. (*Ex transverso impetu facto dirimere intestas acies*). | An attempt to stop a battle. |
| 672-640 | 1.23.3 | Albans | Romans | | | The Albans invade Roman territory with a great army. (*Albani priores ingenti exercitu in agrum Romanum impetum fecere*). | General use of 'attack'. |
| 672-640 | 1.25.9 | Romans | Albans | | | Horatius attacks the first of the Curiatii brothers with great vigour (*in eum magno impetu rediit*). | As an adverb meaning vigour. |
| 672-640 | 1.27.10 | Romans | Veientes | Infantry | Infantry | Veientes failed to withstand the Roman attack (*Nec illi tulere impetum*). | Roman infantry attack. |
| 616-578 | 1.41.4 | | | | | The shouting and vigour (*clamor impetusque multitudinis*) of a crowd. | Meaning vigour. |
| 534-510 | 1.57.3 | Romans | City of Ardea | | | The Romans attempt to capture Ardea by assault. (*Temptata res est, si primo impetu capi Ardea posset*). | Attack on a city. |
| 508 | 2.10.3 | Etruscans | Romans | | | The Etruscans attack Rome. (*Cum captum repentino impetu Ianiculum*). | Attack on a city. |
| 508 | 2.10.4 | Etruscans | Romans | Infantry | One man | Horatius Cocles promised that he would receive the attack of the enemy, as far as it could be withstood by one body. (*Se impetum hostium, quantum corpore uno posset obsisti, excepturum*). | Non-Roman infantry attack. |
| 508 | 2.10.10 | Etruscans | Romans | Infantry | One man | The Etruscans attack Cocles in order to dislodge him from the bridge. (*Iam impetu conabantur detrudere uirum*). | Non-Roman infantry attack |
| 508 | 2.10.10 | Etruscans | Romans | Infantry | One man | Cocles stood on the bridge while the Etruscans tried to dislodge him by attacks, which he withstood (*pauore subito impetum sustinuit*). | Non-Roman infantry attack. |
| 508 | 2.14.6 | Etruscans | Aricini | Infantry | Infantry | The attack of the Etruscans was so vigorous that they routed the Aricini at the first charge. (*Proelio inito adeo concitato impetu se intulerant Etrusci ut funderent ipso incursu Aricinos*). | As an adverb meaning vigour. |
| 500 | 2.19.7 | Romans | Latins | Cavalry | Cavalry | Aebutius, the master of the horse attacked Octavius Mamilius. (*Et ad alterum cornu Aebutis magister equitum in Octavium Mamilium impetum dederat*). | Roman cavalry attack. |
| 500 | 2.20.13 | Romans | Latins | Infantry | Infantry | So great was the ardour of the Romans that they routed the enemy in one attack, and captured their camp. (*Tantusque ardor fuit ut eodem impetu quo fuderant hostem Romani castra caperent*). | Roman infantry attack. |
| 494 | 2.29.4 | | | | | The Roman mob attack senators. (*Cum conversus in patres impetus esset*). | General use of 'attack'. |
| 494 | 2.30.14 | Romans | Volsci | | | The Romans took the Volscian camp (*castra impetu ceperunt*). | Attack on a camp. |
| 494 | 2.31.3 | Romans | Sabines | | | The Romans captured the Sabine camp. (*Impetu castra capta*). | Attack on a camp. |
| 493 | 2.33.7 | Corioli | Romans | Infantry | Infantry | At Corioli Marcius was able to repel an attack from the town. (*Non modo erumpentium rettudit*...). | Attack from a town. |
| 492 | 2.34.4 | Volsci | Romans | | | Roman agents buying corn were in danger of attack from the people of the Volsci and Pomptini (*ab impetu hominum*). | General use of 'attack' |
| 491 | 2.35.2 | | | | | The Roman people would have attacked Marcius as he came out of the curia. (*In exeuntem e curia impetus factus esset*). | General use of 'attack'. |
| 480 | 2.45.8 | | | | | The Roman consuls wished to stimulate the fury of the already eager soldiers (*incitato semel militi adderent impetum*). | General use meaning vigour. |
| 480 | 2.47.5 | Etruscans | Romans | | | The Etruscans capture the Roman camp. (*In quae haud magno certamine impetu facto*). | Attack on a camp. |
| 480 | 2.47.6 | Etruscans | Romans | Infantry | Infantry | Etruscans forced their way into the Roman camp. Manlius posted men at all the gates to cut off their escape. The Etruscans, in desperation, rushed around in whatever direction there was a hope of escape, and made several attacks to no purpose. (*Vano* | Non-Roman infantry attack. |

| | | | | | | | |
|---|---|---|---|---|---|---|---|
| | | | | | | *aliquotiens impetu issent*) | |
| 477 | 2.50.1 | Romans | Veientes | Infantry | Infantry | Surprise attacks on raiding parties. (*Subiti impetus in incursantes*). | General use of 'attack'. |
| 476 | 2.51.4 | Veientes | Romans | | | The Veientes send out an expedition into Roman territory. (*In Romanum agrum impetus dabant*). | General use of 'attack'. |
| 475 | 2.52.6 | | | | | Attack of the tribunes on Spurius Servilius. (*Gratiaeque tribunicios impetus tulit*). | General use of 'attack'. |
| 475 | 2.53.2 | Veientes | Romans | Infantry | Infantry | Romans sack the Sabine camp. While preoccupied with the camp the Veientes attack the Roman troops. (*Pars Romanos toto impetu intentos in castra adoriuntur*). | Non-Roman infantry attack |
| 471 | 2.57.2 | | | | | Conflicting opinions (*Vbi cum timor atque ira in uicem sententias uariassent, quo magis spatio interposito ab impetu ad consultandum auocabantur*). | Meaning conflicting opinions. |
| 468 | 2.64.6 | Romans | Sabines | Infantry | Infantry | The Roman infantry attack the Sabines (*impetu facto, dum se putant vincere vicere*). | Roman infantry attack |
| 468 | 2.64.11 | Romans | Volsci | Infantry | Infantry | The Volsci anticipate a Roman infantry attack. (*Intentos velut ad impetum hostium tenuit*). | Roman infantry attack. |
| 468 | 2.65.2 | Romans | Volsci | Infantry | Infantry | Fresh Roman infantry attack the weary Volsci, who are beaten back at the first attack. (*Volscum primo impetu perculit*). | Roman Infantry attack. |
| 468 | 2.65.4 | Volsci | Romans | Infantry | Infantry | The Volsci, having discharged their missiles in the first attack, picked up stones… (*Volscus effusis ad primum impetum missilibus telis saxa obiacentia pedibus ingerit in subeuntes*…). | Non-Roman infantry attack. |
| 468 | 2.65.5 | Romans | Volsci | Infantry | Infantry | The Romans on the left wing were nearly overwhelmed by this rain of stones. But the consul, reproaching them for cowardice shamed them into fighting. "First they made a resolute stand; then after holding their ground and returning blow for blow, they even dared to press forward and, renewing their cheers, set the line in motion; then with another attack they struggled upward and scaled the height" (Sage, 1919). (*Restitere primo obstinatis animis; deinde, ut obtinentes locum uim pro ui referebant, audent ultro gradum inferre et clamore renouato commouent aciem; tum rursus impetu capto enituntur*). | Roman infantry attack. |
| 464 | 3.5.1 | Aequi | Romans | | | The Aequi made many attacks on the Romans in one place or another (*multique impetus hinc atque illic facti*), these included: an attack on a camp, destroying Roman fields and if possible attacking the city itself. | Attack on a city or camp. |
| 364 | 3.5.10 | Romans | Aequi | Infantry | Infantry | The Aequi, in Roman territory, were spread out and collecting booty, "when they were attacked by Postumius at several points where he had stationed troops". (*In quos palatos praedom agentes Postumius aliquot locis, quibus opportuna imposuerat praesidia, impetum dedit*). | Roman infantry attack. |
| 461 | 3.10.7 | | | | | Sibylline books warn of attacks on the highest places of the city. (*Qui in loca summa urbis impetus*). | Attack on a city. |
| 461 | 3.11.7 | | | | | Caeso sustains the attacks of the tribunes (*unus impetus tribunicios … sustinebat*). | General use of 'attack'. |
| 461 | 3.13.3 | | | | | Caeso is nearly killed by the fury of the people (*impetu populi*). | Meaning violence of a crowd. |
| 461 | 3.14.3 | | | | | The 'fury' of Caeso's friends after his exile (*impetus suos*). | General use of 'attack'. |
| 460 | 3.18.9 | | | | | 'The ardour and enthusiasm of the [Roman] soldiers'. (*Ardor impetuque*). | Meaning enthusiasm. |
| 459 | 3.22.7 | Romans | Volsci | | | The Volsci were unable to sustain the Roman attack from their entrenchments (*non sustinentes Volscos vallo deturbat*). | Attack on a camp. |
| 457 | 3.30.2 | Aequi | Romans | | | A night attack (*nocturno impetu*) by the Aequi on the garrison at Corbio. | Attack on a camp. |
| 451 | 3.35.7 | | | | | "Open opposition to his [Appius Claudius'] desires being more than they dared to venture" (Foster, 1922). (*Propalam obuiam ire cupiditati parum ausi, obsecundando mollire impetum adgrediuntur*). | Meaning propose |
| 449 | 3.53.1 | Romans | Romans | Crowd | | Valerius and Horatius were ordered to protect the Decemvirs from the 'anger and violence of the Roman people'. (*Decemviris quoque abira et impetu multitudinis praecavere iubentur*). | Meaning violence of a crowd. |
| 449 | 3.60.10 | Romans | Volsci and Aequi | Infantry | Infantry | 'The shouting and fury of the attack' (*Clamore atque impetu invadit*). | As an adverb meaning vigour. |
| 449 | 3.61.8 | Romans | Aequi and Volsci | Cavalry | Infantry | The Roman consul, Valerius, inspires his cavalry by saying that the enemy would not sustain their attack (*non sustinebunt impetum*). | Roman cavalry attack. |
| 449 | 3.63.2 | Romans | Sabines | Cavalry | Infantry | Roman cavalry made an attack against the enemy. (*Simul et in hostes… impetum facit*). | Roman cavalry attack. |
| 445 | 4.3.6 | | | | | Canuleius asks: 'Why men should have almost attacked him in the Senate'. (*Cur in me impetus modo paene in senatu sit factus*). | General use of 'attack'. |
| 437 | 4.18.8 | Romans | Etruscans | Infantry | Infantry | The Roman infantry made a furious attack. At no | Roman infantry |

| | | | | | | | |
|---|---|---|---|---|---|---|---|
| | | | | | | point could the Etruscan legions withstand this attack. (*Secuta peditum acies ingenti vi conflixit. Nulla parte legiones Etruscae sustinuere impetum Romanorum*). | attack. |
| 437 | 4.19.2 | Etruscans | Romans | Cavalry | Cavalry | Tolumnius's attack brought confusion to the Roman squadrons. (*Is cum ad impetum Tolumni, quacumque se intendisset, trepidantes Romanas videret turmas*). | Non-Roman cavalry attack. |
| 431 | 4.28.1 | Romans | Volsci | Cavalry | Cavalry | Marcus Fabius had led a cavalry attack. (*Et Fabius cum equitatu impetum dederat*). | Roman cavalry attack. |
| 431 | 4.29.1 | Volsci | Romans | Infantry | Infantry | Messius attacked with a group of courageous young men over the slain bodies of his enemies, and reached the Volscian camp (*Messium impetus per stratos caede hostes cum globo fortissimorum iuvenum extulit ad castra Volscorum*). | Roman infantry attack. |
| 426 | 4.32.12 | Romans | Etruscans | Infantry | Infantry | The armies came together with great vigour. (*Legiones impetu ingenti configunt*). | An adverb meaning vigour. |
| 426 | 4.33.12 | Romans | Fidenates | | | The Romans push forward in the impetuosity of their pursuit of the Fidenates. (*Eodem et Romanos sequentes impetus rapit*). | Meaning impetuosity. |
| 423 | 4.38.3 | Volsci | Romans | Infantry | Cavalry | A Roman cavalry cohort tried to stop the attack of the Volsci. (*Parmata cohors sistit impetum hostium*). | Non-Roman infantry attack. |
| 423 | 4.38.5 | Romans | Volsci | Cavalry | Infantry | The Roman cavalry dismount and fought as infantry. Wherever they attacked they were successful. (*Restituitur omnibus locis pugna, in quae eos impetus tulit*). | Roman cavalry attack, as infantry. |
| 423 | 4.39.12 | Romans | Volsci | Cavalry | Infantry | Romans gave way to the Volsci, the Roman cavalry dismounted and fought as infantry, and everywhere they attacked they were successful. The Volscian general saw that their attack could not be stopped 'he ordered his men to give ground to the cavalry men, the enemy's new cohort, until, carried forward by their attack, they should be cut off from their comrades.' (*Dat signum Volscus imperator, ut parmatis, novae cohorti hostium, locus detur donec impetu inlati ab suis excludantur*). | Roman cavalry attack, as infantry. |
| 419 | 4.44.6 | | | | | Pompilius and Antistius wished to attack Sempronius but could not. (*Impetus fieri non posset*). | General use of 'attack'. |
| 418 | 4.46.5 | Aequi | Romans | Infantry | Infantry | The Aequi attack (*impetu Aequorum*) the Romans, who fall back and many men were cut down (*obtruncati*). | Non-Roman infantry attack. |
| 416 | 4.47.3 | Romans | Aequi | Infantry | Infantry | So eager for battle were the Roman troops that the Aequi could not hold their attack and they retreated in disordered flight. (*Tantus ardor ad dimicandum fuit ut impetum Aequi no tulerint, victique acie cum fuga effusa petissent castra*). | Roman infantry attack. |
| 403 | 5.6.7 | | | | | Appius Claudius claims that "if a city withstood the brunt of their first assault for a brief time, it need hence forward have no fears" (Foster, 1924). (*Si qua urbs primum illum brevissini temporis sustinuerit impetum, nihil deinde timeat*). | Attack on a city. |
| 403 | 5.6.8 | Romans | | | | The Roman army 'conducts campaigns relying not more on vigour than on perseverance.' (*Nec impetu potius bella quam perseverantia gerat*) | Meaning vigour. |
| 394 | 5.26.9 | Faliscans | Romans | | | Faliscans raid the Roman outposts. (*Interdum per occasionem impetus oppidanorum in Romanus stationes*). | Attack on an outpost. |
| 394 | 5.28.13 | Romans | Aequi | Infantry | Infantry | Postumius 'inspired such ardour that the Aequi could no longer withstand the Roman attack, and were slaughtered while they fled.' (*Tantum iniecit ardoris ut non ultra sustinuerint impetum Aequi. Caedes inde fugientium*) | Roman infantry attack. |
| 390 | 5.38.4 | Romans | Gauls | Infantry | Infantry | Brennus, the Gallic chieftain, feared that if the Gauls made a frontal assault on the Roman legions, the reserves might attack the Gallic flanks and rear. (*Subsidia in aversos transversosque impetum darent*). | Roman infantry attack. |
| 390 | 5.39.6 | Gauls | Romans | | | The Romans expected an immediate attack from the Gauls (*impetus*) on the city. | Attack on a city. |
| 390 | 5.41.4 | Gauls | Romans | | | Gauls capture the city by assault. (*Impetu aut vi capiebant urbem*). | Attack on a city. |
| 390 | 5.41.5 | Romans | Gauls | | | The Gauls left a guard to prevent any attack from the Capitol, on their soldiers, who were searching for booty. (*Inde modico relicto praesidio ne quis in dissipates ex arce aut capitolio impetus fieret*). | Attack from a citadel. |
| 390 | 5.43.1 | Gauls | Romans | | | Gauls, in Rome, attack the citadel. (*Impetum facere in arcem statuunt*) | Attack on a citadel. |
| 390 | 5.43.3 | Romans | Gauls | Infantry | Infantry | The Romans, on the Capitol, launch their attack (*inferebat impetu facto*) from the higher ground and dislodge the Gauls. | Roman infantry attack. |
| 390 | 5.45.7 | Romans | Etruscans | | | The Romans, angry that the Etruscans were taking advantage of their situation, 'could hardly curb the impulse to attack them at once.' (*Vix temperavere animis quin extemplo impetum facerent*). | General use of 'attack'. |
| 389 | 6.2.12 | Romans | Volsci | | | The Romans took the Volscian camp by assault. (*castra impetu cepisset*). | Attack on a camp. |
| 389 | 6.2.14 | Romans | Aequi | | | The Romans capture the Aequian camp and city at | Attack on a |

| | | | | | | | |
|---|---|---|---|---|---|---|---|
| | | | | | | the first assault. (*Impetu primo cepit*). | city. |
| 388 | 6.4.9 | Romans | Etruscan cities | | | Romans took many Etruscan cities on the first assault. (*impetu cepere*) | Attacks on cities. |
| 386 | 6.10.5 | Romans | City of Nepete | | | The Romans took Etruscan held Nepete at the first attack (*primo impetuque*). | Attack on a city. |
| 385 | 6.12.8 | Volsci | Romans | Infantry | Infantry | The Roman dictator urges his men not to charge forward but to await the attack of the Volsci. (*Ne procurri quidem ab acie velim, sed obnixos vos stabili gradu impetum hostium excipere*). | Non-Roman infantry attack. |
| 385 | 6.13.2 | Romans | Volsci | Infantry | Infantry | The Volsci's "boldness went no further than the battle-cry, the discharge of missiles, and the first fury of the onset; the play of swords, when foot met foot, and the glance of the foemen that darted out the fire of his spirit, they could not abide. Their front was driven in…next their ranks were broken at many points, and all was in commotion, and the line resembled a surging wave" (Foster, 1924). (*Clamore tantum missilibusque telis et primo pugnae impetu ferox gladios et conlatum pedum et voltum hostis ardore animi micantem ferre non potuit. Impulsa frons prima…rupti inde multis locis ordines motaque omnia et fluctuanti similis acies erat*). | Meaning 'vigour' in battle. |
| 385 | 6.15.8 | | | | | Manlius claimed that the Roman Patricians were attacking him. (*In se impetum fieri*). | General use of 'attack'. |
| 382 | 6.23.5 | | | | | To storm a camp or city on the first assault (*castra urbesque primo impetu rapere sit*). | Attack on a city or camp. |
| 381 | 6.23.8 | | | | | "Marcus Furius, we can no longer resist the enthusiasm of the soldiers" (Foster, 1924). (*M. Furi, non possumus impetum militum*). | Meaning vigour. |
| 381 | 6.24.4 | Volsci | Romans | Infantry | Infantry | The Romans pursued the Volsci without any order. Reserves from their camp then attacked the disorganised Romans. (*Instant Volsci recentes qui e castris impetum fecerant*). | Non-Roman infantry attack |
| 381 | 6.24.11 | Romans | Volsci | Infantry | Infantry | The Romans put the Volsci to rout, large numbers were killed in the flight and many more were killed in the camp, 'which was captured in the same attack'. (*Capta eodem impetu sunt*). | Infantry attack and rout, but also an attack on a camp. |
| 377 | 6.33.11 | Latins | Tusculans | Infantry | Infantry | The Latins could not resist the attack of the Tusculans, as they rushed down from above (*ne impetus Tusculanorum decurrentium*). | Non-Roman infantry attack. |
| 377 | 6.33.6 | | | | | The Latins, angry that Tusculans had joined Rome, went to Tusculum on impulse. (*Incensos ea rabie impetus Tusculum tulit ob iram*). | Meaning impulse. |
| 362 | 7.7.7 | Romans | Hernici | Cavalry | Infantry | 'At first the battle was in doubt and nothing came of the frequent attempts of the Roman cavalry attacks to break the enemy line'. (*Primo stetit ambigua spe pugna nequiquam saepe conatis equitibus Romanis impetu turbare hostium aciem*). | Roman Cavalry attack. |
| 360 | 7.11.10 | Romans | Tiburtes | Infantry | Civilians | 'A few of the people had gone outside the gates to watch the flight of the Gauls, and found that they too were attacked'. (*Spectatores paucos fugae trepidationisque Gallorum extra portas egressos, postquam in se quoque fieri impetum uiderint*). | Roman infantry attack. |
| 358 | 7.12.4 | Romans | Tiburtes | Infantry | Infantry | The Men of Tibur attack Rome, the consuls bring men to the gates to defend the city. The Tiburtes scarcely withstood the first shock of the Roman attack. (*Adeo vix primum impetum Romanorum sustinuere*). | Roman infantry attack. |
| 358 | 7.12.11 | Gauls | Romans | Infantry | Infantry | The Gauls' strength and courage lay entirely in attacking. (*Ad hoc iis corporibus animusque, quorum omnis in impetu vis esset*). | Non-Roman infantry attack. |
| 358 | 7.15.3 | Romans | Gauls | Infantry | Infantry | The Gauls would have routed the Romans had not the dictator (C. Sulpicius Peticus) called to his men and shamed them into fighting. Because of their shame they attacked forgetting the danger. This near insane attack threw the enemy into disarray. (*Hic primo impetus prope vecors turbavit hostes*). | Roman infantry attack. |
| 357 | 7.16.5 | Romans | Privernates | Infantry | Infantry | Sextus Tullius laid down his *pilum*, drew his sword, and attacked the enemy. (*piloque posito stricto gladio in hostem impetum facit*). | Roman infantry attack. |
| 357 | 7.16.6 | Romans | Privernates | Infantry | Infantry | The Roman front line (*antisignani omnes*), turn the enemy away with the first attack. (*Primoque impetu avertere hostium*). | Roman infantry attack. |
| 349 | 7.24.3 | Romans | Gauls | Infantry | Infantry | 'Romans, suppressing their attack, came to a halt'. (*Stetitque suppresso impetu Romanus*). | Roman infantry attack. |
| 349 | 7.24.8 | Gauls | Romans | Infantry | Infantry | Roused by the Consul they formed into wedges and burst through the middle of the Gallic line. (*Cuneis deinde in medium agmen perrumpunt*). The Gauls were thrown into confusion and began to turn and attack each other (*vertunt impetum in suos*). | Romans infantry attack |
| 344 | 7.37.9 | | | | | Samnite commanders restrain the enthusiasm of their men. (*Ni duces continuissent impetum militum*). | Meaning enthusiasm. |
| 344 | 7.37.13 | Romans | Samnites | | | The Romans took the Samnite camp at the first assault. (*primo clamore atque impetu cepisset*) | Attack on a camp. |
| 342 | 7.38.9 | | | | | Rutulus tried to frustrate the impetuosity of the men. (*Militarem impetum frustrari*). | Meaning impetuosity. |
| 342 | 7.39.16 | | | | | Quinctius is hailed imperator. Then his army | An impulse to |

| | | | | | | | |
|---|---|---|---|---|---|---|---|
| | | | | | | marched to the eight mile stone on the Appian way, "more on their own impulse than by the counsel of their general" (Foster, 1924). (*Suo magis inde impetu quam consilio ducis…*). | action. |
| 342 | 7.40.10 | Romans | Romans | Infantry | Infantry | Marcus Valerius Corvus speaks to a rebellious army: "you shall therefore sooner draw sword on me than I on you. It is on your side that the trumpets will sound, on your side that the battle-cry will be raised and the attack begin, if fight we must" (Foster, 1924). (*Ergo uos prius in me strinxeritis ferrum quam in uos ego; istinc signa canent, istinc clamor prius incipiet atque impetus, si dimicandum est*) | Roman infantry attack. |
| 342 | 7.42.4 | Romans | | | | Night attack on the town house of Manlius. (*In aedes C. Manli nocte impetum factum*). | General use of 'attack'. |
| 340 | 8.6.7 | | | | | The wrath and fury of the Roman people. (*Ira impetuque hominum*). | Meaning fury. |
| 334 | 8.16.6 | Romans | Ausonians | Infantry | Infantry | Roman infantry under Corvus rout the enemy, at the first cheer and attack. (*Clamore atque impetu primo fudisset*). | Roman infantry attack. |
| 326 | 8.23.13 | | | | | Lucius Cornelius's vigorous prosecution of the war. (*Ab impetu belli placebat*). | Adverb meaning 'vigorous'. |
| 325 | 8.30.6 | Romans | Samnites | Cavalry | Infantry | At the suggestion of Lucius Cominius, the cavalry attacked a number of times, but they were unable to break the enemy line. (*Eques etiam auctore L. Cominio tribuno militum, qui aliquotiens impetu capto perrumpere non poterat hostium agmen*). | Roman cavalry attack. |
| 325 | 8.30.7 | Romans | Samnites | Cavalry | Infantry | The Roman's "pulled the bridles off their horses and spurred them on so hotly that nothing could resist the shock, and arms and men went down before them over a wide front. The foot soldiers, following up the cavalry charge, advanced on the disordered enemy" (Foster, 1926). (*Dextraxit frenos equis, atque ita concitatos calcaribus permisit ut sustinere eos nulla vis posset; per arma, per viros late stratagem dedere, secutus pedes impetum equitum turbatis hostibus intulit signa*). | Roman cavalry attack. |
| 322 | 8.38.12 | Samnites | Romans | Cavalry | Baggage train | Cavalry attack the Roman baggage train. (*Impedimeta Romanorum… impetum faciunt*). | Non-Roman cavalry attack. |
| 321 | 9.4.14 | Gauls | Romans | | | Remembering the Gallic assault on Rome of 390. (*Tam hercule quam a Gallorum impetu defendit*). | Attack on a city. |
| 320 | 9.13.4 | Romans | Samnites | Infantry | Infantry | 'So that there might be no delay in coming together while letting loose their pila and drawing their swords, they threw down their pila, as if a signal had been given to them, and having drawn their swords they brought a charge against the enemy. No tactical skill was there employed in ranging centuries or reserves, the wrath of the soldiers drove everything in their mad attack. (*Ne mora in concursu pilis emittendis stringendisque inde gladiis esset, pila uelut dato ad id signo abiciunt strictisque gladiis cursu in hostem feruntur. Nihil illic imperatoriae artis ordinibus aut subsidiis locandis fuit; omnia ira militaris prope uesano impetu egit*). | Roman infantry attack. |
| 315 | 9.23.15 | Romans | Samnites | Infantry | Infantry | The Romans were inspired by their dictator's speech and by a special ruse. He had ordered the front tents of the Roman camp to be burnt in order to fire up his soldiers. The Roman infantry, attacking like madmen, threw the enemy's ranks into confusion on the first assault. (*Itaque velut vecordes inlati signa primo impetu hostium turbant*). | Roman infantry attack. |
| 314 | 9.25.9 | Romans | Ausonians | | | The Romans attacked the towns of the Ausonians, but their leaders were not present at the time (*sed absentibus ducibus impetus est factus*). | Attack on a city. |
| 314 | 9.26.2 | Romans | City of Luceria | | | The Romans captured Luceria at the first assault (*primo impetu*). | Attack on a city. |
| 314 | 9.27.9 | Romans | Samnites | Infantry | Infantry | Poetelius on the Roman left ordered the *principes* to join the *hastati* in the initial attack. "By using all his strength at once, he forced the enemy back at the first assault" (Foster, 1926). (*Additae vires, qui subsidiarias cohortes, quae integrae ad longioris pugnae casus reservabantur, in primum aciem extemplo emisit universisque hostem primo impetu viribus impulit*) | Roman infantry attack |
| 310 | 9.35.7 | Romans | Etruscans | Infantry | Infantry | The Etruscans cast away their missiles to get to grips early with the Romans. "The Romans, on the contrary, fell to pelting them, now with javelins and now with stones, of which later the ground itself provided a good supply and even such of the Etruscans as were not wounded were confused by the blows that rattled down on their helms and shields. It was no easy matter to get close enough for fighting hand-to-hand, and they had no javelins for long-range work. There they stood, exposed to missiles, with no adequate cover of any sort, and as some of them gave ground and the line began to waver and be unsteady the Roman first and second lines, giving a | Roman infantry attack. |

| | | | | | | | |
|---|---|---|---|---|---|---|---|
| | | | | | | fresh cheer attacked them sword in hand... the Etruscans could not withstand their attack " (Foster, 1926, slightly adapted). (*Romanus contra nunc tela, nunc saxa, quibus eos adfatim locus ipse armabat, ingerere. Igitur scuta galeaeque ictae cum etiam quos non uolnerauerant turbarent-neque subire erat facile ad propio rem pugnam neque missilia habebant quibus eminus rem gererent-stantes et expositos ad ictus cum iam satis nihil tegeret, quosdam etiam pedem referentes fluctuantemque et instabilem aciem redintegrato clamore strictis gladiis hastati et principes inuadunt... eum impetum non tulerunt Etrusci*). | |
| 310 | 9.39.9 | Romans | Etruscans | Infantry | Infantry | The battle was contested with such rage that neither side threw a missile. The battle began with swords... (*Tantoque irarum certamine gesta res est ut ab neutra parte emissa sint tela. Gladiis pugna coepit...*). The infantry fight bitterly, until Roman cavalry dismount and make their way to the front of the infantry line. As fresh troops they cause havoc with the Etruscans. 'Then the rest of the infantry, following up their attack, despite exhaustion, at last broke through the enemy's ranks'. (*Secuta deinde impetum eorum, utcumque adfecta erat, cetera multitudo tandem perrumpit ordines hostium*). | Roman infantry attack. |
| 310 | 9.39.11 | Romans | Etruscans | | | The Romans capture the Etruscan camp (*impetu capta*). | Attack on a camp. |
| 306 | 9.43.15 | Romans | Samnites | Infantry | Infantry | While the Samnites were occupied with Marcius' troops, the Roman army under Cornelius attacked them in the flank. They burst through at the point where they attacked, advanced through the line and went on to take the enemy camp. (*Qua impetum dederat perrumpit... raptimque eductis in aciem militibus transuersam hostium aciem ...Qua impetum dederat, perrumpit aciemque per mediam in castra hostium tendit.*) | Roman infantry attack on the enemy flank. |
| 302 | 10.2.10 | Patavians | Greeks | | | The Patavians killed some guards and attacked some ships (*in naves ignaris custodibus interemptis impetus factus*). | General use of 'attack'. |
| 302 | 10.4.12 | Etruscans | Romans | Infantry | Infantry | Gnaeus Fulvius's detachment of infantry resisted the attacks of the larger Etruscan force. (*Interea ipse impetus hostium sustinet*). | Non-Roman infantry attack. |
| 302 | 10.5.2 | Romans | Etruscans | Infantry | Infantry | The Romans could hardly be restrained from attacking at a run. (*Vix ab impetu et cursu tenebantur*). | Roman infantry attack. |
| 302 | 10.5.6 | Romans | Etruscans | Infantry and cavalry | Infantry and cavalry | Although the Romans advanced slowly, they had little space to attack in, especially the horse (*Quamquam lente procedunt, iam tamen ad impetum capiundum, equiti utique, modicum erat spatium*). | Roman infantry and cavalry attack. |
| 297 | 10.14.12 | Romans | Samnites | Cavalry | Infantry | The Roman cavalry attacked the Samnites. (*omnem reliquam spem in impetu esse equitum*) | Roman cavalry attack. |
| 296 | 10.19.14 | | | | | The Samnites enter the battle more as impulse guided them than on anyone's orders. (*Suoque impetu magis quam cuiusquam ductu aut imperio pugnam capessebant*). | An impulse to action. |
| 295 | 10.28.3 | Gauls | Romans | Infantry | Infantry | The Romans decide to await the attack of the Gauls and Samnites, as Fabius had persuaded them that they only fought fiercely in the first attack. (*Quia ita persuasum erat duci et Samnites et Gallos primo impetu feroces esse, quos sustinere satis sit*). | Non-Roman infantry attack. |
| 295 | 10.28.7 | Romans | Gauls | Cavalry | Infantry | Decius encouraged all the young nobles to join him in a [cavalry] attack. (*Iuventutis in hostem ut secum impetum faciant*). | Roman cavalry attack. |
| 295 | 10.28.11 | Gauls | Romans | Cavalry and chariots | Infantry | The Gauls attacked with horse and chariots (*impetu equorum ac vehiculorum*). | Non-Roman cavalry attack. |
| 295 | 10.29.9 | Romans | Samnites | Cavalry | Infantry | Roman Cavalry attack, on flanks, with all possible vigour. (*Ut signo dato in transuersos quanto maximo possent impetu incurrerent*). | As an adverb meaning vigour. |
| 295 | 10.29.9 | Samnites | Romans | Infantry | Infantry | The shouts, assaults and missiles of the Samnite infantry, had less force. (*Postquam nec clamor hostium nec impetus nec tela missa eandem uim habere uisa*). | Non-Roman infantry attack. |
| 295 | 10.29.11 | Romans | Samnites | Cavalry and Infantry | Infantry | The Samnites could not withstand the attack of the Roman infantry in their front and the cavalry on their flank. (*Nec sustinuerunt Samnites impetum*). | Roman infantry and cavalry attack. |
| 295 | 10.29.13 | Romans | Gauls | Cavalry | Infantry | The Roman cavalry attacked the Gallic line, then the *principes* were to follow up where the line had been broken and cut down the Gauls. (*Que turbatum agmen hostium viderent impetu equitum, instare ac territos caedere*). | Roman cavalry attack. |
| 294 | 10.32.9 | Samnites | Romans | | | The Samnites attack the Roman camp. (*Ab tergo castrorum decumana porta impetus factus*) | Attack on a camp. |
| 294 | 10.34.1 | Romans | City of Milionia | | | The Romans assault Milionia. (*Postumius Milioniam oppugnare adortus ui primo atque impetu*). | Attack on a city. |
| 294 | 10.36.2 | Romans | Samnites | Infantry | Infantry | Both battle-lines were drawn up and they approached. "And now there was but a little space between the armies, and they halted, each waiting for | Roman infantry attack. |

| | | | | | | | |
|---|---|---|---|---|---|---|---|
| | | | | | | the other to be the first to attack and the first to raise a cheer" (Foster, 1926). (*Iam exiguum inter duas acies erat spatium, et stabant exspectantes dum ab hostibus prius impetus prius clamor inciperet*). | |
| 293 | 10.41.2 | Romans | Samnites | Infantry | Infantry | The Samnites would not have held out against the first battle cry and attack of the Romans. (*Nec sustinuissent primum clamorem atque impetum Romanorum*) had not religious fervour pulled them through. | Roman infantry attack. |
| 293 | 10.41.9 | Romans | Samnites | Cavalry | Infantry | Lanes were opened in the files of the Roman infantry; the cavalry charged out, and with spears levelled charged the enemy formation and broke its ranks wherever they attacked. (*Panduntur inter ordines uiae; prouolat eques atque infestis cuspidibus in medium agmen hostium ruit perrumpitque ordines quacumque impetum dedit*). | Roman cavalry attack. |
| 293 | 10.43.2 | Romans | Latins | | | Delayed Roman assault on the city of Cominium. (*ab impetu moratus est*). | Attack on a city. |
| 219 | 21.14.2 | Phoenicians | City of Saguntum | | | A cohort of Phoenicians assault Saguntum. (*Turris diu quassata prociderat, perque ruinam eius cohors Poenorum impetu facto*). | Attack on a city. |
| 218 | 21.25.3 | Boii | Carthaginians | | | After Hannibal had crossed the Ebro, the Boii invaded that very district and spread terror and confusion. (*Impetu facto tantum terroris ac tumultus fecerunt*). | General use of 'attack', meaning invade. |
| 218 | 21.25.5 | Boii | Romans | | | Roman commissioners were attacked as they were measuring off land. (*An in triumviros agrum metantes impetus sit factus*). | General use of 'attack'. |
| 218 | 21.27.8 | | | | | Current of a river. (*Impetum fluminis*). | Flow of a river. |
| 218 | 21.28.2 | | | | | Carthaginian sailors try to force their way through the current of a river. (*Perrumpere impetum fluminis*). | Flow of a river. |
| 218 | 21.28.5 | | | | | Hannibal's elephants attempt to cross a river; the current swept them over to the other side. (*Impetu ipso fluminis in alteram ripam rapiente*). | Flow of a river. |
| 218 | 21.33.9 | Carthaginians | Gauls | Light Infantry | Infantry | Hannibal charges down and routs the enemy at the first attack. (*Decurrit ex superiore loco et cum impetu ipso fundisset hostem*). | Roman light infantry attack. |
| 218 | 21.47.5 | | | | | Current of the river Po (*impetum fluminis*). | Flow of a river. |
| 217 | 22.5.6 | Romans | Carthaginians | Infantry | Infantry | Romans, surrounded by the Carthaginians, attempt to breakout. 'When attacks on all parts were unable to breakthrough and they found themselves shut in on the flanks by the mountains and lake, and in front and rear by the enemy..." (*Deinde, ubi omnes partes nequiquam impetus capti et ab lateribus montes ac lacus, a fronte et ab tergo hostium acies claudebant...*). | Roman infantry attack. |
| 217 | 22.6.4 | Ducarius | Roman Consul (G. Flaminius) | Cavalry | Cavalry | Ducarius, an Insubrian horseman 'attacked through the crowd of enemies and transfixed the Roman Consul. (*Subditisque calcaribus equo per confertissimam hostium turbam impetum facit obtruncatoque prius armigero, qui se infesto uenienti obuiam obiecerat, consulem lancea transfixit*). | Single cavalry combat. |
| 217 | 22.23.10 | Carthaginians | Romans | Infantry | Infantry | Hannibal sent two thirds of his army out to gather corn, the other third was to protect against any attack on the foragers. (*Circumspectans necunde impetus in frumentatores fieret*). | Roman infantry attack on foragers. |
| 217 | 22.24.2 | Romans | Carthaginians | Infantry | Infantry | The Romans planned to attack the Carthaginian foragers. (*Ut impetus aut in frumentatores palatos aut in castra*). | Roman infantry attack |
| 217 | 22.36.5 | | | | | The Roman legions proceeded with more effort and vigour than in former years. (*Maiore conatu atque impetu rem actam quam prioribus annis*). | As an adverb meaning vigour. |
| 216 | 22.50.12 | | | | | An impulse of courage (*impetu animorum*). | Meaning impulse. |
| 216 | 23.15.5 | | | | | Citizens of Neopolis dispersed wherever impulse (*impetus*) carried them. | Meaning impulse. |
| 216 | 23.16.9 | Romans | Carthaginians | | | The Romans post a guard by their baggage in case of an attack while the legions were fighting. (*Subsidiaque destinata impedimentis data, ne occupatis proelio legionibus in ea impetus fieret*). | General use of 'attack'. |
| 216 | 23.16.12 | Romans | Carthaginians | Cavalry and Infantry | Infantry | The Roman infantry and cavalry were ordered to sally out of a city against the enemy with all possible vigour. (*Quanto maximo possent impetu in hostem*). | Meaning 'vigour'. |
| 216 | 23.26.4 | Carthaginians | Romans | | | Describing Hasdrubal's organisation of the war in Spain: "In the very flush of renewed operations..." (Moore, 1940). (*In ipso impetu movendarum...*). | Meaning vigour. |
| 216 | 23.29.9 | Romans | Carthaginians | Infantry | Infantry | Hasdrubal drew his line up so his weak Celtiberians faced the legions, therefore at the first clash, when they had barely hurled their javelins, the centre fell back, and as the Romans advanced with a great attack, retreated. (*Primo igitur concursu, cum uix pila coniecta essent, rettulit pedem media acies inferentibusque se magno impetu Romanis uertit terga*). | Roman infantry attack. |
| 215 | 23.44.4 | Romans | Carthaginians | Infantry | Infantry | Hannibal had the town of Nola surrounded. Marcellus drew up his infantry line inside the gate | Roman Infantry attack. |

| | | | | | | | |
|---|---|---|---|---|---|---|---|
| | | | | | | and burst out. Many were terrified by the first attack and slain. (*Aliquot primo impetu perculsi caesique sunt*). | |
| 215 | 24.2.10 | Bruttians | City of Croton | | | Bruttians take the city of Croton by assault. (*Acceptique ab plebe primo impetu omnem praeter arcem cepere*). | Attack on a city. |
| 215 | 24.7.5 | | | | | Assasins attack Hieronymus of Syracuse. (*Cum in praetereuntem sine armatis regem impetus fieret*). | General use of 'attack'. |
| 214 | 24.10.8 | | | | | The force of a torrent of an underground spring under the *Vicus Insteius*. (*Impetus torrentis*). | Flow of a river. |
| 214 | 24.26.12 | Syracusans | Family of Hieronymus | | | The wife of Hieronymus is slaughtered and the people of Syracuse then turned their attack on her daughters. (*In virgines deinde respersas matris cruore impetum faciunt*). | General use of 'attack'. |
| 214 | 24.29.4 | Syracusans | Romans | Infantry | Infantry | Hippocrates of Syracuse began raiding territory on the border of the Roman province. When Appius sent troops to protect the farms, Hippocrates attacked the unit on guard. (*Omnibus copiis impetum in oppositam stationem cum caede multorum fecit*). | Non-Roman infantry attack. |
| 214 | 24.30.1 | Romans | City of Leontini | | | Marcellus took Leontini at the first assault (*primo impetu*). | Attack on a city. |
| 214 | 24.31.11 | Syracusan Mercenaries | Rebel Syracusans | Infantry | Infantry | The Mercenaries repeatedly made attacks on the Syracusan soldiers. (*Impetusque in Syracusanos milites fiebant*). | General use of 'attack'. |
| 214 | 24.32.4 | Romans | City of Hexapylon. | | | Roman assault on Hexapylon (*impetu Romanorum*). | Attack on a city. |
| 214 | 24.32.8 | Romans | City of Achradina | | | Achradina was also taken on the first assault. (*Ita Achradina quoque primo impetu capitur*). | Attack on a city. |
| 214 | 24.33.9 | Romans | City of Leontini | | | The Romans took Leontini by the first assault. (*Sicut Leontinos terrore ac primo impetu ceperant*). | Attack on a city. |
| 214 | 24.34.1 | Romans | Syracuse | | | The Romans assault the city of Syracuse. (*Et habuisset tanto impetu coepta res fortunam, nisi unus homo Syracusis ea tempestate fuisset*). | Attack on a city. |
| 214 | 24.40.4 | Macedonians | City of Oricum | | | Philip took the city of Oricum by assault (*primo impetu oppressam esse*) | Attack on a city. |
| 212 | 25.11.2 | Romans | Tarentines | Infantry | Infantry | The Romans held the citadel, near Tarentum, Hannibal feared that the Romans might make an attack from the citadel on the Tarentines. (*Tarentinos impetum ex arce…Romani facerent*) | Hypothetical Roman infantry attack from a citadel. |
| 212 | 25.11.4 | Romans | Carthaginians | Infantry | Infantry | Hannibal tried to build an earthwork to separate the Tarentines from the Roman held citadel. When work began the Romans attacked the men at work. (*Ubi coeptum opus est, patefacta repente porta impetum in munientes fecerunt Romani*). | Roman infantry attack. |
| 212 | 25.11.5 | Carthaginians | Romans | Infantry | Infantry | The Romans having attacked the men digging an earthwork were drawn out of the citadel. On Hannibal's signal the Carthaginian infantry, who had been lying in ambush, attacked and the Romans were not able to withstand the attack. (*Nec sustinuere impetum Romani*). | Non-Roman infantry attack. |
| 212 | 25.13.12 | Romans | Carthaginians | | | Romans could have captured a camp on the first assault. (*Primo impetu capi potuerint*). | Attack on a camp. |
| 212 | 25.16.19 | Romans | Lucanians | Cavalry (on foot) | Infantry | Gracchus, surrounded by the Lucanians tries to inspire his small band of men into angry attack. (*Exspectandoque euentu in impetum atque iram uersi*). | General use of 'attack'. |
| 212 | 25.16.21 | Romans | Lucanians | Cavalry (on foot) | Infantry | Gracchus decides to fight, and so wound his cloak around his left arm as they had no shields and attacked the enemy. (*Inter haec dicta paludamento circa laeuum bracchium intorto—nam ne scuta quidem secum extulerant—in hostes impetum fecit*). | Roman infantry attack. |
| 212 | 25.21.5 | | | | | Fulvius was dragged into battle by the impulse of his soldiers. (*Nec Fuluius est cunctatus, non tam sua ulla spe quam militum impetu fortuito tractus*). | An impulse to action. |
| 212 | 25.21.7 | Carthaginians | Romans | Infantry | Infantry | The Romans form two long lines, the first legion and the left ala in the first line, the second legion and the right ala in the second. "Although the tribunes shouted that in depth it had no power to resist, and that wherever the enemy should make an attack they would pierce it..." (Moore, 1940) the men did not listen. (*Prima legio et sinistra ala in primo instructae et in longitudinem porrecta acies. clamantibus tribunis nihil introrsus roboris ac uirium esse et quacumque impetum fecissent hostes perrupturos*). | Hypothetical non-Roman infantry attack. |
| 212 | 25.21.8 | Carthaginians | Romans | Infantry | Infantry | The Roman line then could not withstand even the shout and first attack of the Carthaginians. (*Ergo ne clamorem quidem atque impetum primum eorum Romani sustinuere*). | Non-Roman infantry attack. |
| 212 | 25.25.8 | Romans | Carthaginians | | | Marcellus posted detachments to stop any attack on his camp while his men were foraging. (*Ne quis in discursu militum impetus in castra fieri posset*). | Attack on a camp. |
| 212 | 25.30.9 | Romans | City of Achradina | | | The defenders of Achradina gather men to ward off the violent Roman attack. (*Ad vim et impetum Romanorum arcendum*). | Attack on a city. |
| 212 | 25.31.1 | Romans | Syracusans | | | The attack of the soldiers [on Achradina] being checked'. (*Suppresso impetu militum…*). | Attack on a city. |
| 212 | 25.34.11 | Carthaginians | Romans | Infantry | Infantry | "Those of the enemy who in a wedge had made an | Non-Roman |

| | | | | | | | |
|---|---|---|---|---|---|---|---|
| | | | | | | attack on the men pressing close about the general, on seeing the dying Scipio slipping from his horse, dashed everywhere along the line, wild with delight, shouting and announcing that the Roman commander had fallen" (Moore, 1940). (*Cuneusque is hostium, qui in confertos circa ducem impetum fecerat, ut exanimem labentem ex equo Scipionem uidit, alacres gaudio cum clamore per totam aciem nuntiantes discurrunt imperatorem Romanum cecidisse*). | infantry attack. |
| 212 | 25.36.3 | Numidians | Romans | Cavalry | Infantry | The Roman infantry surrounded their baggage and with the cavalry in the centre, they held off the attacks of the Numidians without difficulty. (*Ibi primo impedimentis et equitatu in medium receptis circumdati pedites haud difficulter impetus incursantium Numidarum arcebant*). | Non-Roman cavalry attack. |
| 212 | 25.36.13 | Carthaginians | Romans | Infantry | Infantry | Gnaeus Scipio was killed in the first attack of the enemy (*Cn. Scipionem alii in tumulo primo impetu hostium caesum tradunt*). | Non-Roman infantry attack. |
| 212 | 25.37.14 | Romans | Carthaginians | Infantry | Infantry | Romans broke the Carthaginian line. There would have been "a reckless and dangerous attack by the pursuers". (*Temerarius periculosusque sequentium impetus*) had Marcius not sounded the recall. | Roman infantry attack. |
| 212 | 25.38.17 | Romans | Carthaginians | | | The Romans planned to take Hasdrubal's camp at the first attack. (*Primus impetus castra ceperit*). | Attack on a camp. |
| 212 | 25.41.6 | Romans | Carthaginians | Infantry | Infantry | The Carthaginians were deserted by the Numidians, and so feared that they would be attacked by their own best troops, the Roman's were inspired by the news. The battle was decided on the first shout and attack. (*Itaque haud magni certaminis fuit; primus clamor atque impetus rem decreuit*). | Roman infantry attack. |
| 211 | 26.2.11 | Carthagians | Romans | Infantry | Infantry | Gnaeus Fulvius had allowed such vices in his troops that they could not withstand the battle cry of the Carthaginians let alone the attack. (*Nec impetum modo Poenorum sed ne clamorem quidem sustinere possent*). | Non-Roman infantry attack. |
| 211 | 26.4.7 | Romans | Capuans | Light Infantry | Cavalry | The Roman legions are forced to create new tactics: the swiftest of the legionaries were given seven small javelins and a small round shield. They were transported on the backs of the cavalry. They rode out to face the Capuan cavalry. The velites then leapt down and dashed out of the cavalry and while attacking, hurled one javelin after another. (*Pedestris inde acies ex equitatu repente in hostium equites incurrit iaculaque cum impetu alia super alia emittunt*). | Roman light infantry attack. |
| 211 | 26.5.17 | Romans | Spanish | Infantry | Infantry | Quintus Navius, the first Centurion, fought his way through to the standards of the Spanish. All the Spanish turned on him, "but neither the numbers of the enemy nor the mass of weapons could beat off the attack of such a man" (Moore, 1943). (*Sed neque multitudo hostium neque telorum uis arcere impetum eius uiri potuerunt*). | Roman infantry attack. |
| 211 | 26.6.5 | Romans | City of Capua | | | The Romans attack Capua, but this attack is checked by the wounding of Appius Claudius. (*Et suppressit impetum Romanorum volnus imperatoris Ap. Claudi*). | Attack on a city. |
| 211 | 26.13.12 | | | | | Impulse of wild beasts. (*Feras bestias caeco impetu ac rabie concitatas*). | Meaning impulse. |
| 211 | 26.18.10 | | | | | The enthusiasm for giving Scipio command in Spain (*impetus animorum*). | Meaning enthusiasm. |
| 211 | 26.19.1 | | | | | An act of impulsiveness (*tanto impetu acta*). | Meaning impulse. |
| 211 | 26.25.16 | Aetolians | Acarnania | | | The Aetolians had to delay their attack on Acarnania. (*Aetolorum impetum tardaverat*). | General use of 'attack'. |
| 211 | 26.7.3 | | | | | Hannibal has the impulse to go to Rome. (*Animum impetus caput*). | Impulse to action. |
| 210 | 26.39.23 | Romans | City of Tarentum | | | The Romans all but take the city by the same assault. (*Urbs eodem impetu caperetur*). | Attack on a city. |
| 210 | 26.46.6 | Romans | City of New Carthage | | | The Romans assault the city of New Carthage. (*Et mox caedendo confectis ac distractis ne iter impediretur foribus armati impetum fecerunt*). | Attack on a city. |
| 210 | 26.46.9 | Romans | Carthaginians | Infantry | Infantry | The Roman forces take a hill at the first assault. (*Et tumulus primo impetu est captus*). | Romans infantry attack |
| 209 | 27.15.8 | Carthaginians | Romans | Infantry | Infantry | Roman auxiliary units were besieging Caulonia. "To avoid being surprised, just before Hannibal's arrival, [they] withdrew to a hill that was safe from immediate attack" (Moore, 1943). (*In Bruttiis interim Cauloniae oppugnatores sub aduentu Hannibalis ne opprimerentur in tumulum a praesenti impetu tutum, ad cetera inopem, concessere*). | General use of 'attack'. |
| 209 | 27.16.1 | Romans | Tarentines | Infantry | Infantry | Battle was joined at the entrance of the Tarentine forum with more vigour than persistence. (*Proelium in aditu fori maiore impetu quam perseuerantia commissum est*). The Tarentines were no match for the Romans and "after merely throwing their javelins, they retreated almost before they engaged". (*Igitur pilis tantum coniectis, prius paene quam* | As an adverb meaning vigour. |

| | | | | | | | |
|---|---|---|---|---|---|---|---|
| | | | | | | *consererent manus terga dederunt*). | |
| 209 | 27.18.2 | Romans | Carthaginians | Light infantry | Cavalry | The Roman light infantry attacked the cavalry outposts of Hasdrubal's army. (*In eas uelites antesignanique et qui primi agminis erant aduenientes ex itinere priusquam castris locum acciperent, adeo contemptim impetum fecerunt*). | Roman attack on cavalry outposts. |
| 208 | 27.27.5 | Numidians | Romans | Cavalry | Infantry | Numidian cavalry make an attack on Roman troops. (*Tum undique omnes exorti, et clamore sublato impetum fecere*). | Non-Roman cavalry attack. |
| 208 | 27.32.5 | Romans | Macedonians | Infantry | Philip | Philip fell off his horse, the Romans made an attack on the king and his guards try to defend him. (*Ab Romanis impetu in regem facto et protegentibus regiis*). | Roman infantry attack. |
| 208 | 27.33.2 | | | | | Philip was dashed against a tree by his horse. (*In arborem inlatus impetu equi*). | Meaning smash violently. |
| 207 | 27.41.9 | Romans | Carthaginians | Cavalry | Infantry and cavalry | Gaius Aurunculeius sends out the Roman cavalry of the third legion with all possible momentum (*maximo impetu possit*). | As an adverb meaning vigour. |
| 207 | 27.48.10 | Carthaginians | Romans | Elephants | | "The elephants threw the front lines into confusion by their first charge". (*Eodem uersi elephanti, qui primo impetu turbauerant*). | Elephant charge. |
| 207 | 28.3.12 | Romans | Celtiberians | Infantry | Civilians | Scipio laid siege to Orongis. The townspeople came out with shields but no swords. The Romans, thinking it a trick, attacked and cut them down like an opposing battle-line. (*Impetus hostilis in transfugas factus, nec secus quam aduersa acies caesi*). | Roman infantry attack. |
| 206 | 28.13.9 | Romans | Carthaginians | Infantry | Cavalry | The Carthaginians retreated from the Roman infantry, but without breaking ranks. The Romans fell more fiercely on their rear and the attack could not be withstood, so the Carthaginians scattered and were routed. (*Dein, postquam acrius ultimis incidebat Romanus neque sustineri impetus poterat*). | Roman infantry attack. |
| 206 | 28.15.7 | Romans | Carthaginians | Infantry | Infantry | The Romans on seeing that the tide of the battle had changed, attacked more sharply everywhere along the line, and it was not easy to withstand their attack. (*Sed cum eo ipso acrius ubi inclinatam sensere rem uictores se undique inueherent, nec facile impetus sustineri posset*). | Roman infantry attack. |
| 206 | 28.15.11 | Romans | Carthaginians | | | The Romans would have captured the Carthaginian camp, had it not been for the weather. (*Cepissetque tanto impetu castra*). | Attack on a camp. |
| 206 | 28.22.13 | Celtiberians | Romans | Light Infantry | Cavalry and Light Infantry | The battle was fierce in courageous onslaught rather than regular in formation. (*Acrior impetu atque animis quam compositior ordine ullo pugna fuit*). | Generic attack word |
| 206 | 28.22.14 | Townsfolk of Astapa | Romans | Infantry | Infantry | The inhabitants burst out and attacked the Roman cavalry and light infantry outposts. The legion drew up its battle-line. For a while even they were in trouble, until "the veteran soldiers, steadfast against rash attacks, by slaying the first men checked those who followed" (Moore, 1949). (*Dein uetus miles, aduersus temerarios impetus pertinax, caede primorum insequentes suppressit*). | Non-Roman infantry attacks. |
| 206 | 28.30.11 | Romans | Carthaginians | Naval battle | | A Roman ship swept away the oars on one side of a Carthaginian ship. (*Unius, praelata impetu, lateris alterius remos detersit*). | Naval battle. |
| 206 | 28.33.3 | Romans | Celtiberians | Cavalry | Infantry | Scipio ordered Laelius to make an attack with the cavalry from a place of ambush. (*Laelium cum equitatu impetum ex occulto facere iubet*) | Roman cavalry ambush. |
| 206 | 28.36.2 | Carthaginians | Romans | | | Mago hired Gauls so that a war that had begun with the greatest vigour and even greater good fortune would not decline now. (*Conducta ibi Gallorum ac Ligurum quanta maxima posset iuuentute coniungeret se Hannibali neu senescere bellum maximo impetu maiore fortuna coeptum sineret*). | As an adverb meaning vigour. |
| 205 | 29.2.3 | Spanish | Romans | Cavalry | Infantry | An attack was made upon foragers by Spanish horse (*cum in pabulatores Romanos impetus repente ab equitibus Hispanis factus esset*). | Non-Roman cavalry attack. |
| 205 | 29.2.14 | Romans | Spanish | Infantry | Infantry | The Spanish line was broken by the Roman cavalry and the Roman infantry are urged to attack before the enemy can reform. 'The barbarians would not have been able to withstand such an aggressive attack'. (*Non sustinuissent tam infestum impetum barbari*). | Roman infantry attack. |
| 205 | 29.6.12 | Romans | Carthaginians | | | The Romans attacked a Carthaginian citadel (*impetus est factus*). | Attack on a citadel. |
| 205 | 29.9.6 | | | | | Roman soldiers assault Pleminius Scipio's legate. (*In legatum impetum lictoribus prius indignum in modum mulcatis faciunt*). | General use of 'attack'. |
| 204 | 29.30.6 | Numidians | City of Thapsus | | | Massinissa took the city in the first assault (*primo impetu capit*). | Attack on a city. |
| 204 | 29.34.13 | Carthaginians | Numidians | Cavalry | Cavalry | Massinissa attempted to draw the Carthaginian cavalry into a trap by meeting their attacks. (*Sed cedendo sensim impetus eorum accipiebat donec ad tumulos tegentes Romanum equitatum pertraxit*). | Non-Roman cavalry attack. |
| 203 | 30.4.12 | Romans | Carthaginians | | | Scipio made preparations to stop an attack on his camp, in which he had only left a small garrison force. (*Eruptio ex urbe et impetus in castra sua* | Attack on a camp. |

| | | | | | | | |
|---|---|---|---|---|---|---|---|
| | | | | | | *relicta cum leui praesidio fieret*). | |
| 203 | 30.8.7 | Romans | Carthaginians | Infantry and cavalry | Infantry and cavalry | At the battle of the Great Plains: 'by the first attack both wings, Numidians and Carthaginians alike, were beaten back at the same time'. (*Ita instructi concurrunt. primo impetu simul utraque cornua, et Numidae et Carthaginienses, pulsi*). | Attack of Cavalry. |
| 203 | 30.10.9 | Carthaginians | Romans | Naval battle | | The Carthaginian first attack would have been overpowering when everything was confused by the mass of men dashing about. (*Carthaginienses, qui, si maturassent, omnia permixta turba trepidantium primo impetu oppressissent, perculsi terrestribus cladibus*). | Naval battle. |
| 203 | 30.10.14 | Romans | Carthaginians | Naval battle | | A Ship is sunk by the momentum and mass of the warships. (*Primo ipsae tantum impetu ac magnitudine rostratarum obruebantur*). | Naval battle. |
| 203 | 30.11.11 | Romans | Masaesulians | Infantry | Infantry | 'The Masaesulians fail to sustain not only the first attack but even the sight of the standards and arms'. (*Tum uero Masaesulii non modo primum impetum sed ne conspectum quidem signorum atque armorum tulerunt*). | Roman infantry attack. |
| 203 | 30.12.4 | Romans | Carthaginians | | | Roman attack on a Carthaginian camp. (*Minus dimidium eius hominum captum est impetu in castra facto*). | Attack on a camp. |
| 203 | 30.25.8 | Romans | Carthaginians | Naval battle | | Carthaginian ship was run on to the shore with all possible momentum. (*Maximo impetu poterant*). | As an adverb meaning vigour. |
| 202 | 30.33.3 | Carthaginians | Romans | Elephants | Infantry | Charge of the Carthaginian elephants (*impetum elephantorum*). | Elephant charge. |
| 202 | 30.34.3 | Romans | Carthaginians | Infantry | Infantry | "For the Romans [Zama was] a battle of little movement, as they pressed on into the enemy by their own weight and that of their arms; on the other side repeated attacks at high speed but with less power. Consequently by the first attack the Romans at once dislodged the enemy's line. Then beating back with their shoulders and the bosses of their shields, being now in close contact with men forced from their position, they made considerable progress, as no one offered any resistance, while as soon as they saw that the enemy's line had given way, even the rear line pressed upon the first, a circumstance which of itself gave them great force in repulsing the enemy. Among the enemy so far was their second line, the Africans and Carthaginians, from supporting the auxiliaries as they gave way, that on the contrary they even drew back for fear the enemy by slaying the men of the first line if these stoutly resisted, should reach themselves. Accordingly the auxiliaries suddenly retreated…" (Moore, 1949). (*pugna Romana stabilis et suo et armorum pondere incumbentium in hostem, concursatio et uelocita illinc maior quam uis. igitur primo impetu extemplo mouere loco hostium aciem Romani. ala deinde et umbonibus pulsantes in summotos gradu inlato aliquantum spatii uelut nullo resistente incessere, urgentibus et nouissimis primos ut semel motam aciem sensere, quod ipsum uim magnam ad pellendum hostem addebat. apud hostes auxiliares cedentes secunda acies, Afri et Carthaginienses, adeo non sustinebant ut contra etiam, ne resistentes pertinaciter primos caedendo ad se perueniret hostis, pedem referrent. igitur auxiliares terga dant repente…*). | Roman infantry attack. |
| 202 | 30.35.2 | Romans | Carthaginians | Cavalry | Infantry | At Zama, Laelius and Masinissa's timely attack on the rear of the Carthaginian infantry finally broke the enemy. (*Is demum equitum impetus perculit hostem*). | Roman cavalry attack. |
| 202 | 30.35.6 | Carthaginians | Romans | Elephants | | The haphazard charge of the elephants. (*Fortuitus impetus*). | Elephant charge. |
| 202 | 30.35.8 | Romans | Carthaginians | Infantry | Infantry | Hannibal placed his mercenaries in the front line to exhaust the first attack of the Romans. (*Simul primum ardorem atque impetum hostium excipientes fatigarent*). | Roman infantry attack. |
| 201 | 31.2.8 | Gauls | Romans | Infantry | Infantry | The Gauls made an unexpected attack on the Romans (*improviso impetu Gallorum*). | Non-Roman infantry attack. |
| 200 | 31.16.4 | Macedonians | City of Maronea | | | Philip took Maronea at the first assault. (*Maroneam quidem primo impetu expugnauit*). | Attack on a city. |
| 200 | 31.18.7 | Macedonians | People of Abydus | | | Philip took the city, and the men of the city ran to kill their wives and children. So Philip stopped the assaults of his troops (*impetum militum*) and announced that he would give the people of Abydus three days to die. | Non-Roman Infantry attack on townsfolk. |
| 200 | 31.21.16 | Romans | Gauls | | | Romans rout the Gauls; soon the legions followed and attacked the camp. (*Mox et legiones insecutae in castra impetum fecerunt*). | Attack on a camp. |
| 200 | 31.22.2 | Gauls | Romans | Infantry | Infantry | Two thousand Romans and allies were killed, mostly from the right squadron, who were in the van, against whom at the first attack the enemy's main effort had been directed. (*In quam primo impetu uis hostium* | Non-Roman infantry attack |

| | | | | | | | |
|---|---|---|---|---|---|---|---|
| | | | | | | *ingens inlata est*). | |
| 200 | 31.26.3 | Eleusians | Macedonians | | | The Macedonians left an ambush in case the Eleusians attacked from their citadel, while they were foraging. (*Si ex castello ab Eleusine in praedantes suos impetus fieret*). | Attack from a citadel. |
| 200 | 31.27.2 | Romans | Various cities | | | The Romans took Corrhagum, Gerronius and Orgessum at the first assault. (*Corrhago et Gerrunio et Orgesso castellis primo impetu captis*). | Attacks on cities. |
| 200 | 31.27.7 | Romans | Macedonians | Infantry | Infantry | Athenagoras, one of the King's prefects, assaulted the Roman marching line in the rear. The Romans were able to draw up into a line of battle, and the King's soldiers did not withstand the Roman attack. (*Non tulere impetum Romanorum militum regii*). | Roman infantry attack. |
| 200 | 31.35.3 | Macedonians | Romans | Light Infantry | Light Infantry | The swift movements of the Illyrians being useful for sallies and sudden attacks. (*Illyriorum uelocitas ad excursiones et impetus subitos usui esset*). | Non-Roman light infantry attack. |
| 200 | 31.35.4 | Romans | Macedonians | Light Infantry | Light Infantry and Cavalry | The Roman *velites* fought more like heavy infantry in a stationary battle and so defeated the Macedonians: "The Roman attack was no more vigorous than stubborn, prevented the carrying out of this plan; for just as if they were in regular line of battle, both the skirmishers, after hurling their spears, came to hand-to-hand combat with their swords, and the cavalry, as soon as they had charged the enemy stopping their horses either fought from horseback or leaped from their saddles and fought mingled with the footmen" (Sage, 1935). (*Turbauit hunc ordinem pugnandi non acrior quam pertinacior impetus Romanorum; nam haud secus quam si tota acie dimicarent, et uelites emissis hastis comminus gladiis rem gerebant et equites, ut semel in hostem euecti sunt, stantibus equis, partim ex ipsis equis, partim desilientes immiscentesque se peditibus pugnabant*). | Roman light infantry attack. |
| 200 | 31.38.6 | Macedonians | Romans | Cavalry and Light Infantry | Infantry | Philip planned to attack the Roman foragers scattered over the fields. (*Quo impetum in frumentatores palatos per agros fecit*). | Non-Roman infantry attack. |
| 200 | 31.39.12 | Romans | Macedonians | Infantry | Infantry | The Macedonian phalanx was made useless by forests, as were the Thracians, only Philip's Cretan archers were of service, but 'if there was an attack'. (*Si quis impetum faceret*), their arrows would not be able to penetrate the Roman shields. | Hypothetical Roman infantry attack. |
| 200 | 31.40.1 | Romans | Orestis | | | The Romans attack Orestis. (*Inde impetum in Orestidem facit*). | General use of 'attack'. |
| 200 | 31.40.5 | Romans | Macedonians | | | The Romans garrisoned the town of Pelium, for it was favorably situated for making raids into Macedonia. (*Nam et sita opportune urbs erat ad impetus in Macedoniam faciendos*). | General use of 'attack'. |
| 200 | 31.41.14 | Macedonians | Aetolians | Cavalry | Cavalry | Philip's cavalry rout the Aetolians in the first attack. (*Itaque primo impetu fusi uix temptato certamine turpi fuga repetunt castra*). | Non-Roman cavalry attack. |
| 198 | 32.13.11 | Aetolians | Cities of Lymenes and Angeiae | | | Aetolians capture Lymenes and Angeiae at the first assault (*primo impetu*). | Attack on a city. |
| 198 | 32.13.12 | Townsfolk of Callithera | Macedonians | | | The Macedonians assaulted Callithera, and sustained an attack of the townsfolk. (*Callithera inde adgressi similem impetum oppidanorum pertinacius sustinuerunt*). | Attack on a city. |
| 198 | 32.16.15 | Romans | City of Chalcis | | | Quinctius attacks with scaling ladders and captured the town. (*Quinctius noctu ab ea parte quae minime suspecta erat impetu facto scalis urbem cepit*). | Attack on a city. |
| 198 | 32.17.15 | Romans | Macedonians | Infantry | Infantry | Romans face a phalanx, fighting in a broken part of a rampart, which protected the phalanx from flank attack. The Romans could not get past the Macedonian spears, 'nor was it possible either to retire or to attack from a distance, a manoeuvre which usually throws the ranks in to disorder'. (*Nec ex longo spatio aut cedendum aut impetus faciendus erat, quae res turbare ordines solet*). | Roman infantry attack. |
| 198 | 32.18.6 | Romans | City of Phanotea | | | Romans take the city of Phanotea at the first assault (*primo impetu*). | Attack on a city. |
| 198 | 32.18.9 | Romans | City of Daulis | | | The Romans assault the city of Daulis (*impetum Romani facerent*). | Attack on a city. |
| 198 | 32.23.12 | City of Sicyon | Romans | | | The Romans besiege Sicyon - they feared that the attacks from the Royal guards could not easily be resisted. (*Praesidia regia nec facile erumpentium impetus sustineri posse*) and so they abandoned the seige. | Attack from a city. |
| 198 | 32.24.4 | Romans | City of Elatia | | | The Elatian guard rushed to the point where the Romans attacked. (*Impetu hostium locum concurrerunt*). | Attack on a city. |
| 197 | 32.30.10 | Romans | Insubrians | Infantry | Infantry | The Roman consul vowed a temple to Juno Sospita if the enemy were routed, the soldiers shouted that they would bring about the fulfilment of the Consul's vow, and their attack began. (*A militibus clamor sublatus compotem uoti consulem se facturos, et impetus in hostes est factus*). | Roman infantry attack. |
| 197 | 33.8.6 | Romans | Macedonians | Infantry | Infantry | At Cynoscephalae there was a skirmish between the | Roman infantry |

| | | | | | | | |
|---|---|---|---|---|---|---|---|
| | | | | | | Roman and Macedonian light infantry. Flamininus brought up his left wing to help - encouraged by the arrival of the general, 'they renewed the battle, attacked and turned back the enemy'. (*Pugnam renouant impetuque facto rursus auertunt hostem*). | attack. |
| 197 | 33.9.6 | Romans | Macedonians | Infantry | Infantry | At Cynoscephalae, the Macedonian left flank was in disorder. "Quinctius, although he saw his men retreating on the right, first sending his elephants against the enemy, attacked, thinking that the defeat of a part would involve the rest" (Sage, 1935). (*In hos incompositos Quinctius, quamquam pedem referentes in dextro cornu suos cernebat, elephantis prius in hostem actis impetum facit, ratus partem profligatam cetera tracturam*). | Roman infantry attack. |
| 197 | 33.10.5 | Romans | Macedonians | Infantry | Infantry | At Cynoscephalae, on surrendering Macedonian infantry. The Roman infantry, ignorant of the Macedonian custom of raising their spears in surrender, attacked, cut down the first and put the rest to flight. (*Impetus in eos est factus et primis caesis ceteri in fugam dissipati sunt*). | Roman infantry attack. |
| 197 | 33.15.6 | Achaeans | Macedonians | Infantry | Infantry | Thracians in the Achaean forces "made an attack upon the enemy, foraging and scattered through the fields" (Sage, 1935). (*Et Thracum quidam in uagos palatosque per agros hostes impetum fecerant*). | Non-Roman infantry attack. |
| 197 | 33.15.9 | Achaeans | Macedonians | Infantry | Infantry | The Macedonians could not withstand the Achaean attack. (*Primum hostium impetum non tulerunt*). | Non-Roman infantry Attack. |
| 197 | 33.18.14 | Achaeans | Macedonians | Infantry | Infantry | The Achaeans (1000 strong) attacked the Agrianes (400 strong). (*Achaei primi torrente superato in Agrianas impetum fecerunt*). | Non-Roman infantry attack. |
| 196 | 33.36.11 | Romans | Gauls | Cavalry | Infantry | The Gauls attacked the Roman infantry. Marcellus sent all the squadrons of the latin cavalry against the Gauls. Their first and second attacks dulled the enemy's ferocious attack. (*Equitum Latinorum omnes turmas in hostem emisit. quorum cum primus secundusque impetus rettudisset inferentem se ferociter hostem*). | Roman cavalry attack. |
| 196 | 33.40.6 | Thracians | City of Lysimachia | | | Lysimachia had to be destroyed by an attack of the Thracians. (*Lysimachiam deletam Thracum impetu*). | Attack on a city. |
| 195 | 34.15.2 | Romans | Celtiberians | Infantry | Infantry | The Roman front line grew weary, and so Cato brought up reserves from the second line. 'A new line was formed, fresh troops with unused weapons attack the enemy and first with a violent attack in wedge formation, beat them down, then scattered them and put them to flight'. (*Noua acies facta. integri recentibus telis fatigatos adorti hostes primum acri impetu uelut cuneo perculerunt, deinde dissipatos in fugam auerterunt*). | Roman infantry attack. |
| 195 | 34.15.7 | Romans | Celtiberians | | | Romans attacked the camp of the Celtiberians, the guards stationed at the gates did not resist it. (*Non sustinuit impetum eorum statio quae portae apposita erat*). | Attack on a camp. |
| 195 | 34.20.7 | Lacetani | Suessetani | Infantry | Infantry | The Suessetani could scarcely withstand the shout of the Lacetani let alone their attack. (*Uix clamorem eorum, nedum impetum Suessetani tulere*). | Non-Roman infantry attack. |
| 195 | 34.29.8 | Romans | City of Gytheum | | | Romans attacked the town of Gytheum (*impetum*). | Attack on a city. |
| 195 | 34.39.8 | Romans | Sparta | | | The Romans in 'testudo' entered Sparta - the violence of their attack could no longer be resisted. (*Non ultra uis eorum atque impetus sustineri poterant*). | Attack on a city. |
| 195 | 34.39.12 | Romans | Spartans | | | The Romans attacked Sparta (*itaque et qui extra urbem erant Romanorum, tum maxime impetus facientes*…). | Attack on at city. |
| 195 | 34.41.9 | Romans | Spartans | Infantry | Foraging troops | The Romans made an attack on foragers. (*Impetu in pabulatores suos a Romanis facto*). | Roman infantry attack. |
| 194 | 34.47.5 | Romans | Gauls | Infantry | Infantry | After fighting until noon the Gauls became tired and retreated. The Romans attacked the few that remained and drove them into the camp. (*In paucos restantes impetum Romani fecerunt fusosque compulerunt in castra*). | Roman infantry attack. |
| 193 | 35.5.4 | Romans | Gauls | Cavalry | Infantry | "Quintus and Publius Minucius, [were ordered] to lead the cavalry of these legions beyond the flanks of the battle-line into open ground, whence, when the signal was given, they were to attack from the open" (Sage, 1935). (*Equites earum extra aciem in locum patentem Q. et P. Minucios tribunos militum educere iussit, unde cum signum dedisset impetum ex aperto facerent*). | Roman cavalry attack. |
| 193 | 35.5.4 | Gauls | Romans | Infantry | Irregular Infantry | Tiberius Sempronius Longus was informed that the irregulars were not holding the attack of the Gauls. (*Non sustinere extraordinarios impetum Gallorum*). | Non-Roman infantry attack. |
| 193 | 35.5.7 | Romans | Gauls | Infantry | Infantry | The second legion was brought in and when the irregular troops were relieved, the battle was restored. The Gauls, although tired from the sun, withstood the attacks of the Romans. (*Sustinebant impetus Romanorum*). | Roman infantry attack. |
| 193 | 35.11.5 | Romans | Ligures | | | Numidian cavalry attack on a town (*impetum facturum*). | Attack on a town. |

| | | | | | | | |
|---|---|---|---|---|---|---|---|
| 192 | 35.21.5 | | | | | "The Tiber attacks the city with a more violent rush than the year before, swept away two bridges" (Sage, 1935). (*Tiberis infestiore quam priore <anno> impetu inlatus urbi duos pontes... evertit*). | Flow of a river. |
| 192 | 35.29.5 | Achaeans | Spartans | Infantry | Infantry | The Achaean *caetrati* 'made their attack against an enemy in disorder, scattered and exhausted by exertions and wounds.' (*In hostes inordinatos, effusos, labore etiam et uolneribus fessos impetum faciunt*). | Non-Roman infantry attack. |
| 192 | 35.30.4 | Achaeans | Spartans | | | "Straight away the Achaean caetrati attacked the camp and plundered it". (*Extemplo caetrati Achaeorum in castra impetum faciunt et diripiunt*). | Attack on a camp. |
| 192 | 35.35.18 | Alexamenus | Nabis | Cavalry | Cavalry | In single combat, "when Nabis approached, [Alexamenus] charged and piercing his horse overthrew the tyrant" (Sage, 1935). (*Postquam adpropinquabat, impetum facit et transfixo equo tyrannum deturbat*). | Cavalry single combat. |
| 192 | 35.45.5 | | | | | Thoas asserts that Phaeneas was trying to delay preparations for war, so that through tiredness the vigor of Antiochus might relax. (*Ut taedio et impetus relanguescat regis*). | Meaning vigour. |
| 191 | 36.5.4 | Romans | Epirotes | | | The Epirotes fear that if Antiochus went to war with Rome they would be in the forefront of the Roman attacks. (*Primos impetus Romanorum excepturos*). | General use of attack. |
| 191 | 36.6.3 | Antiochus | Romans | | | Attack on a Roman garrison at Delium. (*Ad Delium impetu in praesidium Romanum facto*). | Attack on a garrison. |
| 191 | 36.8.6 | Antiochus | Thessaly | | | Antiochus invaded Thessaly (*Antiochum in Thessaliam impetum fecisse*). | General use of 'attack'. |
| 191 | 36.9.11 | Antiochus | City of Pherae | | | Pherae withstood Antiochus' first attack. (*Primum impetum oppugnationis satis constanter sustinuerunt*). | Attack on a city. |
| 191 | 36.13.3 | Macedonians | Various cities | | | Many cities fell to Philip at the first assault. (*Primo prope impetu capto*) | Attacks on cities. |
| 191 | 36.24.11 | Romans | Aetolians | | | The Romans attack a citadel held by the Aetolians (*impetum*). | Attack on a citadel. |
| 191 | 36.29.1 | | | | | Aetolians were so angered by a Roman order that "if they had been at peace, they would by that onset of passion have been provoked to war" (Sage, 1935). (*Si in pace fuissent, illo impetu irae concitari potuerint ad bellum*). | Onset of emotion |
| 191 | 36.30.1 | Romans | Aetolians | | | The Aetolians assembled at Naupactus, in order that they might "endure the whole violence of the war" (Sage, 1935). (*Totum impetum belli sustinerent).* | Meaning violence. |
| 191 | 36.38.3 | Romans | Ligures | Infantry | Infantry | The Ligures surrounded the Roman camp. At first light the Romans burst out of two gates at once. However the first attack did not drive the Ligures away. (*Prima luce duabus simul portis eruptionem fecit. nec primo impetu, quod sperauerat, Ligures pulsi sunt*). | Roman infantry attack |
| 190 | 37.19.5 | | | | | Eumenes discussed the advantage they had in the war. (*Si ex hoc impetu rerum nihil prolatando remittitur*). | Meaning advantage. |
| 190 | 37.21.2 | Seleucids | Achaeans | | | 'For many hours both sides waited as if an attack were about to come'. (*Per multas horas intenti utrimque uelut iam futurum impetum expectauere*) | General use of 'attack'. |
| 190 | 37.21.3 | Achaeans | Antiochus | Infantry | Infantry | An impetuous attack by Diophanes falling violently on the rear of the enemy troops. (*Deinde eodem, quo pridie, impetu in postremum agmen incurrit*). | Meaning impetuous. |
| 190 | 37.21.5 | Antiochus | Various cities | | | Antiochus took Cotto, Corylenus, Aphrodisas and Prinne at the first assault (*primo impetu*). | Attacks on cities. |
| 190 | 37.24.3 | Rhodians | Antiochus | Naval battle | | Rhodian naval attack. (*In puppim impetum dabat*). | Naval attack. |
| 190 | 37.31.2 | Romans | Antiochus | | | City of Lysimactia easy to defend against the first assault of the Romans (*primo impetu*). | Attack on a city. |
| 190 | 37.32.4 | Romans | City of Lampter | | | The Romans attacked the city of Lampter over the ruins of their walls. (*Ad quorum casum cum impetum Romani milites per ipsam stragem ruinarum facerent*). | Attack on a city. |
| 190 | 37.38.3 | Antiochus | Romans | Cavalry | Roman Outposts | 1000 Galatian and Dahae cavalry cross the River Phrygius and attack the Roman outposts. (*Eo mille ferme equites... tumultuose amni traiecto in stationes impetum fecerunt*). | Cavalry attack on Roman outposts. |
| 190 | 37.41.11 | Antiochus | Romans | Cavalry | Light Infantry | Antiochus' cavalry were frightened by a shower of missiles and were scattered in all directions - their attacks were easily avoided by the light infantry. (*Impetus et levis armatura... declinabant*). | Non-Roman cavalry attack. |
| 190 | 37.42.2 | Romans | Antiochus | Cavalry | Cavalry | The Roman cavalry reached the heavy armed horse who did not even sustain the first attack. (*Ne primum quidem impetum sustinuerunt*). | Roman cavalry attack. |
| 190 | 37.42.5 | | Romans | Elephants | Infantry | Roman soldiers had learnt from the wars in Africa 'to avoid the charges of elephants'. (*Vitare impetum beluae*). | Elephant charge. |
| 190 | 37.42.7 | Antiochus | Romans | Cavalry | Infantry and cavalry | Antiochus made an attack on the Roman left wing with his auxiliary and heavy armed horse. (*Impetum in eam partem cum auxiliis et cataphracto equitatu fecit*). | Non-Roman cavalry attack. |
| 190 | 37.43.5 | Romans | Macedonians | Infantry | Infantry | Antiochus' army was routed on the left flank by the Romans at the first attack (*primo impetu*). | Roman infantry attack. |

| | | | | | | | |
|---|---|---|---|---|---|---|---|
| 190 | 37.43.11 | Romans | Antiochus | | | Romans expected to capture Antiochus' camp on the first attack. (*Quae se impetu ipso capturos crediderant*). | Attack on a camp. |
| 189 | 38.5.8 | Nicodamus | City of Ambracia | | | Nicodamus attacked the city of Ambracia. (*Et Nicodamus intempesta nocte, cum alias custodias fefellisset, per alias impetu constanti perrupisset*). | Attack on a city. |
| 189 | 38.6.3 | Aetolians | Romans | Infantry | Infantry | The Romans were conducting siege works, which the Aetolians then attacked. The Roman guards were cut down on the first attack. (*Multos primo impetu custodes oppresserunt*). | Non-Roman infantry attack. |
| 189 | 38.13.12 | Pisidians | Romans | Cavalry | Infantry | Romans in marching order. 'At this time the cavalry threw the Roman column into no small amount of confusion by their first attack'. (*Tum quoque equites in agmen Romanum eruptione facta haud modice primo impetu turbauere*). | Non-Roman Cavalry attack on troops in marching order. |
| 189 | 38.14.1 | Romans | City of Eriza | | | The Romans took the city on the first assault. (*Inde profecti Erizam urbem primo impetu ceperunt*). | Attack on a city. |
| 189 | 38.17.7 | Gauls | Romans | Infantry | Infantry | The Romans must sustain the first Gallic attack, "into which they pour forth with glowing enthusiasm and blind passion" (Sage, 1936). (*Si primum impetum, quem feruido ingenio et caeca ira effundunt, sustinueris…*). | Non-Roman infantry attack. |
| 189 | 38.21.8 | Gauls | Romans | Infantry | Light Infantry | "Arrows, sling-bullets, darts, coming from all sides wounded them unexpectedly, nor did they see what to do, as their minds were blinded by rage and fear, and they were involved in a kind of battle for which they were very ill-adapted. For, as in hand-to-hand fighting, where they can receive and inflict wounds in turn, passion inflames their minds, so when they are struck by light weapons, coming from unseen and distant sources, and when they have no place at which they can charge with blind violence, like wounded animals they rush headlong upon their friends" (Sage, 1938). (*Sagittis glande iaculis incauti [et] ab omni parte configebantur nec, quid agerent, ira et pauore occaecatis animis cernebant, et erant deprensi genere pugnae, in quod minime apti sunt. Nam quemadmodum comminus, ubi in uicem pati et inferre uulnera licet, accendit ira animos eorum, ita, ubi ex occulto et procul leuibus telis uulnerantur, nec, quo ruant caeco impetu, habent, uelut ferae transfixae in suos temere incurrunt*). | Non-Romans infantry attack |
| 189 | 38.22.9 | Romans | Gauls | Infantry | Infantry | The Romans hurled their missiles at Gauls and forced them back inside their rampart. The *antisignani* of the legions threw their pila at the men guarding the gates. "The men were not injured by them, but their shields in many cases were pierced and fastened together, nor did they resist the attack of the Romans for longer' (*Nec diutius impetum Romanorum sustinuerunt*). | Roman infantry attack. |
| 189 | 38.25.11 | Gauls | Romans | Cavalry | Cavalry | Gallic cavalry move in full gallop. (*Repente concitatis equis cum impetu hostili uidet Gallos uenientis*). | Non-Roman cavalry attack. |
| 189 | 38.25.15 | Romans | Gauls | Cavalry | Infantry | The Gauls were routed at the first attack of the Roman cavalry. (*Et primo impetu fusi Galli sunt*). | Roman cavalry attack. |
| 189 | 38.27.1 | Romans | Gauls | Infantry | Infantry | The Gauls, wearied by standing and by wounds, 'did not endure even the first attack and shout of the Romans'. (*Ne primum quidem impetum et clamorem Romanorum tulerunt*). | Roman infantry attack. |
| 189 | 38.27.2 | | | | | Flight of the Gauls: "they fled where the course of each led" (Sage, 1936). (*Praelati, qua quemque impetus tulit, fugerunt*). | Meaning impulse. |
| 189 | 38.33.6 | Spartan Exiles | Spartans | Infantry | Infantry | "They formed in a body and met the Lacedaemonians as they came to the gates of the camp; and at first they assailed them with insults and then, as a quarrel broke out and the passions were aroused the most impetuous of the exiles attacked the Lacedaemonians" (Sage, 1936). (*Hi uenientibus Lacedaemoniis ad portam castrorum agmine facto occurrerunt; et primo lacessere iurgiis, deinde, altercatione orta, cum accenderentur irae, ferocissimi exulum impetum in Lacedaemonios fecerunt*). | Non-Roman infantry attack. |
| 188 | 38.41.7 | Romans | Thracians | Infantry | Infantry | 'They moved forward in close array and attacking with a shout they first dislodged the enemy and then broke the line'. (*Conferti subeunt et cum clamore impetu facto primum expulere loco hostis, deinde auertere*). | Roman infantry attack. |
| 186 | 39.21.10 | Romans | Celtiberians | | | "And if the arrival of his successor had not prevented the victor from exploiting his success, the Celtiberians might have been subdued" (Sage, 1936). (*Et nisi successor aduentus suo inhibuisset impetum uictoris, subacti Celtiberi forent*). | General use meaning sucessful attack. |
| 185 | 39.31.10 | Romans | Celtiberians | Infantry | Infantry | The Romans were being beaten back by the enemy in wedge formation. Calpurnius inspired the infantry by his and the cavalry's bravery. "The shouting was renewed by all: an attack was launched as if from | Roman infantry attack. |

| | | | | | | | |
|---|---|---|---|---|---|---|---|
| | | | | | | higher ground. And so they swept forward like a torrent and overwhelmed the panic-stricken enemy, nor as they attacked wave after wave could they be resisted" (Sage, 1936, slightly adapted). (*Renouatur ab omnibus clamor: impetus fit uelut ex superiore loco. haud secus ergo quam torrentis modo fundunt sternuntque perculsos, nec sustineri alii super alios inferentes sese possunt*). | |
| 184 | 39.36.10 | Spartans | Peloponnesian cities | | | Spartans capture coastal towns in the Peloponnese by a 'night attack'. (*Nocturno impetu occupauerunt*). | Attack on a city. |
| 184 | 39.36.15 | Spartan Exiles | Spartans | Infantry | Infantry | Spartan exiles made an attack on the Spartan main force (*impetum fecerunt*). | Non-Roman infantry attack. |
| 183 | 39.49.3 | Mesene | Achaeans | Infantry | Cavalry | The enemy made an attack on Philopoemen's cavalry, which he sustained. (*Sustinens impetus hostium*). | Non-Roman cavalry attack. |
| 182 | 40.1.3 | Apuani | Pisani | | | A danger that the Apuani might invade the territory of Pisa. (*Periculumque esse, ne impetum in agrum Pisanum facerent*). | General use of 'attack'. |
| 182 | 40.10.7 | | | | | Perseus claimed that he was attacked by soldiers. (*Vidisti hesterno die impetum militum in me*) | General use of 'attack'. |
| 180 | 40.40.3 | Celtiberians | Romans | Infantry | Infantry | The Celts realised that they could not face the legions in a normal pitched battle. 'They made a thrust in a wedge shape, in which formation they are so powerful that no matter against whom they attack they cannot be resisted' (*cuneo impressionem fecerunt, quo tantum ualent genere pugnae, ut quamcumque [in] partem perculere impetu suo, sustineri nequeant*). | Non-Roman infantry attack. |
| 179 | 40.48.6 | Romans | Carthaginians | Infantry | Infantry | The Celtiberians attack the Roman camp, the Romans burst out of all the gates at once. The enemy could not withstand the unexpected attack. (*Non sustinuere impetum necopinatum hostes*). | Roman attack from a camp. |
| 179 | 40.49.3 | Romans | City of Alce | | | Romans attack the town of Alce, the citizens withstood the first assault. (*Oppidani primum impetum hostium sustinuerunt*). | Attack on a city. |
| 178 | 41.2.6 | Histrians | Romans | | | Imaginary assault on the gates of the Roman camp. (*Ut ubi nulla esset statio, quae sustineret impetum*). | Attack on a camp. |
| 178 | 41.2.9 | Histrians | Romans | | | The Histrians capture an empty Roman camp. (*Hunc in uacua castra impetu facto Histri*). | Attack on a camp. |
| 177 | 41.10.4 | Histrians | Romans | Infantry | Infantry | The Histrians fought at the first clash more sharply than with perseverance. (*Acrius primo impetu quam perseuerantius pugnauit*). | Non-Roman infantry attack. |
| 177 | 41.14.2 | Romans | City of Mutina | | | The Romans assault the city of Mutina. (*Repentino impetu coloniam ipsam ceperunt*). | Attack on a city. |
| 174 | 41.26.4 | Romans | Celtiberians | Infantry | Infantry | The Celtiberians attack the Roman camp. The Romans under Appius Claudius try to force their way out, 'they burst out so unexpectedly that the Celtiberians were unable to withstand the attack' (*ita repente inruperunt, ut sustinere impetum eorum Celtiberi nequirent*). | Roman infantry attack. |
| 172 | 42.29.11 | | | | | Gentius, King of the Illyrians would side with either the Romans or the Macedonians on impulse rather than planning. (*Impetuque magis quam consilio*). | Impulse to action. |
| 172 | 42.36.9 | Illyrians | Macedonians | | | Illyrians request Roman garrisons in order that they might be better protected against Macedonian attack (*impetu Macedonum*). | General use of 'attack'. |
| 171 | 42.59.4 | Macedonians | Romans | Cavalry | Cavalry | Macedonian cavalry turned back the Roman Aetolian cavalry with the first attack. (*Graecos primo impetu auertit*). | Non-Roman cavalry attack. |
| 171 | 42.67.4 | Thracians | Cotys | | | The Thracians made an attack on the territory of Cotys. (*In Cotyis fines impetum fecisse*). | General use of 'attack'. |
| 171 | 42.67.7 | Romans | City of Malloea | | | Malloea was taken at the first assault. (*Malloea primo impetu capta*). | Attack on a city. |
| 169 | 44.13.4 | Romans | City of Meliboea | | | Romans unable to take Meliboea at the first assault. (*Spemque extemplo inciderunt capi primo impetu posse*). | Attack on a city. |
| 168 | 44.30.13 | | | | | Anicius the praetor moves urgently (*impetum*) to relieve the siege of Bassania. | Non military use, meaning urgency. |
| 168 | 44.35.7 | Romans | Macedonians | Infantry | Infantry | Perseus had fortified a strong position on the bank of the River Elpeüs. Some of the younger Romans believed that attacking in a single column, the Macedonians would not be able to resist. (*Uno <agmine impetum> facientibus…*). | Hypothetical Roman infantry attack. |
| 168 | 44.41.5 | Romans | Macedonians | Elephants | | The charge of the elephants was followed by the Latin allies, who routed the left wing (*elephantorum impetum subsecuti sunt socii nominis Latini pepuleruntque laeuom cornu*). | Elephant charge. |

## Appendix 1.6: the occurrences of *inferre* in Livy

| *Date* | *Reference* | *Offensive Army* | *Defensive Army* | *Attacking Arm* | *Defensive Arm* | *Notes* | *Comments* |
|---|---|---|---|---|---|---|---|
| >753 | 1.2.1 | | | | | Turnus, King of the Rutulians, attacked both Aeneas and Latinus at the same time. (*Simul Aeneae Latinoque bellum intulerat*). | Wage war |
| 753-717 | 1.11.3 | | | | | Romulus set out to meet the Crustuminians who were marching to attack him. (*Inde contra Crustuminos profectus bellum inferentes*). | Wage war |
| 753-717 | 1.11.5 | | | | | Sabines did not parade war until they made it. (*Nec ostenderunt bellum prius quam intulerunt*). | Wage war |
| 753-717 | 1.13.1 | | | | | Sabine women "dared to go amongst the flying missiles" (Sage, 1919). (*Ausae se inter tela volantia inferre*). | Carry forward. |
| 753-717 | 1.14.5 | | | | | Exodos of farmers from the country to the city announced war. (*Tumultusque repens ex agris in urbem inlatus pro nuntio fuit*). | Enter a city. |
| 715-672 | 1.21.3 | | | | | "Numa would often withdraw, without witnesses, as if to meet the goddess" (Sage, 1919). (*Quo quia se persaepe Numa sine arbitris velut ad congressum deae inferebat*). | Go to meet. |
| 672-640 | 1.30.8 | Romans | Samnites | | | Success depended on which army "should first take the field" (Sage, 1919). (*Utri prius arma inferrent*). | Offensive move |
| 534-510 | 1.51.2 | | | | | Many swords secretly brought into a house. (*Magnam gladiorum inferri clam*). | Carry forward. |
| 534-510 | 1.51.3 | | | | | 'Just as if it had been brought forward by the providence of the gods'. (*Velut deorum quadam providentia inlatam*). | Carry forward. |
| 508 | 2.14.6 | Etruscans | Aricia | Infantry | Infantry | "When the battle began, the attack of the Etruscans was so impetuous that they routed the Aricini at the first charge" (Sage, 1919). (*Proelio inito adeo concitato impetu se intulerant Etrusci ut funderent ipso incursu Aricinos*). | Non-Roman infantry attack |
| 502 | 2.17.5 | Romans | Pometia | | | Rome attacked Pometia (*Pometia arma inlata*). | Wage war |
| 495 | 2.26.5 | Romans | Aricia | | | It was impossible to offer a peaceful answer "to a people who had already drawn the sword, while they themselves were also arming" (Sage, 1919). (*Nec pacatum responsum arma inferentibus arma ipsi capientes*). | Offensive move. |
| 494 | 2.30.13 | Volsci | Romans | Infantry | Infantry | Roman consul ordered his men to plant their *pila* in the ground (*defixi pilis*) and stand still until the enemy had come to close quarters. "The Volsci, weary with running and shouting, hurled themselves upon the Romans, who seemed numb with fear" (Sage, 1919). (*Volsci cursu et clamore fessi cum se velut stupentibus metu intulissent Romanis*). | Non-Roman infantry attack |
| 477 | 2.50.7 | Etruscans | Romans | Infantry | Infantry | The Romans were surrounded "and as the Etruscans drew together and the Romans were now fenced in by a continuous line of armed men, the harder the enemy pressed them the smaller was the space within which they themselves were forced to contract their circle" (Sage, 1919). (*Coeuntibusque Etruscis iam continenti agmine armatorum saepti, quo magis se hostis inferebat, cogebantur breviore spatio et ipsi orbem colligere*). | Non-Roman infantry attack |
| 475 | 2.53.1 | Romans | Sabines | | | P. Valerius captured the gate [of the Sabine camp] against which he had directed his first assault. (*Ea porta cui signa primum intulerat caperetur*). | Attack on a camp |
| 471 | 2.59.2 | Volsci | Romans | | | The Roman army were only willing to make a stand when they saw the Volsci advancing on their fortifications. (*Signa inferentem Volscum munimentis*). | Advancing standards |
| 469 | 2.63.7 | | | | | Volscians accepted greater losses than they had themselves inflicted. (*Plus cladium quam intulerant acceperunt*). | Inflict casualties |
| 468 | 2.65.5 | Romans | Volsci | Infantry | Infantry | The Volsci, having discharged their missiles in the first attack, picked up stones. The Romans on the left wing were nearly overwhelmed by this rain of stones. But the consul, reproaching them for cowardice shamed them into fighting. "First they made a resolute stand; then after holding their ground and returning blow for blow, they even dared to press forward and, renewing their cheers, set the line in motion; then with another attack they struggled upward and scaled the height" (Sage, 1919, slightly adapted). (*Restitere primo obstinatis animis; deinde, ut obtinentes locum vim pro vi referebant, audent ultro gradum inferre et clamore renovato commouent aciem; tum rursus impetu capto enituntur*). | Roman infantry attack. |
| 464 | 3.5.7 | Romans | Aequi | Cavalry | Infantry | The Roman camp was surrounded by the Aequi. Furius, the brother of the consul, got caught up and killed by the enemy. "The consul too, upon learning that his brother was surrounded, set his face towards the battle and plunged into the midst of the mellay" (Foster, 1922), receiving a wound. (*Et consul nuntio* | Roman cavalry attack |

| | | | | | | | |
|---|---|---|---|---|---|---|---|
| | | | | | | *circumvenit fratris conversus ad pugnam, dum se temere magis quam satis caute in mediam dimicationem infert*). | |
| 464 | 3.5.11 | Romans | Aequi | | | "Heavy losses were inflicted and sustained on both sides at that time" (Foster, 1922). (*Magnae clades ultro citroque illis diebus et inlatae et acceptae*). | Inflict wounds |
| 462 | 3.8.4 | | | | | Rome is strong enough to defend itself and to make war. (*Satis valida civitate ut non solum arcere bellum sed ultro etiam inferre posset*). | Wage war |
| 462 | 3.8.5 | | | | | Veturius was sent to make war against the Volsci. (*Veturius missus in Volscos ad bellum ultro inferendum*). | Wage war |
| 460 | 3.16.6 | | | | | Herdonius attacked the capitol by night. (*Quem nocturnus hostis intulerat*). | Generic attack word |
| 460 | 3.18.8 | Romans | Romans | Infantry | Infantry | The enemy held the Capitoline, but "as they stood there quaking the Romans and allies assailed them" (Foster, 1922). (*Trepidantibus inferrunt signa Romani sociique*). | Roman infantry attack |
| 460 | 3.19.7 | | | | | Cincinnatus haraunges the Roman people: "did you carry your standards against the Capitoline hill before clearing these enemies out of the forum?" (Foster, 1922). (*Prius clivium Capitolinum signa intulistis quam hos hostes de foro tolleretis?*) | Advancing standards |
| 449 | 3.42.7 | Romans | Sabines | | | Romans take the offensive (*inferendo*) against the Sabines. | Offensive move |
| 449 | 3.53.9 | | | | | A lowly citizen when enjoying equal rights, neither inflicts an injury nor receives one. (*Nec inferendo iniuriam nec patiendo*). | Inflict wounds |
| 449 | 3.60.5 | Romans | Latins | | | "On perceiving this the consul repaid the fear he had previously been made to feel" (Foster, 1922). (*Quod ubi consul sensit, reddit inlatum antea terrorem*). | Inspire fear. |
| 449 | 3.60.8 | Romans | Aequi and Volsci | Infantry | Infantry | After spending the day waiting for the enemy give battle, the Roman consul ordered an advance. (*Iubet signa inferri consul*). | Advancing standards |
| 449 | 3.60.9 | Romans | Aequi and Volsci | Infantry | Infantry | "A part [of the enemy army] had already passed out through the gates and the rest were following in good order, each man coming out into his proper place; when the Roman consul, not waiting till the enemy's line should be strongly posted in full force, advanced to the charge" (Foster, 1922). (*Iamque pars egressa portis erat, deincepsque alii servabant ordinem in suum quisque locum descendentes, cum consul Romanus, priusquam totis viribus fulta constaret hostium acies, intulit signa*). | Advancing standards |
| 449 | 3.62.8 | Sabines | Romans | Infantry | Infantry | The two sides fought equally, while the Sabines had 2,000 in reserve to attack the Roman left wing. "These troops, attacking in flank, had almost encompassed that wing, and were beginning to overpower it" (Foster, 1922). (*Quae ubi inlatis ex transvero signis degravabant prope circumventum cornu*). | Non-Roman infantry attack |
| 446 | 3.70.10 | Romans | Aequi | Infantry | Infantry | "Agrippa, young, active and courageous perceived that the battle was everywhere going better than on his own front, snatched the standards from the men who bore them, and began to carry them forward himself, and even to fling some of them into the press of the enemy" (Foster, 1922). (*Ibi Agrippa, aetate viribusque ferox, cum omni parte pugnae melius rem geri quam apud se videret, arrepta signa ab signiferis ipse inferre, quaedam incere etiam in confertos hostes coepit*). | Advancing standards |
| 445 | 4.1.2 | | | | | The suggestion that one consul should be plebian was put forward (*inlata*) by the tribunes. | Offer a suggestion |
| 443 | 4.8.4 | | | | | The subject of the censorship was brought forward (*inlata*) in the senate. | Offer a suggestion |
| 437 | 4.18.5 | Romans | Faliscans and Veientes | | | The dictator advanced on the right, against the Faliscan, and Q. Capitolinus on the left, to meet the Veientes. (*Dictator dextro cornu adversus Faliscos, sinistro contra Veientem Capitolinus Quinctius intulit signa*). | Advancing standards |
| 437 | 4.20.6 | | | | | A. Cornelius Cossus brought (*intulisse*) the second spoils of honour to the temple of Jupiter Feretrius. | Carry in. |
| 435 | 4.21.7 | | | | | The pestilence was so bad that no one left the Roman land to pillage. (*Ex agro Romano exiret bellive inferendi*) | Generic invasion. |
| 431 | 4.28.4 | Volscians | Romans | | | Volscians made war on Rome (*bellum intulistis*). | Wage war |
| 431 | 4.29.4 | Romans | Volsci | | | "The dictator too had reached the rampart and had already carried the fighting into the camp" (Foster, 1922). (*Et dictator proruto vallo iam in castra proelium intulerat*). | Offensive move |
| 430-27 | 4.30.9 | | | | | Romans found strange rights introduced into their homes. (*Novus ritus sacrificandi vaticinando inferentibus in domos*). | Carry forward. |
| 426 | 4.32.4 | | | | | Aulus Cornelius had carried (*intulerit*) the spoils of honour to the temple of Jupiter Feretrius. | Carry forward. |
| 426 | 4.33.5 | Romans | Veii, Fidenates and Etruscans | Infantry | Infantry | The Dictator said: "will you not seize these self-same brands, and each for himself - if we must fight with | Generic attack word |

| | | | | | | | |
|---|---|---|---|---|---|---|---|
| | | | | | | fire, not with javelins - attack them with their own weapons?" (Foster, 1922). (*Non faces has ipsas pro se quisque, si igni, non telis pugnandum est, ereptas ultro inferetis?*). | |
| 426 | 4.33.7 | Romans | Veii, Fidenates and Etruscans | | | The master of the horse was carried up by his unbridled mount into the midst of the flames. (*Ipse princeps calcaribus subditis evectus effreno equo in medios ignes infertur*). | Carry forward. |
| 426 | 4.33.10 | Romans | Veii, Fidenates and Etruscans | Infantry | Infantry | The Fidenates, having come out of their city carrying torches, scared the Roman line. The dictator (M. Aemilius Mamercinus) ordered Quinctius to go around and attack the enemy from the rear with his cavalry. After exhorting his infantry to fight on with torches if necessary, battle was engaged. After some fighting the "dictator called out that Quinctius the lieutenant and his followers had assailed the enemy in the rear, the cheering was renewed, and he pressed home his own attack more sharply" (Foster, 1922). (*Dictator exclamat Quinctium legatum et suos ab tergo hostem adortes; ipse redintegrato clamore infert acrius signa*). The enemy were caught between two forces and fled. | Roman infantry attack |
| 426 | 4.33.11 | Romans | Veii, Fidenates and Etruscans | Infantry | Infantry | 'In fear their flight carried them into the middle of the slaughter'. (*Infert pavidos fuga in mediam caedem*). | Carry forward. |
| 423 | 4.37.10 | Vosci | Romans | Infantry | Infantry | "In the first battle, which Sempronius entered without caution or deliberation, his line was not strengthened with reserves nor was his cavalry skilfully posted, when fighting began. The battle-cries were the first intimation how the affair was likely to go; for the enemy's was louder and fuller, that of the Romans dissonant and uneven and, dragging more with each repitition, betrayed the faintness of their hearts. This caused the enemy to charge the more boldly, thrusting with shields and making play with swords" (Foster, 1922). (*Primo proelio, quod ab Sempronio incaute inconsulteque commissum est, non subsidiis firmata acie, non equite apte locato concursum est. Clamor indicium primum fuit quo res inclinatura esset, excitatior crebriorque ab hoste sublatus: ab Romanis dissonus, impar, segnius saepe iteratus prodidit pauorem animorum. Eo ferocior inlatus hostis urgere scutis, micare gladiis*). | Non-Roman infantry attack |
| 423 | 4.37.11 | Volscians | Romans | Infantry | Infantry | The Romans were in disorder after the preliminary battle, "the Volscians advanced (their standards) and bore hard against the Roman line, but saw more of their enemies killed than running away" (Foster, 1922). (*Volscus inferre signa, urgere aciem, plus caedis hostium videre quam fugae*). | Advancing standards |
| 423 | 4.38.4 | Romans | Volsci | Cavalry fighting as infantry | Infantry | "Wherever they went they forced a passage; holding their targets up before them, they charge where they saw the distress of their friends was greatest. The fortune of the day was restored at every point where their onset carried them" (Foster, 1922). (*Quacumque incedunt, vi viam faciunt, eo se inferunt obiectis parmis ubi suorum plurimum laborem vident. Restituitur omnibus locis pugna, in quae eos impetus tulit*). | Roman infantry attack |
| 423 | 4.39.2 | Romans | Volsci | Cavalry fighting as infantry | Infantry | After cavalry men began to fight as infantry, the Volscian general ordered his men to give ground, until carried forward by their force, they should be cut off from the rest. (*Donec impetu inlati ab suis excludantur*). | Roman infantry attack |
| 421 | 4.43.4 | | | | | Tribunes of the plebs made a fight (*intulerunt*) to have half of the *quaestors*. | Offer a suggestion |
| 419 | 4.44.7 | | | | | Tribunes repeatedly brought forward (*inlata*) the division of public lands. | Offer a suggestion |
| 418 | 4.47.2 | Romans | Aequi | Infantry | Infantry | "When the dictator had attacked with his cavalry and had thrown the enemy's front ranks into confusion, he ordered the legions to advance rapidly..." (Foster, 1922). (*Itaque primo statim proelio cum dictator equitatu immisso antesignanos hostium turbasset, legionum inde signa inferri propere iussit...*). | Advancing standards |
| 416 | 4.47.6 | | | | | The senate proposes a division of the Labician territory before the tribunes could stir up (*inlata*) any agrarian troubles. | Stir up |
| 414 | 4.49.4 | Bolarii | Labici | | | These people had made incursions into the neighbouring territory of Labici and attacked the new settlers (*bellum inlatum*). | Wage war |
| 402 | 5.8.7 | Etruscans | Romans | | | Etruscan forces attacked the Roman camp and inspired great terror. (*Ingentemque terrorem intulere*). | Inspire fear. |
| 399 | 5.13.11 | Romans | Faliscans | | | The battle brought terror to the Faliscans. (*Faliscis intulit terrorem*). | Inspire fear. |
| 398 | 5.14.4 | | | | | A pestilence had descended [made war on] the fields and the city. (*Pestilentiam agris urbique inlatum*). | Wage war |
| 396 | 5.21.11 | Romans | Veii | | | The Romans attacked the Veientine citadel from their | Carry forward. |

| | | | | | | | |
|---|---|---|---|---|---|---|---|
| | | | | | | cover in a mine. Some soldiers, "when the women and slaves cast down stones and tiles from the roofs, fetched fire against them" (Foster, 1924). (*Pars cum ex tectis saxa tegulaeque a mulieribus ac servitiis iacerentur, inferunt ignes*). | |
| 396 | 5.22.8 | | | | | Veii had inflicted considerably heavier losses than it sustained. (*Plus aliquanto cladium intulisset quam accepisset*). | Inflict casualties |
| 390 | 5.39.7 | | | | | The Gauls opt to enter the city at night to strike terror into the enemy. (*Quo plus pavoris inferrent*). | Inspire fear. |
| 390 | 5.39.8 | | | | | Hostile forces entered the city. (*Cum signa infesta portis sunt inlata*) | Attack on a city |
| 390 | 5.43.3 | Romans | Gauls | Infantry | Infantry | "They made their stand about the middle of the declivity, and there, launching their attack from higher ground, which seemed of itself to hurl them against the foe, dislodged the Gauls, with such havoc and destruction the they never attempted to attack in that manner again" (Foster,1924). (*Medio fere clivo restitere, atque inde ex loco superiore, qui prope sua sponte in hostem inferebat impetu facto, strage ea ruina fudere Gallos ut nunquam postea nec universi temptauerint pugnae genus*). | Roman infantry attack |
| 390 | 5.43.8 | | | | | Camillus pushed his way into the middle of the council of the Ardeates. (*In mediam contionem intulisset*) | Carry forward. |
| 390 | 5.50.5 | | | | | A voice foretelling disaster before the Gallic war was disregarded. (*Neglectaque esset mentio inlata*). | Offer a suggestion |
| 389 | 6.2.9 | | | | | The Etruscans were struck with fear on hearing that Camillus was the general (*Camillus auditus imperator terroris intulerat*). | Inspire fear. |
| 386 | 6.6.4 | | | | | Fugitives from the Pomptine district suddenly appeared in Rome. (*Fugientium ex agro Pomptino agmen repente inlatum in urbem*). | Enter the city. |
| 386 | 6.8.6 | | | | | Camillus carried victory with him wherever he went. (*Ita quocumque se intulisset victoriam secum haud dubiam trahebat*). | Carry forward. |
| 385 | 6.12.5 | | | | | Always the same nation made war. (*Eadem semper gens bellum intulerit*). | Wage war |
| 385 | 6.12.9 | Voslci | Romans | Infantry | Infantry | "I would have none run out from the line, but all stand firmly planted and receive the onset of our enemies. When they have discharged their missiles without effect, and come thronging upon you where you stand, then let your blades flash out" (Foster, 1924). (*Ne procurri quidem ab acie velim, sed obnixos vos stabili gradu impetum hostium excipere. Ubi illi vana iniecerint missilia et effusi stantibus vobis se intulerint, tum micent gladii*). | Non-Roman infantry attack |
| 385 | 6.13.3 | Romans | Volsci | Infantry | Infantry | The Vosci's "boldness went no further than the battle-cry, the discharge of missiles, and the first fury of the onset; the play of swords, when foot met foot, and the glance of the foemen that darted out the fire of his spirit, they could not abide. Their front was driven in and communicated its disorder to the supports... next their ranks were broken at many points, and all was in commotion, and the line resembled a surging wave" (Foster, 1924). (*Clamore tantum missilibusque telis et primo pugnae impetu ferox gladios et conlatum pedum et voltum hostis ardore animi micantem ferre non potuit. Impulsa frons prima et trepidatio subsidiis inlata...rupti inde multis locis ordines motaque omnia et fluctuanti similis acies erat*). | Offer a suggestion |
| 385 | 6.13.3 | Romans | Latins | | | Roman cavalry inspired a terror of their own. (*Suum terrorem intulit eques*). | Inspire fear. |
| 381 | 6.23.2 | Volscians | Romans | | | The Volsci marched almost to the rampart of the Romans. (*Vallo pope hostium signa inferendo*). | Generic attack word. |
| 381 | 6.26.4 | Romans | Tusculans | | | Romans made war on Tusculans (*bellum intulistis*) | Wage war |
| 380 | 6.27.11 | Praenestini | Romans | | | "The only thing that was able to allay the quarrel in the city was the approach of the enemy to its very walls" (Foster, 1924). (*Neque aliud ad seditionem exstinguendam in urbe quam prope inlatum moenibus ipsis bellum valuit*). | Advancing standards |
| 380 | 6.28.2 | Praenestini | Romans | | | The Praenestini advanced against the Colline Gate. (*Ad portam Collinam signa intulere*). | Attack on a city |
| 380 | 6.29.2 | Romans | Latins | Infantry | Infantry | Cincinnatus ordered Sempronius to attack the Latin troops, with his cavalry, at the gallop. Then he said: "I, with the legions, will attack them when they are in disorder and confusion" (Foster, 1924). (*Ego cum legionibus in turbatos trepidantesque inferam signa*). | Roman infantry attack |
| 380 | 6.29.5 | | | | | The Praeneste, having been routed by the Romans, abandoned their defences and entered the city of Praeneste. (*Depopulatisque omnibus obsidio urbi inferretur*). | Attack on a city |
| 377 | 6.32.8 | Romans | Latins | Cavalry | Infantry | The Latin legions were able to resist the Romans until "the cavalry were sent against them and threw their ranks into confusion" (Foster, 1924). (*Sed eques immissus ordines turbauit, turbatis signa peditum* | Standards thrown into confusion |

| | | | | | | *inlata*). | |
|---|---|---|---|---|---|---|---|
| 362 | 7.8.3 | Romans | Hernici | Cavalry fighting as infantry | Infantry | The Roman horse unable to break the Hernici line, dismounted and attacked on foot. They were met by the enemy's special cohorts (*extraordinariae cohortes*) and were equally matched in battle, while the rest of the soldiers stood and watched. The cavalrymen encouraged each other to further efforts: "stirred by these mutual reproaches , they advanced and renewed cheering, and first they made the enemy yield, then forced them back, and finally routed them in no uncertain fashion" (Foster, 1924). (*his inter se uocibus concitati clamore renouato inferunt pedem et primum gradu mouerunt hostem, deinde pepulerunt, postremo iam haud dubie auertunt*) | Roman infantry attack |
| 355 | 7.17.5 | Romans | Faliscans and Tarquinienses | Infantry | Infantry | Priests of the Faliscans and Tarquinienses carrying snakes and fire rush out against the Romans, this scared the soldiers who became frantic and disordered. When the Consul upbraided them for being scared, the soldiers hurled themselves against the real armed men and routed the whole army. (*In ipsos armatos se intulissent, averterunt totam aciem*). | Roman infantry attack |
| 349 | 7.24.6 | Romans | Gauls | Infantry | Infantry | The Roman consul exhorts his troops: "…cover the plain with the same carnage you have spread upon the mountains. Do not wait for the enemy to flee from you, while you stand still; you must move forward and attack them" (Foster, 1924). (*…complete eadem strage campos qua montes replestis. Nolite exspectare dum stantes uos fugiant; inferenda sunt signa et uadendum in hostem*). | Roman infantry attack |
| 347 | 7.27.6 | Romans | Volsci | | | Valerius, the consul, ordered to make war on the Volsci before more enemies should arise. (*Priusquam plus hostium fieret Volscis arma inferre iussus*) | Wage war |
| 345 | 7.28.4 | Aurunci | Romans | | | The Aurunci had been the aggressors in the war. (*Quia et ultro bellum intulerant*). | Offensive move |
| 345 | 7.29.4 | Samnites | Sidicini | | | The Samnites made war on (*intulissent*) the Sidicini. | Wage war |
| 344 | 7.31.10 | Samnites | Romans | | | Samnites to make no incursion in to Roman territory. (*In eum agrum qui populi Romani factus esset hostilia arma inferrent*). | Wage war |
| 344 | 7.33.12 | Samnites | Romans | | | The Samnites received more wounds than they delivered. (*Quamquam plura accipiunt quam inferunt vulnera*). | Inflict wounds |
| 340 | 8.5.1 | | | | | Rome pleads with the Latins not to make war on the Samnites (*ne Samnitibus foederatis bellum inferrent*). | Wage war |
| 326 | 8.27.6 | | | | | Certain young Lucanians exhibited (*intulissent*) their scarred bodies before a council of citizens. | Carry forward. |
| 325 | 8.30.7 | Romans | Samnites | Infantry | Infantry | [See *impetus* section for information on the cavalry charge] "The foot soldiers, following up the cavalry charge, advanced on the disordered enemy of whom it is said that twenty thousand were slain that day" (Foster, 1926). (*Secutes pedes impetum equitum turbatis hostibus intulit signa, Viginti milia hostium caesa eo die traduntur*). | Advancing standards |
| 323 | 8.37.4 | | | | | War was not waged against the Apulians. (*Sunt qui non ipsis Apulis bellum inlatum*). | Wage war |
| 323 | 8.37.5 | | | | | The Samnites did not attack the Apulians. (*Non Apulis ab Samnitibus arma inlata*) | Wage war |
| 322 | 8.38.3 | Samnites | Romans | | | The Samnites "entrenched themselves close to the Roman outposts" (Foster, 1926). (*Ut vallum usqu ad stationem Romanum inferrent*). | Carry forward. |
| 322 | 8.39.5 | Romans | Samnites | Infantry | Infantry | During the battle the Roman cavalry attacked the Samnites in the rear. "The dictator (A. Cornelius Cossus Arvina), seeing the men in their fighting line glance nervously behind them and their standards become disordered, and their line began to waver, then cried out to his men, then urged them on, and called by name on tribunes and company-commanders to join him in a new attack. With fresh cheer the ranks pressed forward, and at each advance perceived the Samnites to be more and more confused" (Foster, 1926). (*Et dictator, ubi respectantes hostium antesignanos turbataque signa et fluctuantem aciem uidit, tum appellare, tum adhortari milites, tribunos principesque ordinum nominatim ad iterandam secum pugnam uocare. nouato clamore signa inferuntur, et quidquid progrediebantur magis magisque turbatos hostes cernebant*). | Roman infantry attack |
| 319 | 9.15.6 | | | | | The Romans wanted to send the Samnites under the yoke, "inflicting on them no new disgrace, but requiting that which had first been put upon the Romans" (Foster, 1926). (*Sub iugum missurum, ulciscentem inlatam, non novam inferentem ignominiam*). | Inflict disgrace |
| 319 | 9.15.6 | | | | | Inflicting on them no new disgrace (*non novam inferentem ignominiam*). | Inflict disgrace |
| 319 | 9.16.3 | | | | | Roman consul ordered the Samnite garrison to be killed. "A saying which struck more terror into their | Inspire fear. |

| | | | | | | | |
|---|---|---|---|---|---|---|---|
| | | | | | | hearts than the threatened assault" (Foster, 1926). (*Plus ea voce quam armis inlatis terroris colonis iniectum*). | |
| 316 | 9.21.3 | Saticulani and Samnites | Romans | | | Rome had fear brought forth from two quarters. (*Duplex inde terror inlatus Romanis*). | Inspire fear. |
| 315 | 9.23.15 | Romans | Samnites | Infantry | Infantry | The Romans were inspired by their dictator's speech and by a special ruse. He had ordered the front tents of the Roman camp to be burnt in order to fire up his soldiers. The Roman infantry, attacking like madmen, threw the enemy's ranks into confusion on the first assault. (*Itaque velut vecordes inlati signa primo impetu hostium turbant*). | Roman infantry attack |
| 314 | 9.25.2 | | | | | The Consuls made war on the land and cities of the Ausones. (*In agros atque urbes Ausonum bellum intulerunt*) | Wage war |
| 314 | 9.27.10 | Romans | Samnites | Cavalry | Cavalry | "As the Samnite infantry wavered, their cavalry moved up to support them. But while they came obliquely onward, in the interval between the armies, the Roman cavalry charged them at the gallop" (Foster, 1926). (*Commota pedestri acie Samnitium eques in pugnam succedit. In hunc transverso agmine inter duas acies se inferentem Romanus equitatus*). | Roman cavalry attack |
| 314 | 9.27.12 | Samnites | Romans | Infantry | Infantry | "The Romans had been driven out of their position, and the victorious enemy were charging their disordered ranks" (Foster, 1926). (*Romanos loco pulsos, victorem hostem signa in perculsos inferentem*). | Roman infantry attack |
| 312 | 9.29.4 | Romans | Etruscans | | | Sulpicius did not plan for an offensive war (*inferendo bello*) against the Etruscans, intending to remain inactive. | Wage war |
| 312 | 9.29.5 | Etruscans | Romans | | | Romans would not attack unless the Etruscans should take the field first. (*Nisi ultro arma Etrusci inferrent*). | Wage war |
| 311 | 9.32.6 | Etruscans | Romans | Infantry | Infantry | After a long period of stand-off the Etruscans decide to attack: they set up a shout, and with sound of trumpets advanced their standards. (*Clamor ab Etruscis oritur concinuntque tubae et signa inferuntur*). | Advancing standards |
| 308 | 9.40.9 | Romans | Samnites | Infantry | Infantry | Junius with the Roman left. "Declaring that he offered up these men to Orcus, Junius charged, threw their ranks into disorder, and clearly made their line recoil" (Foster, 1926). (*Eos se Orco mactare Iunius dictitans cum intulisset signa turbauit ordines et haud dubie impulit aciem*). | Roman infantry attack |
| 308 | 9.40.13 | Romans | Samnites | Infantry | Infantry | The Roman cavalry "charged obliquely against the enemy's flanks. Thus a new and appalling danger enveloped their line on either side, and when the Roman legions, observing the terror of the Samnites, pressed forward with redoubled shouts, the enemy began to flee" (Foster, 1926). (*In transuersa latera hostium incurrunt. Is nouus additus terror cum ex parte utraque circumuasisset aciem et ad terrorem hostium legiones Romanae redintegrato clamore intulissent gradum, tum fuga ab Samnitibus coepta*). | Roman infantry attack |
| 306 | 9.43.24 | | | | | The people of Anagnia and those others who had borne arms (*arma Romanis intulerant*) against the Romans were admitted to the citizenship without the right of voting | Wage war |
| 302 | 10.2.13 | | | | | Some of Cleonymus's ships had been run aground in confusion. (*Qua trepidatio in vada intulerat*). | Carry forward |
| 302 | 10.5.9 | Romans | Etruscans | Infantry | Infantry | "The routed enemy fled back to their camp, and when the Roman standards-bearers pressed in after them, they gave way and huddled up together in the furthest part of the enclosure" (Foster, 1926). (*Fusi hostes castra repetunt inferentibusque iam signa Romanis cedunt et in ultimam castrorum partem conglobantur*). | Advancing standards |
| 299 | 10.10.9 | | | | | Make war on Rome (*belli Romanis inferendi*) | Wage war |
| 298 | 10.12.8 | | | | | "Not only was the soil left bare for the enemy, but even the strongholds and villages were burned" (Foster, 1926). (*Nec solum modo vastum hosti relictum sed castellis etiam vicique inlatus ignis*). | Carry forward |
| 296 | 10.19.21 | Romans | Etruscans | | | Volumnius himself led a charge against the gate of the Etruscan camp. (*Et cum Volumnius ipse portae signa inferret*). | Attack on a camp. |
| 295 | 10.28.2 | Romans | Samnites | Infantry | Infantry | The Romans were defending themselves rather than attacking (*Romani apud Fabium arcebant magis quam inferebant pugnam*). | Generic attack word. |
| 295 | 10.28.18 | Romans | Gauls | Cavalry | Cavalry | Decius, on horse back, "hurling himself against the weapons of the enemy met his death" (Foster, 1926). (*Inferensque se ipse infestis telis est interfectus*). | Single cavalry attack |
| 295 | 10.29.9 | Romans | Samnites | Infantry | Infantry | Roman Cavalry attack the enemy flanks (*in transverso*), which disrupted the Samnite line. At the same time Fabius ordered his own men to advance the standards slowly and rout the enemy. (*Sensim suos signa inferre iussit et commovere hostem*). | Advancing standards |
| 295 | 10.30.1 | Romans | Samnites | | | Fulvius, besides the enormous damage which his forays inflicted on the people of the land, fought also | Inflict damage |

| | | | | | | | |
|---|---|---|---|---|---|---|---|
| | | | | | | a victoriuous battle with the enemy. (*Praeter ingentum inlatam populationibus agrorum hosti cladem pugnatum etiam egregie est*). | |
| 295 | 10.31.10 | Romans | Samnites | | | M. Valerius and A. Cornelius (343) were the first to make war on Samnium. (*Qui primi Samnio arma intulerunt*). | Wage war |
| 294 | 10.33.4 | Romans | Samnites | Infantry | Infantry | The Samnites attacked the Roman camp by the Decuman gate, the Romans gave ground. After being exhorted by the consul "they gave a cheer, and, exerting themselves, first made a successful stand, and afterwards pushed forward and forced their enemies back, and, having once repulsed them, left them no time to recover their first dismay, but thrust them out of the gate and rampart". (*Clamore sublato conixi primo resistunt, deinde inferunt pedem urgentque et impulsos semel terrore eodem [agunt] quo coeperunt expellunt extra portam uallumque*). | Roman infantry attack |
| 294 | 10.36.10 | Romans | Samnites | Infantry | Infantry | The Roman line had broken and the men were in flight. The consul managed to stop them with threats and turn them around. "the centurions snatched the standards from the standard-bearers and carried them forward, pointing out to their men that the enemy were few in number and were coming on in irregular and ill formed ranks... and renewing the struggle cut to pieces and overcame the legions of the Samnites" (Foster, 1926). (*Centuriones ab signiferis rapta signa inferre et ostendare suis paucos et ordinibus inconpositis effuse venire hostes... redintegratoque proelio cecidisset vicissetque legiones Samnitium*). | Reform of an infantry line |
| 293 | 10.39.7 | Romans | Samnites | | | Romans spent days provoking the Samnites, more feinting rather than attacking. (*comminandoque magis quam inferendo pugnam dies absumebatur*). | Generic attack word |
| 293 | 10.41.1 | Samnites | Romans | Infantry | Infantry | The Samnites resist rather than to attack. (*Samnitium magnam partem necessitas ac retigio invitos magis resistere quam inferre pugnam cogit*). | Generic attack word |
| 293 | 10.42.4 | Romans | City of Aquilonium | | | The Roman consul "gave orders that the withdrawn troops should be called back and advance against the city" (Foster, 1926). (*Acciri quas receperat copias signaque in urbem inferri iussit*). | Attack on a city |
| 293 | 10.46.6 | | | | | "If the consul had forgone the glory of depositing the captured money in the Treasury, the booty would have afforded the soldiers a donative" (Foster, 1926). (*Si spreta gloria fuisset captiuae pecuniae in aerarium inlatae, et militi tum <donum> dari ex praeda et stipendium militare praestari potuisset*). | Carry forward |
| 218-201 | 21.1.3 | Carthaginians | Romans | | | The Romans were enraged that the defeated were bearing arms against the victors. (*Romanis indignantibus quod victoribus victi ultro inferrent arma*). | Wage war |
| 237-29 | 21.2.2 | Carthaginians | Romans | | | Had he lived longer the Carthaginians would have invaded Italy under the leadership of Hamilcar. (*Si diutius uixisset, Hamilcare duce Poenos arma Italiae inlaturos fuisse*). | Wage war |
| 237-229 | 21.2.2 | Carthaginians | Romans | | | Carthaginians would have invaded Italy under Hamilcar (*intulerunt*). | Wage war |
| 221 | 21.5.3 | Carthaginians | Saguntines | | | Hannibal resolves himself to attacking the Saguntines. (*Saguntinis inferre bellum statuit*). | Generic invasion. |
| 218 | 21.21.10 | | | | | Hannibal took equal concern for attack and defense (*inde partiens curas inferendum atque arcendum bellum*). | Wage war |
| 218 | 21.24.2 | | | | | Hannibal's war was aimed at Italy. (*Italiae bellum inferri audiebant*). | Wage war |
| 218 | 21.44.3 | | | | | The spirit of an attacker is greater than that of a defender. (*Maior est animus inferentis vim quam arcentis*) | Offensive move. |
| 217 | 22.5.5 | Romans | Carthaginians | Infantry | Infantry | Fog obscured the vision and some [Romans] were swept into a crowd of combatants. (*Alii fugientes pugnantium globo inlati haerebant*). | Carry forward |
| 217 | 22.28.12 | | | | | As the Roman light infantry were driven back down hill they caused a panic among the cavalry. (*Terrorem... intulit equitem*). | Inspire fear. |
| 217 | 22.29.6 | Romans | Carthaginians | Infantry | Infantry | Minucius' troops were being routed by Hannibal, until Fabius arrived and checked their retreat, made them face the enemy and formed the defeated army and his own fresh troops into one line, ready to advance against the enemy. (*... ac iam prope una acies facta erat victi atque integri exercitus inferebantque signa in hostem*). | Reform of an infantry line |
| 217 | 22.31.4 | | | | | Roman soldiers spread out to pillage and so an ambush was quickly inflicted on them (*Itaque in insidias temere inlati*) | Offensive move |
| 217 | 22.32.4 | | | | | Envoys from Neapolis brought in (*inlatae*) forty golden bowls to the senate. | Carry forward |
| 216 | 22.47.6 | Romans | Carthaginians | Infantry | Infantry | "At first they were evenly matched in strength and courage, as long as the Gauls and Spaniards maintained their rank; but at last the Romans, by prolonged and frequent efforts pushing forward with | Roman infantry attack |

| | | | | | | | |
|---|---|---|---|---|---|---|---|
| | | | | | | an even front and a dense line, drove in the wedge-like formation which projected from the enemy line, for it was too thin to be strong; and then, as the Gauls and the Spaniards gave way and fell back in confusion, pressed forward and without once stopping forced their way through the crowd of fleeing, panic-stricken foes" (Foster, 1929). (*Primo et uiribus et animis par dum constabant ordines Gallis Hispanisque; tandem Romani, diu ac saepe conisi, aequa fronte acieque densa impulere hostium cuneum nimis tenuem eoque parum ualidum, a cetera prominentem acie. Impulsis deinde ac trepide referentibus pedem instirere ac tenore uno per praeceps pauore fugientium agmen in mediam primum aciem inlati*). | |
| 216 | 23.16.13 | Romans | Carthaginians | Cavalry and infantry | Infantry | The Roman infantry and cavalry attack out of a city against the enemy and carry panic and confusion into the centre. (*Satis terroris tumultusque in aciem mediam intulerant*). | Inspire fear. |
| 216 | 23.24.11 | | | | | Spoils and the head of Postumius were carried (*intulere*) in triumph by the Boians. | Carry forward |
| 216 | 23.27.6 | Tartesii | Carthaginians | Infantry | Infantry | Hasdrubal ordered his men to march in battle order to the Tartesii camp. The Tartesii attacked from their camp in separate groups (*catervatim currerent*), and frightened the Carthaginians by their audacity. "Then, as stragglers advancing against dense ranks, finding no safety in small numbers ... and beaten back from every side formed a circle" (Moore, 1940). (*Deinde rari in confertos inlati, cum paucitas parum tuta esset...undique pulsi coire in orbem*). | Non-Roman infantry attack |
| 216 | 23.29.9 | Romans | Carthaginians | Infantry | Infantry | Hasdrubal placed his Spaniards in the centre of his line. The Spaniards at the first clash, when they had barely hurled their javelins, the centre fell back, and, as the Romans carried themselves with great violence, they retreated. (*Primo igitur concursu, cum vix pila coniecta essent, rettulit pedem media acies, inferentibusque se magno impetu Romanis vertit terga*). | Roman infantry attack |
| 215 | 23.33.5 | | | | | Macedonian ambassadors sent to Hannibal 'encountered the centre of the Roman forces' near Apulia. (*Media in praesidia Romana inlati sunt*). | Carry forward |
| 215 | 23.38.6 | Romans | Macedonians | | | The Romans attempt, by aggressive warfare (*inferendo belli*) to keep the Macedonians away from Italy. | Wage war |
| 214 | 24.16.1 | Romans | Carthaginians | Infantry | Infantry | "Gracchus finally declared that they had no reason to hope for freedom, unless on that day the enemy should be routed and put to flight." "Those words so fired their courage that, as though they were suddenly different, they raised a shout again and charged the enemy with such force that could no longer be withstood. At first the front line of the Carthaginians, then the second was in confusion, finally the whole line was forced back" (Moore, 1940). (*Ea demum vox ita animos accendit ut renovato clamore, velut alii repente facti, tanta vi se in hostem intulerint ut sustineri ultra non possent. Primo antesignani Poenorum, dein signa perturbata, postremo tota inpulsa acies*). | Infantry attack |
| 212 | 25.34.9 | | | | | The Numidian cavalry, by outflanking them, inspired great alarm. (*Ceterum et equites Numidae repente, quos fefellisse se dux ratus erat, ab lateribus circumfusi magnum terrorem intulere*). | Inspire fear. |
| 212 | 25.37.19 | Romans | Carthaginians | | | Marcius plans to attack the camp of Hasdrubal. (*Tamen ultro inferendo arma contemptum sui dempturum*). | Attack on a camp |
| 212 | 25.39.18 | Romans | Carthaginians | | | Both sides after receiving and inflicting such losses upon each other, hesitated to risk a decisive engagement (*Utrisque post tantas in vicem acceptas inlatasque clades cunctantibus periculum summae rerum facere*) | Inflict casualties |
| 212 | 24.38.8 | | | | | Practising treachery (*inferendae fraudis*). | Treachery |
| 212 | 24.42.5 | | | | | Scipio carried into the battle line in a litter. (*Lecticula in aciem inlatus*). | Carry forward |
| 212 | 25.9.14 | | | | | Two men carrying in (*inferentes*) a boar. | Carry forward |
| 212 | 25.9.9 | | | | | Philemenus brought in (*inferens*) his game. | Carry forward |
| 211 | 26.5.15 | Romans | Celtiberians | Infantry | Infantry | Navius inspired by his commander, "snatched a standard of the second maniple of the *hastati* from the standard-bearer and carried it towards the enemy, threatening that he would throw it into their midst if the soldiers did not quickly follow him and take a hand in the battle" (Moore, 1943). (*Secundi hastati signum ademptum signifero in hostes infert, iacturum in medios eos minitans ni se propere sequantur milites et partem capessant pugnae*). | Advancing standards |
| 211 | 26.6.1 | Romans | Celtiberians | Infantry | Infantry | Quintus Navius attacks the enemy with an *impetus*, then "Marcus Atilius, the lieutenant, started to carry the standard of the first maniple of the *principes* of | Advancing standards |

| | | | | | | | |
|---|---|---|---|---|---|---|---|
| | | | | | | the same legion towards the cohort of Spaniards" (Moore, 1943). (*M. Atilius legatus primi principis ex eadem legione signum inferre in cohortem Hispanorum coepit*). | |
| 211 | 26.20.5 | | | | | Inspiring fear (*maiorem inferens metum*). | Inspire fear. |
| 211 | 26.21.6 | | | | | M. Marcellus during his ovation carried a great amount of booty before him into the city. (*Inde ovans multam prae se praedam in urbem intulit*). | Carry forward |
| 211 | 26.24.13 | | | | | Philip should have no right to invade the land of the Aetolians. (*Ne ius ei belli inferendi Aetolis*). | Wage war |
| 211 | 26.25.9 | Aetolians | Acarnania | | | Aetolians prepare to invade Acarnania. (*Bellum inferre Acarnaniae parat*). | Wage war |
| 210 | 26.28.2 | | | | | Philip on the point of invading Aetolia. (*Philippum inferentem bellum Aetolis*). | Wage war |
| 209 | 27.14.11 | Romans | Carthaginians | Infantry | Infantry | After a period of fighting the Carthaginian elephants attack in order to disrupt the Roman line. C. Decimius Flavus commands the Legionaries to hurl their pila at the elephants, which then in terror turned on the Carthaginian line. "Into the line thrown into confusion by the brutes dashing through it the Roman infantry carried their standards and with no great struggle they made the scattered and wavering line enemy retreat" (Moore, 1943). (*In perturbatam transcursu beluarum aciem signa inferunt Romani pedites et haud magno certamine dissipatos trepidantesque auertunt*). | Advancing standards |
| 209 | 27.15.16 | Romans | Tarentum | | | Dimocrates feared that the Roman consul might attack the city and bring in his troops. (*Vim faceret ac signa inferret*) | Attack on a city |
| 209 | 27.15.19 | Romans | Tarentum | | | "Then also the nearest gate was broken open, so that a dense column might march in" (Moore, 1943). (*Inde et proxuma refracta porta, ut frequenti agmine signa inferrentur*). | Attack on a city |
| 209 | 27.18.3 | Romans | Carthaginians | Light infantry and some heavy | Cavalry | At Baecula, the Roman light infantry and those heavy infantry at the head of the marching column made an attack on Hasdrubal's cavalry outposts stationed in front of the camp. "The horsemen were forced into the camp in alarm and flight, and the Roman standards were all but carried inside the very gates" (Moore, 1943). (*In castra trepida fuga conpulsi equites sunt, signaque Romana portis prope ipsis inlata*). | Advancing standards |
| 208 | 27.28.3 | | | | | Employ a ruse (*inferendam…fraudem*) | Treachery |
| 208 | 27.33.2 | | | | | Philip was dashed against a tree by his charging horse. (*In arborem inlatus impetu equi*). | Dash against. |
| 207 | 27.37.15 | | | | | A sacrifice to Juno Reginae: on the *clivus Publicius* two victims were sacrificed and the Cypress statues borne into the temple. (*Simulacra cupressea in aedem inlata*). | Carry forward |
| 207 | 27.38.8 | | | | | Livius had also brought forward a proposal to recall the slave volunteers to their standards. (*Intuleratque mentionem de volonibus revocandis ad signa*). | Offer a suggestion |
| 207 | 27.40.1 | | | | | The first coming of Hannibal had brought disasters into Italy. (*Quas primus adventus Hanniblis intulisset Italiae clades*). | Inflict casualties |
| 207 | 27.40.11 | Romans | Carthaginians | | | C. Hostilius Tubulus attacked Hannibal's army in marching order and inflicted terrible confusion in the column. (*Agmini terribilem tumultum intulit*). | Inflict confusion |
| 207 | 27.42.10 | Romans | Carthaginians | | | Romans came up so close to the Carthaginian gates that they almost seemed to advance into the camp. (*Ut prope inferre signa videretur*). | Advancing standards |
| 207 | 27.42.13 | Romans | Numidians | | | The consul ordered an advance into the empty Numidian camp. ([In castra] inferri signa iussit). | Enter a camp |
| 207 | 28.8.14 | | | | | Attalus withdrew into his own kingdom in order to make war on the Dardanians. (*Retro in regnum concessit, ut Dardanis bellum inferret*). | Wage war |
| 206 | 28.15.5 | | | | | The elephants, frightened by the skirmishing, had shifted from the wings into the centre. (*E cornibus in mediam aciem sese intulerant*). | Carry forward |
| 206 | 28.15.10 | Romans | Carthaginians | Infantry | Infantry | Scipio dragged out the day to tire the Carthaginians. "Weakened therefore in body and spirit the men [Carthaginians] retreated, keeping their ranks nevertheless, just as if by order of the general the line was giving way intact" (*fessi igitur corporibus animisque rettulere pedem, ordines tamen servantes, haud secus quam si imperio ducis cederet integra acies*). The Romans seeing the tide of the battle changing had more spirit, 'so that it was not easy to withstand their attack (*nec facile impetus sustineri posset*). Hasdrubal tried to hold his army back. Nevertheless fear overtook them and they turned about and took to flight. "And at first the standard-bearers began to halt at the foot of the hills and to call the soldiers back into ranks, while the Romans hesitated to advance their line up the hill. Then when the enemy saw the standards coming bravely on, they | Advancing standards |

| | | | | | | | |
|---|---|---|---|---|---|---|---|
| | | | | | | resumed their flight and were driven panic-stricken into camp" (Moore, 1949). (*Ac primo consistere signa in radicibus collium ac reuocare in ordines militem coeperant cunctantibus in aduersum collem erigere aciem Romanis; deinde ut inferri impigre signa uiderunt, integrata fuga in castra pauidi compelluntur*). | |
| 206 | 28.17.15 | | | | | Sails, catching wind from the open sea, brought (*intulerunt*) *quinqueremes* in to harbour. | Carry forward |
| 206 | 28.22.13 | Celtiberian | Romans | | | "The horsemen who had been first to confront the enemy were beaten back and brought panic to the light armed" (Moore, 1949). (*Itaque pulsus eques qui primus se hosti obtulerat terrorem intulit levi armaturae*). | Inspire fear. |
| 206 | 28.22.15 | Romans | Townsfolk of Astapa | Infantry | Infantry | After the *triarii* checked the enemy *impetus*, the Romans, "venturing to take the offensive, when they saw no one giving way and every man resolutely dying in his tracks, they extended their line, as superior numbers of armed men made it possible for them to do, outflanked the enemy, and as they fought in circular formation slew them to the last" (Moore, 1949). (*Conatus paulo post ultro inferre pedem, ut neminem cedere atque obstinatos mori in vestigio quemque suo vidit, patefacta acie, quod ut facere posset multitudo armatorum facile suppeditabat, cornua hostium amplexus, in orbem pugnantes ad unum omnes occidit*). | Advancing standards |
| 206 | 28.30.9 | | | | | Naval battle - the tide of the strait decided the battle: "one might have seen a fleeing ship swung about by a swirl and borne against the victors" (Moore, 1949). (*Fugientem navem videre vertice retro intortam victoribus inlatam*). | Carry forward |
| 206 | 28.33.6 | Romans | Celtiberians | Cavalry | Infantry | "Not only did they trample down those they met by a frontal attack…" (Moore, 1949). (*Neque ex adverso tantum inlati obvios obtrivere…*). | Cavalry attack |
| 205 | 28.41.9 | | | | | "Let our fear abate before we use fear as an offensive weapon against others" (Moore, 1949). (*Et nobis prius decedat timor quam ultro aliis inferatur*). | Generic attack word. |
| 205 | 28.44.1 | | | | | Scipio advised using fear against the enemy ("as a weapon" (Moore, 1949)). (*Ultro metum inferre hosti*). | Generic attack word. |
| 205 | 28.44.3 | | | | | "More spirit has an agressor than a defender" (Moore, 1949). (*Plus animi est inferenti periculum quam propulsanti*). | Offensive move. |
| 205 | 28.44.12 | | | | | Romans were not only to defend Italy but invade Africa (*inferenda*). | Generic invasion. |
| 205 | 29.3.8 | | | | | Laelius lays waste to the African countryside. "Since everybody was free from concern, as if in peace-time, great losses were inflicted" (Moore, 1949). (*Omnibus pacis modo incriose agentibus magna clades inlata*). | Inflict casualties |
| 205 | 29.10.5 | | | | | "If ever a foreign enemy should invade the land of Italy…" (Moore, 1949). (*Quandoque hostis alienigena terrae Italiae bellum intulisset*). | Wage war |
| 204 | 29.27.11 | | | | | On the way to Africa night and fog make it difficult for the Roman fleet and so "they cast anchor, that the ships might not collide or drift onto the shore" (Moore, 1949). (*Nox deinde incertiora omnia fecit; itaque ancoras, ne aut inter se concurrerent naves aut terrae inferrentur*). | Carry forward |
| 204 | 29.28.4 | | | | | The Romans inspire terror in the Carthaginian cities. (*Terrorem inferebant*). | Inspire fear. |
| 204 | 29.31.7 | | | | | Syphax made war upon Massinissa. (*Syphax Masinissae bellum infert*). | Wage war |
| 203 | 30.13.9 | | | | | Syphax had made war on Rome (*bellum intulisset*). | Wage war |
| 203 | 30.18.2 | Romans | Carthaginians | Infantry | Infantry | "And from in front of the two wings praetor and proconsul kept urging the soldiers to advance their ranks against the enemy with all their strength" (Moore, 1949). (*Proque duobus cornibus praetor ac proconsul milites ad inferenda in hostes signa summa vi hortabantur*). | Advancing standards |
| 203 | 30.22.3 | Carthaginians | Romans | | | Hannibal made war on Romans and Saguntines on his own responsibility. (*Privato consilio bellum intulisse*). | Wage war |
| 202 | 30.30.3 | Carthaginians | Romans | | | Hannibal was the first to make war on the Roman people. (*Qui primus bellum intuli populo Romano*). | Wage war |
| 202 | 30.30.17 | | | | | Hannibal said that not long ago "[I] was advancing my standards and now almost scaling the walls of Rome" (Moore, 1949). (*Signa inferentum ac iam prope scandentum moenia Romana*). | Advancing standards |
| 202 | 30.34.3 | Romans | Carthaginians | Infantry | Infantry | "Consequently by the first attack the Romans at once dislodged the enemy's line. Then beating them back with their shoulders and the bosses of their shields, being now in close combat with men forced from their position, they made considerable progress, as no one offered any resistance" (Moore, 1949). (*Igitur primo impetu extemplo mouere loco hostium aciem Romani. ala deinde et umbonibus pulsantes in summotos gradu inlato aliquantum spatii uelut nullo* | Infantry attack |

| | | | | | | | |
|---|---|---|---|---|---|---|---|
| | | | | | | *resistente incessere*). | |
| 201 | 31.1.4 | | | | | Appius Claudius, who began the first war with the Carthaginians. (*Qui primum bellum Carthaginiensibus intulit*). | Wage war |
| 200 | 31.6.1 | | | | | Philip had inflicted injuries on Roman allies. (*Armaque illata sociis*). | Wage war |
| 200 | 31.7.4 | | | | | Laevinus and the fleet had been sent to begin an offensive campaign against Philip. (*Misso cum classe Laevino qui ultro ei bellum inferret*). | Wage war |
| 200 | 31.11.9 | | | | | Philip had attacked the allies of the Roman people. (*Inferendo sociis populi Romani*). | Wage war |
| 200 | 31.14.9 | Acarnanians | Athenians | | | Acarnanians asked Philip if they could attack Athens. (*Bellum se inferre Atheniensibus*). | Wage war |
| 200 | 31.15.6 | | | | | First mention of the tribe called 'Attalis'. (*Tum primum mentio inlata tribu quam Attalida*). | Offer a suggestion |
| 200 | 31.18.1 | | | | | Philip attacked Attalus and the Rhodians (*Attalo Rhodiisque arma inlata*). | Wage war |
| 200 | 31.18.3 | | | | | Paulus ask Philip "did the people of Abydus also take up arms against you, unprovoked?" (*"num Abydeni quoque" inquit "ultro tibi intulerunt arma?"*). | Wage war |
| 200 | 31.22.2 | Gauls | Romans | Infantry | Infantry | Two thousand Romans and allies were killed, mostly from the right squadron, who were in the van, against whom at the first attack the enemy's main effort had been directed. (*In quam primo impetu vis hostium ingens inlata est*). | Non-Roman infantry attack |
| 200 | 31.25.7 | Macedonians | Spartans | | | Philip would make war on Nabis and the Spartans. (*Bellum Nabidi inferam et Lacedaemoniis*) | Wage war |
| 200 | 31.36.11 | | | | | Roman fugitives slipped back to camp carrying (*intuerunt*) in their fear confused rumours. | Carry forward |
| 200 | 31.37.3 | Romans | Macedonians | Infantry | Infantry | "Most of the Romans encountered them [Macedonian royal guard]" (Sage, 1935). (*Plurimi in eam inferebantur*). | Generic attack word |
| 200 | 31.42.9 | | | | | "Aimless wandering in the disorderly flight threw no large number into the hands of the Macedonian cavalry" (Sage, 1935). (*Non ita multos in dispersa fuga error intulit in Macedonum equites*) | Carry forward |
| 198 | 32.10.6 | | | | | He who had been the aggressor in war. (*Qui prior arma intulisset*). | Wage war |
| 198 | 32.14.3 | | | | | The surrender of the Gomphi caused great terror to the Thessalians. (*Haec traditio Gomphorum ingentum terrorem Thessalis intulit*). | Inspire fear |
| 198 | 32.21.18 | Aetolians | Macedonians | | | Aetolians made war on Macedonia. (*Macedoniae intulerunt*). | Wage war |
| 198 | 32.24.5 | | | | | Romans carry scaling ladders to the walls of Elatia. (*Scalas ad stantia moenia inferebant*). | Carry forward |
| 197 | 33.15.14 | | | | | Drifting of disordered soldiers (*illati sunt*). | Carry forward |
| 197 | 33.15.6 | | | | | Sudden panic gripped the camp of Androsthenes. (*Repens terror castris infertur*). | Inspire fear. |
| 197 | 33.16.8 | | | | | Enter the assembly (*concilio intulissent*). | Carry forward |
| 196 | 33.27.4 | | | | | Stertinius deposited (*intulit*) in the treasury fifty thousand pounds of silver. | Carry forward |
| 196 | 33.36.11 | Gauls | Romans | Infantry | Infantry | The Gauls attacked the Roman infantry. Marcellus sent all the squadrons of the latin cavalry against the Gauls. Their first and second attacks dulled the enemy's ferocious attack. (*Equitum latinorum omnes turmas in hostem emisit. Quorum cum primus secundusque impetus reftudisset inferentum se ferociter hostem*). | Non-Roman infantry attack |
| 196 | 33.36.12 | Romans | Gauls | Infantry | Infantry | Marcellus saw the Roman line wavering, "and fearing that once broken they would be routed, he threw in a cohort of the Marsi and sent all the Latin cavalry against the enemy. Their first and second attacks dulled the edge of the enemy's spirited attack, and the rest of the Roman line, with renewed courage, first resisted and then attacked fiercely" (Sage, 1935, slightly adapted). (*Quod ubi Marcellus animaduertit, ueritus ne moti semel pellerentur, cohortem Marsorum cum opposuisset, equitum Latinorum omnes turmas in hostem emisit. quorum cum primus secundusque impetus rettudisset inferentem se ferociter hostem, confirmata et reliqua acies Romana restitit primo, deinde signa acriter intulit*). | Roman infantry attack |
| 195 | 34.4.4 | | | | | Statues brought from Syracuse to Rome. (*Signa ab Syracusis illata sunt huic urbi*). | Carry forward |
| 195 | 34.12.3 | Celtiberians | Romans | | | Roman consul decided not to weaken his forces, in case he should suffer the disgrace of a defeat by the enemy. (*Ne quid interim hostes inferant ignominiae*). | Suffer defeat. |
| 195 | 34.14.6 | | | | | Roman cavalry retreating caused panic among the infantry. (*Cedentesque trepidi etiam pediti terrorem intulere*). | Inspire fear |
| 195 | 34.31.1 | Romans | Spartans | | | Rome had made war on Nabis (*bellum... inferretis*) | Wage war |
| 195 | 34.33.11 | Romans | Spartans | | | Roman standards almost carried into the gates. (*Signa portis prope inferri cernerent*). | Carry forward |
| 193 | 35.1.9 | Romans | Lusitani | Infantry | Infantry | "At first they had thrown the Romans into confusion, later the battle became gradually more even. At this crisis the *propraetor* vowed games to Jupiter if he | Roman Infantry attack |

| | | | | | | | |
|---|---|---|---|---|---|---|---|
| | | | | | | should rout and slaughter the enemy. At length the Romans pressed on with greater vigour and the Lusitani gave way and finally fled" (Sage, 1935). (*Turbaverant primo Romanos; deinde aequata paulisper pugna est. In hoc discrimine ludos Iovi, si fudisset cecidissetque hostes, propraetor vovit. Tandem gradum acrius intulere Romani, cessitque Lusitanus, deinde prorsus terga dedit*). | |
| 193 | 35.5.12 | Romans | Gauls | Infantry | Infantry | The Gauls, after the Romans had attacked them with infantry *impetus* and cavalry attacks, grew tired, disordered and afraid (*turbatos et trepidantes*). "The consul ordered the standard bearers to advance. All joined in the effort and at last turned the enemy to flight" (Sage, 1935). (*Inferre vexillarios iussit signa. Omnes conisi tandem averterunt hostem*). | Advancing standards |
| 193 | 35.11.11 | Numidians | Spanish | | | Numidians, fighting for Rome, "hurled their torches upon the nearest village" (Sage, 1935). (*Proximo deinde vico inferunt ignem*). | Carry forward |
| 192 | 35.21.5 | | | | | "The Tiber, attacking the city with a more violet rush than the year before, swept away two bridges" (Sage, 1935). (*Tiberis infestiore quam priore anno impetu illatus urbi duos pontes... evertit*) | Generic attack word |
| 192 | 35.46.6 | | | | | Aetolians claimed that Antiochus had come not to make war (*inferendi belli*), but to liberate Greece. | Wage war |
| 192 | 35.51.5 | | | | | Justification for Romans declaring war on Antiochus. (*Ad ius inferendi Antiocho belli*). | Wage war |
| 191 | 36.5.3 | | | | | The Elei thought the Achaeans would attack their city after they had declared war on Antiochus (*arma illaturos*). | Wage war |
| 191 | 36.6.1 | | | | | Quinctius carrys on a campaign at Coronea by reason of the slaughtering of Roman soldiers. (*Bellum a Quinctio Coroneae propter Romanorum militum caedes illatum*). | Wage war |
| 191 | 36.17.7 | | | | | Antiochus planned to make war on the Roman people. (*Ad inferendum populo Romano bellum*). | Wage war |
| 191 | 36.18.6 | Romans | Macedonians | Infantry | Infantry | The Macedonians, standing outside their rampart, were driven back inside their fortifications when "a greater and more irresistible pressure was placed upon them by the enemy" (Sage, 1935). (*Ut maior nec iam toleranda vis hostium inferebant*). | Infantry attack |
| 191 | 36.44.8 | Romans | Antiochus | | | "the two [ships] which had just surrounded the Carthaginian ship came up, hoping to repeat their tactics..." (Sage, 1935). (*Adversus quam eadem spe duae quae Punicam unam navem circumvenerant cum inferrentur*) | Carry forward |
| 190 | 37.15.9 | | | | | Regillus ordered to move the fleet into the harbour of Ephesus "in order to strike terror into the enemy" (Sage, 1935). (*Ad inferendum hostibus terrorem*). | Inspire fear. |
| 190 | 37.20.12 | | | | | "Achaeans causing far more terror than was warrented by the number of troopers" (Sage, 1935). (*Maiorem quam pro numero equitum terrorem Achaeis inferentibus*). | Inspire fear. |
| 190 | 37.32.11 | Romans | Phocaea | | | After the Phocaeans had surrendered the standards were carried in to the city. (*Cum signa in urbem inferrentur*). | Advancing standards |
| 190 | 37.42.4 | Romans | Antiochus | Infantry | Infantry | "The whole left flank then wavered, and when the auxiliaries were broken, who were between the cavalry and those who were called the *phalangitae*, the panic spread as far as the centre. There, as soon as the ranks were thrown into disorder and the use of the very long spears - the Macedonians call them *sarisae*- was prevented by their own friends rushing among them, the Roman legions advanced and hurled their javelins into the disordered mass" (Sage, 1935). (*Totum deinde laeuum cornu inclinauit, et turbatis auxiliaribus, qui inter equitem et quos appellant phalangitas erant, usque ad mediam aciem terror peruenit. ibi simul perturbati ordines et impeditus intercursu suorum usus praelongarum hastarum—sarisas Macedones uocant—, intulere signa Romanae legiones et pila in perturbatos coniecere*). | Advancing standards |
| 189 | 37.49.7 | Aetolians | Dolopia | | | The Aetolians were invading Dolopia and Athamania (*Dolopiae atque Athamaniae bellum inferebant*). | Wage war |
| 189 | 38.5.5 | | | | | The people of Acarnania "by sallies conducted both by night against the guards of the engines and by day against the outposts they did their part in spreading terror" (Sage, 1936). (*Ad hoc eruptionibus et nocturnis in custodias operum et diurnis in stationes ultro terrorem inferebant*). | Inspire fear. |
| 189 | 38.10.6 | | | | | The Aetolians were dashed upon Antiochus as upon a rock. (*Quae ad Antiochum eas sicuti in scopulum intulisset*). | Dash against. |
| 189 | 38.18.3 | | | | | Romans asked not to make war on the Tectosagi. (*Ne Tectosagis bellum inferret*). | Wage war |
| 189 | 38.21.8 | Gauls | Romans | | | In hand-to-hand fighting the Gauls could receive and inflict wounds in turn. (*Nam quemadmodum comminus, ubi in vicem pati et inferre vulnera licet*) | Inflict wounds |

| | | | | | | | |
|---|---|---|---|---|---|---|---|
| 189 | 38.34.6 | | | | | Submission (*illata*) of a report. | Offer a suggestion |
| 188 | 38.37.3 | | | | | The servitude imposed on the people of Asia by Antiochus was more endurable than the ferocity of the savage barbarians and the constant and uncertain fear that the Gauls might attack them like a storm. (*Tolerabilior regia servitus fuerat quam feritas immanium barbarorum incertusque in dies terror, quo velut tempestas eos populantes inferret*). | Wage war |
| 188 | 38.38.9 | | | | | Antiochus should only have a ship of one bank for a war in which he himself was the agressor (*belli causa quod ipse illaturus erit*). | Wage war |
| 188 | 38.38.16 | | | | | "If any of the allies of the Roman people shall without provocation make war upon Antiochus, he shall have the right to oppose force with force" (Sage, 1936). (*Si qui sociorum populi Romani ultro bellum inferent Antiocho, vim vi arcendi ius esto*). | Wage war |
| 187 | 38.45.11 | | | | | Manlius "was waging war under no law of nations" (Sage, 1936). (*Nullo gentium iure bellum inferentis*). | Wage war |
| 187 | 38.45.5 | | | | | Galatians, "a people against whom war had not been declared by the authority of the senate or the vote of the assembly" (Sage, 1936) (*Cui nationi non ex senatus auctoritate, non populi iussu bellum illatum*). | Wage war |
| 187 | 38.48.3 | | | | | The Gauls despoiled Delphi, and the Romans did not on that account declare or wage a war upon them (*nec ideo populus Romanus his bellum indixit aut intulit*). | Wage war |
| 187 | 38.55.12 | | | | | Publius Scipio had brought two million into the treasury. (*Bis milliens in aerarium intulisset*). | Carry forward |
| 187 | 38.59.8 | | | | | Much wealth had been brought in (*illatum*) to the house of Lucius Scipio. | Carry forward |
| 186 | 39.10.7 | | | | | A violent attack on a Bacchic initiate's virtue. (*Cum per vim stuprum inferatur*). | Generic attack word. |
| 186 | 39.11.1 | | | | | A mother mentions. (*Mater mentionem intulit*). | Offer a suggestion |
| 186 | 39.11.6 | | | | | The consul brought forward an allusion to Aebutius. (*Sermonem de Aebutio… infert*). | Offer a suggestion. |
| 186 | 39.14.8 | | | | | "Before all it was decreed that an inquiry should be conducted regarding those persons who had come together or conspired for the commission of any immorality or crime" (Sage, 1936). (*Ante omnia ut questio de iis habeatur, qui coierint coniuraverintve, quo stuprum flagitiumve inferretur*). | Carry forward |
| 185 | 39.23.10 | | | | | The Roman consul had permitted Philip to make war on Athamania and Amynander. (*Philippo permisit Athamaniae et Amynandro bellum inferret*). | Wage war |
| 185 | 39.26.14 | | | | | Injuries inflicted (*illatas*). | Inflict wounds |
| 185 | 39.31.9 | Romans | Spanish | Infantry | Infantry | The Romans were in distress, Calpurius, the praetor, inspired the infantry by his and the cavalry's bravery. "Shame moved the senior centurions when they saw the praetor amid the weapons of the enemy. And so each for himself urged on the standard-bearers, ordered them to advance and the soldiers to follow at once" (Sage, 1936). (*Pudor mouit primos centuriones, qui inter tela hostium praetorem conspexerunt. itaque urgere signiferos pro se quisque, iubere inferre signa et confestim militem sequi*). | Advancing standards |
| 185 | 39.31.10 | Romans | Spanish | Infantry | Infantry | The Romans were being beaten back by the enemy in wedge formation. Calpurnius, the praetor, inspired the infantry by his and the cavalry's bravery. "The shouting was renewed by all: an attack was launched as if from higher ground. And so they swept forward like a torrent and overwhelmed the panic-stricken enemy, nor as they attacked wave after wave could they be resisted" (Sage, 1936, slightly adapted). (*Renouatur ab omnibus clamor: impetus fit uelut ex superiore loco. haud secus ergo quam torrentis modo fundunt sternuntque perculsos, nec sustineri alii super alios inferentes sese possunt*). | Roman infantry attack |
| 181 | 40.32.4 | Spanish | Spanish (Roman auxiliaries) | Infantry | Infantry | The Spanish, failing to make any headway against the legion were able to advance with greater confidence against the Roman auxiliaries of their own race. (*Adversus laevem cornu, in quo sui generis provincialia auxilia instruxisse Romanos cernebant, cum maiore fiducia intulerunt signa*) | Non-Roman infantry attack |
| 180 | 40.36.7 | | | | | Roman army ordered to make war upon the Ligurian Apauni. (*Cum hoc exercitu Apaunis Liguribus ut bellum inferrent*). | Wage war |
| 179 | 40.47.6 | Romans | Spanish | | | A Spanish ambassador was sent by his people to find out why the Romans were attacking them. (*"Missi sumus" inquit "a gente nostra qui sciscitaremur qua tandem re fretus arma nobis inferres"*). | Wage war |
| 178 | 41.4.1 | Romans | Histrians | | | Aulus Baeculonius, a notably brave man, is ordered to carry forward the standard (*sub haec A. Baecolonium, signiferum suum, notae fortitudinis virum, inferre signum iussit*). He threw it over the | Advancing standards |

| | | | | | | | |
|---|---|---|---|---|---|---|---|
| | | | | | | Histrian's rampart and led the men through the gates. | |
| 173 | 42.8.5 | Romans | Ligurians | | | The Statellates had been attacked, although they had not begun a war. (*Tum quoque oppugnatos, non ultro inferentes bellum*). | Wage war |
| 173 | 42.10.7 | | | | | Such great clouds of locusts from the sea suddenly appeared (*illatae sunt*) over Apulia that they covered the fields. | Carry forward |
| 172 | 42.13.11 | | | | | Perseus brought war to Italy. ( *ad bellum inferendum*). | Wage war |
| 172 | 42.13.8 | | | | | Perseus made war on Dolopia. (*Dolopiae bellum intulit*). | Wage war |
| 172 | 42.21.3 | | | | | Popilius had made war (*bellum intulisset*) on surrendered tribe. | Wage war |
| 171 | 42.30.10 | | | | | Philip made war on allies of the Roman people. (*Sociis populi Romani arma intulisset*). | Wage war |
| 172 | 42.41.10 | | | | | In a treaty with Rome, the King was not allowed to protect himself or his kingdom, even if someone attacked him. (*Nam si est in foedere ita scriptum, ut ne si bellum quidem quis inferat, tueri me regnumque meum liceat*). | Wage war |
| 172 | 42.42.9 | | | | | 'You rush to arms and declare war on your royal allies'. (*Arma capitis et regibus sociis bella infertis*). | Wage war |
| 171 | 43.1.8 | | | | | War against the Carnians or Histrians. (*Carnis forsitan aut Histris bellum illatum*). | Wage war |
| 170 | 43.4.13 | | | | | An unjust war had been undertaken against the people of Abdera. (*Abderitis iniustum bellum illatum*). | Wage war |
| 170 | 43.8.6 | Romans | Macedonians | | | Roman people declared war on Perseus and Philip to liberate Greece. (*Bellum Persei et ante Philippo, patri eius, intulisse populum Romanum pro libertate Graeciae*). | Wage war |
| 169 | 43.18.7 | Perseus | City of Uscana | | | Perseus' men brought fire agains the city gates. (*Pars ignem portis inferrent*). | Carry forward. |
| 169 | 43.23.5 | Romans | Macedonians | | | The Macedonians moved their camp closer to that of the Romans so that "no more violence might be inflicted by the Roman army on their allies" (Schlesinger, 1951). (*Ne qua vis sociis suis ab Romano exercitu inferri possit*). | Wage war |
| 169 | 44.4.3 | Romans | Macedonians | | | "Many wounds were both received and inflicted by either side in the hasty encounter (Schlesinger, 1951). (*Multa utrimque volnera temerario incursu et accepta et inlata*). | Inflict wounds |
| 169 | 44.12.3 | Romans | City of Cassandrea | | | Romans were summoned from variuos points to advance into the city. (*Qui alii aliunde coibant convocabanturque, ut signa in urbem inferrent*). | Attack on a city |
| 169 | 44.14.3 | | | | | Pamphylians brought a golden crown into the Senate. (*In curiam intulerunt*). | Carry forward |
| 168 | 44.31.5 | | | | | River Oriundes "falls into the Adriatic sea" (Schlesinger, 1951). (*Mari Hadriatico infertur*). | Flow of river. |
| 168 | 44.31.9 | | | | | Defeated Macedonians bring fear in (*intulerunt terrorem*) to the camp | Inspire fear |
| 168 | 45.5.7 | | | | | Court to try those who are judge to bring unclean hands into the sacred precincts of the temple. (*Qui incests manus intulisse intra terminos sacratos templi*). | Carry forward |
| 167 | 45.24.10 | | | | | The senate were able to declare war. (*Quod inferre potestis*). | Wage war |

## Appendix 2.1: the occurrences of *concurrere* in Caesar

| *Reference* | *Offensive Army* | *Defensive Army* | *Attacking Arm* | *Defending Arm* | *Notes* | *Comments* |
|---|---|---|---|---|---|---|
| *B Gall.* I, 8 | Romans | Helvetii | Infantry | Infantry | The Helvetii were repulsed by the crowd of Roman soldiers and by missiles. (*Militum concursu et telis repulsi*). | Gathering crowd. |
| I, 48 | | | | | The German fighting involved mixed cavalry and infantry. The horse would retire on the infantry, and gather quickly if more serious difficulty arose. (*Hi, si quid erat durius, concurrebant*). | Gathering crowd. |
| II, 20 | | | | | Caesar had everthing to do at one time: the flag to raise, which was a signal of a general call to arms… (*Caesari omnia uno tempore erant agenda: vexillum proponendum, quod erat insigne, cum ad arma concurri oporteret*… ) | Rush to arms |
| II, 33 | | | | | As Caesar had ordered, "the detachments from the nearest forts doubled in to the point" (Edwards, 1917). (*Ex proximis castellis eo concursum est*). | Gathering crowd. |
| III, 22 | Men of Sotiates | Romans | | | Men, led by Adiatunnus, attempted a sortie but the Roman soldiers rushed to arms. (*Cum ad arma milites concurrissent* ). | Rush to arms |
| IV, 14 | | | | | The German alarm was notified by the uproar and crowd. (*Quorum timor cum fremitu et concursu significaretur*). | Gathering crowd. |
| V, 10 | | | | | The collision of ships caused damage. (*Itaque ex eo concursu navium magnum esse incommodum acceptum*). | Collision of ships |
| V, 39 | Romans | Eburones, Nervii and Aduatuci | | | The enemy attacked and the Roman troops quickly ran to arms and mounted the rampart. (*Nostri celeriter ad arma concurrunt, vallum conscendunt*). | Rush to arms |
| V, 40 | | | | | Cicero is persuaded to spare himself by the protests of his soldiers who crowd round him. (*Ut ultro militum concursu ac vocibus sibi parcere cogeretur*). | Gathering crowd. |
| V, 55 | | | | | Deputations rushed to Indutiomarus from all directions. (*Ut undique ad eum legationes concurrerent*). | Rush together to a point |
| VI, 8 | Romans | Gauls | Infantry | Infantry | When the enemy saw the Romans advancing in formation, they could not sustain the attack and on the first collision they were routed. (*Illi*… *impetum modo ferre non potuerunt ac primo concursu in fugam coniecti*). | Infantry attack. |
| VI, 13 | | | | | A great number of young men gather about the Druids to be taught. (*Ad hos magnus adulescentium numerus disciplinae causa concurrit*). | Gathering crowd. |
| VII, 3 | | | | | The Carnutes rushed on Cenabum on a given signal and killed Roman citizens settled there. (*Carnutes*… *Cenabum signo dato concurrunt civesque Romanos*… *interficiunt*). | Rush together to a point |
| VII, 4 | | | | | Vercingetorix inspires a general rush to arms among his dependants. (*Ad arma concurritur*). | Rush to arms |
| VII, 24 | | | | | The whole crowd from the camp rush to put out a fire. (*Ut*… *ex castris multitudo ad restinguendum concurreret*). | Rush together to a point |
| VII, 28 | | | | | A crowd (*concursu*). | Gathering crowd |
| VII, 38 | | | | | Litaviccus of the Aedui asks whether they can doubt that the Romans were already hurrying here to kill them. (*An dubitamus quin nefario facinore admisso Romani iam ad nos interficiendos concurrant*). | Rush together to a point |
| VII, 43 | | | | | The Haedui rush to Aristius. (*Concurrunt ad Aristium*). | Rush together to a point |
| VII, 48 | | | | | The Gauls hurry to a town in a great crowd. (*Magno concursu eo contenderunt*). | Gathering crowd. |
| VII,62 | Romans | Gauls | Infantry | Infantry | "At the first encounter on the right wing, where the seventh legion was posted, the enemy were driven back and put to rout" (Edwards, 1917). (*Primo concursu ab dextro cornu, ubi septima legio constiterat, hostes pelluntur atque in fugam coniciuntur*). | General word for infantry engagement |
| VII, 79 | | | | | At the sight of reinforcements the people of Alesia gather together [in congratulation]. (*Concurrunt his auxiliis visis*). | Gathering crowd. |
| VII, 84 | Romans | Gauls | Infantry | Infantry | "The fight went on simultaneously in all places, and all expedients were attempted, with a rapid concentration on that section which was seen to be the least strong" (Edwards, 1917). (*Pugnatur uno tempore omnibus locis, atque omnia temptantur: quae minime visa pars firma est, huc concurritur*). | General word for infantry engagement |
| VIII, 23 | | | | | Deputies meet. (*Concurrunt reliquarum civitatium legati*). | Gathering crowd. |
| VIII, 38 | | | | | Caesar was compelled to execute Gutruatrus by the troops who gathered in a great crowd. (*Cogitur in eius supplicium Caesar contra suam naturam concursu maximo militum*). | Gathering crowd. |
| | | | | | | |
| *B Civ.* I, 3 | | | | | The enemies of Caesar, by their voices and crowd intimidate the senate. (*Quorum vocibus et concursu terrentur infirmiores*). | Gathering crowd |
| I, 53 | | | | | A large crowd gathered at the house of Afranius. (*Magni domum concursus ad Afranium*…*fiebant*). | Gathering crowd |
| I, 71 | | | | | Legates, centurions and military tribunes rushed to Caesar [advising him to join battle]. (*Concurrebant legati, centuriones tribunique militum*). | Rush together to a point |
| I, 76 | | | | | A crowd quickly gathered in the Praetorium. (*Fit celeriter concursus in praetorium*). | Gathering crowd |
| II, 6 | | | | | Two ships were damaged by a collision. (*Ut vehementissime utraque ex concursu laborarent*). | Collision of ships |
| II, 22 | | | | | Two ships, terrified by the gathering of our ships, took shelter in the harbour. (*Duo perterrita concursu nostrarum navium*). | Naval approach |
| II, 25 | Romans | Numidians | Cavalry | Cavalry | Curio ordered his cavalry to retain property, being transported outside Utica, as booty. Varus sends his Numidian cavalry to protect it and the two squads of cavalry meet in conflict. (*Concurrunt equites inter se*). | General word for cavalry engagement. |
| III, 72 | Romans | Romans | | | The Pompeians failed to consider that they had not fought in a sharp encounter or in a pitched battle. (*Non concursu acri facto, non proelio* | General word for infantry |

| | | | | | *dimicatum*). | engagement |
|---|---|---|---|---|---|---|
| III, 80 | | | | | Caesar advises attacking a town quickly before reinforcements could come together. (*Id fieri celeriter, priusquam auxilia concurrerent*). | Rush to arms |
| III, 86 | Romans | Romans | | | Pompey asserted that Caesar's army would be repulsed before the lines engaged. (*Priusquam concurrerent acies, fore uti exercitus Caesaris pelleretur*). | General word for infantry engagement. |
| III, 89 | Romans | Romans | | | Caesar commanded the third line and the whole army not to join battle without orders from himself. (*Tertiae aciei totique exercitui imperavit, ne iniussu suo concurreret*). | General word for infantry engagement. |
| III, 92 | Romans | Romans | | | At Pharsalus between the two lines there was only enough space necessary for the coming together of each army. (*Inter duas acies tantum erat relictum spatii, ut satis esset ad concursum utriusque exercitus*). | General word for infantry engagement. |
| III, 93 | Romans | Romans | Infantry | Infantry | At Pharsalus, Pompey's men waited for the attack of Caesar's troops, but Caesar's troops observed that the Pompeians were not advancing. (*Animadvertissent non concurri a Pompeianis*). | General word for infantry engagement |
| III, 106 | | | | | At Alexandria Caesar sees a crowd gathering to meet him. (*Concursum ad se fieri videt*). | Gathering crowd |
| III, 106 | | | | | Frequent disturbances occurred from the crowd. (*Ex concursu multitudinis concitationes fiebant*). | Gathering crowd |

## Appendix 2.2: the occurrences of *incurrere* in Caesar

| *Reference* | *Offensive Army* | *Defensive Army* | *Attacking Arm* | *Defending Arm* | *Notes* | *Comments* |
|---|---|---|---|---|---|---|
| *B Gall.* VII, 36 | | | | | Caesar creates a defensive point which allowed soldiers to pass safely from a sudden enemy attack. (*Ut tuto ab repentino hostium incursu etiam singuli commeare possent*). | General word for attack |
| VIII, 18 | Bellovaci | Romans | Cavalry | Cavalry | The Bellovaci attack the Roman cavalry, but the Romans withstood the charge without crowding together. (*Nostri constanter incursum sustinent insidiatorum neque plures in unum locum conveniunt*). | Cavalry attack |
| | | | | | | |
| *B Civ.* I, 25 | | | | | A blockade is made with rafts covered in soil with a raised causeway so that "there might be no obstacle in the way of approach or ingress for the purpose of defence". (Peskett, 1914). (*Ne aditus atque incursus ad defendendum impediretur*). | A defensive sortie. |
| I, 41 | Romans | Afranians | Infantry | Infantry | Caesar pitches camp near the mountains so that his men might not be surprised by a sudden onset of the enemy and stopped in their task. (*Ne in opere faciundo milites repentino hostium incursu exterrerentur atque opere prohiberentur*). | Infantry advance/general word for attack |
| I, 71 | Romans | Afranians | Cavalry | Cavalry | The Afranians were scarcely withstanding the Roman cavalry attacks. (*Quod vix equitum incursus sustinerent* ). | Cavalry attack |
| I, 82 | Romans | Afranians | Infantry | Infantry | The two camps were separated by two thousand paces, the two battle-lines took up two thirds of this space, while the remaining third was left empty for the onset and attack of the troops. (*Tertia vacabat ad incursum atque impetum militum relicta*). | Infantry advance. |
| II, 8 | | | | | The Romans construct a tower, at first of small size to defend against small onsets. (*Quam primo ad repentinos incursus humilem parvamque fecerunt*). | Infantry sallies |
| III.92 | Romans | Romans | Infantry | Infantry | "Pompeius had previously ordered his men to await Caesar's attack without moving from their position, and to allow his line to fall into disorder. He is said to have done this on the advice of Gaius Triarius, in order that the first charge and impetus of the troops might be broken and their line spread out" (Peskett, 1914). (*Sed Pompeius suis praedixerat, ut Caesaris impetum exciperent neve se loco moverent aciemque eius distrahi paterentur; Idque admonitu C. Triarii fecisse dicebatur, ut primus incursus visque militum infringeretur aciesque distenderetur*). | Infantry attack. |

## Appendix 2.3: the occurrences of *procurrere* in Caesar

| *Reference* | *Offensive Army* | *Defensive Army* | *Attacking Arm* | *Defending Arm* | *Notes* | *Comments* |
|---|---|---|---|---|---|---|
| *B Gall.* I, 52 | Germans | Romans | Infantry | Infantry | "Our troops attacked the enemy so fiercely when the signal was given, and the enemy dashed forward so suddenly and swiftly, that there was no time to discharge javelins upon them". (*Ita nostri acriter in hostes signo dato impetum fecerunt itaque hostes repente celeriterque procurrerunt, ut spatium pila in hostes coniciendi non daretur.*). | Infantry attack |
| V, 34 | Romans | Gauls | Infantry | Infantry | As often as each cohort dashed forward a great number of the enemy would fall at that point. (*Quotiens quaeque cohors procurrerat, ab ea parte magnus numerus hostium cadebat*). | Infantry attack |
| V, 44 | Gauls | Titus Pullo | Infantry | Infantry | Pullo attacks the enemy. At short range, Pullo sent his *pilum* at the enemy and hit one man who ran forward from the crowd. (*Mediocri spatio relicto Pullo pilum in hostes immittit atque unum ex multitudine procurrentem traicit*). | Infantry attack |
| VI, 40 | | | | | The camp followers dashed forward to the nearest hill. (*Calones in proximum tumulum procurrunt*). | Rush forward to a point |
| VII, 26 | | | | | Matrons rush outside. (*Cum matresfamiliae repente in publicum procurrerunt*). | Rush forward to a point |
| VIII, 10 | Romans | Gauls | Infantry | Infantry | "There were frequent encounters across the marsh that lay between the two camps, for a few men would dash forward from either side" (Edwards, 1917). (*Interim crebro paucis utrimque procurrentibus inter bina castra palude interiecta contendebatur*). | Infantry attack |
| | | | | | | |
| *B Civ.* I, 43 | Romans | Romans | Infantry | Infantry | Caesar orders a guard to advance and occupy a mound. (*Unius legionis antesignanos procurrere atque eum tumulum occupare iubet*). | Advance of a small group. |
| I, 44 | Romans | Romans | Infantry | Infantry | The method of fighting adopted by the enemy was to at first attack with great vigour, boldly seize a position, take no trouble preserving their ranks, but fight singly and dispersed. (*Genus erat pugnae militum illorum, ut magno impetu primo procurrerent, audacter locum caperent, ordines suos non magnopere servarent, rari dispersique pugnarent*). | Infantry attack |
| I, 44 | Romans | Romans | Infantry | Infantry | Influenced by Lusitanian tactics, the enemy kept charging singly and Caesar's men thought they were being surrounded on their flank. (*Circumiri enim sese ab aperto latere procurrentibus singulis arbitrabantur*). | Infantry attack |
| I, 55 | Romans | Romans | Light infantry | Cavalry | One light armed cohort had rashly advanced out of the battle line before the others. (*Quae temere ante ceteras extra aciem procurrerat*). This was then surrounded by the cavalry. | Advance of a cohort out of a battle-line. |
| I, 69 | | | | | The African troops joyfully run out of their camp to see the spectacle. (*Ac primo Afraniani milites visendi causa laeti ex castris procurrebant*). | Rush forward to a point |
| II, 8 | Romans | Romans | Infantry | Infantry | The Romans built a shelter to defend themselves against assaults. From this they ran out to repel and pursue the enemy. (*Hinc ad repellendum et prosequendum hostem procurrebant*). | Infantry attacks |
| II, 34 | Romans | Romans | Light infantry and Cavalry | Cavalry | Curio sends his cavalry against Attius' cavalry and some light infantry. The cavalry could not withstand the attack and flee. The light infantry, who had advanced with them, were surrounded. (*Relicti ab his, qui una procurrerant levis armaturae, circumveniebantur* ). | Cavalry and light infantry advance |
| II, 41 | Romans | Numidians | Infantry | Cavalry | Whenever cohorts came out of the battle-line and charged, the Numidians by their quickness fled from the Roman attacks, and as the Romans returned again to their own ranks, the Numidians would surround them and cut them off from the battle line… (*Cum cohortes ex acie procucurrissent, Numidae integri celeritate impetum nostrorum effugiebant rursusque ad ordines suos se recipientes circuibant et ab acie excludebant*). | Infantry attack |
| II, 41 | Romans | Numidians | Infantry | Cavalry | …Thus it seemed unsafe to either stay in one place and to preserve their ranks or to make an attack. (*Sic neque in loco manere ordinesque servare neque procurrere et casum subire tutum videbatur*). | Infantry attack |
| III, 91 | Crastinus | Romans | Infantry | Infantry | Crastinus ran forward first from the right wing, and about one hundred and twenty picked soldiers from the same cohort [*MSS. centuriae*] as volunteers followed him. (*Primus ex dextro cornu procucurrit, atque eum electi milites circiter CXX voluntarii eiusdem cohortis sunt prosecuti*). | Infantry attack |
| III, 93 | Romans | Romans | Infantry | Infantry | The Roman soldiers on the given signal rushed forward with their *pila* raised. (*Sed nostri milites dato signo cum infestis pilis procucurrissent*). | Infantry attack |
| III, 93 | Romans | Romans | Cavalry | Cavalry | The cavalry on Pompey's left wing, as ordered, made an attack in a body. (*Equites ab sinistro Pompei cornu, ut erat imperatum, universi procucurrerunt*). | Cavalry attack |
| III, 93 | Romans | Romans | Infantry | Infantry | The advance of Caesar's fourth line. (*Illi celeriter procucurrerunt*). | Advance of a battle-line |
| III, 94 | Romans | Romans | Infantry | Infantry | The advance of Caesar's third line. (*Tertiam aciem Caesar...procurrere iussit*). | Advance of a battle-line |

## Appendix 2.4: the occurrences of *decurrere* in Caesar

| *Reference* | *Offensive Army* | *Defensive Army* | *Attacking Arm* | *Defending Arm* | *Notes* | *Comments* |
|---|---|---|---|---|---|---|
| *B Gall.* II, 19 | Gauls | Romans | | | After repulsing the Roman cavalry the Gauls rushed down to the river with incredible speed. (*Incredibili celeritate ad flumen decucurrerunt*). | Rushing down from high ground |
| II, 21 | | | | | Caesar ran down in a chance direction to harangue the troops. (*Caesar... ad cohortandos milites, quam [in] partem fors obtulit, decucurrit*). | Rushing down from high ground |
| III, 2 | Gauls | Romans | Infantry | Infantry | The Seduni and Veragri held the high ground over Galba's Legion. The Gauls believed they would be successful since they themselves would charge down from the heights into the valley and throw their missiles, so that they thought it would not be possible to withstand their first attack. (*Cum ipsi ex montibus in vallem decurrerent et tela coicerent, ne primum quidem impetum suum posse sustineri existimabant*). | Attack from high ground |
| III, 4 | Gauls | Romans | Infantry | Infantry | The Gallic attack on Galba's camp: the enemy, upon a given signal, charged down from all sides, and hurled stones and missiles against the Roman rampart. (*Hostes ex omnibus partibus signo dato decurrere, lapides gaesaque in vallum coicere*). | Attack from high ground |
| VIII, 41 | Townsfolk of Uxellodunum | Romans | | | The townsfolk ran down from the higher ground and engaged the Romans, wounding many. (*Oppidani enim loco superiore decurrunt et eminus sine periculo proeliantur multosque pertinaciter succedentes vulnerant*). | Rushing down from high ground |
| | | | | | | |
| *B Civ.* I, 5 | | | | | Decision to pass an SCU. (*Decurritur ad illud extremum atque ultimum senatus consultum*). | Metaphorical use meaning 'flowing' of opinion. |
| I, 28 | | | | | Men placed on the wall for garrison duty ran down to the ships by familiar routes. (*Notisque itineribus ad naves decurrunt*). | Rushing down from high ground |

## Appendix 2.5: the occurrences of *impetus* in Caesar

| *Reference* | *Offensive Army* | *Defensive Army* | *Attacking Arm* | *Defending Arm* | *Notes* | *Comments* |
|---|---|---|---|---|---|---|
| *B Gall.* I, 22 | Romans | Helvetii | Infantry | Infantry | Labienus had orders to wait for Caesar's troops so that an assault might be made upon the enemy camp from both sides at once. (*Ut undique uno tempore in hostes impetus fieret*) | Attack on a camp |
| I, 24 | Romans | Helvetii | Cavalry and infantry | Cavalry | Caesar sends his cavalry to check the enemy advance. (*Equitatumque qui sustineret hostium impetum misit*). | General word for attack |
| I, 25 | Romans | Gauls | Infantry | Infantry | The legionaries from higher ground, easily broke the mass-formation of the enemy by a volley of *pila*. When it was scattered, they drew their swords and made an attack. (*Milites loco superiore pilis missis facile hostium phalangem perfregerunt. Ea disiecta gladiis destrictis in eos impetum fecerunt*). | Roman infantry attack |
| I, 26 | Romans | Helvetii | Infantry | Infantry | The enemy could no longer withstand the Roman attacks. (*Diutius cum sustinere nostrorum impetus non possent*). | Roman infantry attack |
| I, 44 | | | | | A hypothetical Gallic attack on Roman territory. (*Ut ipsi concedi non oporteret, si in nostros fines impetum faceret*). | General word for attack |
| I, 46 | Gauls | Romans | Cavalry | Cavalry | The Roman soldiers learned how arrogantly, at a parley, Ariovistus had allowed his cavalry to attack the Roman troops. (*Qua arrogantia... impetumque in nostros eius equites fecissent*). | Non-Roman cavalry attack |
| I, 52 | Germans | Romans | Infantry | Infantry | "Our troops attacked the enemy so fiercely when the signal was given, and the enemy dashed forward so suddenly and swiftly, that there was no time to discharge javelins upon them" (*Ita nostri acriter in hostes signo dato impetum fecerunt itaque hostes repente celeriterque procurrerunt, ut spatium pila in hostes coniciendi non daretur.*). | Non-Roman infantry attack |
| I, 52 | Romans | Germans | Infantry | Infantry | The javelins were thrown aside, and it was a fight with swords. But the Germans, according to their custom, quickly massed together to form a phalanx, and received the attack of the swords. There were many Roman soldiers brave enough to jump into the phalanx, rip away shields and deal a wound from above. (*Relictis pilis comminus gladiis pugnatum est. At Germani celeriter ex consuetudine sua phalange facta impetus gladiorum exceperunt. Reperti sunt complures nostri qui in phalangas insilirent et scuta manibus revellerent et desuper vulnerarent*). | Roman infantry attack |
| II, 6 | Belgae | Town of Bibrax | | | The Belgae turned from their march to attack this town with great violence. (*Id ex itinere magno impetu Belgae oppugnare coeperunt*). | Adverb meaning violence |
| II, 11 | Romans | Gauls | Cavalry | Infantry | The Gallic rearguard withstands the attack of the Roman cavalry. (*Cum ab extremo agmine, ad quos ventum erat, consisterent fortiterque impetum nostrorum militum sustinerent*). | Roman cavalry attack |
| II, 19 | Gauls | Romans | Cavalry | Cavalry | The Gallic cavalry attack the Romans from out of a forest. (*cum... rurus ex silva in nostros impetum facerent*). | Non-Roman cavalry attack |
| II, 19 | Gauls | Romans | Infantry | Cavalry | The Gauls, having drawn up their battle-lines under the cover of the forest, attacked the Roman cavalry. (*Intra silvas aciem ordines... subito omnibus copiis provolaverunt impetumque in nostros equites fecerunt*). | Non-Roman infantry attack |
| II, 21 | Romans | Gauls | Infantry | Infantry | Caesar encouraged his tenth legion to bravely withstand the enemy attack. (*Uti... hostiumque impetum fortiter sustinerent*). | Roman infantry attack |
| II, 24 | Gauls | Romans | Cavalry | Cavalry and light infantry | The Roman cavalry and light infantry had been repulsed by the first attack of the enemy. (*Quos primo hostium impetu pulsos*). | Non-Roman cavalry attack |
| II, 25 | Gauls | Romans | Infantry | Infantry | Caesar joins the infantry fighting himself, urging his men to advance and extend the companies so that they could fight with swords more easily. In this way the attack of the enemy was checked a little. (*Centurionibusque nominatim appellatis reliquos cohortatus milites signa inferre et manipulos laxare iussit, quo facilius gladiis uti possent...paulum hostium impetus tardatus est*). | Non-Roman infantry attack |
| III, 2 | Gauls | Romans | Infantry | Infantry | The Seduni and Veragri held the high ground over Galba's Legion. The Gauls believed they would be successful since they themselves would charge down from the heights into the valley and throw their missiles, so that they thought it would not be possible to withstand their first attack. (*Cum ipsi ex montibus in vallem decurrerent et tela coicerent, ne primum quidem impetum suum posse sustineri existimabant*). | Non-Roman infantry attack |
| III, 8 | | | | | The great swell of the sea (*in magno impetu maris*). | Movement of the sea |
| III, 13 | | | | | The natives thought that the great forces of ocean winds could not be withstood. (*Quod tantas tempestates Oceani tantosque impetus ventorum sustineri... non... posse*). | Force of the wind |
| III, 19 | Romans | Gauls | Infantry | Infantry | The Gauls hurried to the Roman camp. The Romans came out of two gates to attack the enemy. Because of the Roman courage and the tiredness of the Gauls, without standing even one Roman attack the Gauls turned and fled. (*Factum est... ut ne unum quidem nostrorum impetum ferrent*). | Roman infantry attack |
| III, 28 | Gauls | Romans | Infantry | Infantry | When the Romans were dispersed at work, the Gauls suddenly dashed out of all parts of the forest and attacked the Roman troops. (*Subito ex omnibus partibus silvae evolaverunt et in nostros impetum fecerunt*). | Non-Roman infantry attack |
| III, 29 | | | | | Caesar cuts down the trees to prevent any flank attack on unarmed and unprepared troops. (*Ne quis inermibus imprudentibusque militibus ab latere impetus fieri posset*). | Hypothetical infantry attack |
| IV, 12 | Germans | Romans | Cavalry | Cavalry | The enemy attacked and speedily threw the Roman cavalry into confusion. (*Impetu facto celeriter nostros perturbaverunt*). | Non-Roman cavalry attack |
| IV, 17 | | | | | Force and onrush of the river Rhine. (*Contra vim atque impetu fluminis conversa statuebat*). | Rush of a river |
| IV, 26 | Romans | Britons | Infantry | Infantry | The Romans were having trouble with amphibious fighting. However, as soon they stood on dry, they attacked the enemy with all their comrades | Roman infantry attack |

| | | | | | | |
|---|---|---|---|---|---|---|
| | | | | | following and put the enemy to rout. (*Nostri, simul in arido constiterunt, suis omnibus consecutis, in hostes impetum fecerunt atque eos in fugam dederunt*). | |
| IV, 35 | Romans | Gauls | Infantry | Infantry | The Gauls could not endure the Roman attack for long. (*Diutius nostrorum militum impetum hostes ferre non potuerunt*). | Roman infantry attack |
| IV, 37 | Britons | Romans | Infantry | Infantry | The Romans by forming a close-order formation, defended themselves against six thousand shouting Britons, who attacked them quickly. The Romans withstood the enemy's attack and fought bravely for more than four hours. (*Cum illi orbe facto sese defenderent, celeriter ad clamorem hominum circiter milia sex convenerunt ...nostri milites impetum hostium sustinuerunt atque amplius horis quattour fortissime pugnaverunt*). | Non-Roman infantry attack |
| V, 15 | Britons | Romans | Infantry | Infantry | The Britons dashed out of the woods and attacked the Roman troops stationed in front of the camp. (*Ex silvis eiecerunt impetuque in eos facto qui erant in statione pro castris collocati*). | Non-Roman infantry attack |
| V, 17 | Romans | Britons | Cavalry and infantry | Cavalry and infantry | The Britions made an assault on the Roman line, the Romans attacked them fiercely and drove them back. (*Nostri acriter in eos impetu facto reppulerunt*). | Roman infantry attack |
| V, 18 | | | | | Roman troops cross the Thames with great speed and vigour. (*Ea celeritate atque eo impetu milites ierunt*). | Adverb meaning vigour |
| V, 18 | Romans | Britons | Cavalry and infantry | Infantry | The Romans attempt to cross the Thames, with a large force of Britons awaiting them on the other side. But, the soldiers crossed with such speed and vigour, even though they only had their heads above water, that the enemy could not withstand the attack of the legions and cavalry. (*Sed ea celeritate atque eo impetu milites ierunt, cum capite solo ex aqua exstarent, ut hostes impetum legionem atque equitum sustinere non possent*). | Roman cavalry and infantry attack |
| V, 21 | Romans | Britons | Infantry | Infantry | The enemy delayed for a short while, but did not stand the assault of the Roman troops, and broke away from another side of the stronghold. (*Hostes paulisper morati militum nostrorum impetum non tulerunt seseque alia ex parte oppidi eiecerunt*). | Attack on a camp |
| V, 28 | Germans | Romans | Infantry | Infantry | The Romans had bravely withstood the first attack of the enemy, and had dealt them many wounds. (*Quod primum hostium impetum multis ultro vulneribus illatis fortissime sustinuerint*). | Non-Roman infantry attack |
| V, 34 | Romans | Gauls | Infantry | Infantry | As often as each cohort dashed forward a great number of the enemy would fall at that point. Ambiorix noticed this and ordered his men to give way wherever the Romans made an attack, and that when the Romans retired back to their standards, his men should pursue in their turn. (*Quotiens quaeque cohors procurrerat, ab ea parte magnus numerus hostium cadebat ...Ambiorix... iubet... quam in partem Romani impetum fecerint, cedant... rursus se ad signa recipientes insequantur*). | Roman infantry attack |
| V, 35 | Romans | Gauls | Infantry | Infantry | The Gauls followed Ambiorix's order: When any cohort came out from the mass and made an attack, the enemy would quickly run back. Meanwhile that group of men was left exposed, and a volley of missiles was received on their flank. When they attempted to return to the place in the line which they had left, they were often surrounded by those who had retreated and those of the enemy who were nearest to them. (*Cum quaepiam cohors ex orbe excesserat atque impetum fecerat, hostes velocissime refugiebant. Interim eam partem nudari necesse erat et ab latere aperto tela recipi. Rursus cum in eum locum unde erant egressi reverti coeperant, et ab eis qui cesserant et ab eis qui proximi steterant circumveniebantur*). | Roman infantry attack |
| V, 37 | Gauls | Romans | Infantry | Infantry | Ambiorix's troops threw the Roman ranks into disorder with an attack. (*Impetuque in nostros facto ordines perturbant*). | Non-Roman Infantry attack |
| V, 47 | Romans | Treveri | | | Labienus feared that he would not be able to withstand the attack of the enemy. (*Labienus... veritus... ut hostium impetum sustinere posset*). | General word for attack |
| VI, 8 | Romans | Gauls | Infantry | Infantry | When the enemy saw the Romans advancing in formation, they could not sustain the attack and on the first collision were routed. (*Illi... impetum modo ferre non potuerunt ac primo concursu in fugam coniecti*). | Roman infantry attack. |
| VI, 37 | Germans | Romans | Cavalry | Infantry | The Germans assault the Roman camp, and the cohort stationed as defenders scarcely withstand the first attack. (*Vix primum impetum cohors in statione sustinet*). | Cavalry attack on a camp |
| VI, 39 | Germans | Romans | Infantry | Infantry | Owing to the small numbers of Roman troops the enemy made an attack from all sides. (*Postea despecta paucitate ex omnibus partibus impetum faciunt*). | Non-Roman infantry attack |
| VI, 40 | Romans | Germans | Camp followers and cavalry | | Trebonius and the infantry attack the enemy and break through to the camp. Closely following G. Trebonius into camp came the camp followers and the cavalry, in the same onrush, saved by the bravery of the soldiers. (*Hos subsecuti calones equitesque eodem impetu militum virtute servantur*). | Rush of cavalry and camp followers. |
| VII, 10 | Gauls | Boii | | | Caesar urged the Boii to remain loyal and to bravely withstand the assault of the enemy. (*Hortenturque ut in fide maneant atque hostium impetum magno animo sustineant*). | General word for attack |
| VII, 13 | Germans | Gauls | Cavalry | Cavalry | Caesar sent his four hundred German cavalry against the Gauls, who could not withstand their attack. (*Eorum impetum Galli sustinere non potuerunt*). | Non-Roman cavalry attack |
| VII, 28 | | | | | The Gauls were surrounded in the town by the Romans, the Gauls cast aside their weapons and make for the farthest parts of the town in a continuous rush. (*Abiectis armis ultimas oppidi partes continenti impetu petiverunt*). | Rush of men. |
| VII, 29 | | | | | The Gauls decide to fortify their camp in order that they could more easily withstand sudden attacks of the enemy. (*Ut castra munire instituerent, quo facilius repentinos hostium impetus sustinerent*). | Attack on a camp |
| VII, 46 | Romans | Gauls | | | The Gauls put up a wall to check the attack of the Romans. (*Qui nostrorum impetum tardaret*). | Attack on a city. |
| VII, 62 | Romans | Gauls | Infantry | Infantry | The enemy could not withstand the attack of the victorious Roman troops. (*Neque nostrorum militum victorum impetum sustinere potuerunt*). | Roman infantry attack |
| VII, 80 | Romans | Gauls | Cavalry | Archers and light | The Gauls had placed archers and light infantry among their cavalry to resist the attack of the Roman cavalry. (*Sagittarios expeditosque levis armaturae... nostrorum equitum impetus sustinerent*). | Roman cavalry attack |

| | | | | | | |
|---|---|---|---|---|---|---|
| | | | | infantry | | |
| VII, 80 | Germans | Gauls | Cavalry | Cavalry | The Germans, in one part of the field, massed their cavalry and attacked the enemy. (*Germani una in parte confertis turmis in hostes impetum fecerunt*). | Non-Roman cavalry attack |
| VIII, 18 | Romans | Bellovaci | Cavalry | Cavalry | The Romans attack the nearest troops of enemy cavalry. (*In proximas turmas impetum fecit*). | Roman cavalry attack |
| VIII, 19 | Bellovaci | Romans | Infantry | Cavalry and light infantry | The Roman cavalry and light infantry were able to withstand the first attacks of the ambushing enemy infantry. (*Qui sustinuerant primos impetus insidiarum*). | Non-Roman infantry attack |
| VIII, 24 | Men of Tergeste | Bandits | | | The men of Tergeste had been overwhelmed by an attack of bandits. (*Qui repentino latrocinio atque impetu illorum erant oppressi*). | Attack on a city. |
| VIII, 30 | | | | | Lucterius had desired to attack the province. (*Facere in provinciam voluisse impetum cognitum est*). | General word for attack |
| VIII, 35 | Romans | Gauls | | | Caninius moved quickly with armed cohorts from the nearest forts and attacked the corn carriers. (*Caninius celeriter cum cohortibus armatis ex proximis castellis in frumentarios sub ipsam lucem impetum fecit*). | General word for attack |
| VIII, 36 | Romans | Gauls | Infantry | Infantry | The cohorts attacked at once from all sides. (*Confestim cohortes undique impetum faciunt*). | Roman infantry attack |
| VIII, 48 | Romans | Gauls | Cavalry | Cavalry | Quadratus, the Roman commander, is killed. The Roman horse attack the enemy, and a number of the enemy were crushed and wounded by the attack. (*Complures hostium magno nostrorum impetu perculsi vulnerantur*). | Roman cavalry attack |
| | | | | | | |
| *B Civ.* I, 25 | | | | | An attempt to better defend rafts against attacks from ships and fire. (*Quo commodius ab impetu navium incendiisque defenderet*). | General word for attack |
| I, 26 | | | | | "Though [Caesar's] frequent attempts at an understanding were hindering energetic action and policy" (Peskett, 1914). (*Ea res saepe tentata etsi impetus euis consiliaque tardabat, tamen…*). | General word for attack |
| I, 27 | Romans | Romans | | | Pompey blocks gates and barricades roads to more easily check any attack of Caesar's. (*Quo facilius impetum Caesaris tardaret*). | Attack on a city. |
| I, 40 | Romans | Romans | Cavalry and infantry | Infantry | L. Plancius and his legions, eventhough outnumbered, withstand great attacks of the legions and cavalry. (*Ita congressus impari numero magnos impetus legionum equitatusque sustinet*). | Roman cavalry and infantry attack |
| I, 44 | Romans | Romans | Infantry | Infantry | The method of fighting adopted by the enemy was to at first attack with great vigour, boldly seize a position, take no trouble preserving their ranks, but fight singularly and dispersed. (*Genus erat pugnae militum illorum, ut magno impetu primo procurrerent, audacter locum caperent, ordines suos non magnopere servarent, rari dispersique pugnarent*). | Roman infantry attack |
| I, 46 | Romans | Romans | Infantry | Infantry | The enemy held the high ground and Caesar's ninth legion was receiving blows from every missile. When they had fought in this way continuously for five hours, Caesar's men, having used all their missiles, drew their swords and attacked the enemy cohorts uphill. (*Hoc cum esset modo pugnatum continenter horis quinque nostrique...consumptis omnibus telis gladiis destrictis impetum adversus montem in cohortes faciunt*). | Roman infantry attack |
| I, 47 | Romans | Afranians | Infantry | Infantry | The Afranians had withstood the attack of the Romans. (*Nostrorum impetum sustinuissent*). | Roman infantry attack |
| I, 58 | Romans | Massilians | Ships | Ships | The Massilians eluded the Romans and parried their attacks. (*Nostros eludebant impetusque eorum excipiebant*). | Naval battle. |
| I, 64 | Romans | Romans | Infantry | Infantry | At times the enemy standards where advanced and Caesar's men were driven back by an attack of the enemy cohorts in a body. (*Alias inferri signa et universarum cohortium impetu nostros propelli*). | Roman infantry attack |
| I, 70 | Romans | Romans | Cavalry | Light infantry | Afranius sent four light armed cohorts to gain a mountain. When Caesar's cavalry saw this they attacked them. (*IIII cetratorum cohortes in montem… mittit… conspicatus equitatus Caesaris in cohortes impetum fecit*). | Roman cavalry attack |
| I, 79 | Romans | Romans | Infantry | Cavalry | In order to defeat the enemy, they were forced to halt the legions and to repel the enemy cavalry a great attack. (*Ut… magnoque impetu equitatum repellerent*). | Roman infantry attack |
| I, 82 | Romans | Afranians | Infantry | Infantry | The two camps were separated by two thousand paces; the two battle line took up two thirds of this space, while the remaining third was left empty for the onset and attack of the troops. (*Tertia vacabat ad incursum atque impetum militum relicta*). | Roman infantry advance. |
| II, 6 | Romans | Romans | Ships | Ships | Brutus' ships attack two disabled ships. (*In eas impeditas impetum faciunt*). | General word for attack |
| II, 14 | Romans | Massilians | Infantry | Infantry | Caesar's men attack the enemy, who were burning their entrenchment. (*Fit in hostis impetus*). | Roman infantry attack |
| II, 25 | Romans | Numidians | Cavalry | Cavalry | Roman and Numidian cavalry meet in conflict; the Numidians could not withstand the first attack of the Romans. (*Concurrunt equites inter se; neque vero primum impetum nostrorum Numidae ferre potuerunt*). | Roman cavalry attack |
| II, 26 | Romans | King Juba | Cavalry and infantry | Cavalry | Curio hears about the king's approach and sends cavalry to meet and delay the first onset. (*Qui primum impetum sustineant ac morentur*). | General word for attack |
| II, 32 | | | | | Within a speech: 'with my having scattered the enemy fleet on my arrival with the first attack'. (*An poenitet vos… quod classem hostium primo impetu adveniens profligaverim*). | Naval battle |
| II, 34 | Romans | Romans | Cavalry | Cavalry | Attius' cavalry could not withstand the attack of Curio's cavalry. (*Quorum primum impetum equites hostium non tulerunt*). | Roman cavalry attack |
| II, 41 | Romans | Celtiberians and Gauls | Cavalry | Cavalry | The Roman cavalry forced the enemy to give way at whichever point they attacked. (*Hi, quamcumque in partem impetum fecerant, hostes loco cedere cogebant*). | Roman cavalry attack |
| II, 41 | Romans | Numidians | Infantry | Cavalry | Whenever cohorts came out of the battle-line and charged, the Numidians by their quickness fled from the Roman attacks, and as the Romans returned again to their own ranks, the Numidians would surround them and cut them off from the battle-line… (*Cum cohortes ex acie procucurrissent, Numidae integri celeritate impetum nostrorum effugiebant rursusque ad* | Roman infantry attack |

| | | | | | | |
|---|---|---|---|---|---|---|
| | | | | | *ordines suos se recipientes circuibant et ab acie excludebant*). | |
| III, 9 | Romans | Romans | | | With a similar assault they attacked the second camp. (*Eodem impetu altera (castra) sunt adorti*). | Attack on a camp |
| III, 21 | | | | | The mob attacked G. Trebonius. (*Impetuque multitudinis in C. Trebonium facto*). | General word for attack |
| III, 24 | Romans | Romans | Ships | Ships | At the first attack Antonian ships captured one of the enemy *quadriremes*. (*Primo... impetu unam ex his quadremem... ceperunt*). | Naval battle. |
| III, 26 | Romans | Romans | Ships | Ships | Caesar's men feared an attack of the fleet. (*Nostri usi fortunae beneficio tamen impetum classis timebant*). | General word for attack |
| III, 36 | | | | | "Scipio made his way to Domitius with great speed". (*Hic nullo in loco Macedoniae moratus magno impetu tetendit ad Domitium*). | Adverb meaning vigour |
| III, 37 | Romans | Romans | Cavalry | Cavalry | Scipio's cavalry ambushed Domitius' men as they were collecting fodder. This attack was bravely withstood. (*Sed nostri fortiter impetum eorum tulerunt*). | Roman cavalry attack |
| III, 37 | Romans | Romans | Cavalry | Cavalry | After withstanding an enemy attack, Varus' troops regained their ranks and the whole group then attacked the enemy. (*Que ordines rediit, atque ultro universi in hostes impetum fecerunt*). | Roman cavalry attack |
| III, 46 | Romans | Romans | Infantry | Infantry | Caesar ordered his men to attack the enemy. (*In hostes impetum fieri iussit*). | Roman infantry attack |
| III, 51 | Romans | Romans | Infantry | Infantry | The Pompeians could not endure the sight nor the attack of Sulla's men, and when the first had been overthrown the rest turned and yielded their position. (*Neque vero conspectum aut impetum nostrorum tulerunt, primisque deiectis reliqui se verterunt et loco cesserunt*). | Roman infantry attack |
| III, 52 | Romans | Romans | Infantry | Infantry | In one place Volcatus Tullus, with three cohorts, withstood the attack of a legion and drove it from its position. (*Uno loco Volcatius Tullus impetum legionis sustinuit cohortibus tribus atque eam loco depulit*). | Roman infantry attack |
| III, 63 | Romans | Romans | Infantry | Infantry | The Pompeians, disembarking from their ships, attacked Caesar's men in the rear. (*Pompeiani navibus expositi in aversos nostros impetum fecerunt*). | Roman infantry attack |
| III, 64 | Romans | Romans | Infantry | Infantry | Marcellinus' troops failed to sustain the attack of the Pompeians. (*Neque ipsae hostium impetum tulerunt*). | Roman infantry attack |
| III, 69 | Romans | Romans | Infantry | Infantry | A Pompeian legion attempted to resist Caesar's men, and began to attack the enemy. (*Ultro in nostros impetum faciebat*). | Roman infantry attack |
| III, 84 | Romans | Romans | Cavalry and light infantry | Cavalry | One thousand cavalry, when fighting with light armed troops, even in the open ground, could attempt to withstand the attack of seven thousand Pompeian horse. (*Ut equitum mille etiam apertioribus locis VII milium Pompeianorum impetum... sustinere auderent*). | Roman cavalry attack |
| III, 92 | Romans | Romans | Infantry | Infantry | Pompey had previously ordered his men to await Caesar's attack without moving, and to allow Caesar's line to fall into disorder. (*Sed Pompeius suis praedixerat, ut Caesaris impetum exciperent neve se loco moverent aciemque eius distrahi paterentur*). | Roman infantry attack |
| III, 93 | Romans | Romans | Infantry | Infantry | The Pompeians parried missiles and withstood the attack of Caesar's legions, while preserving their ranks, and after throwing their *pila* attacked with swords. (*Nam et tela missa exceperunt et impetum legionum tulerunt et ordines suos servarunt pilisque missis ad gladios redierunt*). | Roman infantry attack |
| III, 93 | Romans | Romans | Cavalry | Cavalry | Caesar's cavalry could not withstand the attack of Pompey's cavalry. (*Quorum impetum noster equitatus non tulit*). | Roman cavalry attack |
| III, 93 | Romans | Romans | Infantry | Cavalry | Caesar's fourth line advance and attack Pompey's cavalry with such violence, that not one of them stood their ground. (*Illi celeriter procucurrerunt infestisque signis tanta vi in Pompei equites impetum fecerunt, ut eorum nemo consisteret*). | Roman infantry attack |
| III, 93 | Romans | Romans | Infantry | Infantry | After routing the cavalry, Caesar's fourth line, with the same attack surrounded the left wing and attacked the Pompeians in the rear. (*Eodem impetu cohortes sinsitrum cornu... circumierunt eosque a tergo sunt adorti*). | Roman infantry attack |
| III, 101 | Romans | Romans | Ships | Ships | An attack on the Cassian fleet. (*Impetuque facto in Cassianam classem*). | Naval battle. |
| III, 111 | Achillas | Romans | Infantry | Infantry | Caesar, by putting soldiers in the streets of Alexandria withstood the attack of Achillias' troops. (*Caesar dispositis per vias cohortibus impetum eius sustinuit*). | General word for attack |
| III, 111 | Achillas | Romans | | | Achillias tries to burst into Caesar's house on the first assault. (*Primo impetu domum eius irrumpere conatus*). | Attack on a city. |

## Appendix 2.6: the occurrences of *inferre* in Caesar

| ***Reference*** | ***Offensive Army*** | ***Defensive Army*** | ***Attacking Arm*** | ***Defending Arm*** | ***Notes*** | ***Comments*** |
|---|---|---|---|---|---|---|
| *B Gall.* I, 2 | | | | | The chances of waging war with their neighbours were less easy. (*Minus facile finitimis belum inferre possent*). | Wage war |
| I, 12 | | | | | The Helvetii brought a calamity upon the Roman people. (*Quae pars civitatis Helvetiae insignem calamitatem populo Romano intulerat*). | Bring danger |
| I, 14 | | | | | Injuries inflicted upon the Aedui and their allies. (*Si Aeduis de iniuriis, quas ipsis sociisque eorum intulerint*). | Wage war |
| I, 25 | Romans | Boii, Tulingi and Helveti. | Infantry | Infantry | The Boii and Tulingi attacked the exposed Roman right flank and overlapped them. Seeing this, the Helvetii, who had previously retired to higher ground, renewed their attack. "The Romans wheeled, and advanced in two divisions, the first and second line to oppose the part of the enemy which had been defeated and driven off, the third to check the fresh assault" (Edwards, 1917). (*Romani conversa signa bipertito intulerunt: prima et secunda acies, ut victis ac submotis resisteret, tertia, ut venientes sustineret*). | Massed movement in response to an attack |
| I, 30 | | | | | The Helvetii wish to make war on Gaul. (*Uti toti Galliae bellum inferrent*). | Wage war |
| I, 35 | | | | | Ariovistus ought not make war with the Aedui. (*Eorum bellum inferret*). | Wage war |
| I, 36 | | | | | Ariovistus agreed not to make war on the Aedui. (*Bellum illaturum*). | Wage war |
| I, 39 | | | | | Caesar's tribunes offer reasons [to leave him]. (*Quorum alius alia causa illata*). | Offer a suggestion |
| I, 40 | | | | | Make war. (*Bellum intulisset*). | Wage war |
| I, 43 | | | | | Ariovistus must not make war on the Aedui. (*Ne aut Aeduis... bellum inferret*). | Wage war |
| I, 44 | | | | | The Gauls had made war on Ariovistus. (*Sed Gallos sibi bellum intulisse*). | Wage war |
| I, 44 | | | | | Ariovistus' warfare had not been offensive. (*Quod bellum non intulerit*). | Wage war |
| I, 50 | | | | | "At sunset, when many blows had been dealt and taken, Ariovistus led his forces back to camp" (Edwards, 1917). (*Solis occasu suas copias Ariovistus multis et inlatis et acceptis vulneribus in castra reduxit*). | Inflict wounds |
| II, 14 | | | | | The Bellovaci made war on the Romans. (*Populo Romano bellum intulisse*). | Wage war |
| II, 14 | | | | | The leaders of a plot, realising the calamity they had brought upon the Roman people, fled to Britain. (*Qui eius consilii principes fuissent, quod intellegerent quantam calamitatem civitati intulissent, in Britanniam profugisse*). | Bring danger |
| II, 15 | | | | | The Nervii did not allow wine nor any other luxuries to be imported. (*Nihil pati vini reliquarumque rerum inferri*). | Carry forward |
| II, 25 | Romans | Gauls | Infantry | Infantry | Caesar came to his twelfth legion and saw that many men were injured and the rear ranks were beginning to withdraw. "The enemy were not ceasing to move upwards in front from the lower ground, and were pressing hard on either flank. The condition of affairs, as he saw, was critical indeed, and there was no support that could be sent up. Taking therefore a shield from a soldier of the rearmost ranks, as he himself was come thither without a shield, he went forward into the first line, and, calling on the centurions by name, and cheering on the rank and file, he bade them advance and extend the companies, that they might ply swords more easily" (Edwards, 1917). (*Hostes neque a fronte ex inferiore loco subeuntes intermittere et ab utroque latere instare et rem esse in angusto vidit, neque ullum esse subsidium quod submitti posset, scuto ab novissimis [uni] militi detracto, quod ipse eo sine scuto venerat, in primam aciem processit centurionibusque nominatim appellatis reliquos cohortatus milites signa inferre et manipulos laxare iussit, quo facilius gladiis uti possent*). | Massed movement in response to an attack |
| II, 25 | | | | | Caesar's arrival brought hope. (*Cuius adventu spe inlata militibus* ). | Inspire hope |
| II, 26 | Romans | Gauls | Infantry | Infantry | Following above: "Perceiving that the seventh legion, which had formed up near at hand, was also harassed by the enemy, Caesar instructed the tribunes to close the legions gradually together, and then, wheeling, to advance against the enemy" (Edwards, 1917). (*Caesar, cum VII. legionem, quae iuxta constiterat, item urgeri ab hoste vidisset, tribunos militum monuit ut paulatim sese legiones coniungerent et conversa signa in hostes inferrent*). | Massed movement in response to an attack |
| II, 29 | | | | | Offensive warfare. (*Alias bellum inferrent*). | Wage war |
| II, 32 | | | | | Caesar ordered that injuries should not be committed against surrendered subject of Rome. (*Ne quam dediticiis populi Romani iniuriam inferrent*). | Wage war |
| IV, 7 | | | | | The Germans were not the first to make war with the Roman people. (*Germanos neque priores populo Romano bellum inferre*). | Wage war |
| IV, 7 | | | | | Germans attack anyone who made war on them. (*Bellum inferant*). | Wage war |
| IV, 13 | | | | | Make war. (*Bellum intulissent*). | Wage war |
| IV, 16 | | | | | Sugambri make war on Caesar. (*Bellum intulissent*). | Wage war |
| IV, 27 | | | | | Make war without cause. (*Bellum sine causa intulissent*). | Wage war |
| IV, 30 | | | | | Make war on Britain. (*Belli inferendi cause in Britanniam*). | Wage war |
| V, 12 | | | | | Make war. (*Belli inferendi*). | Wage war |
| V, 16 | Britons | Romans | Cavalry | Cavalry | The British cavalry tactics brought about the same danger for the Romans in retirement as in pursuit. (*Equestris... proeli ratio et cedentibus et insequentibus par atque idem periclum inferebat*). | Bring danger |
| V, 28 | | | | | The Romans had withstood the first attack of the Germans, and had actually dealt them many wounds. (*Quod primum hostium impetum multis ultro vulneribus illatis fortissime sustinuerint*). | Inflict wounds |
| V, 54 | | | | | Make war. (*Inferendi belli*). | Wage war |
| VI, 15 | | | | | The Gauls would every year make war or defend against it. (*Uti aut ipsi iniurias inferrent aut illatas propulsarent*). | Wage war |
| VI, 19 | | | | | Gauls cast everything in to the fire at a funeral. (*Omnia..., quae vivis cordi fuisse arbitrantur, in ignem inferunt, etiam animalia*). | Carry forward. |
| VI, 23 | | | | | When a state makes or resists aggressive war... (*Cum bellum civitas aut illatum defendit aut infert*). | Wage war |
| VI, 24 | | | | | Gauls make war on Germans. (*Ultro bella inferrent*). | Wage war |
| VI, 30 | | | | | One of Ambiorix's supporters sets him on a horse. (*His pugnantibus illum in* | Carry forward. |

| | | | | | | |
|---|---|---|---|---|---|---|
| | | | | | *equum quidam ex suis intulit*). | |
| VI, 43 | | | | | Hope of catching fugitives. (*Spe consequendi illata*). | Inspire hope |
| VII, 8 | | | | | Strike as much terror into the enemy as possible. (*Ut... quam maximum hostibus terrorem inferant*). | Inspire fear |
| VII, 22 | | | | | In day and night raids there are attempts to set fire to a ramp (*crebris diurnis nocturnisque eruptionibus aut aggeri ignem inferebant*). | Carry forward. |
| VII, 54 | | | | | Caesar did not wish to seem like he was inflicting an injury. (*Ne... inferre iniuriam videretur*). | Wage war |
| VII, 62 | Romans | Gauls | Infantry | Infantry | At the first engagement the 7th legion, on the right wing, put the enemy left to rout. On the Roman left the 12th attacked and although many were killed by missiles, the remainder resisted strongly. 'Victory was still uncertain, but when the tribunes of the 7th legion were told what was happening on the left wing, they brought out their legion behind the rear of the enemy and attacked. Not even then did any man yield his position, but all were surrounded and slain'. (*Incerto nunc etiam exitu victoriae, cum septimae legionis tribunis esset nuntiatum quae in sinistro cornu gererentur, post tergum hostium legionem ostenderunt signaque intulerunt. Ne eo quidem tempore quisquam loco cessit, sed circumventi omnes interfectique sunt*). | Roman infantry attack |
| VII, 64 | | | | | Make war on the Allobroges. (*Bellumque inferri Allobrogibus*). | Wage war |
| VII, 67 | Romans | Gauls | Infantry | Infantry | "At any point where our troops seemed to be distressed or too hard pressed Caesar would order the standards to advance and the line of battle to be formed" (Edwards, 1917). (*Si qua in parte nostri laborare aut gravius premi videbantur, eo signa inferri Caesar aciemque constitui iubebat*). | Massed movement in response to an attack |
| VII, 77 | | | | | The Cimbri devastated Gaul, and brought about calamity. (*Depopulata Gallia Cimbri magnaque illata calamitate*). | Bring danger |
| VIII, 1 | | | | | Make war. (*Bella... intulissent*). | Wage war |
| VIII, 4 | | | | | Make war. (*Intulisse bellum*). | Wage war |
| VIII, 16 | | | | | Horsemen brought about great havoc upon the Roman foraging parties. (*Magna detrimenta Romanis in pabulationibus inferebant*). | Bring danger |
| VIII, 21 | | | | | If Caesar could have inflicted punishment without a battle... (*Si sine dimicatione inferre integris posset*). | Inflict punishment |
| VIII, 52 | | | | | The armed domination of Pompey was causing much terror in the forum. (*Quoniam Pompei dominatio atque arma non minimum terrorem foro inferrent*). | Inspire fear |
| | | | | | | |
| *B Civ.* I, 35 | | | | | Make war. (*Inferendi belli*). | Wage war |
| I, 64 | Romans | Romans | Infantry | Cavalry | Caesar sent his cavalry to harass the enemy marching column. "At early dawn it was observed from the higher ground adjacent to Caesar's camp that the enemy's rear was being hard pressed by the attack of our cavalry, and that sometimes the end of the column was being held up and cut off from the rest, while at other times their standards were advanced and our men were driven off by an attack of the cohorts in a body" (Peskett, 1914) (*Prima luce ex superioribus locis, quae Caesaris castris erant coniuncta, cernebatur equitatus nostri proelio novissimos illorum premi vehementer ac nonnumquam sustineri extremum agmen atque interrumpi, alias inferri signa et universarum cohortium impetu nostros propelli, dein rursus conversos insequi*). | Massed movement in response to an attack |
| I, 82 | Romans | Romans | Infantry | Infantry | "If battle were joined, the propinquity of the camps afforded the conquered a speedy retreat in their flight. For this reason he had made up his mind to resist them if they advanced their colours, but not to be the first to attack" (Peskett, 1914). (*Si proelium committeretur, propinquitas castrorum celerem superatis ex fuga receptum dabat. Hac de causa constituerat signa inferentibus resistere, prior proelio non lacessere*). | Advancing standards |
| I, 86 | | | | | A discussion is introduced about the time and place of an arrangement. (*Cum de loco et tempore eius rei controversia inferretur*). | Offer a suggestion |
| II, 2 | | | | | Fire brought against towers and earthworks. (*Ignesque aggeri et turribus inferebantur*). | Carry forward |
| II, 2 | | | | | Inflict losses. (magnisque ultro illatis detrimentis). | Inflict loses |
| II, 6 | | | | | "Showers of missiles hurled from the smaller vessels at a distance inflicted many wounds on our men" (Peskett, 1914). (*Simul ex minoribus navibus magna vis eminus missa telorum multa nostris de improviso imprudentibus atque impeditis vulnera inferebant*). | Inflict wounds |
| II, 14 | | | | | Set fire to earthworks. (*Secundo magnoque vento ignem operibus inferunt*). | Carry forward |
| II, 14 | | | | | Set fire to earthworks. (Multumque ignem intulerunt). | Carry forward |
| II, 42 | | | | | Curio's men were scared and so Caesar saw one hope of safety: he ordered them in a body to occupy the nearest hills and the standards to be moved to there. (*Proximos colles capere universos atque eo signa inferri iubet*). | Massed movement |
| III, 27 | | | | | Danger on Caesar's ships... (*Qui nostris navibus periculum intulerant*). | Bring danger |
| III, 38 | | | | | Neighing of horses brings suspicion. (*Ex fremitu equorum illata suspicione*) | Suspicion |
| III, 65 | | | | | The Pompeians, approaching, caused great terror in the camp of Marcellinus. (*Iamque Pompeiani magna caede nostrorum castris Marcellini appropinquabant non mediocri terrore illato reliquis cohortibus*). | Inspire fear |
| III, 67 | | | | | Pompey had left his camp, but scouts reported back to Caesar that the standards of the legion had been brought back there. (*Eo signa legionis illata speculatores Caesari renuntiarunt*). | Massed movement |
| III, 72 | | | | | False suspicion, a sudden alarm, or a religious scruple brought about great disasters. (*Quam parvulae saepe causae vel falsae suspicionis vel terroris repentini vel obiectae religionis magna detrimenta intulissent*). | Bring danger |
| III, 75 | | | | | Pompey did not allow any delay in pursuit. (*Neque vero Pompeius... moram ullam ad insequendum intulit*). | A delay |
| III, 77 | | | | | Delay brought by the first day. (*Primi diei mora illata*). | A delay |
| III, 80 | | | | | Caesar aims to strike terror into the remaining communities. (*Simul reliquis civitatibus huius urbis exemplo inferre terrorem*). | Inspire fear |

## Bibliography

### *Texts and Translations*


*Historicorum Romanorum Fragmenta*, ed. H. Peter (Teubner: Leipzig, 1883)

T. Livius, *Ab Urbe Condita*, Libri I-VI, ed. W. Weissenborn (Teubner: Leipzig, 1867)

T. Livius, *Ab Urbe Condita*, Libri VII-XXIII, ed. W. Weissenborn (Teubner: Leipzig, 1866)

T. Livius, *Ab Urbe Condita*, Libri XXIV-XXX, ed. W. Weissenborn (Teubner: Leipzig, 1868)

T. Livius, *Ab Urbe Condita*, Libri XXXI-XXXV, ed. W. Weissenborn (Teubner: Leipzig, 1867)

T. Livius, *Ab Urbe Condita*, Libri XLI-XLV, ed. W. Weissenborn and M. Mueller (Teubner: Stuttgart, 1981)

T. Livius, *Ab Urbe Condita*, Libri XXXI-XXXV, ed. J. Briscoe (Teubner: Stuttgart, 1991)

T. Livius, *Ab Urbe Condita*, Libri XXXVI-XL, ed. J. Briscoe (Teubner: Stuttgart, 1991)

*Livy: Ab Urbe Condita Book VI*, ed. C. S. Kraus, (Cambridge, 1994).

*Oratorum Romanorum Fragmenta Liberae Rei Publicae*, ed. H. Malcovati (Paraviae, 1967).

*Appian: Civil Wars*, trans. J. Carter (London, 1996).

*Caesar: The Gallic War*, trans. H. J. Edwards (Loeb: Cambridge, MA, 1917)

*Caesar: The Civil Wasr*, trans. A. G. Peskett (Loeb: Cambridge, MA, 1914)

*Julius Caesar. The Civil War, Books 1&2*, ed. and trans. J. Carter (Warminster, 1991).

*Julius Caesar. The Civil War, Book 3*, ed. and trans. J. Carter (Warminster, 1993).

*C. Iuli Caesaris Commentarii: Rerum in Gallia Gestarum VII; A. Hirti Commentarius VIII*, T. Rice Holmes (Oxford, 1914).

*Die Historien des Coelius Antipater. Fragmente und Kommentar*, ed. W. Herrman (Meisenheim am Glan, 1979).

*Livy: Books 1-2*, ed. and trans. B. O. Foster (Loeb: Cambridge, MA, 1919)

*Livy: Books 3-4*, ed. and trans. B. O. Foster (Loeb: Cambridge, MA, 1922)

*Livy: Books 5-7*, ed. and trans. B. O. Foster (Loeb: Cambridge, MA, 1924)

*Livy: Books 8-10*, ed. and trans. B. O. Foster (Loeb: Cambridge, MA, 1926)

*Livy: Books 21-22*, ed. and trans. B. O. Foster (Loeb: Cambridge, MA, 1929)

*Livy: Books 23-25*, ed. and trans. F. G. Moore (Loeb: Cambridge, MA, 1940)

*Livy: Books 26-27*, ed. and trans. F. G. Moore (Loeb: Cambridge, MA, 1943)

*Livy: Books 28-30*, ed. and trans. F. G. Moore (Loeb: Cambridge, MA, 1971)

*Livy: Books 31-34*, ed. and trans. E. T. Sage (Loeb: Cambridge, MA, 1967)

*Livy: Books 35-37*, ed. and trans. E. T. Sage (Loeb: Cambridge, MA, 1935)

*Livy: Books 38-39*, ed. and trans. E. T. Sage (Loeb: Cambridge, MA, 1949)

*Livy: Books 40-42*, ed. and trans. A. C. Schlesinger (Loeb: Cambridge, MA, 1938)

*Livy: Books 43-45*, ed. and trans. A. C. Schlesinger (Loeb: Cambridge, MA, 1951)

*Tite-Live Histoire Romaine: Tome XIX, Livre XXIX*, trans. P. François (Paris, 1994)

*Livy: The Early History of Rome*, trans. A. De Selincourt (London, 2002)

*Livy: Rome and Italy*, trans. B. Radice (London, 1982)

*Livy: Hannibal's War*, trans. J. C. Yardley (Oxford, 2006)

*Livy: The Dawn of the Roman Empire*, trans. J. C. Yardley (London, 2000)

*Livy: Rome's Mediterranean Empire*, trans. J. D. Chaplin (London, 2007)

*Frontinus: The Strategems and The Aqueducts of Rome*, trans. C. E. Bennett and M. B. McElwain (Loeb: Cambridge, MA, 1925)

*Polybius: Books 1-2*, trans. W. R. Paton (Loeb: Cambridge, MA, 1922)

*Polybius: Books 3-4*, trans. W. R. Paton (Loeb: Cambridge, MA, 1922)

*Polybius: Books 5-8*, trans. W. R. Paton (Loeb: Cambridge, MA, 1923)

*Polybius: Books 9-15*, trans. W. R. Paton (Loeb: Cambridge, MA, 1925)

*Polybius: Books 16-27*, trans. W. R. Paton (Loeb: Cambridge, MA, 1927)

*Polybius: Books 28-39*, trans. W. R. Paton (Loeb: Cambridge, MA, 1927)

*Polybius: The Rise of the Roman Empire*, trans. Ian Scott-Kilvert (London, 1979)

*Vegetius: Epitoma Rei Militaris*, trans. L. F. Stelten (New York, 1990)

*Vegetius: Epitome of Military Science*, trans. N. P. Milner (Liverpool, 1996)


### *Lexicographical Material*


Glare, P.G.W. (ed.) (1984) *The Oxford Latin Dictionary*, Oxford.

Lewis, C.T. and Short, C. (1955 [1879]) *A Latin Dictionary*, Oxford.

Liddell, H. G. and Scott, R. (1968 [1843]) *A Greek to English Lexicon*, Oxford.

Mauersberger, A. (1961) *Polybios – Lexikon*, Berlin.

Merguet, H. (1961 [1886]) *Lexikon zu den Schriften Cäsars und Seiner Fortsetzer mit Angabe Sämtlicher Stellen*, Hildesheim.

Meusel H. (1887-93) *Lexicon Caesarianum*, 3 vols., Berlin.

Packard, D. W. (1968) *A Concordance to Livy*, volumes I-IV, Cambridge, MA.

Various (eds.) (1900 - ) *Thesaurus Linguae Latinae*, Tuebner: Leipzig.


### *General Works*


Adams, J. N. (2003) *Bilingualism and the Latin Language*, Cambridge.

Adcock, F. (1970 [1940]) *The Roman Art of War under the Republic*, Cambridge, MA.

Anderson, W. B. (1908) 'Contributions to the Study of the Ninth Book of Livy' *Transactions of the American Philological Association* 39, 89-103.

Ash, R. (1999) 'An exemplary conflict: Tacitus' Parthian battle narrative (*Annals* 6.34-35)', *Phoenix* 53, 114-35.

Ash, R. (2002) 'Epic Encounters? Ancient Historical Battle Narratives and the Epic Tradition', in Levene and Nelis (eds.) (2002), 253-273.

Astin, A. E. (1978) *Cato the Censor*, Oxford.

Badian, E. (1993) 'Livy and Augustus' in Schuller (1993), 9-38.

Batstone, W. W. and Damon, C. (2006) *Caesar's* Civil War, Oxford.

Batstone, W. W. (1990) 'A tendentious hypotaxis in Caesar's plain style', *The American Journal of Philology* 111.3, 348-60.

Batstone, W. W. (1991) 'A narrative gestalt and the force of Caesar's style', *Mnemosyne* 4th Series, 44.1/2, 126-36.

Begbie, C. M. (1967) 'The epitome of Livy', *Classical Quarterly* 17, 332-338.

Bishop and Coulston (1993) *Roman Military Equipment*, London.

Bishop and Coulston (2006) *Roman Military Equipment*, 2nd edition, London.

Bosworth, A. B. (1980) *A Historical Commentary on Arrian's History of Alexander, Vol. I.*, Oxford.

Briscoe, J. (1973) *A Commentary on Livy Books 31-33*, Oxford.

Briscoe, J. (1978) 'Review of Luce (1977)' *Journal of Roman Studies* 68, 227-8.

Briscoe, J. (1981) *A Commentary on Livy Books 34-37*, Oxford.

Briscoe, J. (1993) 'Livy and Polybius' in Schuller (1993), 39-53.

Briscoe, J. (2008) *A Commentary on Livy Books 38-40*, Oxford.

Briscoe, J. (2009) 'Some misunderstandings of Polybius in Livy', forthcoming.

Brouqier-Reddé, V. (1997) 'L'équipment militaire d'Alésia d'après les nouvelles recherches (prospections et fouilles)', *Journal of Roman Military Equipment Studies* 8, 277-88.

Brown, R. (1999) 'Two Caesarian battle-descriptions: A study in contrast', *The Classical Journal* 94.4, 329-57.

Brunt, P. A. (1993) *Studies in Greek History and Thought*, Oxford.

Buckland, P. (1978) 'A First Century Shield from Doncaster, Yorkshire', *Britannia* 9, 247-69.

Burck, E. (1971) 'The Third Decade', in Dorey (1971) 21-46.

Campbell, B. (2004) *Greek and Roman Military Writers: Selected Readings*, London and New York.

Campbell, D. (1997) 'Review Article: The Roman Art of War', *Britannia* 28, 473-478.

Cawkwell, G. L. (1978) *Philip of Macedon*, London.

Coarelli, F. (1968) 'L'"ara di Domizio Enobarbo" e la cultura artistica in Roma nel II secolo a.C.', *Dialoghi di Archeologia* 2, 302-68.

Collins, J. H. (1972) 'Caesar as Political Propagandist', in *Aufstieg und Niedergang der römischen Welt* I.i, 922-66.

Connolly, P. (1987) 'The Roman Saddle' in Dawson (1987), 7-27.

Connolly, P. (1989) 'The Roman Army in the Age of Polybius', in Hackett (1989), 149-168.

Connolly, P. (1990) 'The Saddle Horns from Newstead', *Journal of Roman Military Equipment Studies* 1, 61-6.

Connolly, P. (1991), 'The Roman Fighting Technique Deduced from Armour and Weaponry', in Maxfield and Dobson (1991), 358-363.

Connolly, P. (1997), 'Pilum, gladius and pugio in the Late Republic', *Journal of Roman Military Equipment Studies* 8, 41-56.

Connolly, P. (1998) *Greece and Rome at War*, London.

Connolly, P. (2000) 'The Reconstruction and Use of Roman Weaponry in the Second Century BC', *Journal of Roman Military Equipment Studies* 11, 43-46.

Cornell, T. J., Rankov, B and Sabin, P. (1996) *The Second Punic War a Reappraisal* BICS Supplement 67

Cornell, T. J. (1986) 'The Value of the Literary Tradition Concerning Archaic Rome', in Raaflaub (1986), 52-76.

Cornell T. J. (1995) *The Beginnings of Rome: Italy and Rome from the Bronze Age to the Punic Wars (c. 1000-264 BC)*, London and New York.

Coutagne, D. (ed.) (1987) *Archéologie d'Entremont au Musée Granet*, Aix-en-Provence.

Culham, P. (1989) 'Chance, command and chaos in ancient military engagement', *World Futures* 27, 191-205.

Curchin, L. (1991) *Roman Spain: Conquest and Assimilation*, London.

Daly, G. (2002) *Cannae: the Experience of Battle in the Second Punic War*, London.

Dawson, M. (ed.) (1987) *Roman Military Equipment: the Accoutrements of War. Proceedings of the Third Roman Military Equipment Research Seminar*, B.A.R. International Series 336, Oxford.

Delbruck, H. (trans. 1975) *History of the Art of War, Volume 1, Warfare in Antiquity*, translated by Walter Renfroe jr., Lincoln, NE.

Deroux, C. (2000) *Studies in Latin Literature and Roman History X* [Collection *Latomus* ccliv], Brussels.

Derow, P. (1979) 'Polybius, Rome and the East', *Journal of Roman Studies* 69, 1-15.

De Sanctis, G. (1916) *Storia dei Romani*, volume iii, *L'età delle Guerre Puniche*, Torino: Bocca.

Dillon, S. and Welch, K. E. (2006) *Representations of War in Ancient Rome*, Cambridge.

Dobson, M. (2008) *The Army of the Roman Republic: The Second Century BC, Polybius and the Camps at Numantia, Spain*, Oxford.

Dorey, T. A. (ed.) (1971) *Livy*, London and Toronto.

Eden, P. T. (1962) 'Caesar's style: inheritance versus intelligence', *Glotta* 40, 74-117.

Feugère, M. (trans. 2002) *Weapons of the Romans*, translated by D. G. Smith, Stroud.

Feugère, M. (1994) 'L'equipement militaire d'époque républicaine en Gaule', *Journal of Roman Military Equipment Studies* 5, 3-23.

Fuller, J. F. C. (1965) *Julius Caesar: Man, Soldier, and Tyrant*, New Brunswick.

Gabriel, R. A. and Metz, K. S. (1991) *From Sumer to Rome: the Military Capabilities of Ancient Armies*, New York.

Gelzer, M. (1968 [1921]) *Caesar: Politician and Statesman*, translated by P. Needham, Cambridge, MA.

Gilliver, C. (1996) 'The Roman army and morality in war' in Lloyd (1996), 219-238.

Gilliver, C. (1999) *The Roman Art of War*, Stroud

Gilliver, C. (2007) 'Display in Roman warfare: the appearance of armies and individuals on the battlefield', *War in History* 14.1, 1-21.

Glover, R. F. (1948) 'The tactical handling of the elephant', *Greece and Rome*, 1st Series 17.49, 1-11.

Glover, R. F. (1950) 'Some curiosities of ancient warfare', *Greece and Rome* 19.55, 1-9.

Goldsworthy, A. (1996) *The Roman Army at War 100BC-200AD*, Oxford.

Goldsworthy, A. K. (1997) 'The *othismos* myths and heresies: the nature of hoplite battle' *War in History* 4.1, 1-26.

Goldsworthy, A. K. (1998) '"Instinctive Genius": the depiction of Caesar the general', in Welch and Powell (1998) 193-219.

Goldsworthy, A. (2000) *Roman Warfare*, London.

Goldsworthy, A. (2003) *In the Name of Rome*, London.

Goenman-van Waateringe, W. (1967) *Romeins Lederwerk uit Valkenburg Z.H.*, Nederlandse Oudheden 2, Groningen.

Gotoff, H. C. (1984) 'Towards a practical criticism of Caesar's prose style', *Illinois Classical Studies* 9, 1-18.

Grossman, D. (1995) *On Killing: the Psychological Cost of Learning to Kill in War and Society*, New York

Gulbekian, E. (1987) 'The origin and value of the stadion unit used by Eratosthenes in the Third Century B.C.' *Archive for History of Exact Sciences* 37.4, 359-360.

Hackett, J. (ed.) (1989) *Warfare in the Ancient World*, London.

Hammond, N. G. L. and Walbank, F. W. (1988), *A History of Macedonia: volume 3, 336-167*, Oxford.

Hammond, N. G. L. (1988), 'The campaign and the battle of Cynoscephalae in 197 BC', *Journal of Hellenic Studies* 107, 60-82.

Hammond, N. G. L. (1984) 'The Battle of Pydna', *Journal of Hellenic Studies* 104, 31-47.

Hanson, V. D. (1989) *The Western Way of War: Infantry Battle in Classical Greece*, London.

Hanson, V. D. (ed.) (1991) *Hoplites: The Classical Greek Battle Experience*, New York.

Hanson, V. D. (1999) 'The Status of Ancient Military History: Traditional Work, Recent Research, and On-Going Controversies', *Journal of Military History* 63.2, 379-413.

Hanson, V. D. (2007) 'The modern historiography of ancient warfare', in P. Sabin, H. Van Wees and M. Whitby (2007) 3-21.

Harris, W. V. (1979) *War and Imperialism in Republican Rome 327-70BC*, Oxford.

Henderson, J. (1996) 'XPDNC/Writing Caesar (*Bellum Ciuile*)', *Classical Antiquity* 15.2, 261-88.

Hill, P. R. (2002) *Polybius to Vegetius: Essays on the Roman Army and Hadrian's Wall presented to Brian Dobson*, The Hadrianic Society.

Holmes, R. (2004) *Acts of War*, London.

Hölscher, T. (2003) 'Images of war in Greece and Rome: between military practice, public memory and cultural symbolism', *Journal of Roman Studies* 93, 1-17.

Hopkins, K. (1978) *Conquerors and Slaves*, Cambridge.

Hornblower, S. (2007) 'Warfare in ancient literature: the paradox of war', in P. Sabin, H. Van Wees and M. Whitby (2007) 22-53.

Horvat, J. (1997) 'Roman Republican weapons from Šmihel in Slovenia', *Journal of Roman Military Equipment Studies* 8, 105-20.

Hoyos D. (2006) 'Introduction', in J. C. Yardley (2006) ix-xxxviii.

Hoyos, D. (2003) *Hannibal's Dynasty: Power and Politics in the Western Mediterranean, 247-183 BC*, London.

Hoyos, D. (ed.) (2010), *A Companion to the Punic Wars*, Oxford, forthcoming.

Hölscher, T. (2003) 'Images of war in Greece and Rome: between military practice, public memory, and cultural symbolism', *Journal of Roman Studies* 93, 1-17.

Horsfall, N. (1985) 'Illusion and reality in Latin topographical writing', *Greece and Rome* 32.2, 197-208.

Hyland, A. (1990) *Equus: The Horse in the Roman World*, London.

Kagan, K. (2006) *The Eye of Command*, Ann Arbor.

Kähler, H. (1965) *Der fries vom Reiterdenkmal des Aemilius Paullus in Delphi*, Berlin.

Keay, S. J. (1988) *Roman Spain*, London.

Keegan, J. (1976) *The Face of Battle*, London.

Keegan, J. (1993) *A History of Warfare*, London.

Keppie, L. (1987) 'Review of Ulbert (1985)' *Britannia* 18, 401-2.

Keppie, L. (1991) 'A centurion of *legio Martia* at Padova?', *Journal of Roman Military Equipment Studies* 2, 115-22.

Keppie, L. (1998 [1984]) *The Making of the Roman Army*, London.

Kimmig, W. (1940) 'Ein Keltenschild aus Aegypten', *Germania* 24, 106-11.

Klotz, A. (1953) 'Caesar und Livius' in *Rheinisches Museum für Philologie*, 62-67.

Kmetic, D., Horvat, J. and Vodopivec, F. (2004) 'Metallographic examinations of the Roman Republican weapons from the hoard from Grad near Šmihel' *Arheološki vestnik* 55, 291-312.

Koon, S. (2010) 'Phalanx and legion: the 'face' of Punic War battles' in D. Hoyos (forthcoming).

Kraus, C. S. and Woodman, A. J. (1997) *Latin Historians*, Oxford.

Krentz, P. (1985a) 'Casualties in hoplite battles', *Greek, Roman and Byzantine Studies* 26.1, 13-20.

Krentz, P. (1985b) 'The Nature of Hoplite Battle', *Classical Antiquities* 4.1, 50-61.

Krentz, P. (1994) 'Continuing the *Othismos* on the *Othismos*', *Ancient History Bulletin* VIII (2) 45-49.

Kromayer, J. and Veith, G. (1912) *Antike Schlachtfelder in Italien und Afrika*, vol. 3 part 1, Berlin.

Kromayer, J. and Veith, G. (1928) *Heerwesen und Kriegführung der Griechen und Römer*, München.

Lang, J. (1988) 'Study of the metallography of some Roman swords', *Britannia* 19, 199-216.

Lazenby, J. F. (1978) *Hannibal's War: A Military History of the Second Punic War*, Warminster.

Lazenby, J. F. (1985) *The Spartan Army*, Warminster.

Lazenby, J. F. (1991) 'The Killing Zone' in Hanson (1991), 87-109.

Le Bohec, Y. (1997) 'L'armement des Romains pendant les Guerres Puniques d'après les sources littéraires', *Journal of Roman Military Equipment Studies* 8, 13-24.

Lee, A. D. (1996) 'Morale and the Roman Experience of Battle' in Lloyd (1996), 199-218.

Lendon, J.E. (1999) 'The rhetoric of combat: Greek military theory and Roman culture in Julius Caesar's battle descriptions', *Classical Antiquity* 18/1, 273-329.

Lendon, J.E. (2005) *Soldiers and Ghosts: a History of Battle in Classical Antiquity*, London.

Levene, D. S. and Nelis, P. (eds.) (2002) *Clio and the Poets: Augustan Poetry and the Traditions of Ancient Historiography*, Brill.

Levithan, J. (2006) ''Picked Men:' Heroic Volunteerism in the Roman Army', American Philological Association Annual Meeting 2006. http://www.apaclassics.org/AnnualMeeting/06mtg /abstracts/Levithan.pdf.

Lipovsky, J. (1981) *A Historiographical Study of Livy Books VI to X*, New York.

Lloyd, A. (ed.) (1996) *Battle in Antiquity*, London.

Luce, T.J. (1965) 'The dating of Livy's first decade', *Transactions of the American Philological Association* 96, 209-40.

Luce, T.J. (1977) *Livy, the Composition of his History*, Princeton.

Luginbill, R. (1994) 'Othismos: the importance of the massed shove in hoplite warfare', *Phoenix* 48.1, 51-61.

Mcdonald, A. H. (1957) 'The Style of Livy', *Journal of Roman Studies* 47, 157-172.

Marsden, E. W. (1973), 'Polybius as a Military Historian', *Entretiens de la Fondation Hardt XX: Polybe*, Geneva.

Marshall, S. L. A. (1947) Men against Fire: the Problme of Battle Command, Washington.

Maxfield, V. and Dobson, M. (1991) *Roman Frontier Studies 1989*, Exeter.

McCall, J. (2002) *The Cavalry of the Roman Republic: Cavalry Combat and Elite Reputations in the Middle and Late Republic*, London.

Meier, C. (1995 [1982]) *Caesar*, translated by D. McLintock, New York.

Mitchell, S. (1996) 'Hoplite Warfare in Ancient Greece' in Lloyd (1996), 87-106.

Morello, R. (2002) 'Livy's Alexander digression (9.17-19): counterfactuals and apologetics', *Journal of Roman Studies*, 62-85.

Nolan, L. (1853) *Cavalry: Its History and Tactics*, London. Republished (2006) Yardley, PA.

Northwood, S. J. (2000) 'Livy and the Early Annalists', in Deroux (2000), 45-55.

Oakley, S. P. (1985) 'Single Combat in the Roman Republic', *Classical Quarterly* 35.2, 392-410.

Oakley, S. P. (1992) 'Livy and Clodius Licinius', *Classical Quarterly* 42.2, 547-551.

Oakley, S. P. (1997) *A Commentary on Livy Books VI-X*, vol. 1: book vi, Oxford.

Oakley, S. P. (1998) *A Commentary on Livy Books VI-X*, vol. 2: books vii-viii, Oxford.

Oakley, S. P. (2005a) *A Commentary on Livy Books VI-X*, vol. 3: book ix, Oxford.

Oakley, S. P. (2005b) *A Commentary on Livy Books VI-X*, vol. 4: book x, Oxford.

Ogilvie, R. M. (1965) *A Commentary on Livy Books 1-5*, Oxford.

Ogilvie, R. M. (1971) 'Introduction', in A. De Selincourt (2002), 1-25.

Ogilvie, R. M. (1979) 'Review of Luce (1977)', *Classical Review* 29. 1, 58-60.

Parker, H. M. D. (1961, [1928]) *The Roman Legions*, Oxford.

Philips, Brig. Gen. T. R. (1987) *Roots of Strategy*, Book 2, Harrisburg, PA.

Plathner, H. G. (1934) *Die Schlachtschilderungen bei Livius*, Breslau.

Pritchett, W. K. (1985) *The Greek State at War*, Part IV, Berkeley.

du Picq, A (trans. 1987 [1868]) *Battle Studies*, translated by J. Greely and R. Cotton, in Philips (1987), 9-300.

Prosen, A. (1965) 'Livy's and Sallust's Rhetorical Style', *Classical Bulletin* 41.5, 68-71.

Quesanda Sanz, F. (1997) '*Gladius hispaniensis*: an archaeological view from Iberia', *Journal of Roman Military Equipment Studies* 8, 251-70.

Raaflaub, K. A. (1986) *Social Struggles in Archaic Rome*, Berkeley, Los Angeles and London).

Rapin, A. (2001) 'Des épées romaines dans la collection d'Alise-Sainte-Reine', *Gladius* XXI, 31-56.

Rawson, E. (1971) 'Literary Sources of the Pre-Marian Army', *Papers of the British School at Rome* 39 ns 26, 13-31.

Reddé, M., von Schnurbein, S., Barral, P., Bénard, J., Brouquier-Reddé, V., Goguey, R., Joly, M., Köhler, H.-J., Petit, C., and Sievers, S. (1995) 'Fouilles et recerches nouvelles sur les travaux de César devant Alésia (1991-1994)', *Bericht der Römisch-Germanischen Kommission* 76, 73-158.

Reinach, A. (1907) 'L'origine du pilum', *Revue archéologique* 10, 226-44.

Richardson, J. S. (1996) *The Romans in Spain*, Oxford.

Riggsby, A. (2006) *Caesar in Gaul and Rome: War in Words*, Austin, TX.

Rivet, A. L. F. (1988) *Gallia Narbonensis*, London.

Rosenstein, N. (1990) *Imperatores Victi: Military Defeat and Aristocratic Competition in the Middle and Late Republic*, University of California Press.

Roth, J. P. (2006) 'Siege narrative in Livy: representation and reality' in S. Dillon and K. E. Welch (2006) 49-67.

Sabin, P. (1996) 'The Mechanics of Battle in the Second Punic War' in T. Cornell, B. Rankov, and P. Sabin (1996) 59-80.

Sabin, P. (2000) 'The Face of Roman Battle', *Journal of Roman Studies* 90, 1-17.

Sabin, P. (2007a) *Lost Battles: Reconstructing the Great Clashes of the Ancient World*, London.

Sabin, P. (2007b) 'Land battles', in P. Sabin, H. Van Wees and M. Whitby (2007) 399-433.

Sabin, P., Van Wees, H. and Whitby, M (eds.) (2007) *Cambridge History of Greek and Roman Warfare*, vol. 1, Cambridge.

Sage, M. M. (2008) *The Republican Roman Army : a Sourcebook*, London.

Sandars, H. (1913) 'The Weapons of the Iberians', *Archaeologia* 64, 205-94.

Schuller, W. (ed.) (1993) *Livius: Aspekte Seines Werkes*, Konstanz.

Schulten, A. (1911), 'Der Ursprung des Pilums', *Rheinisches Museum* 66, 573-84.

Schulten, A. (1927) *Numantia: die Ergebnisse der Ausgrabungen 1905-19*, vol. 3, München.

Schulten, A. (1929) *Numantia: die Ergebnisse der Ausgrabungen 1905-19*, vol. 4, München.

Scullard, H. H. (1974) *The Elephant in the Greek and Roman World*, Cambridge.

Sekunda, N. (1996) *Republican Roman Army 200 - 106BC*, Oxford.

Sekunda, N. (2001) *Hellenistic Infantry Reform in the 160s*, Lódz.

Sekunda, N. (2007) 'Land forces', in P. Sabin, H. Van Wees and M. Whitby (2007) 325-357.

Sidnell, P. (2006) *Warhorse: Cavalry in Ancient Warfare*, London.

Sievers, S. (1997) 'Alseia and Osuna: Bemerkungen zur Normierung der spätrepublikanischen Bewaffnung und Ausrüstung', *Journal of Roman Military Equipment Studies* 8, 271-6.

Stadter, P.A. (1972) 'The structure of Livy's history', *Historia* 21, 287-307.

Stuart Jones, H, (1919) 'Review of De Sanctis (1916)', *English Historical Review*, 93-96.

Syme, R. (1958) *Tacitus*, Oxford.

Syme, R. (1959) 'Livy and Augustus', *Harvard Studies in Classical Philology* 64, 27-87.

Torelli, M. (1982) *Typology and Structure in Roman Historical Reliefs*, Ann Arbor.

Tränkle, H. (1971) *Cato in Der Vierten und Fünften Dekade des Livius* [Akademie der Wissenschaften und der Literatur, Mainz, Abhandlungen der geistes- und sozialwissenschaftlichen Klasse iv], Mainz.

Treloar, A. (1971) 'The Roman Shield: Polybius VI.23.2', *Classical Review* 21.1, 3-5.

Ulbert, G. (1985) *Cáceres el Viejo. Ein spätrepublikanisches Legionslager in Spanisch-Extremadura*, Mainz.

Van Wees, H. (1996) 'Heroes, Knights and Nutters: Warrior Mentality in Homer' in Lloyd (1996), 1-86.

Van Wees, H. (2004) *Greek Warfare: Myths and Realities*, London.

Walbank, F. W. (1957) *A Historical Commentary on Polybius*: vol. 1, London.

Walbank, F. W. (1967) *A Historical Commentary on Polybius*: vol. 2, London

Walbank, F. W. (1979) *A Historical Commentary on Polybius*: vol. 3, London

Walbank, F. W. (1979) 'Introduction', in I. Scott-Kilvert (1979), 9-40.

Walbank. F. W. (2002) 'Polybius as military expert' in Hill (2002) 19-30.

Walsh, P. G. (1958) 'The Negligent Historian: "Howlers" in Livy', *Greece and Rome* 2nd series 5, 83-88.

Walsh, P. G. (1970 [1961]) *Livy: His Historical Aims and Methods*, Cambridge.

Walsh, P. G. (1974) 'Livy' *Greece and Rome New Surveys in the Classics* 8, Oxford.

Walsh, P. G. (1978) 'Review of Luce (1977)', *Phoenix* 32. 2, 171-174.

Warry, J. (1980) *Warfare in the Classical World*, London.

Webster, G. (1985) *The Roman Imperial Army of the First and Second Centuries AD*, 3rd ed., London.

Welch, K. and Powell, A. (1998) *Julius Caesar as Artful Reporter: The War Commentaries as Political Instruments*, London.

Wheeler, E. L. (1979) 'The Legion as Phalanx' *Chiron* 9, 303-318. '

Whitby, M. (2007) 'Reconstructing Ancient Warfare', in P. Sabin, H. Van Wees and M. Whitby (2007) 54 - 81.

Wiseman, T. P. (1979) *Clio's Cosmetics*, Leicester.

Witte, K. (1910) 'Über die Form der Darstellung in Livius' Geschichtswerk', *Rheinisches Museum für Phililogie* 65, 270-305, 359-419.

Woodman, A. J. (1988) *Rhetoric in Classical Historiography*, London.

Woodman, A. J. (1998) *Tacitus Reviewed*, Oxford.

Syme R, (1958) *Tacitus*, vol. 1, Oxford.

Zhmodikov, A. (2000) 'Roman Republican heavy infantrymen in battle (IV-II centuries B.C.)', *Historia* 49, 67-78.

www.ingramcontent.com/pod-product-compliance
Lightning Source LLC
LaVergne TN
LVHW071217210926
848482LV00015B/833